Air War 1941:
The Turning Point

Part one

by

John Foreman

Air Research Publications

First published 1993 by
Air Research Publications
PO Box 223, Walton on Thames,
Surrey, KT12 3YQ,
England.
Second Impression April 1994

Typeset in Great Britain by
A.C.E. Services
Radlett, Herts WD7 8LU

Printed in Great Britain by
MBA Group Ltd
London N17 OHW

ISBN 1 871187 22 2

Air War 1941:
The Turning Point

The day by day account of air

operations over northwest Europe

Part One
From the Battle of Britain to the Blitz

by

John Foreman

Air Research Publications

Contents

Foreword
by
Air Vice-Marshal Sir Ivor Broom
KGB CBE DSO DFC AFC

This book is a remarkably detailed day-by-day account of air operations over the United Kingdom and northwest Europe during the first six months of 1941. The *Luftwaffe* had lost the battle for air superiority over England in the summer of 1940 and this book shows the subsequent emergence of changing rôles in both the Royal Air Force and the *Luftwaffe*. John Foreman shows how the Royal Air Force progressively went over to the offensive in 1941 and thus caused the *Luftwaffe* to change to a more defensive rôle.

Developments in the air defence of the United Kingdom were somewhat more advanced than developments in bomber operations in 1939/40 and it is salutary to be reminded that early in 1941 Bomber Command was still relying largely on obsolescent aircraft and navigation techniques of pre-1939 vintage. The small but effective air defence force provided the shield to blunt the effectiveness of the powerful *Luftwaffe* and provided a breathing space for industry to produce additional aircraft and for the Royal Air Force to recruit and train additional crews. It is good that this book, by reviewing in detail events in the first half of 1941, implicitly reminds us of the timescale needed to produce additional and improved modern weapons and trained manpower in times of emergency.

A glance at the extensive information sources used by John Foreman will intantly show why he has spent some twenty years studying the British and German records in order to produce this history of air warfare during the first half of 1941. His access to *Luftwaffe* fighter claims and aircraft losses - as well as RAF records - has enabled him to provide many interesting checks on claims made by either side. He frequently correlates the RAF and *Luftwaffe* records and is thus able to comment on many specific operations during early 1941. He has looked at these operations from both sides and the information he has acquired will, I believe, provide new and interesting material for the student of air operations and for all those who participated in the air war during the first half of 1941.

Ivor Broom
Sarrat
Hertfordshire

Introduction

This work began from curiosity. Many years ago I first realised
that, in the published history of the Royal Air Force, there were
large 'grey areas' that had never fully been researched; details
of certain battles and campaigns were of course available, as
were various biographies and unit histories, but these gave only
a tiny view of the whole. One period that intrigued me
immensely was that immediately following the Battle of Britain,
when a remarkable change had taken place in the whole aspect
of the air war in the west - the beginning of the Non-stop
Offensive.

As I began to research the details, I found that the changes in
both equipment and outlook of the RAF were indeed profound
and were materially to affect the course of air operations for the
remainder of the war. They deserve to be recorded in detail.

Within those short six months, Fighter Command had
reversed its policy completely. During the summer and into the
winter of 1940, the aspect had been totally defensive, waging a
bitter battle to protect the United Kingdom from the threat of
invasion and occupation. Yet by mid-June 1941 those same
exhausted fighter squadrons were to be found high over France
daily - and often twice daily - escorting bombers. Their task was
now to lure the German fighter pilots into a battle of attrition
and to destroy them. By night, the radar-equipped Beaufighter
had emerged as a powerful weapon and, by June 1941, the Blitz
upon Britain had all but ceased.

Bomber Command had also changed considerably. The
wide-ranging 'penny-packet' attacks of 1940 were now being
abandoned in favour of mass attacks upon specific targets. This
was to be a portent of the long and bitter struggle to come that
would cost Bomber Command some two-thirds of the 70,000
casualties that would eventually be suffered by the Royal Air
Force in air operations. Both Bomber and Coastal Commands

would also become increasingly involved in the marine war against German shipping, developing the techniques that were to pave the way for the Coastal Command Strike Wings of later years.

For the Germans too the changes were to be great. By the end of June 1941 their massed bomber fleets had departed for other theatres, their task in the west abandoned as a failure. The *Luftwaffe* fighter force that in 1940 had cleared the way for the victorious German summer advances across Europe had shrunk to a shadow of its former power, taking the part of besieged defenders. The German aircrews had fought bravely and with considerable skill, but this professional air force had, in the end, been defeated by poor leadership, by a task that was never within their capability to fulfil and by the courge and sacrifices of the British aircrews. This is the story of how those changes came to pass.

Mainly however, this book is about the men who made those changes possible. Many books have been written about aircraft, but without the men who crew and fight in them, military aircraft are but useless, lifeless machines. It is therefore to the men, particularly those who lost their lives for their beliefs - of whichever nationality - that this book is respectfully dedicated.

Here, a word of apology is necessary. It had always been the intention to produce this work as one volume, but the ever-increasing amount of information, particularly from the German side, has resulted in the manuscript reaching an unmanageable size. Technical and economic considerations have thus compelled me to produce the book in two volumes, with tentative plans to extend the series through 1941 and into 1942.

John Foreman,
Radlett,
Hertfordshire.
October 1993

Acknowledgements, Sources and Notes

In a work that has taken so long to research and complete, many people have been involved and to attempt to list them all would be to risk omissions. My particular thanks must go to my good friend and colleague Christopher Shores; Chris taught me the business of research and his encouragement, support and active help throughout the years and his reading and editing of this very large manuscript made its appearance possible. I also owe especial thanks to Air Vice-Marshal Sir Ivor Broom KCB, CBE, DSO, DFC, AFC who made many helpful comments and suggestions as well as consenting to write the foreword. Also to my friend and publisher Simon Parry, who so willingly gave his time and expert knowledge on the fates of Luftwaffe aircraft lost on operations over the United Kingdom; to my colleagues in Germany, Hans Ring, Winfried Bock, Heinrich Weiss and Herbert Scholl, for their help with Luftwaffe claims and losses; to Air Commodore Henry Probert at Air Historical Branch, who afforded me the facilties of his department and whose staff, particularly Mrs Boyd, answered my questions so promptly.

I would also like to thank Air Chief Marshal Sir Christopher Foxley-Norris GCB, OBE, DSO, MA; Air Vice Marshal J E Johnson CB, CBE, DSO, DFC; Wing Commander L C Gregory DFC, Squadron Leader S V Holloway OBE; Squadron Leader B Drobinski DFC; Group Captain Sir Douglas Bader CBE, DSO, DFC; Group Captain J A Kent DFC, AFC; Wing Commander H R Allen DFC; Major Josef Fözö (the latter four men now deceased); Squadron Leader J.G.P.Millard; Flight Lieutenant Christopher Deanesly DFC; Flight Lieutenant M V Weight DFC; Group Captain J R Goodman DFC, AFC; Mr I K S Wilson, Mr H D Denchfield; Frank Twitchett; Make Tagg and Ken Hunter of the RAF Museum Archives; Brian Cull; Phillipa Hodgkiss; Bruce Lander; Bryce Gomersall; Peter Sharpe; Frank Marshall; Norman Didwell; Don Clark; Peter Wood; Ron Collier and Harry

Moyle. Finally -and especially - to my wife Pam, for putting up with my often chaotic filing system, my clattering computer printer and my late nights. Thank you all!

Main Sources

Public Record Office, Kew.
Squadron Operation Record Books AIR27 series
Group Operation Record Books AIR25 series
Command Operation Record Books AIR24 series
Fighter Command Combats and Casualties AIR16 961
Miscellaneous Bomber, Coastal and Fighter Command documents AIR14, AIR15 and AIR16 series.
Intelligence documents AIR40 series
Daily Resumé of Air Operations AIR22 series
Combat Reports AIR50 series.

<u>Royal Air Force Museum Archives, RAF Hendon</u>
Accident Cards Aircraft Movement Cards

<u>Ministry of Defence Air Historical Branch</u>
Bomber Command Loss Cards (now held at the RAF Museum)

<u>Luftwaffe Documents</u>
KTB I./Jagdeschwader 3.
KTB I./Kampfgeschwader 4.
Unpublished history Kampfgeschwader 1.
Quartermaster General Loss Returns.
The Luftwaffe Fighter Forces in World War Two (unpublished history by Hans Ring)

<u>Published Works</u>

Aders G	:	Geschichte der Deutschen Nachtjagd.
Allen, W/C H R	:	Fighter Squadron (quoted with author's permission).
Baker E C R	:	The Fighter Aces of the RAF.
Barker R	:	The Ship Busters.
Bekker C D	:	Swastika At Sea
	:	Angriffshöhe 4000
Bowyer C	:	Guns in the Sky.
	:	Fighter Command 1936-68.
Bowyer M J F	:	Fighting Colours.
	:	Bombing Colours.
	:	2 Group RAF.
Braham W/C J R D	:	Scramble.

Brickhill P	:	Reach for the Sky.
Brookes A J	:	Photo Reconnaissance.
Caldwell D	:	JG 26 - Top Guns of the Luftwaffe.
Chisholm, Air Com R	:	Cover of Darkness.
Collier B	:	The defence of the United Kingdom.
Dierich W	:	Kampfgeschwader 55 Greif.
	:	Kampfgeschwader 51 Edelweiss.
	:	Die Verbände der Luftwaffe.
Forrester L	:	Fly For Your Life.
Galland A	:	The First and the Last.
Gibson W/C G P	:	Enemy Coast Ahead.
Gomersall B	:	The Stirling File.
Halley J J	:	The Squadrons of the Royal Air Force.
HMSO	:	British Vessels Lost At Sea 1939-45.
Houart J	:	Lonely Warrior.
Jefford W/C C G	:	RAF Squadrons.
Johnson, AVM J E	:	Wing Leader (quoted with author's permission).
Jones Dr R V	:	Most Secret War.
Kent Gp Capt J A	:	One of the Few.
Knoke H	:	I Flew For The Führer.
Lanchberry E	:	Against The Sun.
Lee W/C A	:	Blitz on Britain.
Middlebrook M & Everitt C	:	The Bomber Command War Diaries.
Mohlenbeck O & Leihse M	:	Ferne Nachtjagd.
Morgan E B & Shacklady E	:	Spitfire. The History.
Nesbitt R C	:	Torpedo Airmen.
Noyes P	:	Bomber Squadrons of the Royal Air Force.
Obermaier E	:	Die Ritterkreuzträger der Luftwaffe. Band I Jagdflieger.
Parry S W	:	Intruders over Britain.
Price A	:	Instruments of Darkness.
Priller J	:	Geschichte eines Jagdgeschwaders.
Ramsay W (Ed)	:	After the Blitz vols 2 & 3.
Rawlings J R	:	Fighter Squadrons of the Royal Air Force.
Rawnsley C F & Wright R	:	Night Fighter.
Richards D & Saunders H St.J	:	The Royal Air Force 1939-45.
Robertson B	:	The Lancaster Bomber.

Rohwer J		
& Hümmelchen G	:	Chronology of the War at Sea.
Shores C F		
& Williams C	:	Aces High.
Sims E	:	Fighter Exploits.
Terraine J	:	The Right of the Line.
Toliver R F		
& Constable T	:	Horrido!
Webster Sir Charles		
& Frankland N	:	The Strategic Air Offensive Against Germany.
Wallace G	:	RAF Biggin Hill.
Witherbotham F W	:	The Ultra Secret.
Zwanenberg G	:	En Nooit was Het Stil....

Notes

The presentation is on a daily 'diary' basis, with facts, when it seems appropriate, brought out in 'boxes' to avoid cluttering the text. Night operations usually narrate RAF bombing raids, followed by *Luftwaffe* attacks. The daily losses are presented in tabular form at the end of each day or night as in my foregoing work *'The Battle of Britain: The Forgotten Months'*. The main sources for these have been for the RAF the Operation Record Books and Accident Cards. However, these latter are not complete since it is by now well known that many cards are missing. Indeed, those recording almost all fatalities in Spitfire accidents were stolen many years ago from AHB, a fact regarded with total disgust and contempt by all reputable historians. A painstaking attempt has been made to reconstruct these, but I freely admit that many items may be inaccurate and I would welcome corrections. Similarly, the Luftwaffe Quartermaster General loss returns contain a few omissions and many errors, mainly of date. The fact that no indication is given as to whether a loss or casualty occurred by day or by night is of course another problem, thus considerable 'detective work', aided by Intelligence Summaries and Y-Service Reports and by German unit histories, has been used to present a coherent picture. It must be stressed however that the result is my own interpretation of the facts and I am well aware that other conclusions are possible. Similarly the air combats - particularly in the case of the Luftwaffe fighter claims - must necessarily require a measure of educated guesswork, assisted by many years study of the German fighter forces. Thus I accept again that other conclussions could well be drawn.

At the beginning of each month will be found a general 'overview' of events taking place during that month, (unit movements, re-equipment, squadron formations etc.) that would clutter the main text unnecessarily.

J F

Orders of Battle

Royal Air Force

Fighter Command

No 9 Group,
West Midlands and Wales

Speke Sector

96 Squadron	Hurricane I	Cranage
229 Squadron	Hurricane I	Speke
312 Squadron	Hurricane I	Speke, det Penrhos
307 Squadron	Defiant I	Jurby, dets Cranage & Squires Gate

Ternhill Sector

306 Squadron	Hurricane I	Ternhill

No 10 Group
Southwest England

Middle Wallop Sector

32 Squadron	Hurricane I	Middle Wallop
93 Squadron	Harrow II/Havoc I	Middle Wallop
604 Squadron	Beaufighter If	Middle Wallop, det Coltishall
152 Squadron	Spitfire I	Warmwell
609 Squadron	Spitfire I	Warmwell
238 Squadron	Hurricane I	Chilbolton

Filton Sector

87 Squadron	Hurricane I	Charmy Down
501 Squadron	Hurricane I	Exeter
504 Squadron	Hurricane I	Exeter
263 Squadron	Whirlwind I	Exeter, det St.Eval

St.Eval Sector

234 Squadron	Spitfire I	St.Eval
247 Squadron	Gladiator I /Hurricane I	Roborough, Det St.Eval
79 Squadron	Hurricane I	Pembrey

No 11 Group
Southeast England

Biggin Hill Sector
66 Squadron	Spitfire IIa	West Malling
74 Squadron	Spitfire IIa	Biggin Hill
92 Squadron	Spitfire I	Biggin Hill
141 Squadron	Defiant I	Gravesend
421 Flight	Spitfire I	Hawkinge

Debden Sector
85 Squadron	Hurricane I	Debden (from 1.1.41)
17 Squadron	Hurricane I	Martlesham Heath
242 Squadron	Hurricane I	Martlesham Heath

Northolt Sector
1 Squadron	Hurricane I	Northolt
601 Squadron	Hurricane I	Northolt

Tangmere Sector
65 Squadron	Spitfire I	Tangmere
145 Squadron	Hurricane I	Tangmere
302 Squadron	Hurricane I	Westhampnett
610 Squadron	Spitfire I	Westhampnett
23 Squadron	Blenheim If	Ford
FIU	Blenheim If /Beaufighter If	Ford

Kenley Sector
253 Squadron	Hurricane I	Kenley
615 Squadron	Hurricane I	Kenley
605 Squadron	Hurricane IIa	Croydon
219 Squadron	Beaufighter If	Tangmere, det Valley

Hornchurch Sector
41 Squadron	Spitfire IIa	Hornchurch
64 Squadron	Spitfire I	Hornchurch
611 Squadron	Spitfire I	Southend (Rochford)

North Weald Sector
56 Squadron	Hurricane I	North Weald
249 Squadron	Hurricane I	North Weald
264 Squadron	Defiant I	Gravesend

No 12 Group
West Midlands

Digby Sector

46 Squadron	Hurricane IIa	Digby
2 (RCAF) Squadron	Hurricane I	Digby
29 Squadron	Blenheim If /Beaufighter If	Wellingore

Wittering Sector

151 Squadron	Hurricane I/Defiant I	Wittering, det Coltishall
266 Squadron	Spitfire I	Wittering
25 Squadron	Blenheim If /Beaufighter If	Wittering

Kirton-in-Lindsay Sector

71 Squadron	Hurricane I	Kirton-in-Lindsay
616 Squadron	Spitfire I	Kirton-in-Lindsay
255 Squadron	Defiant I	Kirton-in-Lindsay

Duxford Sector

19 Squadron	Spitfire IIa	Duxford
310 Squadron	Hurricane I	Duxford

Church Fenton Sector

213 Squadron	Hurricane I	Leconfield
303 Squadron	Hurricane I	Leconfield

Coltishall Sector

222 Squadron	Spitfire I	Coltishall
257 Squadron	Hurricane I	Coltishall

Baginton Sector

308 Squadron	Hurricane I	Baginton

No 13 Group
Northern England, Northern Ireland and Southern Scotland

Aldergrove Sector

245 Squadron	Hurricane I	Aldergrove, dets Ballyhalbert & Limavady

16

Catterick Sector

54 Squadron	Spitfire I	Catterick
600 Squadron	Blenheim If	
	/Beaufighter If	Catterick, dets Drem,
		Acklington & Prestwick
256 Squadron	Defiant I	Catterick (Note 1.)

Turnhouse Sector

43 Squadron	Hurricane I	Drem
603 Squadron	Spitfire IIa	Drem
602 Squadron	Spitfire I	Prestwick

Usworth Sector

72 Squadron	Spitfire I	Acklington
258 Squadron	Hurricane I	Acklington
607 Squadron	Hurricane I	Usworth

No 14 Group
Northern Scotland

Kirkwall Sector

3 Squadron	Hurricane I	Castletown
1 (RCAF)		
Squadron	Hurricane I	Digby
260 Squadron	Hurricane I	Skitten

Dyce Sector

111 Squadron	Hurricane I	Dyce, det Montrose
232 Squadron	Hurricane I	Elgin

Bomber Command

No 1 Group

12 Squadron	Wellington II	Binbrook
142 Squadron	Wellington II	Binbrook
88 Squadron	Battle I	Long Kesh
226 Squadron	Battle I	Long Kesh
103 Squadron	Wellington IC	Newton
150 Squadron	Wellington IC	Newton
300 Squadron	Wellington IC	Swinderby
301 Squadron	Wellington IC	Swinderby
304 Squadron	Wellington IC	Syerston
305 Squadron	Wellington IC	Syerston

Note 1. Non-operational

17

No 2 Group

18 Squadron	Blenheim IV	Great Massingham
21 Squadron	Blenheim IV	Watton
82 Squadron	Blenheim IV	Watton
101 Squadron	Blenheim IV	Oakington
105 Squadron	Blenheim IV	Swanton Morley
107 Squadron	Blenheim IV	Wattisham
110 Squadron	Blenheim IV	Wattisham
114 Squadron	Blenheim IV	Oulton
139 Squadron	Blenheim IV	Horsham St.Faith

No 3 Group

7 Squadron	Stirling I	Oakington (Note 2.)
9 Squadron	Wellington Ic	Honington
15 Squadron	Wellington Ic	Wyton
40 Squadron	Wellington Ic	Wyton
57 Squadron	Wellington Ic	Feltwell
75 Squadron	Wellington Ic	Feltwell
99 Squadron	Wellington Ic	Newmarket
115 Squadron	Wellington Ic	Marham
218 Squadron	Wellington Ic	Marham
214 Squadron	Wellington Ic	Stradishall
311 Squadron	Wellington Ic	East Wretham
149 Squadron	Wellington Ic	Mildenhall
109 Squadron	Wellington Ic /Whitley V /Anson I	Boscombe Down
1419 Flight	Whitley V	Newmarket (Note 3.)
3 PRU	Spitfire I	Oakington

No 4 Group

77 Squadron	Whitley V	Topcliffe
102 Squadron	Whitley V	Topcliffe
10 Squadron	Whitley V	Leeming
35 Squadron	Halifax I	Linton-on-Ouse (Note 4.)
58 Squadron	Whitley V	Linton-on-Ouse
78 Squadron	Whitley V	Linton-on-Ouse
51 Squadron	Whitley V	Dishforth

No 5 Group

44 Squadron	Hampden I	Waddington

Note 2. Non-operational
Note 3. Special Duties
Note 4. Non-Operational

207 Squadron	Manchester I	Waddington (Note 5.)
49 Squadron	Hampden I S	Scampton
83 Squadron	Hampden I	Scampton
50 Squadron	Hampden I	Lindholme
61 Squadron	Hampden I	Hemswell
144 Squadron	Hampden I	Hemswell
106 Squadron	Hampden I	Finningley

Coastal Command

No 15 Group
Western Approaches

217 Squadron	BeaufortI/Anson I	St.Eval
236 Squadron	Blenheim IVf	St.Eval
321 Squadron	Anson I	Carew Cheriton
502 Squadron	Whitley V	Aldergrove, dets Kinloss & Limavady
233 Squadron	Hudson I	Aldergrove
272 Squadron	Blenheim IVf	Aldergrove
48 Squadron	Anson I	Hooten Park
210 Squadron	Sunderland I	Oban
240 Squadron	Stranraer I	Stranraer
209 Squadron	Lerwick I	Stranraer
10 (RAAF) Squadron	Sunderland I	Mount Batten

No 16 Group
Channel and Eastern Approaches

22 Squadron	Beaufort I	North Coates
812 Squadron	Swordfish I	North Coates
206 Squadron	Hudson I	Bircham Newton
235 Squadron	Blenheim IVf	Bircham Newton
221 Squadron	Wellington Ic	Bircham Newton (Note 6.)
500 Squadron	Anson I	Detling, det Thorney Island
59 Squadron	Blenheim IV	Thorney Island
53 Squadron	Blenheim IV	Thorney Island

No 17 Group
Western Approaches and Irish Sea

86 Squadron	Blenheim IV	Gosport (Note 7.)
252 Squadron	Beaufighter I	Chivenor (Note 8.)

Note5.Non-operational
Notes6-8.Forming

No 18 Group
North Sea and North Atlantic

201 Squadron	Sunderland I	Sullom Voe
204 Squadron	Sunderland I	Sullom Voe
700 Squadron	Walrus I	Sullom Voe
248 Squadron	Blenheim IVf	Sumburgh
42 Squadron	Beaufort I	Wick
269 Squadron	Hudson I	Wick
254 Squadron	Blenheim IVf	Dyce
220 Squadron	Hudson I	Thornaby-on-Tees
224 Squadron	Hudson I	Thornaby-on-Tees
608 Squadron	Anson I	Thornaby-on-Tees
320 Squadron	Hudson I	Leuchars (Note 9.)
98 Squadron	Battle I	Kaldardarnes

Under Direct Control of HQ Coastal Command

1 PRU	Hudson I/Spitfire I	Heston, Benson and Wick

Luftwaffe

Luftflotte 2

Under Direct Control

Fernaufklärungsgruppe 122

1.(F)/122	Ju88A	Brussels/Evére
2.(F)/122	Ju88A5, Ju88D1, Ju88D2	Brussels
4.(F)/122	Ju88A5, Ju88D1	Brussels/Evére
7.(F)/LG 2	Ju88A5, Ju88D1, He111	Ghent

Fliegerkorps II
Headquarters Ghent

Kampfgeschwader 2 'Holzhammer'

Stab./KG 2	Do17Z	Arras
I./KG 2	Do17Z	Epinay
II./KG 2	Do17Z	Arras
III./KG 2	Do17Z	Cambrai
E./KG 2	Do17Z	Osnabrück

Note 9. Training

Kampfgeschwader 3 'Blitz'

Stab./KG 3	Do17Z	Le Culot
I./KG 3	Do17Z	Le Culot
II./KG 3	Do17Z	Antwerp
III./KG 3	Do17Z	St Trond
E./KG 3	Do17Z	Nivelles

Kampfgeschwader 53 'Legion Condor'

Stab./KG 53	He111H	Lille-Nord
I./KG 53	He111H	Vitry-en-Artois
II./KG 53	He111H	Lille-Nord
III./KG 53	He111H	Germany
E./KG 53	He111H	Lille-Nord

Fliegerkorps X
Headquarters Soesterburg

Under Direct Control

3.(F)/122	Ju88A, Ju88D, He111	Soesterburg

Kampfgeschwader 4 'General Wever'

Stab./KG 4	He111H	Soesterburg
I./KG 4	He111H	Soesterburg (Note 10.)
II./KG 4	He111H	Eindhoven
III./KG 4	He111H	Schipol (Note 11.)
E./KG 4	He111H	Nantes

Kampfgeschwader 30 'Adler'

Stab./KG 30	Ju88A	Eindhoven
I./KG 30	Ju88A	Gilze-Rijn
II./KG 30	Ju88A	Eindhoven
III./KG 30	Ju88A	Schipol

Küstenfliegergruppe 106

Stab./K.Fl.Gr.106	He115	Norderney
3./.KFl.Gr.106	He115	Norderney
3./K.Fl.Gr.506	He115	Borkum

Jagdfliegerführer 2
Headquarters Wissant

Jadgeschwader 3

Stab./JG 3	Bf109E	St.Omer/Wizernes
I./JG 3	Bf109E	St.Omer/Wizernes

Note 10. Less 2 Staffel in Middle East
Note 11. Non-operational

21

II./JG 3	Bf109E	St.Omer/Wizernes
III./JG 3	Bf109E	St.Omer/Wizernes
E./JG 3	Bf109E	St.Omer/Wizernes
I.(J)/LG 2	Bf109E	Calais/Marck

Jadgeschwader 26 'Schlageter'

Stab./JG 26	Bf109E	Abbeville/Drucat
I./JG 26	Bf109E	Crécy
II./JG 26	Bf109E	Abbeville/Gramont
III./JG 26	Bf109E	Abbeville/Drucat
E./JG 26	Bf109E	Cognac

Stukageschwader 1

Stab./St.G.1	Ju87B	Ostend
I./St.G.1	Ju87B	Bergen-op-Zoom
III./St.G.1	Ju87B	Ostend
II.(Sch)/LG 2	Bf109E	St.Omer/Marques
E.Gr.210	Bf110C	Denain
20 Stormo		
56 Gruppo	Fiat G-50	Ursel (Note 12.)

Nachtjagddivision
Headquarters Zeist

Nachjagdgeschwader 1

Stab./NJG 1	Bf110C, Bf110D	Deelen
I./NJG 1	Bf110C, Bf110D	Güterslohe
II./NJG 1	Bf110C, Bf110D	Deelen
III./NJG 1	Bf110C, Bf110D	Rheine
I./NJG 2	Ju88C, Do17Z	Gilze-Rijn
I./NJG 3	Bf110C Vechta,	Oldenburg & Wittmundhafen

Luftgaukommando XI
Headquarters Rotterdam

Stab./JG 1	Bf109E	Jever
I./JG 54	Bf109E	Wesermünde
II./ZG 76	Bf110C	Jever
E./ZG 76	Bf110	Wesermünde

Luftgaukommando Holland
Headquarters Rotterdam

| 1./JG 1 | Bf109E | Katwijk |
| I./JG 52 | Bf109E | Katwijk |

Note 12. Regia Aeronautica

II./JG 52	Bf109E	Bergen-op-Zoom
E./JG 52	Bf109E	Gröningen
E./JG 54	Bf109E	Katwijk

Luftflotte 3

Under Direct Control

1.(F)/123	Ju88A, Ju88D	Jersey
2.(F)/123	Ju88A, Ju88D	Cherbourg/West
3.(F)/123	Ju88, Do17P, Bf110C	Paris/Buc
2.(F)/ObdL	Do215B	Paris/Le Bourget
Wekusta 51	He111, Do17	Paris/Le Bourget

Seenotdienstführer

2./K.Fl.Gr.906	He115	Cherbourg

Fliegerkorps I

5.(F)/122	Ju88A	Amiens
Korpstransport		
-staffel 1	Ju52/3M	Not known

Kampfgeschwader 1 'Hindenburg'

Stab./KG 1	Ju88A	Clairmont
I./KG 1	He111H	Rosiéres-en-Santerre
II./KG 1	Ju88A	Clairmont
III./KG 1	Ju88A	Nijmegen
III./KG 26	He111H	Poix-Nord

Kampfgeschwader 77

Stab./KG 77	Ju88A	Laon
I./KG 77	Ju88A	Abbeville
II./KG 77	Ju88A	Laon
III./KG 77	Ju88A	Laon/Athies
E./KG 77	Ju88A	Laon/Couvron

Fliegerkorps IV
Headquarters Rennes

Under Direct Control

3.(F)/131	Ju88A, Ju88D	Chateaudun & Lannion
Transport		
-staffel IV	Ju52/3M	Not known
I./KG 40	FW200C	Brest
E./KG 40	FW200C, He111	Amiens
K.Gr.100	He111H	Vannes
E./K.Gr.100	He111	Vannes

K.Gr.606	Do17Z	Lannion
Kampfgeschwader 27 'Boelke'		
Stab./KG 27	He111P	Tours
I./KG 27	He111P	Tours
II./KG 27	He111P	Dinard
III./KG 27	He111P	Rennes
IV./KG 27	He111P	Tours
Lehrgeschwader 1		
Stab./LG 1	Ju88A	Orleans/Bricy
I./LG 1	Ju88A	Orleans/Bricy
III./LG 1	Ju88A	Orleans/Bricy
E./LG 1	Ju88A	Langendiebach
Jagdgeschwader 77 'Herz As'		
Stab./JG 77	Bf109E	Brest
II./JG 77	Bf109E	Brest
III./JG 77	Bf109E	Brest

Fliegerkorps V Headquarters Villacoublay

Under Direct Control		
4.(F)/121	Ju88A, Ju88D	Villacoublay
Transport		
-staffel V	Ju52/3M	Not known
Kampfgeschwader 51 'Edelweiss'		
Stab./KG 51	Ju88A	Paris/Orly
I./KG 51	Ju88A	Villaroche
II./KG 51	Ju88A	Paris/Orly
III./KG 51	Ju88A	Bretigny
IV./KG 51	Ju88A	Lechfeld
Kampfgeschwader 54 'Totenkopf'		
Stab./KG 54	Ju88A	Evreux
I./KG 54	Ju88A	Evreux
II./KG 54	Ju88A	St.André l'Eure
K.Gr.806	Ju88A	Caen
E./KG 54	Ju88A	Fritzlar
Kampfgeschwader 55 'Greif'		
Stab./KG 55	He111	Villacoublay
I./KG 55	He111	Dreux
II./KG 55	He111	Chartres
III./KG 55	He111	Villacoublay
E./KG 55	He111	Landsberg/Lech (Note 13.)

Note 13. Formed 10.1.41

Stukageschwader 77

Stab./St.G.77	Ju87B	Cherbourg
I./St.G.77	Ju87B	Cherbourg
II./St.G.77	Ju87B	Théville
III./St.G.77	Ju87B	Caen

Jagdgeschwader 2 'Richthofen'

Stab./JG 2	Bf109E	Beaumont-le-Roger
I./JG 2	Bf109E	Théville
II./JG 2	Bf109E	Beaumont-le-Roger
III./JG 2	Bf109E	Bernay
E./JG 2	Bf109E	Le Havre

Luftflotte 5

Under Direct Control

K.Gr.z.b.V.108	He59, Ju52/3M, Ju52See	Not known
Transportstaf- -fel Norwegen	Ju52/3M	Not known

Kampfgeschwader 26 'Löwen'

Stab./KG 26	He111	} Transferring from
I./KG 26	He111	} Beauvais to Aalborg
E./KG 26	He111	Lübeck/Blankensee
IV.(St)/LG 1	Ju87B	Trondheim

Fernaufklärungsgruppe 22

2.(F)/22	Ju88A, Ju88D	Aalborg
3.(F)/22	Ju88D	Stavanger/Sola
1.(F)/120	Ju88A, Ju88D, He111	Stavanger/Sola
1.(F)/124	Ju88A, Ju88D, He111	Trondheim/Vaernes
Wekusta 5	He111	Stavanger/Sola

Zerstörergeschwader 76

Stab./ZG 76	Bf110C	Stavanger
III./ZG 76	Bf110C	Bergen
Zerst.E-Gruppe	Bf110	Aalborg

Taking an arbitrary figure of twelve serviceable aircraft per fighter Staffel and nine for the bomber and other units, the *Luftwaffe* in theory had a combat ready strength on the Channel front (not including the several important units currently re-equipping in Germany) of:

610 fighter and fighter-bombers

1050 bombers and dive-bombers

27 Coastal aircraft
180 reconnaissance aircraft
200 night fighters
150 others.

Total 2,672

This overall total is misleading however, as the actual number of operational aircraft was much lower. For example *I./NJG 2*, with a nominal strength of around forty fighters, could muster only seven combat ready machines on 1st January. The same strictures obviously applied to the Royal Air Force, the nominal operational strength of 1,700 being heavily reduced by general unserviceability, compounded by the unusual harshness of the winter. The situation was therefore better for the British than it had been during the summer of 1940. However the *Luftwaffe* still proved to be a tough and dangerous opponent.

January 1941 - Overview

The Royal Air Force

Fighter Command

The coming month would see several inter-Group movements. Indeed, on the 1st 85 Squadron was in the process of moving from Gravesend to Debden to begin training for its new rôle of night fighting, changing places with 264 Squadron and taking a few Defiants on strength. 264 Squadron would then, on the 11th, move on to Biggin Hill. On the 3rd, 303 Squadron transferred south from Leconfield to Northolt, exchanging their Hurricane Is for Spitfire Is, while 253 Squadron moved from Leconfield to Kenley and 256 Squadron from Catterick to Pembrey. squadron movements with Groups were:

7th	3 Squadron	Castletown to Skeabrae, sending a detachmentto Sumburgh.
	260 Squadron	Skitten to Castletown.
9th	92 Squadron	Biggin Hill to Manston.
15th	213 Squadron	Leconfield to Driffield.
16th	607 Squadron	Usworth to Macmerry.
27th	64 Squadron	Hornchurch to Rochford.
	307 Squadron	Jurby to Squires Gate, with a detachment at Speke.
	611 Squadron	Rochford to Hornchurch.

On the 7th, 68 Squadron was formed at Catterick with Blenheim Ifs, while on the 21st 315 Squadron was formed at Acklington with Hurricane Is. 255 Squadron became operational for night fighting duties on the 5th and the unique 421 Flight, the shipping reconnaissance unit, was re-numbered as 91 Squadron on the 11th, when it began to re-equip with Spitfire IIs.

Bomber Command

A notable event took place on 7th January when the Stirlings of

7 Squadron became operational. During the month 114 Squadron was temporarily placed under control of Fighter Command. The overall offensive plan for Bomber Command was defined in a Directive issued on 15th January:

"The sole primary objective of your bomber offensive, until further orders, should be the destruction of the German synthetic oil plants.

"It is recognised that conditions of weather and visibility will limits the occasions when it will be profitable to plan attacks against the seventeen oil objectives. Under these conditions your offensive should be directed towards harassing the enemy's main industrial towns and communications and may include periodically heavy concentrations against the former to maintain fear of attack."

This order was modified slightly on the 21st, when a further Directive was issued to Bomber Command HQ. This instructed that German anti-shipping aircraft bases were to be included when operations against enemy aerodromes were being planned.

It was understood that the Blenheims of 2 Group possessed insufficient range materially to implement the Oil Plan attacks for most targets, and were thus issued with the following objectives:

(1) Two squadrons to co-operate with Fighter Command in escorted daylight operations.

(2) To carry out attacks against airfields and marshalling yards by night.

(3) To continue with cloud cover raids.

Despite the above, the naval threat at Brest was occupying quite a large proportion of Bomber Command effort, but the effectiveness of the raid had yet to be determined.

Coastal Command

Only two units changed bases, 248 Squadron moving from Sumburgh to Dyce on 6th, while 502 Squadron transferred from Aldergrove to Limavady on the 27th.

Meanwhile, the scope of Coastal Command strikes had also been increased. On 20th January Air Vice-Marshal A T Harris, Deputy Chief of Air Staff, advised the AOC-inC Coastal Command that his crews now had permission to attack airfields on the Channel Islands, hitherto prohibited targets. Only aircraft in the air or on the ground were to be attacked and also 'men in uniform within the confines of the airfields'.

The short Stirling, first of the new generation of heavy bombers. It went on to serve with Bomber Command until late 1943.

The Luftwaffe

There were few changes; Stab and III./JG 54 arrived at Le Mans from Germany on the 15th (see text) and, two days later, Stab./KG 1 flew into Amiens/Glisy, while II Gruppe took up residence at Achiet. I./KG 40 moved south from Brest to Bordeaux. One unit disappeared from France when the Ju88s of II./LG 1 departed for Sicily for operations against Malta.

Chapter One
The Cold Grey Dawn.

1st January 1941

The New Year opened quietly. Fighter Command flew an uneventful sweep along the northern coastline of France, and nine Blenheims from 2 Group set out to attack towns in the Ruhr and in France. The bombers were recalled but a 110 Squadron machine was briefly engaged by a Bf110 and escaped undamaged.

In the late afternoon nine Hurricanes of 111 Squadron took off from Dyce for convoy protection duties. They split into three sections and headed for the east coast of Scotland. It was almost dark when a reconnaissance Ju88 was spotted off Montrose by Squadron Leader Biggar, Flight Lieutenant Walker and Flying Officer Kellett, who gave chase. Biggar's aircraft was hit by return fire, but he was safely escorted to Montrose airfield and effected a successful crash-landing, 'writing off' his fighter. In this, the first Fighter Command combat of 1941, the enemy aircraft was claimed as 'probably destroyed' for the loss of a Hurricane, pilot unhurt.

Casualties 1st January 1941

Royal Air Force

41 Squadron Spitfire P7548
Crashed landing at Hornchurch. Sgt Swanwick safe.

48 Squadron Anson R3305
Crashed on Hoylake foreshore. P/O Erskins & crew safe.

71 Squadron Hurricane P3459
Crashed at Kirton-in-Lindsay. P/O Keough safe.

111 Squadron Hurricane V6875
Damaged by return fire from Ju88. S/L Biggar safe. Aircraft destroyed.

206 Squadron Hudson T9827
Crashed near Bircham Newton (P/O Featherstone).

257 Squadron Hurricane V7186
Crashed at Coltishall. P/O Capon killed. Aircraft destroyed.

504 Squadron Hurricane TM-
Damaged on runway, P/O Simmon safe.

Luftwaffe

II./LG 2 Bf109E4 2030
crash-landed at Marquise, Uffz Wilhelm Rowold injured. Aircraft 60% damaged.
1./K.Gr.z.b.V.108 Ju52 6929
force-landed at Bodo. Aircraft destroyed.

1/2nd January 1941

This first night operation of 1941 lasted more than three hours. The Hemelingen Focke-Wulf factory was attacked with incendiaries and high explosives, and considerable damage was also caused to other factories.

> **Bomber Command Operations:**
> Bremen 85; Ostend and Flushing 13; Emden 12; Brest 7; Various 24
> **Luftwaffe Operations.**
> Various 52

As the bomber force took off, intruder fighters were patrolling over East Anglia; *Leutnant* Rudolf Stradner of *1./NJG 2* claimed a Wellington shot down at 18.40 hours. Squadron Leader Floryanowicz's 301 Squadron aircraft, approaching Coleby Grange, was seen to burst into flames and crash. In the glare of flames another aircraft was seen passing above at high speed; *I./NJG 2* had claimed its first

Rudolf Stradner (right) with Paul Böhn of I./NJG 2. Stradner scored the first intruder success of 1941 by bringing down a Wellington on the first night of January.

'kill' of 1941. Stradner's aircraft, damaged in the exchange, crashed on return.

Around 50 *Luftwaffe* bombers were over Britain during the night, bombs falling on eastern counties, while minelaying was carried out in Liverpool Bay. Irish neutrality was violated by the Germans.

Casualties 1/2nd January 1941

Royal Air Force

50 Squadron Hampden X3143
Overshot Lindholme P/O Burrough & crew safe.
78 Squadron Whitley T4204
Abandoned near Doncaster, one man from Sgt Davies' crew killed.
87 Squadron Hurricane V7207
Crashed landing at Charmy Down. Sgt Thom safe.
301 Squadron Wellington T2517
Shot down by intruder at Coleby Grange. S/L Floryanowicz & crew killed.
301 Squadron Wellington T2518
Crashed landing at Wellingore (P/O Murawski).
301 Squadron Wellington R1006
Crashed landing at Swinderby, Sgt Koslowski & crew safe.
605 Squadron Hurricane Z2383
Crashed near Brize Norton. P/O Scott killed.

Luftwaffe

I./NJG 2 Ju88C2 0254 R4+KH
Crashed at Gilze-Rijn after combat, Lt R.Stradner & crew unhurt.
Aircraft 60% damaged.

2nd January 1941

Two Spitfires of 234 Squadron took off at 09.38 hours for a routine patrol and were vectored towards a 'bandit' off the south-west coast. This was intercepted, identified as a Ju88, and claimed damaged by Pilot Officer Dewhurst.

The next interception involved a pair of Hurricanes from 79 Squadron, airborne from Pembrey at 13.19 hours. Sergeants Parr and Hughes intercepted a bomber over the sea, again identified as a Ju88. Parr attacked, followed by Hughes, and the two pilots were credited with the bomber as a 'probably destroyed'. It would seem that this aircraft was actually an He111 of *K.Gr.100*, which force-landed at Dinard, badly shot-up and with one crewman wounded.

The third interception occurred to the north east, when Flight Lieutenant Colin MacFie of 616 Squadron engaged a Heinkel of *I./KG 4* near Spurn Head. His fire produced no visible effect,

A section of 1 Squadron Hurricanes raise plumes of snow as they accelerate down the frozen runway. - RAF Museum

and no claim was made, but this aircraft force-landed in Holland with one man wounded.

During the course of the day the *Luftwaffe* claimed two victories by bomber crews, obviously during two of the above actions, but no British aircraft was hit.

Casualties 2nd January 1941

Royal Air Force

264 Squadron Defiant N3313
Crashed landing at Gravesend, S/L Sanders & gunner safe.
269 Squadron Hudson P5147
Crashed on take-off from Skeabrae, P/O Rees & crew safe.

Luftwaffe

II./JG 2 Bf109E4 1373
crash-landed at Bernay. Aircraft 60% damaged.
III./JG 26 Bf109E7 3280
Damaged in collision near Wehnen. Aircraft 30% damaged.
E./JG 26 Bf109E1 3613
Crashed at Cognac. Fw Rudolf Dietze killed. Aircraft 90% damaged.
III./JG 27 Bf109E4 1363
Force-landed at Oldenburg. Aircraft 50% damaged.
1./KG 4 He111P 2690
One man wounded in combat near The Humber. Aircraft 20% damaged.
III./KG 26 He111H5 3614
Force-landed at Le Havre. Aircraft 35% damaged.
4./KG 53 He111H2 5368
Force-landed at Amiens. Aircraft 35% damaged.
I./KG 100 He111H2 ----
One wounded by AA fire; Dinard. Extent of damage not known.
III./ZG 76 Bf109E4 1441
Crashed on take off from Bergen. Aircraft 70% damaged.

3.(F)/123 Bf110C5 2267
Crash-landed at Versailles. Lt Wolfgang Baumung and gunner killed.
Aircraft 80% damaged.
1./K.Gr.z.b.V.108 Ju52 6932
Damaged in storm at Hommelvik. Aircraft destroyed.
E.Gr.(See) Ar196A2 0091
Crashed on take-off Thistedt. Aircraft 80% damaged.

2/3rd January 1941

Intruders from *I./NJG 2* were again operating. *Unteroffizier* Arnold of *1 Staffel* claimed a Whitley destroyed at 18.45 hours, while at 19.02 hours a similar claim was made by *Feldwebel* Hans Hahn of *3./NJG 2*. One Whitley of 4 Group reported a fighter attack shortly after crossing the English coast on the way out. The Ju88 made one inaccurate firing pass from astern, and was hit by return fire from the British rear gunner, who reported that the fighter dived away with smoke pouring from one engine. One of the Junkers - probably that flown by Arnold - crash-landed at Gilze-Rijn on return. A second Whitley, of 102 Squadron, failed to return; Flying Officer Coutts and his crew are presumed lost at sea. It seems probable that this aircraft fell to Hahn, by far the most experienced of the two *Luftwaffe* pilots. One Squadron Hampden crashed on return.

Bomber Command Operations:
Bremen 41; Amsterdam and Emden 6.
Luftwaffe Operations
Cardiff 111. Minor raids elsewhere

A British intruder crew claimed success when Pilot Officer Ensor probably destroyed a Heinkel near Vereul. This was an aircraft from *III./KG 55*, which crashed at Villacoublay and was 'written off'.

Great damage was done to Cardiff, but no claims were made, by the defences. Three Heinkels of *KG 55* crashed on return at Villacoublay. In addition, a Do17 of *6./KG 2* - 'U5+GP' *Leutnant* Heinz Schiffner - failed to return from a sortie to Liverpool. No trace of this aircraft was ever found. A Dornier from *8./KG 2* returned to base with two crewmen wounded by Cardiff defences. Some of the German navigators were in error however, and bombs fell upon Eire, which evoked a sharp protest from the Irish government.

The hunters. A Ju88C and a Do17Z-10 at Gilze-Rijn, as if waiting for darkness to fall.

Casualties 2/3rd January 1941

Royal Air Force

61 Squadron Hampden X3126
Crashed landing at Hemswell. F/L Powdrell & crew safe.
64 Squadron Spitfire X4481
Damaged landing at Hornchurch P/O Jones safe.
82 Squadron Blenheim R3604
Damaged landing at Bodney Sgt Inman & crew safe.
102 Squadron Whitley T4227
Missing from operations. F/O Coutts & crew lost.
234 Squadron Spitfire P9491
Belly-landed at St Eval. F/O Baynham safe.
604 Squadron Beaufighter R2981
Damaged landing at Middle Wallop. Sgt Brown & crew safe.

Luftwaffe

6./KG 2 Do17Z3 2821 U5+GP
Failed to return from sortie. Lt Heinz Schiffner & crew missing.
8./KG 2 Do17Z3 3404 U5+DS
Two crew wounded on sortie to Cardiff. Aircraft 15% damaged.
Stab./KG 55 He111P3 2797
Crash-landed at Villacoublay. Aircraft 60% damaged.
III./KG 55 He111P2 1619 G1+BT
Undercarriage damage at Villacoublay. Aircraft 15% damaged.
III./KG 55 He111P2 2827 G1+LT
Crash-landed at Villacoublay. Aircraft 25% damaged.

3rd January 1941

As dawn broke, a few German aircraft began their daily reconnaissance of the British coastline, but Fighter Command made no interceptions. Coastal Command aircraft flew several patrols, and a Hudson had an inconclusive engagement with Bf110s off Norway.

Casualties 3rd January 1941

Royal Air Force

238 Squadron Hurricane V6758
Damaged beyond repair. No further details.
616 Squadron Spitfire R6980
Belly-landed at Kirton-in-Lindsay. P/O Johnson safe.

Luftwaffe

III./JG 27 Bf109E1 6009
Force-landed at Wehnen. Aircraft 80% damaged.
III./JG 77 FW58C1 0260
Force-landed at Dinard. Aircraft 80% damaged.
III./ZG76 Bf109E1 3540
Crash-landed at Stavanger. Aircraft 25% damaged.
1./196 He115C1 2729
Damaged in storm at Brest. Aircraft 50% damaged.
5(H)./13 Hs126B1 ----
Taxiing accident at Brussels-Evére. Aircraft 50% damaged.
K.Gr.z.b.V.108 Ju52 6755
Force-landed at Dresden. Aircraft 35% damaged.

3/4th January 1941

One bomber was lost, Pilot Officer Trehern's 51 Squadron Whitley apparently falling to

Bomber Command Operations
Bremen 71; Minelaying 6.
Luftwaffe Operations:
Bristol 178.

Flak. A 10 Squadron Whitley flown by Pilot Officer Williams was attacked and damaged near Catterick by *Leutnant* Böhme of *I./NJG 2*, the latter claiming a Whitley destroyed at 19.02 hours. A Wellington of 103 Squadron was also attacked, the nightfighter intercepting near the French coast and attacking from below. Flight Lieutenant Kelly evaded the attack and his rear-gunner claimed the fighter shot down into the sea. Squadron Leader Coleman's 23 Squadron Blenheim fighter failed to return. In the absence of any report of loss or damage to a German nightfighter, it is possible that Coleman attacked the Wellington in error, and was shot down by return fire.

One interception was effected over England. Flight Lieutenant John Cunningham of 604 Squadron claimed an He111 probably destroyed near Lyme Regis at around 19.15 hours. A Ju88, 'V4+FR' of *III./KG 1*, failed to return, *Leutnant* Theuer-

Leutnant Böhme of I./NJG 2. This unit had been formed from the Zerstörer Staffel of KG 30 in mid-1940, specifically for night intruder operations over England.

kauf and his crew being lost at sea, possibly as a result of this action.

Casualties 3/4th January 1941

Royal Air Force

10 Squadron Whitley T4234
Damaged by intruder near Catterick. P/O Williams & crew safe.
23 Squadron Blenheim YP-X
Missing from intruder sortie. S/L Coleman & crew lost.
51 Squadron Whitley P5060
Missing from operations. P/O Trehern & crew lost.
78 Squadron Whitley P4937
Abandoned near Barnstaple due to fuel shortage. P/O James & crew safe.
106 Squadron Hampden P4314
Force-landed near Finningley. Sgt Mapp & crew safe.
217 Squadron Beaufort MW-
Damaged by *Flak*, crew safe.
Fighter Interception Unit Beaufighter R2186
Crashed landing at Ford. W/C Chamberlain & crew safe.

Luftwaffe

III./KG 1 Ju88A5 3186 V4+FR
Failed to return from sortie. Lt Kurt Theuerkauf & crew missing.

4th January 1941

Action commenced at 09.50 hours, when three 65 Squadron Spitfires were vectored onto a 'bandit' 15 miles south of Selsey.

This was intercepted, identified as a Bf110, and claimed destroyed by Flying Officer Finucane. The 'bandit' may have been a Dornier - 'U5+JK' of *I./KG 2*, flown by *Oberleutnant* Joachim Rücker - which crash-landed at Epinoy.

In the early afternoon, two Spitfires from 152 Squadron found a Do17 of *Wekusta 26* flown by *Gefreiter* Werner Seurig near Portland at 14.00 hours. Pilot Officer Marrs DFC attacked, chased it down through the heavy naval barrage and shot it down into the sea southwest of The Shambles. There were no survivors. This victory was credited jointly to Marrs and the AA gunners.

Around noon, Blenheims of 53 Squadron raided warships in Brest harbour. Three hits were reported on a destroyer, but ten Bf109s of *II./JG 77* had been scrambled, and intercepted in the target area. Pilot Officer Gibbs' aircraft was shot down into the sea by *Unteroffizier* Rudolf Schmidt of *5 Staffel*, and that piloted by Pilot Officer Newton was attacked and badly shot about by *Oberleutnant* Horst Carganico, who claimed it 'wirklich beschossen' (badly damaged). This bomber subsequently crash-landed at Exeter. Two more Blenheims, flown by Flying Officer Gatward and Pilot Officer Bannister, were hit apparently following attacks by *Oberleutnant* Drüschle, who claimed strikes on three bombers. *Flak* gunners made two claims.

During the day a German bomber crew claimed a Hurricane destroyed near Ramsgate.

Casualties 4th January 1941

Royal Air Force

7 Squadron Stirling N3637
Damaged in flying accident. F/L Robertson & crew safe.

53 Squadron Blenheim PZ-V
Missing from sortie to Brest. P/O Gibbs & crew lost.

53 Squadron Blenheim PZ-E
Damaged by Bf109 and crash-landed at Exeter. P/O Newton & crew safe.

53 Squadron Blenheim PZ-
Damaged by Flak. P/O Bannister & crew safe.

53 Squadron Blenheim PZ-
Damaged by Flak. P/O Gatward & crew safe.

66 Squadron Spitfire P7660
Hit balloon cable and crash-landed at Chessington. Sgt Wylde safe.

99 Squadron Wellington L7783
Crashed after take-off from Newmarket.
Two men from F/O Davidson's crew killed.

304 Squadron Wellington N2844
Damaged at Litchfield. P/O Onoszko & crew safe.

A Dornier 17P of a long range reconnaissance Gruppe lies forlornly in a cornfield in Holland. - G J Zwanenberg MBE

504 Squadron Hurricane V6695
Force-landed near Exeter. Sgt Masarik safe.

Luftwaffe

1./JG 1 Bf109E4 6018
Crashed on take-off from Bergen. Aircraft 40% damaged.

I./KG 2 Do17Z2 4191 U5+JK
Crash-landed at Epinoy, Oblt J.Rücker & crew unhurt. Aircraft 35% damaged.

I./KG 26 He111H5 3699
Belly-landed at Hagenau. Aircraft 30% damaged.

I./KG 54 Ju88A5 6081
Crash-landed at Evreux, Aircraft 10% damaged.

III./St.G.2 Ju87R2 5843
Crash-landed at Loddenheide, crew injured. Aircraft 40% damaged.

III./St.G.2 Ju87R2 5692
Crashed on take-off from Ernes. Aircraft 15% damaged.

III./StG.2 Ju87R2 %849
Crash-landed at Loddenheide. Aircraft 60% damaged.

Wekusta 26 Do17Z3 2643 5M+J
Failed to return from combat sortie. Gfr Werner Seurig & crew lost.

4/5th January 1941

The weather was not good. At 18.30 hours, a fighter identified as a Bf110 slid out of the low cloud cloudbase above Marham and dived on a 218 Squadron Wellington which had just become airborne. The fighter let fly with a short burst of cannon fire that was answered immediately by the British

---

Bomber Command Operations:

Brest 53; ; Hamburg 24; Rotterdam 4; Duisberg 9; Minelaying 5; OTU 2.

Luftwaffe Operations:

Bristol and Avonmouth 103

---

rear-gunner. No hits were seen and the fighter whipped over the Wellington and disappeared in an almost vertical climb into the clouds.

There were no losses during the raids, but a Whitley crashed on return.

Only one contact was made against the German raiders when Flying Officer Smallwood of 87 Squadron claimed a bomber damaged near the target area. One Ju88 of *KGr.806* force-landed at St Lô, and a Dornier from *8./KG 2* bellied in at Cambrai, one of these possibly due to the Hurricane pilot's attack.

Casualties 4/5th January 1941

Royal Air Force

10 Squadron Whitley T4220
Damaged landing after operations. S/L Holford & crew safe.

Luftwaffe

8./KG 2 Do17Z2 3357
Belly-landed at Cambrai. Aircraft 35% damaged.
K.Gr.806 Ju88A1 7079
Force-landed at St Lô. Aircraft 30% damaged.

5th January 1941

There were again a few raiders out over Britain, mostly around East Anglia where a few bombs fell. Pilot Officer Brewster of 616 Squadron was the only pilot to engage a German aircraft. He intercepted a Do17 north of the Wash and fired one burst before losing it in cloud. He made no claim, but the Dornier in fact crash-landed at St Trond.

Nine Blenheims from 59 Squadron Coastal Command raided Brest and once again Messerschmitts from *I./JG 77* were ready · for them. This squadron fared better however; Pilot Officer Custerson's aircraft was jumped by a Bf109, and his gunner Sergeant Edgar claimed this shot down in flames. Pilot Officer Buchan's bomber was also attacked and damaged, but his gunner claimed to have hit the fighter which half-rolled and dived away pouring smoke. During the fight the Bf109 pilots, hindered by their own *Flak*, claimed hits upon three Blenheims. Despite the claims of the turret gunners, no Messerschmitt was hit.

The Handley-Page Hampden equipped No.5 Group. It was the only medium bomber to have an 'open' rear turret. The gunners froze!

Casualties 5th January 1941

Royal Air Force

59 Squadron Blenheim TR-A
Damaged by Flak. P/O Custerson & crew safe.
59 Squadron Blenheim TR-F
Damaged by Bf109. P/O Buchan & crew safe.
71 Squadron Hurricane V6636
Collided near Scunthorpe. P/O Leckrone killed.
71 Squadron Hurricane XR-
Collided near Scunthorpe. P/O Orbison baled out unhurt.
111 Squadron Hurricane N2489
Belly-landed near Dyce. Sgt Hruby safe.
139 Squadron Blenheim T2134
Damaged by AA fire at Lowestoft. W/C Kyle & crew safe.
206 Squadron Hudson T9368
Crashed landing at Northolt. Sgt Cave & crew safe.
5 FPP Oxford V3540
Lost over Thames estuary. 1st Off.Amy Johnson baled out but missing.*

Luftwaffe

III./JG 77 Bf109E4 1305
Crashed on take-off from Dinan. Aircraft 50% damaged.
8./KG 3 Do17Z2 3328
Crash-landed at St Trond. Aircraft 55% damaged.
III./ZG 76 Bf109E4 0959
Crashed on take-off from Bergen. Aircraft 70% damaged.
4.(F)/14 Ju88A5 0291
Villacoublay; technical failure. Aircraft 20% damaged.

---

*Note: Non-operational, but included for historical interest.

SNFKdo 4 Do24 0019
Crashed at Caen. Ofw W.Nies & one man killed, one injured. Aircraft destroyed.

5/6th January 1941

Twelve Hampdens were sent to lay mines off Brest, Lorient and St. Nazaire harbours. One machine from 49 Squadron flown by Sergeant Price DFM, ditched off Sidmouth.

The *Luftwaffe* was similarly hampered by bad weather, and raids were light and scattered. One Ju88 of *3.(F)/122* failed to return from the Thames estuary area, *Leutnant* Heinz Krafftschick and his crew being lost at sea. This possibly fell victim to A.A. gunsites, whose crews made three claims for 'probables'. Another bomber crash-landed on return.

Casualties 5/6th January 1941

Royal Air Force
49 Squadron Hampden P4366
Ditched off Sidmouth. Sgt Price DFM & crew lost.

Luftwaffe
9./KG 3 Do17Z2 3324
Crashed at Cambrai. Aircraft 45% damaged.
3.(F)/122 Ju88A1 0394 F6+FL
Failed to return from combat sortie. Lt H.Krafftschick & crew missing.

6th - 9th January 1941

The operations of the next four days were greatly hampered by the appalling weather conditions prevailing over north-west Europe.

2 Group sent a small number of cloud cover raiders out on the 6th. A tanker was claimed damaged off Holland, but an 82 Squadron Blenheim crashed on return. A success was claimed by Coastal Command however, when Flying Officer Baker's 210 Squadron Sunderland crew was credited with the destruction of a U-boat whilst on a Biscay patrol.

Next day 421 Flight made two interceptions; Flight Lieutenant Drake and Flying Officer O'Meara claimed a Ju88 damaged near Dover at 12.00 hours, and at 14.00 hours Drake claimed a second Junkers damaged near Hawkinge. No German aircraft had actually been hit, but during one of these engagements a *Luftwaffe* crew claimed a British fighter shot down.

The bitter winter of 1940/41 affected both side equally. This is Westerland, with Bf110s lined up in the snow. - Petrick

On the 8th, more cloud cover Blenheims were despatched, all five returning safely, but Coastal Command lost a 233 Squadron Hudson which crashed near Antrim with the loss of the crew. That night 57 Bomber Command aircraft raided targets in northwest Germany while Coastal Command bombers attacked Brest. A Wellington crashed on take-off, and a Whitley crashed at Dishforth.

Next morning (9th), Fighter Command flew the first offensive sweep over French soil since June 1940 (65, 145 and 610 Squadrons), but drew no reaction from the *Luftwaffe*. A similar operation a little later (1 and 615 Squadrons) proved equally fruitless, but a Hurricane force-landed on return.

The conditions of heavy overcast over Britain had encouraged the cloud cover raiders of the *Luftwaffe*. Apart from from many attacks upon residential and industrial areas, several airfields were bombed. Bircham Newton was raided on the 6th, while Debden, Newmarket, Stradishall and Honington all received a few bombs next day.

Casualties 6th January 1941

Royal Air Force
48 Squadron Anson W1670
Crashed on take-off from Stornoway. Sgt Burton & crew safe.
82 Squadron Blenheim V5375
Crashed at Norwich on return from operations. Sgt Jackson & crew safe.
602 Squadron Spitfire K9970
Belly-landed near West Kilbride. Sgt McDougall-Black safe.

Luftwaffe

E./JG 77 Bf109E1 3632
Crashed on take-off from Bordeaux. Aircraft 30% damaged.
E./LG 1 Ju88A5 4167
Crashed at Langendiebach. Oblt Günther Porth & one crewman killed.
Aircraft destroyed.
I./ZG 26 Bf110D3 4220
Force-landed at Memmingen. Aircraft 80% damaged.

Casualties 7th January 1941

Royal Air Force

48 Squadron Anson K8703
Overshot Stornoway. Aircraft destroyed.
209 Squadron Lerwick L7262
Crashed on take-off from Loch Ryan (F/O Spotswood).
260 Squadron Hurricane V7133
Crashed landing at Castletown. Sgt Crocker safe.

Luftwaffe

8./JG 3 Bf109E7 6196
Damaged taxiing at Desvres. Aircraft 40% damaged.
II./KG 1 Ju88A5 7173
Force-landed at Antwerp. Aircraft 90% damaged.
4./KG 30 Ju88A5 8176
Gilze-Rijn; technical failure. Aircraft 35% damaged.
3.(F)/11 Do17P1 1088
Taxiing accident at Mutford. Aircraft 5% damaged.
1./196 Ar196A2 0047
Crash-landed on Bornholm Island. Aircraft 35% damaged.

Casualties 7/8th January 1941

Royal Air Force

1 (RCAF) Squadron Hurricane V7111
Crashed landing at Castletown. F/L Russel safe.

Luftwaffe

- nil -

Casualties 8th January 1941

Royal Air Force

72 Squadron Spitfire X4167
Belly-landed at Acklington. P/O Elliott safe.
255 Squadron Defiant YD-
Hit Spitfire landing at Kirton-in-Lindsay. Pilot safe.
233 Squadron Hudson T9379
Crashed at Antrim. P/O Stone & crew killed.
301 Squadron Wellington R1366
Crashed landing at Cranwell. P/O Pozyczka safe.
616 Squadron Spitfire X4055
Hit by 255 Squadron Defiant at Kirton-in-Lindsay. No casualty.

The naval threat at Brest. Part of a low level oblique photo taken by 252 Squadron, showing the cruiser Hipper in dock.

Luftwaffe

IV./LG 1 Ju87B1 5508
Taxiing accident at Stavanger. Aircraft 5% damaged.
IV./LG 1 Ju87B1 0215
Taxiing accident at Stavanger. Aircraft 5% damaged.
IV./LG 1 Ju87B2 5729
Taxiing accident at Stavanger. Aircraft 5% damaged.

Casualties 8/9th January 1941

Royal Air Force

51 Squadron Whitley P5020
Crashed at Dishforth. P/O Myers & crew safe.
214 Squadron Wellington T9256
Crashed on take-off from Stradishall. P/O Timmins & crew killed.

Luftwaffe

- nil -

Casualties 9th January 1941

Royal Air Force

32 Squadron Hurricane V7125
Overshot Kenley. Sgt Wolstenholme safe.
214 Squadron Wellington T2542
Belly-landed at Stradishall. P/O Sturdy & crew safe.
229 Squadron Hurricane V7674
Overshot Hawarden. P/O Stegman safe.
263 Squadron Blenheim L1123
Crashed at Topsham, Exeter. Aircraft destroyed.

264 Squadron Defiant PS-
Collided (P/O Bowen).
264 Squadron Defiant PS-
Collided (P/O Melville).
303 Squadron Hurricane V6815
Belly-landed at Hillingdon. P/O Miksza safe.
615 Squadron Hurricane V7339
Force-landed near Kenley on operations. P/O Wydrowski safe.
3 PRU Spitfire X4385
Belly-landed at Oakington. P/O Wilkinson safe.

Luftwaffe

E./JG 3 Bf109E3 1163
Crashed on take-off from Wizernes. Aircraft 60% damaged.
E./JG 51 Bf109E4 1285
Landed at Marquise with engine damage. Aircraft 30% damaged.
II./KG 1 Ju88A5 4190
Crashed on take-off from Münster-Handorf. Aircraft 70% damaged.
III./KG 76 Ju88 ----
Crashed at Insterburg. Oblt W.Georgens & one crewman killed.
Aircraft destroyed.
2.(F)/22 Do17M1 2152
Crash-landed at Sola. Aircraft 25% damaged.
3.(H)/32 Hs126B1 3170
Crashed force-landing at Quimper. Aircraft 90% damaged.
Stab E-St. VIII Fl.K Ju87B1 0363
Crashed at Eikeloh. Ofhr G.Wacker & crew killed. Aircraft destroyed.
Kur.St.O.b.d.L Fs104 0883
Force-landed at Wolbeck. Aircraft 55% damaged.

9/10th January 1941

Better weather resulted in one interception when at 23.18 hours *Oberleutnant* Reinhold Eckardt of *6./NJG 1* intercepted and destroyed Sergeant Smith's 78 Squadron Whitley over Erlekem in Holland. The fighter was also damaged. One Wellington crew from 149 Squadron was attacked by a fighter but escaped. A 2 Group Blenheim crew sighted a Ju88 some 30 miles from Gilze-Rijn, and made a diving attack. *Oberfeldwebel* Johann-Theodor Schmal's *I./KG 30* aircraft was hit in one engine, which burst into flames. The Junkers then rolled over and dived into the ground. Only one man survived, badly wounded.

Bomber Command Operations:

Gelsenkirchen, Hamborn and Essen 13;
Rotterdam 15; Calais 1; Minelaying 4.

Luftwaffe Operations:

Manchester 143; London 62; Liverpool 141

A Coastal Blenheim of 59 Squadron flown by Pilot Officer Cook failed to return from Brest, and is believed to have crashed into the Irish sea. A 53 Squadron Blenheim ditched off Wittering, one man being lost from Pilot Officer Lucas' crew. Intruders from 23 Squadron were operating again and Sergeant Jones' Blenheim did not return.

Over Britain three bombers were claimed destroyed by A.A. sites, while Sergeant Endersby in a 264 Squadron Defiant, claimed a Ju88 damaged over Beachy Head at midnight. Two German bombers were lost; *Oberfeldwebel* Karl Goppert's He111 of *II./KG 27* and *Unteroffizier* Otto Kraher's Ju88C nightfighter from *I./NJG 2* both disappeared without trace. Another Heinkel bellied in at Artois.

Casualties 9/10th January 1941

Royal Air Force

23 Squadron Blenheim L1226
Missing from intruder sortie. Sgt Jones & crew lost.
51 Squadron Whitley T4270
Crashed at Dishforth. Four men from P/O Shaw's crew killed.
53 Squadron Blenheim V5370
Ditched off Wittering. One man from P/O Lucas' crew lost.
59 Squadron Blenheim T2217
Failed to return from sortie. P/O Cook & crew lost.
78 Squadron Whitley T4203
Failed to return from sortie. Sgt Smith & crew lost.
103 Squadron Wellington R3215
Crash-landed near Abergavenny after sortie. Sgt Crich & crew safe.
106 Squadron Hampden X2968
Crashed landing at Finningley. Sgt West & crew safe.
149 Squadron Wellington T2460
Damaged by Royal Naval AA fire. Sgt Goss wounded.
149 Squadron Wellington T2737
Damaged by nightfighter. Crew unhurt.
307 Squadron Defiant N3401
Abandoned off Barmouth. Sgt Joda & gunner safe, aircraft lost.
610 Squadron Spitfire X4263
Overshot Westhampnett. P/O Ross safe.

Luftwaffe

II./KG 27 He111P 1646 1G+FH
Failed to return from sortie. Ofw Karl Goppert & crew missing.
I./KG 30 Ju88A5 0323
Crashed at Etten. Ofw Johann-Theodor Schmal & two crew killed, one wounded. Aircraft destroyed.
I./KG 53 He111H5 3831
Belly-landed at Artois. Aircraft 70% damaged.

47

II./NJG 1 Bf110 ---- G9+HP
Damaged in combat, Oblt R.Eckardt & crew safe. Aircraft 25% damaged.
I./NJG 2 Ju88C2 0227 R4+CL
Failed to return from sortie. Uffz O.Kraher & crew lost.

Chapter Two

"Leaning Forward"

10th January 1941

The first aerial encounter took place in the morning, when Sergeant Gillies of 421 Flight (renumbered 91 Squadron next day) was jumped by Bf109s over Boulogne. He escaped by diving to sea level.

A milestone in the air war was reached with the despatch of *Circus No.1*. For the first time since mid-1940, an escorted bomber force was ordered to penetrate enemy-held airspace, thus beginning the rôle-reversal of the opposing sides maintained since the Dunkiirk evacuation.

At noon, Wing Commander Elsmie led his six Blenheims away from Hornchurch, and made rendezvous with the escorts over Southend. Before the bombers had reached the French coast, 249 Squadron took on a small group of Messerschmitts near Mardyck, where Wing Commander Beamish claimed one damaged. Sergeant Maciejowski became separated and found himself at low level near Guines. He machine-gunned a group of Hs126s on the airfield without effect and then spotted a pair of Bf109Es at his own altitude. He attacked, claiming that one crashed into some trees. The second disappeared. Finding his throttle jammed fully open, he withdrew. He landed at Hornchurch by switching off his engine and gliding in.

Circus No.1 To Fôret de Guines	
6 Blenheims of 114 Sqn	
Close Escort:	56 Sqn
Forward Support:	242 and 249 Sqns
Target Support:	302 and 610 Sqns
Top Cover:	41, 64 and 611 Sqns
Rear Cover:	66, 74 and 92 Sqns

A Blenheim crew returns from 'ops'. During the next few months very many crews would not be so lucky.

As the bombers approached the French coast, the Forward Support Hurricanes crossed out near Calais. Wing Commander Beamish then saw a Bf109 drop onto the tail of Pilot Officer McConnell of 249 Squadron. The Messerschmitt pilot, *Oberleutnant* Michalek of *II./JG 3*, executed a perfect 'bounce', and McConnell baled out hurriedly. He was later picked up by the A.S.R. Service and taken to hospital suffering from splinter wounds. Beamish turned into the attack and claimed to have shot the Bf109 down into the Channel, but Michalek escaped unscathed.

Meanwhile the Blenheims, under heavy and accurate Flak, had bombed the ammunition dumps and were withdrawing. As they re-crossed the French coastline, the Rear Cover squadrons swept in and a strong force of Bf109s then attacked. 74 Squadron was bounced and two of their Spitfires were badly shot-up. Sergeant Freese managed to reach Detling, where he stalled and crashed attempting to force-land. 41 Squadron, high squadron of the Top Cover Wing, were jumped by five Bf109s

Wing Commander F V Beamish claimed a Bf109 destroyed and another damaged on 'Circus No.1'.

Pilot Officer W W McConnell of 249 Squadron, first fighter pilot to be 'bounced' in 1941.

over Wissant. The Spitfire flown by Sergeant Beardsley was badly hit, but he managed to return. Sergeant Baker claimed a 'probable'.

Apart from *II./JG 3*, it is clear that elements of *I Gruppe* were also airborne. *Hauptmann* Hans von Hahn, the *Gruppenkommandeur*, claimed a Blenheim shot down near near Nieuport thirty minutes later, probably accounting for Pilot Officer Alcock's 53 Squadron machine, which was reported missing from a Channel patrol.

In all, the R.A.F. fighters had come off 'second best' in this encounter; for the loss of two fighters and two more damaged, not a single Messerschmitt had even been hit.

A little later two Hurricanes of 145 Squadron patrolled over Littlehampton at 15,000 ft and intercepted a Ju88 at 13.45 hours. Pilot Officer Dunning-White closed on it under intense return fire and fired a three-second burst. One engine caught fire at once and the return fire stopped. Sergeant Turnbull then chased the Junkers for 35 miles, losing contact when the smoke trail thickened and it dived towards the sea. The British pilots claimed a 'shared probable'. It is likely that it was a machine from *III./KG 1* which subsequently force-landed at Arras with one engine ablaze. One Junkers was lost however. *Oberleutnant* Hans-Joachim von Sydow and his crew from *2.(F)/123* were reported missing from a reconnaissance sortie to Manchester. This aircraft crashed into the sea off Newquay due to AA fire.

The *Luftwaffe* sustained a further loss when a FW200 of *I./KG 40* was reported missing near Iceland. It was shot down by a Lewis gun, manned by Mr Reilly, mate of the ocean-going tug *Seaman*, when the vessel was attacked some 200 miles north-west of Ireland at 13.50 hours. *Oberleutnant* Burmeister and his crew were rescued and taken prisoner.

Casualties 10th January 1941

Royal Air Force

23 Squadron Havoc AX922
Crashed landing at Ford. F/S Burton & crew safe.

32 Squadron Hurricane V6927
Damaged landing at Middle Wallop. P/O Waskiewicz safe.

41 Squadron Spitfire P7590
Damaged by Bf109. Sgt Beardsley safe.

53 Squadron Blenheim PZ-H
Failed to return. P/O Alcock and crew lost.

74 Squadron Spitfire P7561
Damaged by Bf109 and crashed at Detling. Sgt Freese safe. Aircraft wrecked.

74 Squadron Spitfire P7310
Damaged by Bf109. Pilot safe.

75 Squadron Wellington T2550
Crashed near Duxford. P/O McNamara & five crew killed.

107 Squadron Blenheim N3629
Overshot Bicester. F/L Simmons & crew safe.

152 Squadron Spitfire X4772
Crashed landing at Warmwell. P/O Fox-Male safe.

213 Squadron Hurricane P3522
Crashed on Yorkshire Moors. Sgt Bruce killed.

214 Squadron Wellington T3542
Belly-landed. Crew safe.

249 Squadron Hurricane P3579
Shot down into Channel by Bf109. P/O McConnell baled out wounded.

264 Squadron Defiant N1763
Crashed landing at Gravesend. Sgt Hibbert & gunner safe.

266 Squadron Spitfire X4021
Belly-landed at Cranwell after scramble. P/O Mitchell safe.

266 Squadron Spitfire R6920
Crash-landed at Swinderby after scramble. Sgt Shirecore safe.

269 Squadron Hudson T9334
Damaged by AA fire from convoy. P/O Heron & crew safe.

604 Squadron Beaufighter R2098
Damaged landing at Middle Wallop. F/L Skinner & crew safe.

Target England. A Heinkel 111 with engines running, prepares to taxi out for a sortie.

812 Squadron Swordfish :Q
Crashed at Halton, crew killed.
10 (RAAF) Squadron Sunderland P9600
Crashed landing at Oban. S/L Cohen & crew safe.

Luftwaffe

III./JG 2 Bf109E7 1964
Crash-landed at Bernay. Aircraft 35% damaged.
III./KG 1 Ju88A5 2219
Force-landed near Arras. Aircraft 80% damaged.
I./KG 40 FW200C3 0035 F8+AB
Failed to return. Oblt F.Burmeister & two crew captured, three killed.
II./KG77 Ju88A1 6179
Tyre damage on take-off from Rheims. Aircraft 25% damaged.
E./NJG 1 Bf110C1 1355
Force-landed near Köln. Aircraft 30% damaged.
E./ZG 26 Bf110C3 1373
Crash-landed at Ingolstadt. Aircraft 50% damaged.
III./ZG 76 Bf110C4 2083
Belly-landed at Stavanger. Aircraft 30% damaged.
2.(F)/123 Ju88A5 0358 4U+FK
Failed to return from sortie. Oblt Hans-Joachim von Sydow & crew lost.
5.(H)/12 Go145A1 1111
Force-landed Luxembourg. Aircraft 20% damaged.
Tr.St. I Fl.K Fi156C2 4242
Taxiing accident at Guyancourt. Aircraft 40% damaged.

10/11th January 1941

Bomber and Coastal Commands despatched 27 aircraft to Brest, and a further 25 Swordfish of the Fleet Air Arm laid mines off

Dieppe. A Hampden crashed on return.

153 *Luftwaffe* bombers punished Portsmouth, causing great damage, but only one fighter pilot engaged. Pilot Officer Dunning-White of 145 Squadron attacked a bomber without effect, which would certainly have been *Oberleutnant* Kuechle's Ju88 from *I./KG 51*, which bellied in at Villaroche after combat.

Casualties 10/11th January 1941

Royal Air Force

49 Squadron Hampden L4045
Crashed at Northope, Lincs. P/O Newhouse & crew killed, aircraft destroyed.

Luftwaffe

I./KG 51 Ju88A5 3234
Crash-landed at Villaroche after combat. Oblt Kuechle & crew safe.

11th January 1941

The 11th began with low-level attacks upon airfields by the *Luftwaffe*, with Bf109s damaging a 92 Squadron Spitfire during a strafe of Manston, while three training aircraft were hit at Bramcote during a Bf110 attack.

A 201 Squadron Sunderland engaged a FW200 of *I./KG 40* over Biscay at 12.54 hours, Flight Lieutenant Lindsay's gunners claiming it damaged. In fact two FW200s crashed, but neither was due to combat. Coastal Command sustained one loss when Pilot Officer Fox's 224 Squadron Hudson crashed at Kildare, Eire.

Bomber Command despatched 19 Blenheims to attack targets in Holland, from which Pilot Officer Poulson's 82 Squadron machine failed to return.

Casualties 11th January 1941

Royal Air Force

72 Squadron Spitfire X4602
Force-landed near Durham. Sgt Casey safe.
82 Squadron Blenheim T2163
Failed to return. P/O Poulson & crew lost.
92 Squadron Spitfire QJ-
Damaged during strafe of Manston. No casualty.
96 Squadron Hurricane V7130
Crashed landing at Cranage. P/O Lauder safe.
219 Squadron Beaufighter R2076
Damaged landing at Tangmere. Sgt Grubb & crew safe.
224 Squadron Hudson N7298
Crashed near Kildare after patrol. P/O Fox & crew lost.

Pilot Officer Tom Smart (left), Flying Officer Walker and Flight Lieutenant Gordon Olive of 65 Squadron. Smart claimed a Ju88 on the night of 11/12th January, a rare achievement for a Spitfire pilot.

306 Squadron Hurricane V7165
Force-landed at Cosford. S/L Rolski safe.
OTU Wellington -----
Three aircraft damaged in raid on Bramcote.

Luftwaffe

II./JG 3 Bf109E4 5359
Crash-landed at Arques. Aircraft 25% damaged.
E./JG 26 Bf109E4 0749
Crash-landed at Dieppe. Aircraft 10% damaged.
I./KG 40 FW200C3 0028
Force-landed on Ile de Ré due to Flak damage. Aircraft destroyed.
I./KG 40 FW200C3 0037
Crashed at Merignac in bad visibility. Aircraft 25% damaged.

11/12th January 1941

35 bombers were sent to attack the battleship *Tirpitz* at Wilhelmshaven, all returning safely. Of eleven bombers sent to bomb Turin, one Wellington of 9 Squadron force-landed near Dijon where Sergeant Parkes' crew were taken prisoner.

London was raided by 137 bombers. Flight Lieutenant Smart of 65 Squadron claimed a Ju88 destroyed near the south coast. This would appear to have been an aircraft from *II./KG 51* which crashed at Arques, killing *Feldwebel* Blusch and two of his crew. AA gunners claimed two bombers. An He111 force-landed near Zandvoort with battle damage.

Casualties 11/12th January 1941

Royal Air Force

9 Squadron Wellington R1244
Failed to return. Sgt Parkes & crew lost.

23 Squadron Blenheim L6737
Belly-landed at Ford. P/O Simpson & crew safe.

Luftwaffe

II./KG 51 Ju88A5 6020
Crashed at Arques. Fw H-G Blusch & two crew killed, one injured. Aircraft destroyed.

1./KG 53 He111H5 3633
Force-landed at Zandvoort due to Flak, one man wounded. Aircraft 80% damaged.

12th January 1941

Two Whirlwinds of 263 Squadron took off at 09.42 hours and intercepted a Ju88, possibly a *K.Gr.806* machine. This was attacked and claimed damaged by Pilot Officer Stein, who thus made the first combat claim by a Whirlwind pilot.

At 11.30 hours, the Hurricanes of Red Section, 3 Squadron, scrambled from Sumburgh and, at 11.40 hours, intercepted a Dornier over Fair Isle. This was attacked and claimed probably destroyed by Flight Lieutenant Berry. Air Intelligence reported that such an aircraft crashed into the sea in this area, but no such loss appears on the German Loss listings.

242 Squadron flew their first *Rhubarbs* during the morning. Squadron Leader Bader and Flight Lieutenant Turner departed at 10.20 hours, finding and strafing two E-boats between Dunkirk and Calais. The rest of the squadron clamoured to join in the new 'game', and at 12.15 hours Pilot Officer Latta and Flying Officer Cryderman took off, followed at 13.25 hours by Flight Lieutenant McKnight and Pilot Officer Brown. Cryderman and Latta made landfall near Gravelines, where they strafed targets just inland before two Bf109s jumped them. Latta was shot down into the sea, but Cryderman escaped. McKnight and Brown proceeded to Calais and had just made a strafing run over beach targets when they too were attacked by Messerschmitts. Brown engaged the leader in a head-on attack, then broke fast for the clouds. Flying Officer W L McKnight, one of the leading R.A.F. aces with 18 victories to his credit, was

Flying Officer Wil-
liam McKnight
DFC, one of several
Canadians to fly
with 242 Squadron.
He fought with dis-
tinction in France
and during the Bat-
tle of Britain. By the
time of his death he
had claimed at least
eighteen confirmed
victories.

never seen again. One of the two Hurricanes was shot down by *Oberleutnant* Georg Michalek of *II./JG 3*.

Another loss was sustained when a Spitfire flown by Flight Lieutenant Marshall of 3 PRU was shot down over Texel by *Oberleutnant*. Kinzinger of *I./JG 54*. Henry Marshall suffered severe leg injuries in the subsequent crash-landing. Although taken prisoner immediately he quickly escaped, but was soon recaptured.

Casualties 12th January 1941

Royal Air Force

15 Squadron Wellington R1169
Overshot. Sgt Garrioch & crew safe.
19 Squadron Spitfire P7318
Crash-landed at base. P/O Howard-Williams safe.
72 Squadron Spitfire X4413
Overshot Acklington. Sgt Lack safe.
96 Squadron Hurricane P3663
Crashed landing at Cranage. Sgt Kneath safe.
115 Squadron Wellington R1004
Damaged by Royal Naval AA fire. Sgt Marriott & crew safe
141 Squadron Defiant N1688
Crashed landing at Gravesend. P/O Benson & gunner injured.

142 Squadron Wellington W5373
Overshot Binbrook. P/O Bilton & crew safe.
242 Squadron Hurricane P2961
Shot down by Bf109. F/O McKnight DFC missing.
242 Squadron Hurricane V7203
Shot down by Bf109. P/O Latta missing.
256 Squadron Defiant N1648
Force-landed near Doncaster. Sgt Hall & gunner safe.
310 Squadron Hurricane P2953
Overshot Duxford. F/L Sinclair safe.
603 Squadron Spitfire P7546
Belly-landed at Drem. Sgt Stokoe safe.
607 Squadron Hurricane P3603
Damaged landing at Usworth. S/L Vincent safe.
3 PRU Spitfire X4386
Failed to return. F/L Marshall lost.

Luftwaffe

E./JG 2 Bf109E7 5378
Undercarriage damage at Octeville. Aircraft 15% damaged.
3./NJG 3 Bf110C4 3559
Belly-landed at Vechta. Aircraft 15% damaged.
K.Gr.806 Ju88A1 4080
Undercarriage damage at Caen. Aircraft 30% damaged.
K.Gr.806 Ju88A1 2165
Undercarriage damage at Caen. Aircraft 15% damaged.

12/13th January 1941

The primary objective for Wellingtons of 149 Squadron was the blocking of the Brenner Pass, with an Italian Navy oil storage depot (situated on an island in the Venice Lagoon) as the secondary target. Pilot Officer Wilson, a Rhodesian, was second pilot to Sergeant Dick Hodgson, and recalled the events of that night clearly:

Bomber Command Operations

Brest 26; Regensburg 3;

Airfields 21; Venice 7; Turin 2;

Minelaying 8; OTU 3.

Luftwaffe Operations

London 141

"The direct route from Suffolk to Venice and back non-stop was a long way for a Wimpey, but our trip was scheduled to be longer because we had to fly on a circular, southwards route to avoid the Flak and nightfighters of the Ruhr. It was a brilliant moonlit night, and after about four hours we saw the glow of the French/Swiss Alps reflecting the blazing moon on their heavily snow-mantled slopes. We crossed into neutral Switzerland, and saw the lights of the cities, farms and villages twinkling gaily up to us in a strong contrast to the rest of drab, blacked-out Europe.

"Suddenly, the most fantastic sight took our breaths away. On our port side, and towering about 4,000 feet above us were the Jungfrau and the Eiger. The full moon shining on them turned them into giant stacks of millions of glistening, polished diamonds.

"As we left this awesome sight, we flew on into Austria, but a blanket of cloud filled the valley around the Brenner Pass. It would have been an elusive target under the best of circumstances, so we headed straight south to Venice. The cloud cleared as we crossed the Dolomite Alps, and we could almost map-read our way there. When we arrived, we could see the city and our target to the south of the Via D'Annunzio quite distinctly.

"We dropped two of our bombs, and watched them curve down and plop harmlessly into the Lagoon. The Italian defences appeared to be virtually nil, and we'd come a long way, so we decided to 'dive bomb' the target.

"It seemed as if the shuddering wings were going to come off, as we hurtled into a speed of well over 250 m.p.h., and we dropped our last two bombs as we flattened out. We saw the flash of at least one of them hit the target.

"By this time we were only about 300 feet over the Lagoon, and our momentum kept us well over 200 m.p.h. I suppose it must have been one of the rare occasions that a bomber crew, at that stage of the war, had seen it's target blow up just beneath them and, in our elation, we decided to fulfill our mission completely by dropping propaganda pamphlets over Venice itself."

The wireless operator went back to carry out the leaflet dropping, but managed instead to fill the rear fuselage of the Wellington with paper. Wilson moved back to help, calling to Dick Hodgson to circle again, but as he began to thrust the packages down the chute:

"....to my horror I felt the 'plane shudder violently as if it had hit a cattle grid, and bullets burst all around Lofty and myself - one between our faces. We looked at each other for a second or two. Then I heard Dick's voice yell over the intercom, 'We're on fire!'

"I pushed my way through the sea of pamphlets and started to run forward. I could see our starboard engine blazing through the windows, the 'plane began to tilt down and the starboard wing headed for the water as the fire spread. As I reached the cockpit we hit the water. Apparently we'd flown over the only naval patrol ship in the lagoon.

"We must have been doing 200 m.p.h. as we hit and, quite frankly, I don't remember the next few minutes; I wasn't injured, just mentally out for the count. I dragged myself to my feet and saw the tail unit of 'another' plane about 200 yards in front of us, and wondered where it had come from. Our engine was still blazing furiously, and we decided to abandon the 'plane quickly before the petrol tank burst into flames. We laboriously climbed out of the astro hatch. Lofty reached the tip of the port wing and I called out to him to dive in and see how deep it was.

"He dived in and then, to our amazement, rose out of the water like a black Phoenix, dripping with mud. We all burst into laughter and began to drop, feet first, into the water. Someone said 'Where's Mac?' I looked around towards the tail unit. It wasn't there! It was our tail unit in front of us. Doubled up with laughter we stumbled towards it. Halfway there another Wimpey swooped down over us. It was the Squadron Commander, Speedy Powell. He waggled his wings and I saw his hand in thumbs up salute. It was the last time I ever saw him. I looked at my watch. It was 1.45 a.m. on the 13th January 1941."

The rear gunner was extricated from the turret, nicking his eyebrow on the wreckage as he emerged, and then a motor-boat appeared to carry the still laughing crew into captivity. The Italians were convinced that they had been under the influence of drugs.

"It would only have complicated matters considerably to have told them that we were under the influence of the most potent of drugs in conditions of stress - 'Facetiae Brittanicae", commonly known as the British sense of humour!'

Over England, one fighter combat took place when Flight Lieutenant John Cunningham of 604 Squadron found and attacked an He111 off Beachy Head around 04.30 hours, but could only claim a 'damaged' due to gun failures. Their opponent was almost certainly a machine from *III./KG 55*, which subsequently crashed on return at Orleans.

Casualties 12/13th January 1941

Royal Air Force

115 Squadron Wellington R1179
Overshot Marham. Sgt Lasbrey & crew safe.
149 Squadron Wellington T2807
Failed to return. Sgt R.Hodgson & crew lost.

Luftwaffe

III./KG 55 He111P2 1560
Crash-landed at Orleans.Aircraft 30% damaged.

13th January 1941

Bad weather curtailed the operations of both sides, the sole fighter action coming at 14.30 hours, when Flying Officer Pegge and Sergeant Warden of 610 Squadron found an intruder identified as a Do17 near Portsmouth. This proved too fast to be caught and was probably a Messerschmitt Bf110.

There was only one offensive operation, a lone Blenheim of 114 Squadron sent to attack Nordhorn. This did not return.

Pilots of 615 Squadron. From left, F/O McClintock, P/O Edmund, F/O Stewart (with his dog) and P/O Cosby. Note the Douglas Boston at extreme left.

Pilot Officer Lowther-Clarke and his crew fell to a Bf109 of *I./JG 1, Leutnant* Mickel claiming a Blenheim destroyed north of Bergen-am-Zee at 10.38 hours.

Casualties 13th January 1941

Royal Air Force

3 Squadron Hurricane R4076
Crashed landing at Skeabrae. P/O Miller safe.

35 Squadron Halifax L9487
Crashed near Dishforth. F/O Henry & five crew killed.

46 Squadron Hurricane PO-
Crashed on Lod Farm, Ancaster. P/O Harper killed.

46 Squadron Hurricane PO-
Crashed at Belton Park, Grantham. Sgt Markham killed.

48 Squadron Anson N5049
Overshot Port Ellen. F/O Holgate & crew safe.

114 Squadron Blenheim T1858
Failed to return. P/O Lowther-Clarke & crew lost.

145 Squadron Spitfire P9562
Overshot Tangmere. P/O Ward safe.

214 Squadron Wellington T2953
Overshot Marham. F/L Coleman & crew safe.

235 Squadron Blenheim R2782
Force-landed at Docking. Sgt Mason & crew safe.

235 Squadron Blenheim T1869
Crashed cause not known. P/O Crawford & crew safe.

306 Squadron Hurricane UZ-
Hit Master landing. Sgt Pietrasiak safe.

502 Squadron Whitley T4221
Crashed near Limavady. P/O Longhurst & crew safe.

Luftwaffe

2,(F)/11 Do17P1 4114
Crashed at Trattenbach. Oblt T.Kruska killed. Aircraft 70% damaged.

3.(F)/31 Bf110C5 2197
St Brieuc; technical failure. Aircraft 30% damaged.

2.(F)/O.b.d.L Do215B4 0071 L2+05
Crashed at Elbing. Lt W.Steinhoff & crew killed. Aircraft destroyed.

13/14th January 1941

36 RAF bombers raided Channel ports without loss, whilst the *Luftwaffe* retaliated by striking at Plymouth and Devonport with 50 aircraft, causing much damage.

Casualties 13/14th January 1941

Royal Air Force

85 Squadron Defiant N1805
Overshot Debden. F/O Carnaby safe.

Luftwaffe

- nil -

14th January 1941

The weather became even worse. Bomber and Coastal Commands made isolated forays, and the former were placed on 'stand down' for the night. Only six Coastal Hudsons operated and all returned safely.

Casualties 14th January 1941

Royal Air Force

25 Squadron Beaufighter R2129
Belly-landed near Wisbech. Sgt Hollowell & crew safe.

48 Squadron Anson W1710
Undershot Port Ellen. F/O Davy & crew safe.

115 Squadron Wellington R1179
Overshot Marham. Crew safe.

213 Squadron Hurricane V7432
Spun into ground at Lockington. P/O David killed.

222 Squadron Spitfire P9516
Force-landed at New Romney. Sgt Cockram safe.

308 Squadron Hurricane P3598
Force-landed at Wittering. F/O Chciuk safe.

605 Squadron Hurricane Z2344
Crashed landing. Sgt Wright safe.

Luftwaffe

II./JG 26 Bf109E7 3780
Crash-landed at St.Aubin. Aircraft 30% damaged.

E./JG 26 Bf109E7 5163
Hit ground near Dieppe. Aircraft 10% damaged.
III./KG 27 He111P2 2667
Crashed at Rennes. Aircraft 60% damaged.
E./KG 51 Ju88A1 7012
Crash-landed at Lechfeld. Aircraft 35% damaged.
E./KG 51 Ju88A1 4090
Crashed at Illesheim. Aircraft 50% damaged.
E./KG 51 Ju88A1 2143
Crashed on take-off from Illesheim. Aircraft 50% damaged.
III./ZG 76 Bf110C4 2215
Belly-landed at Stavanger. Aircraft 25% damaged.
2.(F)/O.b.d.L Do215B4 0019
Crashed at Britz. Lt A.Harak & one crewman killed. Aircraft destroyed
4.(H)/12 Hs126B1 3459
Crashed at Quimper. Aircraft 20% damaged.

Casualties 14/15th January 1941

Royal Air Force

256 Squadron Defiant N1691
Damaged landing at Pembrey. P/O Caldwell & gunner safe.

Luftwaffe

- nil -

15th January 1941

Despite the foul weather a few interceptions were made by Fighter Command. In the afternoon Flying Officer Dundas and Pilot Officer Johnson of 616 Squadron scrambled from Kirton-in-Lindsay. The sky was surprisingly clear and they soon found a convoy threatened by an approaching 'bandit'. In Johnson's own words:

'It was a perfect interception. We were up-sun and higher than the Do17. But he saw us when we streaked down, and whirled round for Holland in a fast diving turn.'[1]

Dundas made the first pass, Johnson following and after a few more passes heavy return fire from the rear gunner stopped, the undercarriage dropped, and smoke issued from the port engine. The two Spitfire pilots turned hard to come in again, but the Dornier dropped into a layer of sea mist and was lost to sight. The two pilots were credited with a 'shared damaged'. Their

1. Wing Leader - AVM J E Johnson. Quoted with authors permission.

opponent was certainly an aircraft of *II./KG 3*, which subsequently crashed at Antwerp, badly damaged.

Pilot Officer Ashton and Sergeant Russell of 145 Squadron, on an afternoon patrol, had an inconclusive fight with a Ju88 near Portsmouth at 14.45 hours.

Yellow Section of 257 Squadron, airborne from Coltishall at 13.56 hours, patrolled near Honington. As they were returning to base, Flight Lieutenant Lazoryk sighted a Heinkel off Sherington, and closed on it under wildly inaccurate return fire. He expended all his ammunition. Although black smoke was seen, no claim was submitted.

Casualties 15th January 1941

Royal Air Force

22 Squadron Beaufort N1152
Crashed on return from sortie. (P/O Hatton).
111 Squadron Hurricane V7361
Belly-landed near Montrose. W/O Blaize safe.

Luftwaffe

8./JG 26 Bf109E4 3728
Crashed at St Valery en Caux. Fw Helmut Brügelmann killed. Aircraft destroyed.
E./JG 27 Bf109E4 1607
Crashed at Mansholt, pilot killed. Aircraft destroyed.
E./JG 53 Bf109E4 5111
Crashed at St Jean d'Angely. Uffz Kopperschläger killed. Aircraft destroyed.
II./KG 3 Do17Z2 1174
Belly-landed near Antwerp. Aircraft 20% damaged.
E./KG 26 He111H1 5093
Crashed at Lübeck-Blankensee. Aircraft 90% damaged.

15/16th January 1941

Bomber Command sent 96 aircraft to Wilhelmshaven, where much damage was caused to both military and civilian installations. Nine more aircraft attacked Emden and Rotterdam, while six Coastal Command Beauforts laid mines in the Jade Bay, a 22 Squadron aircraft failing to return. At 22.46 hours a 78 Squadron Whitley flown by Pilot Officer Peers was intercepted and shot down over Petton, Holland by *Oberleutnant* Zur Lippe Weissenfeld of *II./NJG 1*. *Flak* claimed a further two bombers and three aircraft crashed on return.

Nearly sixty German bombers were sent out to attack industrial complexes at Derby. London and Liverpool also underwent smaller raids. The British nightfighters were sent up

The legendary Richard Stevens of 151 Squadron. Flying a Hurricane at night during the first six months of 1941, he became the most successful fighter pilot, by day or night.

in some strength. The first fight occurred at 23.18 hours when Flight Lieutenant McMullen of 151 Squadron attacked a Ju88 off Cromer, claiming it probably destroyed. Another 151 Squadron Defiant pilot, Flight Lieutenant Blair, claimed a Ju88 'probable' over Kings Lynn at 23.43 hours. The unit also had Hurricanes airborne, the remarkable Pilot Officer Stevens, patrolling over the London area, intercepting a Do17 of *4./KG 3* near Brentwood. His legendary skill and marksmanship gave the crew no chance, and '5K+DM' smashed into Hart's Wood at 01.36 hours, killing all four members of *Unteroffizier* Matthias Schindler's crew. Stevens landed for fuel and ammunition and took off again. At 05.20 hours he managed to find an He111 'A1+JK' of *2./KG 53* near Canvey Island. *Leutnant* Günther Mehring and two of his crew baled out before the bomber went down, hitting a barge as it crashed into the sea near Spit Buoy, Holehaven,

The intruder fighters of *I./NJG 2* were prowling over East Anglia. At Church Fenton, night flying training was being carried out by aircraft from 54 OTU. *Oberleutnant* Schulz of *2*

Staffel claimed a Blenheim and a Defiant destroyed at 02.30 and 02.35 hours respectively. In fact he damaged three aircraft; Pilot Officer Wyrill force-landed his Defiant at Appleton Roebuck, Flight Lieutenant Burns, also in a Defiant, crash-landed his burning aircraft on the runway and a Blenheim flown by Pilot Officer King was also slightly damaged. At Feltwell, two Wellingtons were damaged in a strafe, presumably by an intruder

Casualties 15/16th January 1941

Royal Air Force

22 Squadron Beaufort W6489
Failed to return. No further details available.
51 Squadron Whitley T4175
Force-landed near Driffield. P/O Harrington & crew safe.
72 Squadron Spitfire X4252
Crashed on take-off from Acklington. F/O Davy safe.
75 Squadron Wellington T2881
Crash-landed near Stradishall. P/O McFarlane & crew safe.
75 Squadron Wellington AA-
Two aircraft damaged in attack on Feltwell.
150 Squadron Wellington T2622
Crash-landed near Cranwell. S/L Beall & crew safe.
151 Squadron Hurricane P3813
Abandoned out of fuel. S/L Adam baled out safely, aircraft destroyed.
218 Squadron Wellington P9207
Crashed after take-off. P/O McLaren killed. Aircraft destroyed.
502 Squadron Whitley P5051
Crashed landing at Limavady. P/O Howard-Jones & crew safe.
54 OTU Blenheim -----
Force-landed at Appleton Roebuck. P/O King & crew safe.
54 OTU Defiant L7002
Damaged in attack on Church Fenton. P/O Wyrill & crew safe
54 OTU Defiant N1542
Damaged in attack on Church Fenton. F/L Burns & crew safe

Luftwaffe

4./KG 3 Do17Z 3456 5K+DM
Failed to return from sortie. Uffz Matthias Schindler & crew lost.
2./KG 53 He111H5 3638 A1+JK
Failed to return from sortie. Lt Günther Mehring killed, three crew captured.

16th January 1941

Fighters from 10 Group flew an unopposed sweep over northern France in the morning but, around noon, as the force returned, a Ju88 of *3.(F)/121* was sighted near Portsmouth It was engaged by Pilot Officer Rogers of 234 Squadron. Contact was

Hauptmann Albert Schulz of I./NJG 2 in the cockpit of his Do17Z-10. Note the 'England-blitz' ensignia beneath the cockpit.

lost when he was shot down into the sea by the German rear-gunner.

In the north, Red Section of 3 Squadron took off at 11.35 hours for a defensive patrol, Flight Lieutenant Berry and Pilot Officer Harris finding a Ju88 near Fair Isle. The Junkers was chased away by the Hurricane pilots, who could not close sufficiently to open fire.

Finally, in the early evening Flying Officer Falkowski of 32 Squadron engaged an He111 near Shoreham at 19.30 hours. He claimed to have shot this down, but his Hurricane received severe battle damage and he baled out over Hayling Island. No Heinkel was lost, but an aircraft of *5./KG 53* belly-landed after a combat sortie.

Coastal Command lost a 220 Squadron Hudson, which was ditched whilst on patrol. Pilot Officer George and his crew were safely rescued.

Casualties 16th January 1941

Royal Air Force

18 Squadron Blenheim R3752
Damaged landing at Wyton. W/C Sharp & crew safe.

23 Squadron Blenheim L8655
Overshot Ford. P/O Brown & crew safe.

32 Squadron Hurricane P2984
Shot down by He111 over Hayling Island. F/O Falkowski baled out and safe, aircraft destroyed.

79 Squadron Hurricane P3092
Crashed at Pembrey. Sgt Bradley safe.

111 Squadron Hurricane P3619
Belly-landed near Montrose. Sgt Seaman safe.
219 Squadron Beaufighter R2074
Crashed landing at Tangmere. P/O Sinclair & crew safe.
220 Squadron Hudson P5151
Crashed into sea on convoy escort. P/O George & crew rescued.
233 Squadron Hudson N7243
Belly-landed at White Abbey, Belfast. Sgt Grundy & crew safe.
234 Squadron Spitfire X4428
Failed to return. P/O Rogers lost.
234 Squadron Spitfire N3191
Crashed near Truro. P/O Beech killed. Aircraft destroyed.
504 Squadron Hurricane V6819
Crashed near Exeter in snowstorm. P/O McGregor believed safe.

Luftwaffe

I./JG 26 Bf109E7 5966
Crash-landed at St Aubin. Aircraft 20% damaged.
III./JG 26 Bf109E8 6256
Crash-landed at Abbeville. Aircraft 15% damaged.
III./JG 77 Kl35 4584
Force-landed at Dinant out of fuel, Fw E.Neumann killed. Aircraft 90% damaged.
I./KG 26 He111H4 3211
Crash-landed at Beauvais. Aircraft 25% damaged.
5./KG 53 He111H2 2710
Belly-landed at Staden. Aircraft 40% damaged.

16/17th January 1941

Once again the main target for Bomber Command was the
battleship *Tirpitz* at Wilhelmshaven, to where 81 aircraft were
sent. Five more attacked Rotterdam, Emden and Boulogne,
while four laid mines. The weather was particularly bad and
only slight damage was caused. Five bombers were reported
missing; 311 Squadron and 40 Squadrons each lost a Wellington, flown by Pilot Officer Kubiznalc and Sergeant Jones
respectively. An 83 Squadron Hampden captained by Pilot
Officer Strong and Flying Officer Skyrme's 10 Squadron Whitley
were also lost, as was Sergeant Barlow's 58 Squadron Whitley.
All these aircraft were apparently lost at sea. A further two
Wellingtons crashed on return.

The *Luftwaffe* sent 126 bombers against Avonmouth. One
combat took place when Flight Lieutenant Willans of 23
Squadron, en route for the Continent, encountered a supposed
Do17 off Orfordness at 01.00 hours. This he claimed to have
damaged. It was almost certainly a Bf110 of *3.(F)/123* flown by
Unteroffizier Toni De Lorenzo, which subsequently crashed at

Vire killing the crew. A Heinkel of *K.Gr.100* failed to return; *Feldwebel* Erwin Schüle, flying '6N+CL', was shot down into the Bristol Channel at 09.50 hours by AA fire, with the loss of the crew.

Casualties 16/17th January 1941

Royal Air Force

10 Squadron Whitley T4220
Failed to return. P/O Skyrme & crew lost.
40 Squadron Wellington T2912
Failed to return. Sgt Jones &/ crew lost.
58 Squadron Whitley Z6462
Failed to return. Sgt Barlow & crew lost.
75 Squadron Wellington T2881
Force-landed after sortie. Crew safe.
83 Squadron Hampden AD731
Failed to return. P/O Strong & crew lost.
99 Squadron Wellington R3217
Crash-landed at Newmarket. P/O Marshall & crew safe
99 Squadron Wellington R3295
Overshot Kenley. Sgt Ferguson & crew safe.
101 Squadron Blenheim N6182
Overshot West Raynham. Sgt Gaunt & crew safe.
311 Squadron Wellington P2519
Failed to return. P/O Kubiznalc & crew lost.

Luftwaffe

K.Gr.100 He111H2 5441 6N+CL
Failed to return. Fw Erwin Schüle & crew lost.
3.(F)/123 Bf110C5 2308
Crashed near Vire. Uffz Toni De Lorenzo and gunner killed. Aircraft destroyed.

17th January 1941

Two Hurricanes of 3 Squadron took off in the late morning for a routine patrol and were vectored towards a raider which proved to be a reconnaissance He111 of *Wekusta 1* Flight Lieutenant Berry attacked, crippling *Leutnant* Thurz's 'T5+HU' so severely that it was crash-landed on Fair Isle at 11.02 hours. Two of the five-man crew were killed.

In the early afternoon a pair of 504 Squadron Hurricanes patrolled off Bolt Head at 28,000 ft. An He111 was sighted 17,000 ft below, and Sergeants Haw and Hirst dived, chasing the bomber down to sea level. Fire was seen coming from the starboard engine before the bomber vanished into the sea mist and was claimed as damaged. It was actually a Ju88, 'L1+LK' of

I. /LG 1. targetted to Avonmouth and flown by *Leutnant* Max Zodrow; it failed to return.

Coastal Command attacked a convoy off Holland, mounting two strikes. The first was by torpedo-carrying Beauforts and a second by Blenheims, each with Blenheim fighter escort. Four vessels were claimed sunk in these actions, in which a bomber was slightly damaged by *Flak*.

During the day Flight Lieutenant Miles of 1 PRU set out to photograph the area Boulogne - St. Omer - Calais, but at 15.50 hours he was intercepted over Boulogne by Bf109s of *I. /LG 2*. The Spitfire was shot down by *Hauptmann* Herbert Ihlefeld, killing the pilot.

Casualties 17th January 1941

Royal Air Force

23 Squadron Boston BJ740
Crashed landing at Boscombe Down. P/O Pushman & crew safe.

152 Squadron Spitfire R6801
Belly-landed at Warmwell. F/O True safe.

217 Squadron Beaufort L9862
Crashed on return. P/O Forde & crew safe.

504 Squadron Hurricane L1513
Crashed landing at Exeter. F/O White safe.

603 Squadron Spitfire P7552
Crashed near Nigg Bay, Aberdeen. Pilot believed killed.

1 PRU Spitfire R6906
Failed to return. F/L Miles lost.

Luftwaffe

E./JG 2 Bf109E4 0850
Force-landed at Octeville. Aircraft 30% damaged.

7./JG 3 Bf109E7 6378
Crash-landed at Desvres. Aircraft 40% damaged.

I./JG 27 Bf109E4 2795
Force-landed near Bernay. Uffz Greuel injured. Aircraft 75% damaged.

III./JG 77 Bf109E4 0743
Crashed on take-off from Dinant. Aircraft 20% damaged.

III./JG 77 FW58B2 3132
Crashed on take-off from Dinant. Aircraft 10% damaged.

I./LG 1 Ju88A5 6123 L1+LK
Failed to return. Lt Max Modrow & crew lost.

Stab./St.G 3 He111H5 3700
Belly-landed at Echterdingen. Aircraft 10% damaged.

Wekusta 1 He111H2 2645 T5+EU
Failed to return from sortie. Lt Karl-Heinz Thurz & crew lost.

The Bristol Beaufort was the first really effective torpedo-carrying aircraft to be used by the RAF. It was under-powered and lightly armed, but could take more punishment than the anti-shipping Blenheims.

17/18th January 1941

Bomber Command activity was almost nil; only one leaflet-dropping sortie was flown by an OTU aircraft, but Coastal Command sent Beauforts to Brest and Morlaix. Flight Lieutenant Willans of 23 Squadron was again successful on an intruder mission, catching a Heinkel of *III./KG 26* in the landing circuit at Poix-Nord and shooting it down. The pilot crash-landed without injury to the crew.

The Luftwaffe struck at Swansea with 88 bombers. Despite several AA claims, all 88 aircraft returned, although an He111 of *I./KG 28* crashed at Nantes. St. Eval was also raided. Two Gladiators and a Hurricane were attacked in the circuit, one of the former being slightly damaged. One claim was submitted by a returning *I./KG 28* crew for a nightfighter destroyed.

Casualties 17/18th January 1941

Royal Air Force

247 Squadron Gladiator -----
Damaged in circuit at St Eval. Pilot safe.

604 Squadron Beaufighter R2087
Crashed at Stratford-upon-Avon. P/O Scott & crew baled out.

Luftwaffe

III./KG 26 He111H5 3613
Force-landed at Poix-Nord. Aircraft 60% damaged.
I./KG 28 He111H5 3801
Crash-landed at Nantes. Aircraft 40% damaged.

18th January 1941

The weather worsened sharply, with clouds and snow prevailing. One combat occurred when Squadron Leader Love of 222 Squadron intercepted a Heinkel off East Anglia. He attacked, without apparent effect and the bomber vanished into cloud. A little later AA defences at Coltishall opened fire on a *9./KG 3* Dornier briefed to attack Saxmundham. Both the pilot, *Leutnant* Abel, and his *Bordmechaniker* were wounded.

Casualties 18th January 1941

Royal Air Force

- nil -

Luftwaffe

I./JG 51 Bf109F1 6627
Crash-landed at Mannheim-Sandhofen. Aircraft 75% damaged.
9./KG 3 Do17Z ----
Damaged by enemy gunfire. Lt F.Abel & one man wounded.
Aircraft 20% damaged.
II./KG 76 Ju88A5 6177
Crashed at Ansbach, Fw L.Koch & one man killed. Aircraft destroyed.

19th January 1941

During the afternoon Flight Lieutenant Finucane and Sergeant Orchard of 65 Squadron flew a Channel patrol, intercepting a Ju88 of *4(F)/121* near the French coast. Despite Finucane's Spitfire being badly shot-up by return fire, they claimed it destroyed; it was belly-landed at Caen.

Casualties 19th January 1941

Royal Air Force

3 Squadron Hurricane R5454
Hit Royal Naval target-towing cable at Skeabrae. Sgt Taylor safe.
65 Squadron Spitfire P7752
Damaged by Ju88 over Channel. F/L Finucane safe.

Flight Lieutenant Pugh of 263 Squadron prepares for a sortie. On 19th January he was forced to bale out of P6984 over Devon and escaped without a scratch.
- A Saunders

263 Squadron Whirlwind P6984
Abandoned near Middlemore, Devon. F/L Pugh safe.
605 Squadron Hurricane Z2351
Force-landed at Martlesham Heath. F/O Forde safe.

Luftwaffe

2./JG 52 Bf109E8 4908
Crashed on take-off from Katwijk. Aircraft 35% damaged.
III./JG 77 Bf109E4 1306
Force-landed at Cherbourg. Aircraft 90% damaged.
I./NJG 1 Bf110D1 3176
Crashed at Wipperfürth. Ofw H.Rossbach & gunner killed. Aircraft destroyed.
4./KG 3 Do17Z3 2898
Force-landed at Eckeren. Aircraft 60% damaged.
III./KG 76 Ju88A5 5166
Damaged at Lechfeld. Aircraft 15% damaged.
4.(F)/121 Ju88A1 0314 7A+DM
Belly-landed at Caen due to enemy gunfire. Aircraft 35% damaged.

19/20th January 1941

Darkness brought 62 German bombers to raid Southampton, with smaller forays against other targets in the south including London. No nightfighters made contact, but three of the raiders failed to return. *1./KG 1* lost its *Staffelkapitän, Hauptmann* Gustav Graf zu Castell, when his He111 'V4+FH' crashed on Wyckham Farm, Steyning, at 08.09 hours, killing the crew. A *2./KG 1* Heinkel was lost when *Leutnant* Günther Bockhorn's 'V4+FK' failed to return, believed to have been shot down off Selsey Bill at 09.00 hours by AA fire. The final loss was again an He111, '1H+FT' of *III./KG 26*. This fell to AA fire at Allington Farm, Eastleigh, killing all five of *Unteroffizier* Karl Lindhorst's crew. A further two Heinkels and a Ju88 force-landed on the Continent, while a Ju88 crew baled out over Compéigne.

Casualties 19/20th January 1941

Royal Air Force

219 Squadron Beaufighter R2155
Crashed landing at Tangmere. F/S Grubb & crew safe.
604 Squadron Beaufighter R2187
Undershot Middle Wallop. Sgt Brown & crew safe.

Luftwaffe

1./KG 1 He111H5 3325 V4+FH
Failed to return from sortie. Hptm Graf Zu Castell & crew killed, aircraft lost.
2./KG 1 He111H3 6941 V4+FK
Failed to return from sortie. Lt G. Bockhorn & crew missing.
4./KG 4 He111P4 2981
Force-landed at Haarlem. Lt D.Grassman & three crewmen injured. Aircraft destroyed.
III./KG 26 He111H5 3602 1H+FT
Failed to return from sortie. Uffz K.Lindhorst & crew lost.
Stab./KG 53 He111H3 3308
Crash-landed at Lille. Aircraft 60% damaged.
II./KG 77 Ju88A5 7106
Abandoned over Compéigne. Aircraft destroyed.
K.Gr.806 Ju88A5 4175
Crash-landed at Caen. Oblt H.Forgatsch & one crewman wounded. Aircraft 50% damaged.

20th January 1941

Only one fight occurred, Pilot Officer Tufnell of 43 Squadron engaging a Ju88 over May Island at 13.30 hours. No claim was made, but Tufnell's Hurricane was badly hit by return fire and crashed on return, injuring the pilot. His opponent could possibly have been *Hauptmann* Wolfgang Zechiel's He111 of *Wekusta 5*, which itself crashed in Norway.

Casualties 20th January 1941

Royal Air Force

10 Squadron Whitley P4956
Crashed landing at Leeming. Sgt Byrne & crew safe.
43 Squadron Hurricane P3776
Crashed after combat. P/O Tufnell wounded.

248 Squadron Blenheim Z5973
Crashed on take-off from Dyce. F/L McHardy safe.

Luftwaffe

Wekusta 5 He111H5 3824 1B+CH
Crashed near Vaernes. Hptm W.Zechiel & one crewman injured. Aircraft destroyed.

Tr.St. I Fl.K Ju52/3m 5428
Crashed at Regensburg. Ofw H.Mobius & one man killed, three injured. Aircraft 95% damaged.

21st January 1941

No events of any significance took place.

Casualties 21st January 1941

Royal Air Force

201 Squadron Sunderland T9049
Force-landed at Unst, Shetlands. S/L Cecil-Wright and crew safe.

Luftwaffe

K.Gr.100 He111H3 5629
Belly-landed at Köthen. Aircraft 25% damaged.

3.(H)/LG 2 FW58C1 0006
Damaged by storm at Châlons-sur-Soane. Aircraft 15% damaged.

L.Fl.Res. 3 Ju88A5 0653
Taxiing accident at Fritzlar. Aircraft 40% damaged.

21/22nd January 1941

Luftwaffe activity was minimal. A strange loss occurred when a Heinkel of *4./KG 53* crashed into the sea off Dover. One body was recovered from *Feldwebel* Heinrich Sticht's crew. This aircraft was possibly hit by AA fire near London, a site south of the city claiming a bomber damaged.

Casualties 21/22nd January 1941

Royal Air Force

- nil -

Luftwaffe

4./KG 53 He111H2 2783 A1+FM
Failed to return from sortie. Fw H.Sticht & crew lost.

Chapter Three
Winter War

22nd January 1941

In contrast to the preceding nine days of relative quiet, an improvement in the weather allowed a variety of operations to take place.

In the morning six Blenheims each from 114 and 139 Squadrons were escorted on an unopposed raid against oil installations along the Dutch coastline. On the return flight a 139 Squadron machine flown by Flight Lieutenant Menzies DFC was shot down into the sea by A.A. gunners at Lowestoft.

Fighter Command was in action early when Blue Section of 41 Squadron patrolled over Bradwell Bay at 09.50 hours. Pilot Officer Wells attacked and claimed to have damaged an He111. One Heinkel of *6./KG 53* was indeed damaged in combat while on a sortie to Southend, one member of the crew being wounded.

Later in the morning reconnaissance aircraft were reported in the Dover Straits area. At 11.25 hours two Spitfires of 91 Squadron, patrolled the Thames estuary and intercepted a Ju88 of *III./KG 1* flown by *Leutnant* Wolfgang Lademann. This was chased southward and was finally shot down into the sea between Dover and Folkestone by Pilot Officer

Flying Officer E P Wells (left) of 41 Squadron later became Kenley Wing Leader, with thirteen confirmed victories to his credit

76

Beauforts being refuelled before a shipping strike.

Parrott, in view of naval observers aboard H.M.S. *Wasp*. Forty minutes later two more fighters from this unit discovered a Junkers near Dover, which was claimed damaged by Flying Officer O'Meara. Three Spitfires of 64 Squadron were also airborne, patrolling near Calais. At 12.15 hours Squadron Leader Rankin leading Pilot Officers Rowden and Tidman attacked a Ju88, possibly the same one engaged earlier by O'Meara. The bomber was claimed probably destroyed before it escaped.

Further north, Squadron Leader Bader of 242 Squadron led Flying Officers Edmond and Cryderman on a convoy patrol off East Anglia in the afternoon. They discovered a Ju88 and jointly claimed it shot down into the sea off Yarmouth.

Three Beauforts of 22 Squadron were sent out to Holland seeking shipping. One became detached and the remaining two were jumped by a pair of Bf109s from *1./JG 1* north-west of Terschelling. *Feldwebel* Mickel shot down Pilot Officer Coules' aircraft, and the second Beaufort was damaged. Meanwhile the lone aircraft bombed the seaplane base at De Mok, but was then also engaged by a *I./JG 1* Messerschmitt. This bomber escaped after being badly damaged by *Unteroffizier* Krause, who claimed a 'Blenheim' shot down south-west of Den Helder. One was also claimed by *Flak* gunners, apparently during this engagement.

Both surviving Beauforts - flown by Flying Officers Boycott and Hyde - returned safely to base.

During the day 303 Squadron flew its first offensive operations when Hurricanes carried out *Rhubarbs* along the French coast shortly after midday, more being similarly engaged three hours later. One returned with a large chunk of high tension cable wrapped around it's tailplane. Squadron Leader Lapkowski and Sergeant Strembosz each claimed a Messerschmitt damaged in combat, although no details are available. One Bf109 was in fact lost by the Luftwaffe, *Fähnrich* Friedrich von Uiberacker of *2./JG 26* being shot down and wounded near Liegescourt. A Bf109 of *I./LG 2* crashed and exploded whilst landing at Calais after a combat sortie.[1]

Casualties 22nd January 1941

Royal Air Force

22 Squadron Beaufort OA-T
Failed to return. P/O Coules & crew lost.
22 Squadron Beaufort OA-N
Damaged in action. F/O Boycott & crew safe.
22 Squadron Beaufort OA-E
Damaged in action. F/O Hyde & crew safe.
85 Squadron Hurricane V6857
Belly-landed at Debden. Sgt Walker-Smith safe.
115 Squadron Wellington R3153
Undershot Marham. Sgt Elliott & crew safe.
139 Squadron Blenheim T2435
Shot down at Lowestoft by British AA fire. F/L Menzies DFC & crew killed.
220 Squadron Hudson T9371
Crashed at Osmotherley. (Sgt Smith).
303 Squadron Hurricane V7499
Crashed landing at Redhill. F/O Srzeszczak safe.
1 PRU Spitfire K9959
Crashed landing at Long Marston. P/O Krol safe.

Luftwaffe

2./JG 26 Bf109E7 4147
Shot down by fighter at Liegescourt. Fhr F.von Uiberacker wounded. Aircraft destroyed.
III./KG 1 Ju88A5 0578 V4+HT
Failed to return from sortie. Lt Wolfgang Lademann & crew lost.
I./KG 26 He111H5 3778
Crash-landed at Münster-Handorf. Aircraft 30% damaged.
6./KG 53 He111P5 3833
Damaged by enemy gunfire on sortie to Southend One crewman wounded. Aircraft 5% damaged.

1. The 303 Sqn action is not recorded in the unit ORB, the details having been supplied to the author by Sqn Ldr Boleslaw Drobinski DFC

I./LG 2 Bf109E4 5397
Exploded whilst landing at Calais/Marck. Uffz J.Surkamp killed. Aircraft destroyed.

E./ZG 26 Bf110C4 3505
Crashed at Memmingen. Uffz K.Ullrich & crew killed. Aircraft destroyed.

E./ZG 26 Bf110C4 3068
Force-landed at Ruhmannsfelden. Aircraft 10% damaged.

2.(F)/123 Ju88A5 0401
Crashed landing at Jersey. Aircraft 15% damaged.

L.Fl.Res. 3 Ju87R1 5547
Force-landed at Hesperange. Aircraft 20% damaged.

22/23rd January 1941

Bomber Command sent 40 aircraft to attack Düsseldorf from which all returned. Only isolated German aircraft were noted. No claims were made on either side.

Casualties 22/23rd January 1941

Royal Air Force

82 Squadron Blenheim V3553
Crashed after take-off. P/O Moller & crew killed. aircraft destroyed.

82 Squadron Blenheim T2330
Damaged landing at Bodney. Sgt Smith & crew safe.

Luftwaffe

- nil -

23rd January 1941

The first combat involved fighter Blenheims of 254 Squadron which engaged a small formation of He111s and Bf110s off Sumburgh Head at 10.30 hours. The Blenheims attacked, Pilot Officer Illingworth claiming damage to a Heinkel, while Pilot Officer Sizer reported hits a Messerschmitt. One Ju88 of *3.(F)/122* crashed at Schipol on return with one man wounded, possibly as a result of this engagement.

Pilot Officer Fokes and Sergeant Lloyd of 92 Squadron took off from Manston in the late morning, meeting a Bf110 of *E.Gr.210* piloted by *Leutnant* Dipser east of their base at 11.00 hours. Both pilots attacked, claiming it damaged the Messerschmitt force-landing at Zuydecoote with both crewmen wounded.

During the day *Feldwebel* Hans Stechmann of *9./JG 3* reputedly claimed a Hurricane destroyed near Boulogne.

The BV 138. Although slow and unwieldy, it carried a heavy punch with its 20mm cannon mounted in the nose turret

Casualties 23rd January 1941

Royal Air Force

214 Squadron Wellington R1223
Overshot Stradishall. Sgt Paramore & crew safe.
307 Squadron Defiant N3439
Force-landed at Squires Gate. F/O Antonowicz & gunner safe.
307 Squadron Defiant N3320
Force-landed near Ormskirk. F/O Mikzo & gunner safe.
502 Squadron Whitley P5041
Crashed into Mull of Kintyre. F/O Johnson & crew killed.
607 Squadron Hurricane P3031
Crash-landed near Drem. P/O Davies safe.

Luftwaffe

E./JG 51 Bf109E4 4085
Crashed at Biscarosse. Aircraft 80% damaged.
E.Gr.210 Bf110E1 3831
Force-landed at Zuydecoote due to enemy gunfire. Lt Dipser & gunner wounded.
Aircraft 25% damaged.
3.(F)/122 Ju88A5 0427
Crashed at Schipol due to combat. One crewman wounded. Aircraft 50%
damaged.
1./K.Fl.Gr.906 He115C1 2748
Hit ground near Brest. Aircraft destroyed.

24th January 1941

Few German aircraft were reported around Britain. In the afternoon five Spitfires from 'B' Flight of 603 Squadron patrolled over May Island and drove a Ju88 away. Sergeant Strawson fired a burst at extreme range, but claimed no strikes.

Coastal Command aircraft patrolled Biscay, where a 233 Squadron Hudson flown by Pilot Officer Welply was engaged and badly damaged by a BV138 flying-boat from *K.Fl.Gr.406*. The Hudson was badly hit and force-landed at Sligo, Eire, where the crew were interned. A second aircraft was lost when Flying Officer Ward's 502 Squadron Whitley crashed into the sea off Eire, killing three.

The Germans flew a few sorties off East Anglia. One bomber was claimed damaged by naval gunners aboard H.M. trawlers *Strathannock*, *Philipe* and *Galvani*; this was undoubtedly a Ju88 from *III./KG 30*, which crashed at Zandvoort with battle damage.

Casualties 24th January 1941

Royal Air Force

233 Squadron Hudson P5273
Failed to return from patrol, interned in Eire. P/O Welply & crew lost.
502 Squadron Whitley T4168
Force-landed in Eire. F/O Ward & crew interned.

Luftwaffe

III./KG 30 Ju88A5 4233
Crashed at Zandvoort due to combat. Aircraft 65% damaged.
E./Zerst.Gr Do17E3 2056 DC+NH
Crashed near Warnemünde. Lt K Koch & crew missing.
Wekusta O.b.d.L He111H3 6945
Crash-landed at Oldenburg. Aircraft 50% damaged.

24/25th January 1941

Operations were limited. Coastal Command sent Beauforts to attack Brest, four crashing on return.

Casualties 24/25th January 1941

Royal Air Force

22 Squadron Beaufort OA-A
Crashed on return. Sgt Sullivan & crew safe.
22 Squadron Beaufort OA-
Crashed on return. F/L Oakley & crew safe.
217 Squadron Beaufort L9820
Crashed landing at St.Eval. F/O Reid & crew safe.
217 Squadron Beaufort L9821
Crashed landing at St.Eval. P/O Welsh & crew safe.

Luftwaffe

- nil -

25th January 1941

Coastal Command aircraft were again operating over Biscay. Three Blenheim fighters of 236 Squadron led by Flight Lieutenant McArthur flew an 'anti Focke Wulf' patrol and encountered an He115 of *1/K.Fl.Gr.506* which was attacked by McArthur. No claim was made, but the Heinkel, 'M2+KH' flown by *Oberleutnant zur See* Hans-Dieter Furl, failed to return. To the north, Beauforts of 22 Squadron operated along the Frisian Island chain. One formation of three was attacked by a fighter near Ameland, and Flying Officer Sharman's aircraft returned with a 20 mm cannon shell in one engine.

The weather deteriorated rapidly that night and continued to hamper operations for some days.

Casualties 25th January 1941

Royal Air Force

22 Squadron Beaufort OA-D
Crashed at Bircham Newton after combat. P/O Sharman & crew safe.
51 Squadron Whitley N1504
Crashed landing at Dishforth. Sgt Turner & crew safe.

Luftwaffe

1./K.Fl.Gr.506 He115 2727 M2+KH
Failed to return from sortie. Lt zur See H-D Furl & crew lost.

26th January 1941

Ju88s of *KG 30* flew several strikes against coastal shipping in the Thames estuary and off East Anglia. These attacks caused severe damage to two vessels in Barrow Deep, but one aircraft was lost. At 09.20 hours a Ju88 of *8./KG 30* attacked HM trawler *Galvani,* but *Feldwebel* Walter Guttmann misjudged his height and struck the mast and rigging of the vessel. The crippled, '4D+LS' was crash-landed at Somerton Holmes, Norfolk, where it burnt out. The crew, having successfully evacuated their machine, were subsequently captured by two civilians, who were surprised to find four German airmen towing a dinghy towards the coast - with the obvious intention of paddling home!

In the afternoon further attacks were made by *KG 30*, but the naval gunners exacted a heavy price. A Junkers of *8 Staffel*, '4D+LS', was shot down off Brightlingsea by HM trawlers *Reids* and *Fisher Boy*. One survivor from *Oberleutnant* Ignatz Kraft's

Dawn. A weary Whitley crew heads for debriefing, breakfast and bed.

crew was rescued. A second bomber from the same unit ('4D+GS' piloted by *Oberleutnant* Eberhard Gaul) fell to gunners aboard H.M.S. *Wallace*. There were no survivors from this crew.

Casualties 26th January 1941

Royal Air Force
50 Squadron Hampden AD730
Damaged landing at Lindholme. P/O Srylls & crew safe.
233 Squadron Hudson N7257
Force-landed at East Kilbride. Sgt Grundy & crew safe.
1 PRU Spitfire K9959
Crashed force-landing at Long Marston. Pilot safe.

Luftwaffe
8./KG 30 Ju88A5 0634 4D+LS
Failed to return. Fw W.Guttmann & crew captured.
8./KG 30 Ju88A5 3261 4D+AS
Failed to return. Oblt I Kraft & crew lost.
8./KG 30 Ju88A5 7198 4D+GS
Failed to return. Oblt E.Gaul & crew lost.

26/27th January 1941

Seventeen aircraft from Bomber Command raided Hannover while a handful of Coastal aircraft attacked Cherbourg and Brest. All returned safely. A Bf110 of *I./NJG 3* landed at Vechta with slight battle damage.

Casualties 26/27th January 1941

Royal Air Force

- nil -

Luftwaffe

I./NJG 3 Bf110C4 3586
Crash-landed at Vechta. Aircraft 5% damaged.

27th January 1941

During the afternoon Coastal Command sent small formations of aircraft out on anti-shipping sweeps. The sole Bomber Command sortie, a Blenheim of 139 Squadron, had a short fight with a Ju88, claiming it damaged off Shoeburyness, but Coastal Command lost a Hudson of 224 Squadron flown by Sergeant Lanchberry, which was reported missing over the North Sea. It was shot down by a Bf110 of *III./ZG 76* flown by *Hauptmann* Kaldrack. One aircraft from this unit crashed at Kjevik with engine damage.

Meanwhile a lone Ju88 of *9./KG 30* had carried out a surprise attack upon Grantham, but was hit by the A.A. defences. *Oberleutnant* Friedrich-Karl Rinck, the Staffelkapitän, effected a forced landing at Tilley's Lane, Boston. The crew scrambled out and set fire to '4D+CT' before being captured.

Casualties 27th January 1941

Royal Air Force

43 Squadron Hurricane P3386
Belly-landed near Merryfield. P/O Doll safe.
224 Squadron Hudson QA-
Failed to return. Sgt Lanchberry & crew lost.

Luftwaffe

5./JG 52 Bf109E8 6387
Crash-landed at Haamstede. Aircraft 65% damaged.
E./KG 1 Kl35 4119
Crashed at Güterslohe. Uffz H.Rademacher injured, one man killed. Aircraft destroyed.
III./KG 1 Ju88A5 4225
Tyre damage at Gevilliers. Aircraft 40% damaged.
III./KG 30 Ju88A5 2280 4D+CT
Failed to return from sortie. Oblt F-K.Rinck & crew lost.
III./StG. 2 Ju87R2 5847
Taxiing accident at Kitzingen. Aircraft 35% damaged.

III./ZG 76 Bf110C4 2070
Force-landed at Kjevik. Aircraft destroyed.

28th January 1941

No combats took place during the day, but the *Luftwaffe* was active against shipping in the Western Approaches, where a ship was badly damaged. Three Heinkels from *I./KG 28* were lost, two crashing in France and a third ditching off La Rochelle, probably following these attacks.

Casualties 28th January 1941

Royal Air Force

- nil -

Luftwaffe

I./JG 27 Bf109E1 3268
Crashed near Berlin. Oblt Herbert Maqas killed. Aircraft destroyed.
I./JG 51 Bf109F1 6637
Crashed at Darmstadt. Aircraft destroyed.
E./JG 52 Bf109E1 3203
Crashed at Krefeld. Ofhr H.Voight killed. Aircraft destroyed.
E./JG 52 Bf109E4 1210
Crash-landed at Fontenet. Aircraft 75% damaged.
1./NJG 3 Bf110C4 3085
Crash-landed at Köln-Ostheim. Aircraft 20% damaged.
I./KG 28 He111H5 3559 1T+GK
Ditched off La Rochelle. Hptm P.Claas & crew safe. Aircraft 90% damaged.
I./KG 28 He111H5 3524 1T+EK
Crashed at Nantes. Lt Kurt Bitterlich & crew safe. Aircraft 95% damaged.
I./KG 28 He111H5 3501 1T+AB
Crash-landed at Vannes. Oblt W. Plumecke & crew injured.
Aircraft 75% damaged.
III./KG 76 Ju88A5 4248
Force-landed at Treuchtlingen. Aircraft 25% damaged.

29th January 1941

Again there was little action. Flying Officer Aikman's 210 Squadron crew sighted one of *I./KG 40's* FW200s to the south of Eire at 11.27 hours. The Focke-Wulf made a diving port-quarter attack at 500 yards range. The rear turret of the Sunderland was hit and the gunner wounded, but the crew returned fire. Hits were reported on the cockpit and port engines. The German aircraft 'retired hurt' with the port inner engine windmilling.

Casualties 29th January 1941

Royal Air Force

87 Squadron Hurricane W9173
Belly-landed at Charmy Down. P/O Forsyth safe.
210 Squadron Sunderland L2163
Damaged in combat. F/O Aikman & crew safe.
236 Squadron Blenheim -5432
Crashed on take-off. F/O Cotes-Preedy & crew safe.

Luftwaffe

I./KG 40 FW200C ----
Damaged in combat near Ireland. One man killed. Aircraft 10% damaged.
E./KG 55 He111H2 5309
Crash-landed at Lechfeld. Aircraft 40% damaged.
I./KG 76 Ju88A5 2222
Crash-landed at Giebelstadt. Aircraft 20% damaged.
II./ZG 76 Bf110E1 3838
Crashed on Fano Island. Lt K.Helmer injured. Aircraft destroyed.
4.(F)/122 Ju52/3m 5077
Damaged at Travemünde. Aircraft 10% damaged.
5(H)/12 FW58A1 0049
Crashed at Nellingen, Uffz J Trepziak killed. Aircraft destroyed.
Stab G.d.L. beim O.b.d.H Bloch 175 0133
Crashed on take-off from Saarbrücken. Aircraft 50% damaged.

29/30th January 1941

Thirty-four Bomber Command aircraft raided Wilhelmshaven. All returned, although two bombers crashed. London was raided firstly by 7 aircraft from *I./NJG 2*, then by 36 bombers. The A.A. defences claimed a 'probable' and a 'damaged'. Two Ju88s crashed on return.

Casualties 29/30th January 1941

Royal Air Force

99 Squadron Wellington T2541
Force-landed at Burgh. P/O Smith & crew safe.
149 Squadron Wellington L7812
Crash-landed at Marlborough. Sgt Milsted & crew safe.
214 Squadron Wellington T2841
Crashed on take-off. Sgt Smiles & crew safe.

Luftwaffe

III./KG 1 Ju88A5 5183
Crash-landed at Gevilliers. Aircraft 60% damaged.
III./KG 30 Ju88A1 4123
Crash-landed at Steene. Aircraft 80% damaged.

Developed from a civil design, the FW 200 Condor was often referred to as the 'Scourge of the Atlantic'. It was actually lighter armed and of less sturdy construction than most combat aircraft of the period.

30th January 1941

Only Coastal Command aircraft operated. Sergeant Houchin's 248 Squadron Blenheim crew were initially reported missing from a sortie to Norway, but were subsequently discovered in the wreckage of their aircraft at Chapel Farm, Newmurcham. AA gunners at Clacton shot down a Ju88 of *2./KG 30* at 13.30 hours. This crashed at St. Osyth, killing *Feldwebel* Wilhelm Muth and his crew.

Casualties 30th January 1941

Royal Air Force

110 Squadron Havoc AX922
Hit by British AA fire and crash-landed at Wattisham.
W/C Sutcliffe & crew safe.
149 Squadron Wellington N2769
Crashed near Hornchurch. One man from P/O Gilmour's crew injured.
149 Squadron Wellington R1391
Force-landed Lancashire, lost. P/O Duigan & crew safe.
229 Squadron Hurricane V6821
Damaged landing at Speke. P/O Penny safe.
232 Squadron Hurricane V6849
Overshot Montrose. Sgt Jordan safe.
248 Squadron Blenheim N6233
Crashed at Newmurcham. Sgt Houchin & crew killed.
252 Squadron Blenheim L6792
Crashed landing at Chivenor. Sub Lt Crane & crew safe.
603 Squadron Spitfire P7297
Crashed landing at Drem. Sgt Crawford-Compton safe.

Luftwaffe

2./KG 30 Ju88A5 6053 4D+CK
Failed to return. Fw W.Muth & crew lost.

I./NJG 3 Bf110D0 3149
Taxy accident at Vechta. Aircraft 20% damaged.
I./ZG 26 Bf110C4 2169
Force-landed at Gräfenberg. Aircraft 10% damaged.
I./LLG 1 Hs126B1 4314
Crashed at Hildesheim. Fw F.Bohn killed. Aircraft destroyed.

31st January 1941

Cloud cover sorties by Bomber Command aircraft were dogged by adverse weather conditions. 2 Group recalled Blenheims from sorties over Holland and Flight Lieutenant King's 139 Squadron aircraft was badly shot-up by AA fire near Southwold on the way back.

Luftwaffe bombers were out over England during the day and at 08.05 a Royal Navy patrol boat brought down an He111 of *I,/KG 28* near Treen, Cornwall. This aircraft, flown by the *Staffelkapitän Hauptmann* Reinhold Gottschalk, was shot down into the sea after machine-gunning fishing vessels. There were no survivors.

In the afternoon an He111 of *2./KG 53*, targetted to London, was flying fast and low over East Sussex in bad visibility. At 16.40 hours 'A1+GK' hit anti-landing cables, and crashed on Wales Farm, Plumpton, killing *Leutnant* Wolf Helm and his crew.

One Dornier of *7./KG 3* was hit by A.A. fire near Wattisham, wounding the *Bordfunker*.

Casualties 31st January 1941

Royal Air Force

139 Squadron Blenheim R3903
Damaged by AA fire at Southwold. F/L King & crew safe.

Luftwaffe

3./JG 52 Bf109E7 4955
Crashed on take-off from Katwijk. Aircraft 15% damaged.
7./KG 3 Do17Z ----
Damaged by gunfire near Wattisham, one man wounded. Aircraft 10% damaged.
II./KG 4 He111P4 3075
Force-landed at Rheine. Aircraft 80% damaged.
I/KG 28 He111H5 3757 1T+LH
Failed to return. Hptm R.Gottschalk & crew lost.
4./KG 30 Ju88A5 4227
Crash-landed at Gilze-Rijn. Aircraft 25% damaged.
IV./KG 30 Ju87B1 0316
Crashed at Ludwigslust. Uffz R.Deise & crew killed. Aircraft destroyed.

A 217 Squadron Beaufort. 217 Squadron operated mainly in the Western Approaches while the other two Beaufort units, Nos 22 and 42 Squadrons, operated along the Channel and North Sea respectively.

E./KG 51 Ju88A1 2116
Crashed near Lechfeld. Oblt Dieter Millbrast & crew killed. Aircraft destroyed.
E./KG 51 Ju88A1 5016
Damaged taxiing at Lechfeld. Aircraft 20% damaged.
E./KG 51 Ju88A1 5017
Damaged taxiing at Lechfeld. Aircraft 10% damaged.
2./KG 53 He111H5 3750 A1+GK
Failed to return from sortie. Lt W.Helm & crew lost.
E./KG 54 Ju88A1 6103
Crashed at Ansbach, Fw A.Schwentekowski & crew killed. Aircraft destroyed.
K.Gr.100 He111H3 6910
Crash-landed at Vaernes. Aircraft 10% damaged.
I./LG 1 Ju88A5 0305
Force-landed at Klosterneuburg. Ofw Karl Fuhrmann & crew injured. Aircraft destroyed.
II./NJG 1 FW58C2 0364
Taxy accident at Deelen. Aircraft 40% damaged.

1st February 1941

A cloud cover sortie to Brest by six Beauforts of 217 Squadron was recalled due to bad weather. Two crews either did not hear or disobeyed the signal. Flight Lieutenant Oakley is believed to have attacked the target, but he failed to return. The wreckage of his aircraft was discovered by the Germans near Calais. Sergeant Rutherford also reached Brest, but was intercepted and shot down northwest of Morlaix by *Unteroffizier* Bochmann of *II. / JG 77.*

At 12.15 hours Flying Officer Van Mentz of 222 Squadron intercepted a Ju88, which he claimed to have probably destroyed east of Yarmouth.

Casualties 1st February 1941

Royal Air Force

1 Squadron Hurricane P3042
Crashed landing at Bredhurst. Sgt Prihoda safe.

1 Squadron Hurricane V7464
Fabric lost in flight. P/O Behal safe.

96 Squadron Hurricane P8813
Crashed landing at Cranage. Sgt Peacock safe

213 Squadron Hurricane V6643
Damaged landing at Driffield. Sgt Wallace safe.

217 Squadron Beaufort L9835
Failed to return. F/L Oakley & crew lost.

217 Squadron Beaufort L9866
Failed to return. Sgt Rutherford & crew lost.

252 Squadron Beaufighter R2152
Overshot Carew Cheriton. P/O Davidson & crew safe.

258 Squadron Hurricane P3658
Force-landed near Penrith. Sgt Maney safe.

258 Squadron Hurricane ZT-
Force-landed near Penrith. P/O Bush safe.

258 Squadron Hurricane ZT-
Force-landed near Penrith. Sgt Sodak safe.

258 Squadron Hurricane ZT-
Force-landed near Penrith. Sgt Sticka safe.

306 Squadron Hurricane V6986
Overshot High Ercall. P/O Czapiewski safe.

607 Squadron Hurricane L1577
Crashed at Middle Moneynut, East Lothian.

Luftwaffe

E./JG 51 Bf109E1 4808
Crash-landed at Cazaux. Aircraft 70% damaged.

IV./KG 30 Ju88A5 0210 4D+MZ
Crashed near Rügen. Lt W.Kremer & crew killed. Aircraft destroyed.

K.Gr.z.b.V. 101 Ju52/3m 2860
Crashed Parchau. Aircraft destroyed.

1/2nd February 1941

That night thirteen Wellingtons attacked Boulogne without loss, but there were several accidents to units not on operations.

Casualties 1/2nd February 1941

Royal Air Force

61 Squadron Hampden AD725
Crashed landing at Hemswell. One man from Sgt Lloyd's crew killed.

144 Squadron Hampden P1238
Crashed at Willingham. Two men from Sgt Hawthorne's crew killed.
604 Squadron Beaufighter R2092
Crashed on approach to Middle Wallop. Sgt Poole & crew safe.

Luftwaffe

- nil -

2nd February 1941

In the afternoon *Circus No.2* began, supported by cloud cover attacks upon nearby airfields by six Coastal Command Blenheims. Wing Commander Kyle's Blenheims returned safely despite a claim by the German gunners. Seven Bf109s were seen in the target area, but made no attempt to intervene. One fighter attack came just as the force was moving away from Boulogne when two Bf109Es from *I./JG 3* dived on the bombers. Squadron Leader Whitney-Straight, leading 601 Squadron, fired a burst at the leading Messerschmitt. The German fighter took hits in the fuselage and wing, and *Unteroffizier* Günther Pöpel was wounded in the eye. He managed to crash-land near Boulogne, wrecking his aircraft. His Rottenflieger (wingman) was attacked by Hurricanes of 1 Squadron, Flight Sergeant Kuttelwascher and Flying Officer Hancock each claiming a Bf109 damaged. One of these pilots put four bullets through the fuselage as the '109 hurtled past.

Circus No.2 To Boulogne Docks	
Five Blenheims of 139 Squadron	
Close Escort :	1, 303 and 601 Sqns
Rear Cover :	66, 74 and 92 Sqns
Channel Sweep:	54, 64 and 611 Sqns

The Biggin Hill Spitfires arrived over the target area at 19,000 ft and found six Messerschmitts below them. Squadron Leader Malan took 74 Squadron down to engage. He and Sergeant Payne each claimed one destroyed while a 'probable' was claimed by Sergeant Smith. Squadron Leader Michelmore, on attachment from 611 Squadron, was shot down and killed by *Leutnant* Friedrich Geisshardt of *I./LG 2*. *LG 2* suffered no casualties.

Meanwhile the Coastal Command Blenheims were having problems. Flight Lieutenant Grece managed to bomb Poix airfield, but was then attacked by two Bf109s. He escaped in cloud and headed for home, but was only eight miles out from Dungeness when two more Messerschmitts attacked, severely damaging his Blenheim. Pilot Officer Trim reached the St. Omer airfield complex, but he too was engaged by Bf109s and took violent evasive action, his gunner claiming a Messerschmitt destroyed. The German pilots chased his aircraft as far as Ramsgate, where Trim belly-landed. The crew beat a hasty retreat before the bomb load blew up.

Karel Kuttelwascher of 1 Squadron was to achieve fame as an intruder pilot in 1942.

Further west 56 Squadron were flying a Channel sweep. A Do17 was sighted in mid-Channel, but although three Hurricanes of 'B' Flight gave chase, it escaped in cloud.

The Channel area quietened until 15.35 hours, when two Spitfires of 91 Squadron intercepted a Do17 near Dover. This was attacked and claimed damaged by Flying Officer O'Meara.

An hour later Flying Officer Van Mentz of 222 Squadron found an He111 from *1./KG 53* east of Lowestoft. He attacked and claimed it damaged. This machine eventually crash-landed at Hyseles with the gunner wounded.

Flight Lieutenant Count Manfred Czernin of 17 Squadron led Yellow Section into an attack on a Ju88 off the east coast. His Hurricane caught a burst of return fire and the '88 escaped unscathed.

That night Bomber Command sent twelve aircraft to attack Brest, while two more laid mines. There were no casualties. No appreciable German activity was reported over Britain.

Casualties 2nd February 1941

Royal Air Force

17 Squadron Hurricane V7408
Damaged by return fire from Ju88. F/L Czernin safe.
59 Squadron Blenheim V5531
Damaged by Bf109s and crash-landed. P/O Trim & crew safe.

59 Squadron Blenheim TR-T
Damaged by Bf109s. F/L Grece & crew safe.
64 Squadron Spitfire P7690
Force-landed near Eastchurch; fuel. Sgt Cooper safe.
64 Squadron Spitfire P7748
Force-landed near Faversham; fuel. Sgt Allen safe.
64 Squadron Spitfire P7626
Force-landed near Shepherdswell; fuel. P/O Blake safe.
74 Squadron Spitfire P7741
Failed to return. S/L Michelmore lost.
91 Squadron Spitfire DL-
Force-landed at Hawkinge. F/L Drake safe.
92 Squadron Spitfire X4484
Belly-landed at Manston. F/O Kinder safe.
101 Squadron Blenheim N3570
Crashed near Boston, Lincs. Sgt Langrish & crew killed.
219 Squadron Beaufighter R2134
Overshot Gatwick. S/L Little and crew safe.
238 Squadron Hurricane P3219
Crashed landing at Chilbolton. P/O Seddon safe.
255 Squadron Defiant N3306
Stalled at Kirton-in-Lindsay. Sgt Jacobs safe, gunner killed.
263 Squadron Whirlwind P6973
Damaged landing at Charmy Down. Sgt Jowitt safe.
302 Squadron Hurricane V6753
Crashed at Lagness on training flight. Sgt Markiewicz safe.
312 Squadron Hurricane WX-
Crashed at Penrhos, Sgt Kruta safe.
605 Squadron Hurricane Z2308
Missing. Sgt Pettit lost.
605 Squadron Hurricane Z2329
Missing. Sgt K.H.Jones lost. (captured).
615 Squadron Hurricane P3111
Overshot Kenley. Adj Guerin safe.

Luftwaffe

1./JG 3 Bf109E8 6386
Damaged in combat and crashed at Boulogne. Uffz Pöpel wounded.
Aircraft destroyed
1./JG 3 Bf109E ----
Damaged in combat. Uffz Müller safe.
E./JG 52 Bf109E4 5144
Force-landed near Arques. Aircraft destroyed.
1./KG 53 He111H5 3809
Damaged by fighters and force-landed at Hyseles, one man wounded.
Aircraft 35% damaged.
I./KG 76 Ju88A5 7172 F1+DL
Crash-landed at Giebelstadt. Aircraft 50% damaged.

3rd February 1941

The day was quiet and only one combat occurred. Several
Spitfire Vbs from 92 Squadron patrolled the Thames estuary in

Tony Bartley of 92 Squadron, who was to become another of the great fighter leaders.

the morning and succeeded in finding a Heinkel from *6./KG 53*. This was attacked by Pilot Officer Bartley, whose cannon shells blasted 'A1+AN' apart in mid-air. All of *Leutnant* Max Petry's crew were lost. The night hours brought limited activity by both sides, the RAF sent eighteen aircraft to attack targets in western France without loss and a few German bombers were plotted over Britain. There were no claims by the defences, but two Heinkels crashed on return.

Casualties 3rd February 1941

Royal Air Force

9 Squadron Wellington N2619
Crashed at Stradishall. Crew unhurt.
43 Squadron Hurricane L1968
Missing on training flight. Sgt Stoker lost.
72 Squadron Spitfire X4596
Crashed landing at Acklington. F/O Secretan safe.
85 Squadron Hurricane P2298
Crash-landed in snowstorm. Sgt Webster safe.
96 Squadron Hurricane W9159
Force-landed near Tarporley. Sgt Taylor safe.

Luftwaffe

III./KG 2 Do17Z3 4228
Taxiing accident at Cambrai-Sud. Extent of damage not notified.
6 /KG 53 He111H2 5517 A1+AN
Failed to return. Lt M.Petry & crew missing.
E /KG 55 He111P2 1621
Undercarriage damage at Landsberg. Aircraft 45% damaged.

Casualties 3/4th February 1941

Royal Air Force

308 Squadron Hurricane V7502
Force-landed at Stoney Stratford. F/L Young safe.
311 Squadron Wellington N3010
Crashed on return. Sgt Ocelka & crew safe.

502 Squadron Whitley P5096
Damaged on take-off from Wick. F/L Foster & crew safe.

Luftwaffe

Stab./KG 53 He111H3 3345
Hit by AA fire and landed at Merville. Aircraft 40% damaged.
I./KG 53 He111H5 3549
Crash-landed at Vitry. Aircraft 15% damaged.
4.(H)/31 Hs126B1 4311
Taxy accident at Hoogboom. Aircraft 40% damaged.

4th February 1941

The weather cleared considerably. Several air combats occurred, beginning at dawn when Sergeants Barnes and Brejcha of 257 Squadron flew an airfield protection sortie from Coltishall. They noticed explosions in nearby Lowestoft, and then intercepted *Feldwebel* Heinz Ablonski's Do17 of *4./KG 2*, the crew of which had been briefed to attack Mildenhall. The two fighter pilots attacked, despite accurate return fire which damaged one of the Hurricanes, and 'U5+GM' crashed into the sea at 09.30 hours. The crew baled out, but Ablonski and one other man died when their parachutes failed to open. Two other wounded men were captured, one dying later in hospital. As if in retaliation, Bf109s strafed Hawkinge at 12.40 hours and destroyed the 91 Squadron Spitfire normally flown by Flight Sergeant McKay.

Flight Sergeant D A S McKay of 91 Squadron was to make several claims during early 1941, including two on 4th February.

In the afternoon three Hurricanes from 249 Squadron flew a convoy protection patrol and sighted a Bf110 approaching the ships. Squadron Leader Barton attacked and shot it down near the Kentish Knock Lightship. A second '110 was then seen and Barton, together with Sergeant Palliser, again attacked. One engine stopped and the Messerschmitt slowly descended into the water. These were from *E.Gr.210*, which reported the loss of two aircraft -'S9+EH' and 'S9+FK', flown by *Unteroffizier* Josef Roming and *Unteroffizier* Gustav Drews respectively. Barton was awarded credit for one victory plus a 'shared'.

At 14.40 hours, two Spitfires of 91 Squadron patrolled over Manston, making contact with two Bf109s. Flight Sergeant Donald McKay, in a new aircraft, dived on the nearest one, opened fire from dead astern and claimed that his adversary had exploded. He then attacked the second and claimed it damaged before it slipped into a cloudbank. In fact one Bf109 from *9./JG 3* crash-landed at Etaples with undercarriage damage.

Blenheims of 53 Squadron again attempted to attack Brest, and as before the Bf109s of *II/JG77* were ready for them. The interception was made in the target area where Pilot Officer Morris' aircraft was shot down into the sea by *Unteroffizier* Rudolf Schmidt of *5 Staffel*. Pilot Officer Marriott was obliged to ditch off the English coast and one crewman was lost. Coastal Command sustained a further loss when a 206 Squadron Hudson flown by Pilot Officer Blackett failed to return from a sortie to Norway.

Casualties 4th February 1941

Royal Air Force

41 Squadron Spitfire R7448
Crashed landing at Hornchurch. Sgt Hopkinson safe.
53 Squadron Blenheim T1992
Crashed into sea off Manston. One man from P/O Marriott's crew killed.
53 Squadron Blenheim T2283
Failed to return. P/O Morris & crew lost.
54 Squadron Spitfire KL-
Crashed. P/O Bocca killed.
59 Squadron Blenheim TR-D
Crashed on take-off. Two men from P/O Custerson's crew killed.
64 Squadron Spitfire SH-
Hit balloon cable. Sgt Wylde safe, aircraft repairable.
82 Squadron Blenheim T2118
Force-landed at Mildenhall. F/L Messervy & crew safe.
91 Squadron Spitfire P7735
Burnt in raid upon Hawkinge. No crew casualty.
150 Squadron Wellington N2758
Force-landed near North Coates. F/O Hooper & crew safe.
151 Squadron Defiant N3371
Belly-landed at Wittering. P/O Edmiston safe.

206 Squadron Hudson VX-S
Failed to return. P/O Blackett & crew lost.
214 Squadron Wellington R1385
Missing en route to Middle East. P/O Todd & crew lost.
221 Squadron Wellington N2910
Belly-landed at Bircham Newton. F/L Starling & crew safe.
229 Squadron Hurricane V7078
Crashed into River Mersey. Sgt Arbuthnot killed.
263 Squadron Whirlwind P6971
Damaged landing at Charmy Down. Sgt Skelton safe.
604 Squadron Beaufighter R2137
Crashed landing at Middle Wallop. P/O McLaren & crew safe.

Luftwaffe

6./JG 3 Bf109E4 1485
Crashed at Vendeville. Uffz E.Rybiak killed. Aircraft destroyed.
9./JG 3 Bf109E1 4867
Tyre damage at Etaples. Aircraft 35% damaged.
I./KG 2 Do17Z2 4222 U5+KK
Crashed on take-off from Epinay. Oblt J.Rücker & crew safe.
Aircraft destroyed.
4./KG 2 Do17Z2 1132 U5+GM
Failed to return. Fw H.Ablonski & crew killed.
II./KG 77 Ju88A5 0614 3Z+LN
Belly-landed at Rheims. one man injured. Aircraft 30% damaged.
E./KG 100 He111H2 5297
Crash-landed at Wiener-Neustadt. Aircraft 15% damaged.
1./E.Gr.210 Bf110E1 3849 S4+PK
Failed to return. Uffz G.Drews and &w missing.
1./E.Gr.210 Bf110E1 3852 S9+EH
Failed to return. Uffz J Roming & crew missing.

4/5th February 1941

Bomber Command sent 106 aircraft to raid airfields and Channel ports, thirty more attacking Düsseldorf and four laying mines.

On the outward journey a Hampden, some 30 miles out from Lowestoft, was intercepted by a fighter identified as a Bf110. The fighter opened fire and the Hampden rear gunner replied. The intruder vanished into cloud and suddenly a ball of fire was seen dropping away. This was without doubt *Oberleutnant* Otto-Heinrich Häuser's Do17Z-10 of *2./NJG 2*, which vanished into the North Sea this night. The Hampden force lost two aircraft. Pilot Officer Lewis's 49 Squadron crew were taken prisoner when their machine was shot down by *Flak* near Düsseldorf, while a 106 Squadron aircraft piloted by Flight Lieutenant Burr-Thomas fell to *Flak* near La Gandiniere while engaged upon minelaying the approaches to St. Nazaire. *Flak*

A Bf 110C of II./NJG 1. This particular aircraft was the mount of Leutnant Helmut Lent, later to become the second-highest scoring nightfighter Experte with 102 victories.

batteries claimed three bombers destroyed, two Whitleys and a Wellington crashing on return.

The *Luftwaffe* sent 159 aircraft out on small-scale raids, particularly against London, Derby and the Midlands. Nightfighters were airborne and Pilot Officer Arbon of 85 Squadron gained a 'visual' on a Ju88 south-east of Debden. Closing to fifty yards, he fired a burst, and last saw the Junkers going away in a fast dive. This was claimed as damaged. It could possibly have been an aircraft from *3.(F)/22*, which crash-landed, heavily damaged, at Stavanger. Arbon's CO Squadron Leader Townsend was himself attacked by an enemy aircraft over East Anglia. His Hurricane was not hit, nor did he see his attacker.

At 21.40 hours, Sergeant Bodien from 151 Squadron patrolled west of Wittering, where a Do17 was sighted at 10,000 ft. He closed on it and attacked the *3./KG 2* machine from below and, after a second burst from the Defiant's four-gun turret, 'U5+AR' rolled over and plunged into the ground at Corthwick Lodge, Weldon, Northants. *Oberleutnant* Herbert Krisch and his three crewmen were killed.

Casualties 4/5th February 1941

Royal Air Force

49 Squadron Hampden P3920
Failed to return. P/O Lewis & crew lost.

59 Squadron Blenheim V5374
Damaged landing at Thorney Island. P/O James & crew safe.

77 Squadron Whitley KN-
Crashed at Driffield on return. Sgt Godwin & crew safe.

99 Squadron Wellington P9281
Overshot Mildenhall. Sgt Malcolm & crew safe.

102 Squadron Whitley P5092
Crashed landing at Driffield. P/O Pitt & crew safe.

106 Squadron Hampden AD750
Failed to return. F/L Burr-Thomas & crew lost.

Luftwaffe

I./NJG 2 Do17Z10 2859 R4+BK
Failed to return. Oblt O-H Häuser & crew missing.

II./NJG 1 Bf110C 4223
Crashed near Bonn . Aircraft destroyed.

III./K G2 Do17Z3 2907
Failed to return. Oblt H.Krisch & crew lost.

II./KG 53 He111H3 3350
Crash-landed at Vendeville. Aircraft 15% damaged.

3.(F)/22 Ju88 ----
Crash-landed at Stavanger. Aircraft 35% damaged.

February 1941 - Overview

The Royal Air Force

Fighter Command

The first unit to move during February was 258 Squadron, flying out from Acklington to Jurby on the Isle of Man on the 1st. 253 Squadron moved further north, from Leconfield to Skeabrae on the 10th, while two days later 1 (RCAF) Squadron arrived at Driffield from Castletown, moving on to Digby on the 16th. The units place at Castletown was taken by 213 Squadron, which moved up from Driffield on 18th February. 41 Squadron left Hornchurch for Catterick on the 23rd, changing places with 54 Squadron and, next day, 609 Squadron arrived at Biggin Hill from Warmwell, while 66 Squadron left West Malling for Exeter. Two days later (26th) 616 Squadron arrived at Tangmere from Kirton-in-Lindsay, changing places with 65 Squadron, and 605 Squadron transferred from Croydon to Martlesham Heath, from which 17 Squadron moved two days later to replace 605 at Croydon. Less significant changes during the month were:

6th	19 Squadron	Duxford to Fowlmere.
	256 Squadron	Pembrey to Colerne,
		sending a detachment to Middle Wallop
10th	3 Squadron	Skeabrae to Castletown.
	247 Squadron	Roborough to St. Eval,
		leaving a detachment at Roborough.
	260 Squadron	Castletown to Skitten.
12th	29 Squadron	Digby to Wellingore.
16th	32 Squadron	Middle Wallop to Ibsley.
17th	247 Squadron	returns to Roborough from St. Eval.
20th	74 Squadron	Biggin Hill to Manston.
	92 Squadron	Manston to Biggin Hill
22nd	43 Squadron	Drem to Crail.

24th	71 Squadron	'B' Flight Kirton-in Lindsay to Finningley.
	234 Squadron	St. Eval to Warmwell.
	263 Squadron	Exeter to St. Eval.
28th	46 Squadron	'A' and 'B' Flights Digby to Church Fenton, 'C' Flight to Wellingore.
	603 Squadron	Drem to Turnhouse.

Three new fighter squadrons were formed. 316 Squadron (Hurricane I) was established at Pembrey on the 15th, 118 Squadron (Spitfire I) at Filton on the 20th and 317 Squadron (Hurricane I) at Acklington on the 22nd.

Newer aircraft were now appearing in larger numbers. During the month Hurricane IIs were taken on charge by 1, 17. 56, 242, 249 and 615 Squadrons. Spitfire IIs went to 54, 64, 145, 303, 609 and 616 Squadrons. 85 Squadron continued its conversion to the night fighting rôle at Debden, beginning to re-equip with the twin-engined Douglas Havoc I (a fighter development of the DB-7 Boston light bomber), while 96 Squadron supplemented its Hurricanes with the arrival of some Defiants. 71 (Eagle) Squadron became operational on 7th February.

Bomber Command

There were several changes withing the bomber forces during the month. 40 Squadron moved to Alconbury on the 2nd, a detachment of 110 Squadron Blenheims was sent to Horsham St. Faith on the 16th and smaller detachments from 107 Squadron were sent to Swanton Morley and Newmarket, returning within a few days. On the 23rd, two flights of Hampdens from 106 Squadron transferred to Coningsby. The Manchesters of 207 Squadron finally became operation on the 24th and, next day, 97 Squadron formed at Waddington as the second Manchester unit. In Northern Ireland 226 Squadron began to re-equip with Blenheim IVs in preparation for a move to England for the planned 2 Group offensive. The unit would not, however, become fully operational until July 1941.

The Luftwaffe

Fighter Forces

On the 5th, *JG 3* moved from the Pas de Calais area to Germany, its place being taken *JG 51*. *JG 26* also departed to Germany, flying out on 9th February. Meanwhile, *Stab./JG 52* arrived at Berck-sur-Mer from Germany on the 1st, where it was joined by *II Gruppe* from Bergen-op-Zoom. The stay was to be short, for on the 10th, both units moved on to Maldeghem. Next day *II./JG 54* moved from Laval to Le Mans. *I./JG 52* transferred from Katwijk to Woensdrecht and Vlissingen on 20th. In Norway a new *Gruppe, I./JG 77,* was formed at Stavanger with Bf109Es.

Bomber Forces

There were many unit movements, commencing on the 6th when *I./KG 26* transferred from Aalborg to Stavanger. This was followed on the 14th by *Geschwaderstab,* while *II./KG 53* moved from Lille-Nord to Vendeville on the 10th. *KG 77* moved in mid-February, *Stab, I* and *II Gruppen* going to Rheims, while *III./KG 77* transferred to Juvincourt. On the 16th, the 'pathfinder' *III./KG 26* moved from Poix-Nord to Achiet, while *II Gruppe* dispersed to Aalborg and Woensdrecht two days later. *E.Gr.210* had been in training at Denain for some time and had indeed begun limited operations. Now, on the 22nd, it moved to Ursel in preparation for a return to operations in strength. In late February, *Stab, I* and *II./KG 3* transferred to Cambrai and Schipol, while *III Gruppe* went to Merville. The bomber force was strengthened by the arrival from Germany of *II./KG 76* on the 6th and *III./KG 53* four days later, taking up residence at Chateaudun and Lille-Nord respectively.

Meanwhile many units were leaving the west for other theatres. *St.G. 2* and *St.G. 77* went to Rumania on the 12th, with *7./LG 1.* Next day, *Stab* and *I./LG 1* and *I./KG 3* all left for the Mediterranean area. On the 19th *II* and *III./St.G. 1* went to Sicily. Other departures were *1./NJG 3* and *2.(F)/122,* again bound for the Middle East.

Naval Situation

The German surface raiders were still posing a threat to British Merchant shipping. The battlecruisers *Scharnhorst* and *Gneisenau* ranged across the Indian Ocean, meeting a convoy escorted by the battleship *Ramillies* on 6th February. The two German warships, out-gunned, turned and ran. They had better luck on the 22nd however, getting among a convoy and sinking six vessels. The previous day the battlecruiser *Admiral Scheer* captured a tanker near the Seychelles. Most significant was the sortie of the cruiser *Hipper*, which left Brest on 1st February to work with FW200s of *I./KG 40* and a U-boat. This resulted in the destruction of thirteen merchant ships in the North Atlantic before *Hipper* returned to Brest on the 15th. By this date the other raiders were nearing the point at which they needed to return to base. Brest was the nearest port capable of supplying the heavy warships. If these vessels were allowed to reach port, a formidable striking force would be poised to attack shipping the Western Approaches.

Chapter Four
The Gathering of the Hawks

5th February 1941

Early that morning a FW200C of *1./KG 40* attempted to attack shipping off Scotland and was hit by gunfire from SS *Major C*. It crashed on a hillside between Durrus and Schull at 08.00 hours with one injured survivor from *Oberleutnant* Paul Gömmer's crew.

Four Spitfires of 92 Squadron flew a morning convoy patrol in the Thames estuary. As they neared Manston on the return flight, warning came of a raider approaching the North Foreland. They turned and headed back to the patrol area to discover a Ju87B Stuka diving on the ships. The dive-bomber released its bomb, which hit HM trawler *Tourmaline*, but as it levelled out, the Spitfires cut off its retreat. The German pilot immediately turned towards the English coast with Pilot Officers Saunders, Fokes and Sergeants Ream and Bowen-Morris closing in fast.

Squadron Leader John Kent, CO of 92 Squadron, was at that moment driving his car along the road leading past Manston. He recalled:

"The Stuka came across the airfield twisting and turning, closely followed by Toby Fokes, who was flying my aeroplane (X6923 QJ-J). Coincidentally, a few of us had been talking about this possibility only the night before when the subject of entertaining captured German airmen had been raised - we had heard that they sometimes did this for our shot-down fighter pilots. I really 'tore them off a strip', saying that their job was to defend England and to kill the King's enemies - and nothing else. Toby had obviously taken this to heart. Although the German pilot clearly wanted to surrender, Toby was equally determined that he should not. I heard the deep 'thump-thump-thump' of the cannons and then the gigantic 'whoosh!' as the Stuka blew up and crashed near the road. I ran over to the wreckage. The pilot was sitting upright in his seat, one hand still holding the throttle. He was quite dead."

Above: Saunders, Ream, Bowen-Morris and Fokes inspect the wreckage of J9+BK at Manston.
Right: Ronald Fokes, who was killed in 1944 while leading a Typhoon squadron over Normandy following the D-Day landings.

This aircraft was 'J9+BK' of *7./St.G 1*. Neither *Leutnant* Ernst Schimmelpfennig nor his *Bordschütze* survived. It was the last Stuka to fall on British soil. All four British pilots were awarded a 'share' of this victory.

Shortly after noon, *Circus No.3* took place. The bombers were, according to Fighter Command, a little late. Consequently two of the Close Escort squadrons proceeded independently to France. The target was reached and bombed without interference, bomber crews reporting that a yellow-painted aircraft was set on fire. The War Diary of *I./JG 3* states however: 'Eleven bombs on airfield, causing no damage.'

Circus No.3 to St.Omer/Wizernes		
Six Blenheims each 139 and 114 Sqns		
Close Escort:	1, 56 and 615 Sqns	
Top Cover:	65, 302 and 610 Sqns	
Target Support:	41, 64 and 611 Sqns	

The formation was between St. Omer and the French coast when Bf109Es of *I./JG 3* attacked from above, taking both the Top Cover and Close Escort squadrons by surprise. The price was heavy. 610, top squadron of the High Cover Wing, had seen shadowing '109s in the target area, when suddenly a lone Bf109 flicked over the Spitfires. It rolled swiftly to port and dived away. It was then discovered that Sergeant Denchfield had vanished. He had baled out of his burning Spitfire west of Wizernes. Pilot Officer Fenwick was also attacked but, although wounded, brought his battered fighter home. 611 Squadron, flying Target Support, was bounced just off the coast, losing Pilot Officer Sadler, but a Messerschmitt was claimed shot down by Flight Lieutenant Heath. His wingman Pilot Officer Smith fired on a Bf109 that dived away, obviously damaged. This aircraft was then attacked by Sergeant Gillegan and the two pilots were awarded a shared 'probable'.

As more Bf109s made diving attacks, 65 Squadron separated from the Top Cover Wing and chased them down. Flight Lieutenant Finucane claimed a Bf109 shot down at low level, but both Pilot Officer Hill and Sergeant Orchard failed to return. Hill was taken prisoner near St. Omer. 1 Squadron lost Pilot Officer Lewis, blasted into the sea, 615 Squadron lost Sergeant Jenkins. Sergeant Jones of 56 Squadron also failed to return. Pilot Officer Adams of 41 Squadron attempted to engage a '109, but the German pilot dived away before he could open fire. Finally, two Hurricanes of 615 Squadron collided near Dover on the way back. Pilot Officer Wydrowski baled out safely, but Pilot Officer Czernastek was killed.

Jagdgeschwader 3 had scored a notable victory and the following claims were made: *Leutnant* Meckel two Spitfires, *Oberfeldwebel* Robert Olejnik, *Feldwebel* Hans Ehlers and *Feldwebel* Heesen one apiece, these pilots from *2 Staffel*. One more was claimed by *Oberleutnant* Wulff of the Gruppenstab. It is possible that a claim for a Spitfire by Feldwebel Wilhelm Philipp of *II. / JG 26* was also made during this fight.

As they stand, the German claims show a high degree of accuracy; seven claims against seven losses, plus one badly damaged. However, the story does not end there. At 13.30 hours, a five-squadron Channel patrol was carried out. This was followed, thirty minutes later, by six Blenheims of Coastal Command, escorted by 3, 19 and 257 Squadrons, flying a *Roadstead* to Calais. No air opposition was met. Simultaneously more fighter squadrons swept between St. Inglevert and Boulogne, again finding nothing. The Germans reported a second large combat, *III. / JG 3* finding another formation. *9*

Three of the successful pilots from I./JG 3. From left: Hans Ehlers, Robert Olejnik and Helmut Meckel. Only Olejnik was to survive the war.

Staffel claimed four Hurricanes destroyed by *Oberleutnant* Viktor Bauer, *Feldwebel* Wessling, *Oberleutnant* Jaczak and *Unteroffizier* Schleef. *Hauptmann* Walter Oesau, the Gruppen-kommandeur, claimed a Spitfire near Desvres for his 40th victory. *Oberleutnant* Ostholt claimed no less than three Spitfires, one of which force-landed, and *Feldwebel* Schentke claimed one also. *Flak* gunners claimed a Blenheim and a Spitfire.

From the above it would seem that another fight took place. This is supported by Air Ministry documents[1] which state that during an anti-shipping operation off Calais 'Four Spitfires and five Hurricanes Cat.3 destroyed. Six pilots missing.' A careful search of all Operation Record Books cannot confirm this however. In the opinion of the author this is a duplication of the earlier operation. This view is supported by the testimony of Sergeant H.D.Denchfield of 610 Squadron, who was shot down during this operation. 'Dave' Denchfield was acting as 'weaver' to the the squadron. This task was difficult and dangerous at the best of times, involving steep turns behind the squadron attempting to both scan the sky behind and keep some sort of contact with the squadron in front. He found himself some six hundred yards adrift from his fellow pilots and was endeavour-

---

1. Daily Resumé of Air Operations - PRO Kew

ing to make up ground when suddenly his Spitfire was hit by cannon fire. He broke hard, lost contact with 610 as he was, in his own words, 'weaving like mad'. His fighter was badly hit however and he was obliged to bale out near Wizernes airfield, losing one flying boot on the way down to land adjacent to the airfield. As some German ground staff approached him, he saw two '109s, wheels and flaps down, pass overhead on final approach to the airfield. He was treated with courtesy, even down to the famous 'For you the war is over' and, upon arrival on the airfield, was introduced to the fighter pilots of *JG 3*, including the man credited with shooting him down. This officer held out a silver cigarette case and asked him to sign his name in pencil. Dave, noticing that there were already seven or eight signatures neatly engraved on the inside of the case, did as he was requested and shortly afterwards was whisked away to prison camp and interrogation.[1]

In the combat only one Bf109 was actually hit, a machine from *8 Staffel* force-landing damaged at Etaples. A second Messerschmitt, from 5 *Staffel*, force-landed near Lille out of fuel.

The result of this operation caused a bitter exchange of words between 2 Group and Fighter Command Headquarters. Fighter Command accused the Blenheims of being late, an assertation hotly disputed by 2 Group, who claimed to have been given no definite rendezvous time. The following day Air Marshal Sholto Douglas, AOC in C. Fighter Command, wrote to the Secretary of State for Air:

"The deduction to be drawn from the experience of these patrols is the importance of making thorough arrangements for the rendezvous and the accurate execution of these arrangements, as formations which proceed incomplete, as was the case in the first patrol, are liable to be attacked in detail and to suffer casualties accordingly."

---

1. Many years later, the author sent Dave Denchfield photographs of many of the successful German pilots involved. He unhesitatingly identified Walter Oesau as the man whose cigarette case he had autographed. He had become Oesau's 40th 'kill'. Shortly afterwards, following a careful search by French acquaintances, Dave travelled to France and found the precise spot where his Spitfire had fallen. After gaining a total of 127 combat victories and winning the *Ritterkreuz* with Oak Leaves and Swords, Oesau, often referred to as the 'toughest fighter pilot in the Luftwaffe' was killed in action by American fighters on 11th May 1944.

Top left: Sergeant H D Denchfield of 610 Squadron, minus right flying boot, is introduced to pilots of I. / JG 3 (out of shot) at Wizernes. The 'haystack' behind is actually a camouflaged building.

Top right: Walter Oesau, who was credited with bringing him down.

Below: Germans inspect the wreckage of 'Dave' Denchfields Spitfire N3249 at a roadside near Wizernes.

On the 12th, Air Vice-Marshal Stevenson, AOC No.2 Group, wrote to the Chief of Air Staff, Air Chief Marshal Sir Charles Portal:

"I know that the original idea of using the bombers was that they should act as "bait" - not an attractive proposition to me - but I agree with Douglas. It was worth trying if it produced a tactical situation favourable to his fighters. This so far has not succeeded appreciably, and I notice moreover, that when Fighter Sweeps have been unaccompanied by bombers, engagements have not resulted.

"If we do (and we do) want engagements, then they must be profitable to us either because we shoot down more fighters than we ourselves lose, or because we have inflicted material bombing damage on the enemy. Preferably a combination of both.

"The initiative lies with us. We can pick a time and place; weather and height, also the size of our formation. I am bound to say that I would have thought that we could have produced a tactical situation favourable to ourselves. Yet I don't think the poor results can be entirely due to the bombers having dallied too long over the target. I agree with you that this should never be.

"If I may criticise, I would say that we have not gone big enough; have neither tried to do severe bomb damage, or had sufficient high upper guard to take care of the withdrawal. If we want the enemy to accept battle on our terms we shall, I think, have to bomb in a manner which he cannot ignore, otherwise he will only take us on when it suits him.

"Please regard these as my reflections. I shall continue to leave the tactical handling of the business with Leigh-Mallory (AOC 11 Group Fighter Command) since too many cooks will only contrive a nonsense, but I shall squeal like a wounded steer if I lose Blenheims as 'bait'."

The final action took place in the early evening, when Squadron Leader Malan of 74 Squadron, leading Pilot Officer Armstrong, Flight Lieutenant Freeborn and Pilot Officer Chesters, engaged a Do215 off Boulogne. This was attacked by all four pilots and claimed damaged and was a Do17 from *III./KG 2* flown by *Feldwebel* Walter Gottschlich, which actually failed to return.

Luftwaffe cloud cover raiders were out over England during the day, dropping bombs on southeast Scotland and Kent. Pilot Officer Goodman of 9 Squadron had an interesting experience during the afternoon:

"We were out on an air test over Suffolk. There was a lot of low cloud about. Suddenly a Dornier appeared from the cloudbase right above us. I told my gunners to open fire and it sheered off abruptly into the cloud again. Later we heard that a Dornier had come down in Suffolk, but we didn't claim it, after all, whoever heard of a Wellington fighter?"

JG 3 now prepared to move back to Germany for rest and refitting. To replace them came the Bf109s of *JG 51*. The *Geschwaderstab*, led by the redoubtable *Major* Werner Mölders, went to Mardyck. Mölders had become the top-scoring *Condor Legion* pilot in Spain, where he achieved fourteen 'kills' with *Jagdgruppe 88*. On 29th June 1940 he became the first fighter pilot to be awarded the *Ritterkreuz*, having claimed twenty victories since the outbreak of war. On 21st September 1940 he became the second pilot to win the *Eichenlaub*, after claiming his 40th combat success. His score in February 1941 was now approaching sixty and he was *Oberkanone* (top gun) of the Luftwaffe.

I./JG 51, arriving at Abbeville, was commanded by *Hauptmann* Hermann-Friedrich Joppien, a *Ritterkreuzträger* with a score nearing forty. *II Gruppe* joined the *Stab* at Mardyck and was led by *Hauptmann* Josef Fözö, another *Condor Legion* veteran who had seventeen kills to his credit. *III./JG 51*, commanded by *Hauptmann* Richard Leppa (ten-plus victories) arrived at St. Omer/Wizernes, while *IV Gruppe* under *Hauptmann* Keitel (six) went to Etaples. *I./JG 51* would shortly transfer to Coquelles and *IV./JG 51* to Mardyck.

Casualties 5th February 1941

Royal Air Force

1 Squadron Hurricane P3920
Failed to return from sortie. P/O Lewis lost.
51 Squadron Whitley N1488
Overshot Dishforth. P/O Mattey & crew safe.
56 Squadron Hurricane P3123
Failed to return from sortie. Sgt Jones lost.
65 Squadron Spitfire P7665
Failed to return from sortie. P/O Hill lost.
65 Squadron Spitfire P7733
Failed to return from sortie. Sgt Orchard lost.
304 Squadron Wellington N2910
Damaged landing at Syerston. Sgt Boczkowski & crew safe.
610 Squadron Spitfire N3249
Failed to return from sortie. Sgt Denchfield lost.
610 Squadron Spitfire R6601
Damaged in combat France. P/O Fenwick safe.
611 Squadron Spitfire X4567
Failed to return from sortie. P/O Sadler lost.
615 Squadron Hurricane V6980
Failed to return from sortie. Sgt Jenkins lost.

111

615 Squadron Hurricane V7598
Collided near Dover, P/O Czernastek killed.
615 Squadron Hurricane V6618
Collided near Dover. P/O Wydrowski baled out and safe.

Luftwaffe

5./JG 3 Bf109E7 4113
Force-landed near Lille. Aircraft 15% damaged.
8./JG 3 Bf109E7 4172
Damaged in combat near Etaples. Aircraft 35% damaged.
E./JG 3 Bf109E4 1354
Crashed on Ile de Ré. Fhr Wilhelm Allwang killed. Aircraft destroyed.
E./JG 26 Bf109E7 5591
Crashed at Cognac. Aircraft destroyed
5./JG 52 Bf109E1 3528
Crashed on take-off from Haamstede. Aircraft 50% damaged.
E./JG 53 Bf109E1 6038
Crashed at Curselle. Aircraft 60% damaged.
II./JG 54 Bf109E1 6352
Undercarriage damage at Wevelghem. Aircraft 35% damaged.
III./JG 54 Bf109E4 1646
Force-landed at Le Mans. Aircraft 45% damaged.
3./NJG 1 Bf110C1 0968
Force-landed near Moers, Uffz Werk & crew safe. Aircraft 70% damaged.
III./KG 2 Do17Z2 3386 U5+BS
Failed to return from sortie. Fw W.Gottschlich & crew missing.
Stab./KG 26 He111H5 3764
Force-landed near Aalborg. Aircraft 35% damaged.
I./KG 40 FW200C3 0042
Failed to return from sortie. Oblt P.Gömmer & crew lost.
7./StG 1 Ju87B1 5225
Failed to return from sortie. Lt E.Schimmelpfennig & gunner lost.
I./StG 77 Ju87B1 5329
Force-landed near Champigny. Fw H.Kemmer killed. Aircraft 30% damaged.
II./LG 2 Bf109E7 5899
Crashed at Cognac. Oblt P.Widmann killed. Aircraft destroyed.
4.(H)/12 Hs126 4123
Force-landed near Bordeaux. Aircraft 60% damaged.

6th - 7th February 1941

On the night of the 5th and all the following day, gales lashed the Channel and, apart from a handful of German aircraft plotted, few incidents were noted. The weather eased slightly that night, permitting short-range operations by 49 aircraft from Nos. 3 and 4 Groups. Targets were Channel ports and a Wellington flown by Pilot Officer Cigos of 311 Squadron was lost. It force-landed at La Fleur, Normandy, where the crew were captured. Flak claimed a Whitley. One such aircraft, flown by Pilot Officer Grant of 10 Squadron, had an inconclusive engagement with a twin-engined fighter near Dunkirk.

The *Luftwaffe* laid mines off Liverpool, South Wales and the southeastern counties, but no successes were claimed by the defences.

Next day (7th) the weather clamped down again and the opposing forces were largely grounded. Isolated German shipping raiders were out however. A convoy was attacked off Dundee and SS *Bay Fisher* was sunk off Bell Rock. Navy gunners aboard HMS *Vanity* claimed the destruction of a Dornier. This was possibly a Heinkel of *2./KG 53*, which crashed on return at Zeebrugge and was destroyed. Darkness brought more short-range Bomber Command attacks against French coastal targets by 64 aircraft, with 2 more on leaflet-dropping tasks. All returned safely, although *Flak* gunners at Boulogne claimed a Blenheim.

Casualties 6th February 1941

Royal Air Force

42 Squadron Beaufort L9869
Undercarriage collapsed landing. S/L Hibberd & crew safe.
106 Squadron Hampden AD736
Crashed at Finningley. Sgt Osborne & crew believed safe.
107 Squadron Blenheim L8777
Crashed force-landing near Wattisham. Sgt Clarke & crew safe.
111 Squadron Hurricane P2999
Damaged landing at Dyce. P/O Bain safe.
111 Squadron Hurricane V6562
Undershot Dyce. P/O Skelly safe.
210 Squadron Sunderland P9624
Damaged landing at Oban. P/O Wheeler & crew safe.
304 Squadron Wellington R1014
Crashed on take-off from Syerston. Four men from Sgt Tofin's crew killed.
308 Squadron Hurricane V6937
Belly-landed south of Warwick. S/L Morris safe.
1 (RCAF) Squadron Hurricane P3883
Crashed landing at Highbaldstow. F/O Hyde safe.

Luftwaffe

E.Gr.210 Bf110E1 3824
Taxiing accident at Vechta. Aircraft 20% damaged.
E./KG 54 Ju88A1 6096
Crashed landing at Lechfeld. Aircraft 20% damaged.
8./St.G 1 Ju87R2 5868
Crash-landed at St Pol. Aircraft 15% damaged.

Wellington L7842 of 311 Squadron was force-landed in France on 6/7th February and was later flown by the Germans.

Casualties 6/7th February 1941

Royal Air Force

40 Squadron Wellington L7845
Belly-landed at Little Strakely. P/O Payne & crew safe.

214 Squadron Wellington N2776
Overshot Stradishall. P/O Spooner & crew safe.

307 Squadron Defiant N3432
Belly-landed at Squires Gate. Sgt Ebenrytter & gunner safe.

311 Squadron Wellington L7842
Failed to return from sortie. P/O Cigos & crew lost.

604 Squadron Beaufighter R2054
Crashed at Middle Wallop. F/L Hunter & crew killed.

604 Squadron Beaufighter R2139
Damaged landing at Middle Wallop. P/O McLaren & crew safe.

Luftwaffe

- nil -

Casualties 7th February 1941

Royal Air Force

32 Squadron Hurricane P3981
Damaged landing at Middle Wallop. S/L Lawrence safe.

41 Squadron Spitfire P7689
Crashed landing at Bottisham. F/L MacKenzie safe.

92 Squadron Spitfire R6924
Crashed near Deal in mist. P/O Watling killed.

214 Squadron Wellington P9239
Crashed landing at Stradishall. F/O Thorburn & crew safe.

226 Squadron Boston AW407
Belly-landed at Sydenham. S/L Hurst & crew safe.

502 Squadron Whitley T4223
Crashed into sea. F/O Henderson & crew rescued.

In spite of the heavy-looking floats, the Ar 196B was a very nimble aircraft and was used both as a catapult launched aircraft from heavy warships and to patrol the Biscay area.

Luftwaffe

II./KG 1 Ju88A5 4191
Taxiing accident at Münster-Handorf. Aircraft 25% damaged.
2./KG 53 He111H5 3822
Crashed at Zeebrugge due to enemy gunfire. Aircraft destroyed.
I./KG 40 FW200C3 0029
Crashed near Merignac. Oblt H. Kreimayer & crew killed. Aircraft destroyed.

8th February 1941

At 09.30 hours, south of Dodman Point, two Whirlwinds of 263 Squadron intercepted an Ar196B of *5./196* flown by *Oberleutnant* Adolf Berger, the *Staffelkapitän*. Pilot Officer Graham gave chase, following the floatplane into thick cloud. Seconds later, '6W+ON' briefly reappeared, diving vertically. It fired a flare, then plunged into the sea. Graham's Whirlwind was not seen again. He was credited with the destruction of the Ar196 and is believed to have succumbed to return fire. Neither man from the German crew survived.

In the afternoon, a three-Hurricane patrol from 242 Squadron was vectored onto a Do17 near Clacton. This was attacked and claimed destroyed by Flight Lieutenant Turner, with Pilot Officers Crowley-Milling and Crydermann. The latter pilot failed to return. Gerrie J. Zwanenberg MBE, the noted Dutch air historian saw him flying over north Holland:

"I was skating on a frozen lake with a friend, when we heard the sound of an aeroplane engine. We looked up and saw a Hurricane, flying low towards us. At first we just didn't believe it. It seemed impossible, because we knew that the British fighters simply did not have enough petrol. We waved and he circled around. We could clearly see the pilot waving back. Then he straightened up and flew away to the north. It was an event I'll never forget."

It is presumed that Crydermann then flew out over the North Sea again and perished when his aircraft ran out of fuel.

One further combat took place when Flying Officer Mortimer-Rose of 234 Squadron claimed to have damaged a Ju88 south of Warmwell. This was possibly an He111 of *Wekusta O.b.d.L.* flown by *Feldwebel* Franz Glocke, which crashed on return at Brest and was destroyed.

Shortly after 15.00 hours, a pair of Bf109Es from *5./LG 2* made a surprise attack upon Hawkinge. The AA defences opened fire, claiming hits upon the leader as it turned and hurtled away seaward. The second Messerschmitt stall-turned after strafing two Spitfires and, as it came down to make another firing pass, it took direct hits from light AA sites and spun into the ground at Arpinge Farm, killing the pilot *Leutnant* Werner Schlether.

The *Luftwaffe* claimed two combat victories off Norway. *Leutnant* Weyergand, a Bf110 pilot from the *Zerstörer Staffel* of *JG 77*, shot down Pilot Officer Tingey's 269 Squadron Hudson. *Oberfeldwebel* Lütter of *III./ZG 76* claimed a Beaufort flown by Squadron Leader Hibberd of 42 Squadron, intercepted while attacking warships off Obrestad. Hibberd claimed a 'near miss' for his torpedo attack, but his aircraft was then jumped by the Bf110, which severely damaged the Beaufort and killed the radio operator. The rear gunner claimed the Messerschmitt damaged before the Beaufort escaped.

During the day Hurricanes of 1 Squadron flew a *Rhubarb* to Arques, where a parked Bf109 of *4./JG 3* was strafed and damaged by Squadron Leader Brown, who claimed it destroyed.

Casualties 8th February 1941

Royal Air Force

12 Squadron Wellington W5365
Crashed at Tollerton. S/L Lawrence & crew killed.

25 Squadron Beaufighter R2157
Crashed landing at Wittering. S/L Pleasance & crew safe.

42 Squadron Beaufort L4487
Damaged in combat. S/L Hibberd & crew safe.

91 Squadron Spitfire P7615
Damaged in raid on Hawkinge.
91 Squadron Spitfire P7598
Damaged in raid on Hawkinge.
105 Squadron Blenheim T1930
Belly-landed at Swanton Morley. P/O Dore & crew safe.
219 Squadron Beaufighter R2074
Crashed at Slindon. P/O Head and crew killed.
222 Squadron Spitfire X4067
Crashed landing at Coltishall. Sgt Purcell safe.
232 Squadron Hurricane V6754
Collided with P8810 at Buckie, Renfrew. Fate of pilot not known.
232 Squadron Hurricane P8810
Collided with above. Pilot safe, aircraft repairable.
234 Squadron Spitfire P9446
Belly-landed at Kilmington. Sgt McFarline safe.
242 Squadron Hurricane V6823
Failed to return from sortie. P/O Cryderman lost.
257 Squadron Hurricane V6680
Damaged landing at Coltishall. P/O Blackburn safe.
263 Squadron Whirlwind P6969
Failed to return from sortie. P/O Graham lost.
263 Squadron Whirlwind P6979
Damaged landing at Exeter. Sgt Rudland safe.
269 Squadron Hudson -----
Failed to return from sortie. P/O Tingey & crew lost.

Luftwaffe

4./JG 3 Bf109E4 2036
Strafed at Arques. Aircraft 25% damaged.
6./JG 3 Bf109E4 1243
Crash-landed at Arques. Aircraft 10% damaged.
II./JG 3 Bf109E7 4093
Taxiing accident at Arques. Aircraft 5% damaged.
E./JG 3 Bf109E1 4077
Crash-landed at Brombes. Aircraft 20% damaged.
E./JG 51 Bf109E4 4098
Force-landed at Pitt-Plage. Aircraft 40% damaged.
E./KG 26 He111H3 6858
Force-landed at Kramsforde. Aircraft 75% damaged.
I./KG 27 He111H3 2058
Crashed near Diepholz. Stfw G.Schmidt & one man injured.
Aircraft 60% damaged.
II./LG 2 Bf109E7 6410 'Black T'
Failed to return from sortie. Lt W.Schlether killed.
5./196 Ar196A2 0129 6W+ON
Failed to return from sortie. Oblt A.Berger & crew killed.
Wekusta 1 He111H5 3826
Damaged by gunfire from German destroyer, one man wounded.
Aircraft 25% damaged
Wekusta O.b.d.L. He111H5 3802
Crashed near Brest. Ofw F.Glocke & crew killed. Aircraft destroyed.

L.Fl. Res. 3 Bf109E7 4215
Force-landed at Ehingen. Aircraft 20% damaged.

8/9th February 1941

Fifteen Hampdens of 5 Group struck at Mannheim. All returned, although two aircraft crashed. No claims were submitted by the British defences against the few German aircraft plotted off Yorkshire and the west of England.

Casualties 8/9th February 1941

Royal Air Force

144 Squadron Hampden P4359
Abandoned over Taverham. Sgt Pearman & crew safe.
144 Squadron Hampden AD724
Overshot Waddington. P/O O'Leary & crew safe.
233 Squadron Hudson N7336
Crashed at Leuchars. P/O Alexander & crew safe.
264 Squadron Defiant N1558
Damaged landing at Biggin Hill. P/O Clive & gunner safe.

Luftwaffe

- nil -

9th February 1941

There was a single fighter combat in British airspace. Squadron Leader Jamie Rankin of 64 Squadron, leading Pilot Officer Rowden and Sergeant Savage, intercepted a Ju88 of *II. /KG 30* piloted by *Unteroffizier* Hans Weber over the Thames estuary at 10.25 hours. This was shot down into the sea near Mersea Island, but Rowden's Spitfire was badly hit by return fire.

The Germans claimed another two British aircraft shot down off Norway. 42 Squadron sent several Beauforts out on shipping strikes, two being intercepted by Bf110s of *III. /ZG 76*. Flying Officer Boycott was engaged near Lister and his aircraft badly shot-up, but his gunner claimed the Bf110 damaged. Squadron Leader Miller's aircraft was also badly hit. He ditched some twenty miles from Wick. The pilot was later rescued. The German pilots involved in these actions were *Leutnant* Rolf Hermichen and *Oberfeldwebel* Hans Peterburs, who claimed a Beaufort apiece.

Far to the southwest, *Hauptmann* Fritz Fliegel, Kapitän of *2. /KG 40*, led a formation of five FW200s to attack convoy

A Bristol Beaufort of 42 Squadron heads out across the North Sea seeking German shipping. Note the similarity to the smaller Blenheim.

HG53 inbound from Gibralter, discovered by *U-37* between Portugal and the Azores. Fliegel brought his bombers down to wave-top height to attack and within minutes five vessels had been sunk. *Oberleutnant* Adam's Focke-Wulf was badly hit on the run-up to the target and he finally crashed on the coast of Portugal, where the crew were interned.

Casualties 9th February 1941

Royal Air Force

7 Squadron Stirling N6003
Damaged landing at Oakington. F/O Cox & crew safe.
9 Squadron Wellington R1239
Crashed landing at Alconbury. P/O Wills & crew safe.
22 Squadron Beaufort L9873
Belly-landed at Grainthorpe. F/O Boycott & crew safe
42 Squadron Beaufort L9832
Ditched in North Sea. S/L Miller & two crew lost.
43 Squadron Hurricane V6925
Belly-landed at North Berwick. Sgt Jika injured.
64 Squadron Spitfire P7751
Damaged in combat with Ju88. P/O Rowden safe.
71 Squadron Hurricane V6983
Abandoned in cloud over Donna Nook. P/O Orbison killed.
72 Squadron Spitfire X4486
Crash-landed near Acklington. Sgt Lamberton safe.
105 Squadron Blenheim T1814
Damaged on take-off from Swanton Morley. Sgt King & crew safe.
151 Squadron Defiant N1807
Belly-landed at Wittering. P/O Ellacombe safe.
311 Squadron Wellington L7785
Undershot Honington. Sgt Hajek & crew safe.

119

607 Squadron Hurricane W9189
Crashed at Haddington. P/O Burnell-Phillips killed.

Luftwaffe

E./JG 2 Bf109E4 1418
Abandoned near Cap d'Antifer. Aircraft destroyed.

E./JG 2 Bf109E1 4066
Crashed on take-off from Le Havre. Aircraft 40% damaged.

I./JG 3 Bf109E7 3777
Taxiing accident at Wizernes. Aircraft 10% damaged.

E./JG 3 Bf109E4 1468
Crash-landed at Brombes. Aircraft 50% damaged.

E./JG 3 Bf109E1 6361
Crash-landed at Brombes.Aircraft 10% damaged.

E./JG 3 Bf109E4 3198
Crash-landed at Brombes. Aircraft 30% damaged.

E./JG 3 Bf109E4 1638
Crash-landed at Poix-Nord. Aircraft 85% damaged.

E./JG 26 Bf109E4 0815
Crashed on take-off from Dieppe. Aircraft 95% damaged.

III./JG 51 Bf109F1 6615
Belly-landed at Wizernes. Aircraft 20% damaged.

III./JG 51 Bf109F1 6612
Taxiing accident at Wizernes. Aircraft 10% damaged.

II./JG 54 Bf109E7 3453
Crash-landed at Cherbourg. Aircraft 40% damaged.

II./KG 30 Ju88A5 8102 4D+FH
Failed to return from sortie. Uffz H.Weber & crew missing.

I./KG 40 FW200C1 0003 F8+DK
Failed to return from sortie. Oblt E.Adam & crew interned.

I./LG 2 Bf109E4 1605
Crashed on take-off from Calais/Marck. Aircraft 25% damaged.

I./St.G 1 Ju87R2 5863
Crash-landed at Schweinfurt. Aircraft 5% damaged.

9/10th February 1941

Bomber Command sent 23 aircraft to Wilhelmshaven and fourteen more to the Channel ports. Two aircraft were lost. A Hampden crashed at Culton, killing the crew, and a 103 Squadron Wellington ditched in the Channel. Sergeant Crich and his crew were later rescued.

There were widespread *Luftwaffe* raids totalling 102 bombers, directed mainly against Plymouth, Birmingham and Humberside. One fighter pilot made contact when Sergeant Wagner of 151 Squadron claimed a bomber damaged near Birmingham He crashed at Wittering on return, possibly due to return fire. A Ju88, *Leutnant* Heinz Gibbens' Ju88 'V4+AT' of *III./KG 1* was reported missing from Birmingham, falling victim either to Alan

Wagner or to AA Command, gunners claiming three bombers destroyed.

Casualties 9/10th February 1941

Royal Air Force

83 Squadron Hampden X2972
Crashed landing at Scampton. Sgt Harpham & crew safe.
103 Squadron Wellington T2610
Ditched. Sgt Crich and crew rescued injured.
111 Squadron Hurricane P3106
Crashed landing at Montrose. Sgt Baker safe.
151 Squadron Hurricane -----
Damaged in combat and crash-landed at Wittering. Sgt Wagner unhurt.
307 Squadron Defiant N3410
Crashed into sea off Barmouth. Sgt Joda & gunner rescued.

Luftwaffe

III./KG 1 Ju88A5 0580 V4+AT
Failed to return from sortie. Lt H.Gibbens & crew missing.

10th February 1941

At noon, a *Roadstead* was flown against Boulogne by six Blenheims of 59 Squadron, escorted by thirty Hurricanes of 1, 605 and 615 Squadrons. This drew no reaction.

Almost at the same time as the *Roadstead*, *Circus No.4* took place.

Circus No.4 To Dunkirk Docks	
Six Blenheims 114 Sqn	
Close Escort:	56 Sqn
Top Cover:	17, 249 and 303 Sqns

The Blenheims made a wide feint into France before turning back to bomb their target, where a mixed interception force from *IV./JG 51* and *I./LG 2* dived on the formation. The Messerschmitts jumped 249 Squadron. *Hauptmann* Keitel and *Leutnant* Wiest of *IV./JG 51* each claimed a Hurricane, while *Hauptmann* Herbert Ihlefeld of *I./LG 2* claimed a Spitfire, this highly experienced pilot probably accounting for Pilot Officer David, who failed to return. He baled out wounded to become a prisoner. Two more 249 Squadron Hurricanes sustained damage. Meanwhile the remaining 249 Squadron pilots engaged the '109s, Sergeants Maciejowski and Brzeski each claiming to have shot down a Bf109E. *Unteroffizier* Karl Ryback of *I/LG2* was shot down and killed, his 'White 3' plunging into the Channel. *Leutnant* Adolf

From left: Major Gotthard Handrick with Hauptmann Herbert Ihlefeld, Oberleutnant Wolf-Dietrich Huy and General Förster in the spring of 1941. During 1940/41 Ihlefeld had proved himself to be a master tactician and a deadly shot.

Steckmeyer of *11/JG51* also lost his life when his Messerschmitt crashed at Ardres. A *Staffel* of Bf110s had also been scrambled, but arrived too late to intervene. Had they done so, it seems likely that they would have been badly mauled by the RAF escorts.

Another *Roadstead* departed for Calais at 16.20 hours, comprising six Blenheims of 59 Squadron escorted by 26 Hurricanes and sixteen Spitfires. The bombers hit their target, but the escorts were soon heavily engaged by *Stab* and *I./JG 51*. No claims were made by the RAF pilots, but *Major* Mölders of the *Geschwaderstab* claimed a Hurricane 5 km northnorthwest of Calais at 17.24 hours. *Oberleutnant* Balfanz claimed a second and *Hauptmann* Hartmann Grasser a Spitfire. four Hurricanes were shot down. 601 Squadron lost Pilot Officer Lawson and 46 Squadron lost Pilot Officer Hedley, both reported missing. Sergeant Steadman of the latter unit crashlanded on a sandbank. Although wounded, he managed to swim ashore. Sergeant Mares of 601 Squadron wrecked his fighter while force-landing near Martlesham. Sergeant Hulbert of 601 force-landed near Rochester out of fuel. The *JG 51* pilots were jubilant at their success and their War Diarist wrote: *'Es gehts wieder los!'* - Here we go again!.

Flak gunners claimed three Spitfires, a Hurricane and a Blenheim off Dunkirk.

Coastal Command continued to fly long-range patrols and from these two fighter Blenheims failed to return. Squadron Leader Coates of 248 Squadron crashed near Mandal, while Flying Officer Mackenzie of 254 Squadron was shot down by *Flak* over Trondheim harbour while attacking the tanker *Atria*.

Casualties 10th February 1941

Royal Air Force

9 Squadron Wellington R1239
Damaged landing at Honington. Crew safe.

42 Squadron Beaufort L9869
Crashed landing at Wick. S/L Hibberd & crew safe.

46 Squadron Hurricane V7594
Failed to return from sortie. P/O Hedley missing.

46 Squadron Hurricane V7443
Shot down by Bf109. Sgt Steadman safe, aircraft lost.

54 Squadron Spitfire P9506
Crashed force-landing at Ellerton. Pilot believed safe.

91 Squadron Spitfire DL-W
Crashed. P/O Hartas killed.

92 Squadron Spitfire R6888
Crashed on take-off. P/O Maitland-Thompson safe.

96 Squadron Hurricane V6947
Force-landed on Sutton Hall Farm. F/O Klouboucnik injured.

145 Squadron Hurricane Q4959
Collided. P/O Turner baled out unhurt.

145 Squadron Hurricane Q8553
Collided. P/O Ashton baled out unhurt.

145 Squadron Spitfire X4585
Crashed. No details known.

217 Squadron Beaufort W6490
Crashed landing at St Eval. P/O Livingstone & crew safe.

248 Squadron Blenheim Z5956
Failed to return from sortie. S/L Coates and crew lost.

249 Squadron Hurricane V7171
Failed to return from sortie. P/O David lost.

249 Squadron Hurricane GN-
Damaged in combat. Pilot believed unhurt.

249 Squadron Hurricane GN-
Damaged in combat. Pilot believed unhurt.

254 Squadron Blenheim N3528
Failed to return from sortie. F/O Mackenzie & crew lost.

502 Squadron Whitley T4320
Belly-landed at Port Ballantyne. S/L Stanley & crew safe.

601 Squadron Hurricane V6630
Failed to return from sortie. P/O Lawson lost.

601 Squadron Hurricane V7416
Force-landed at Rochester. Sgt Hulbert safe.
601 Squadron Hurricane V7236
Force-landed near Martlesham Heath. Sgt Mares safe.
615 Squadron Hurricane P3811
Belly-landed near Dungeness. Sgt Ptacek safe.

Luftwaffe

7./JG 3 Bf109E4 5220
Crashed on take-off from Desvres. Aircraft destroyed.
9./JG 3 Bf109E4 1578
Crashed on take-off from Etaples. Aircraft 60% damaged.
11./JG 51 Bf109 6626
Crashed at Ardres. Lt R.Steckmeyer killed. Aircraft destroyed.
1./NJG 1 Bf110C4 3260
Hit obstruction at Stade. Aircraft 15% damaged.
I./LG 2 Bf109E4 1084 White 3
Failed to return from sortie. Uffz K.Ryback missing.
1.(F)/121 Ju88A1 5049
Crash-landed at Elmas. Aircraft 60% damaged.
Kur. St. 5 Bü131D2 4514
Force-landed at St André. Aircraft 25% damaged.

10/11th February 1941

Luftwaffe nightfighters were patrolling and a 15 Squadron Wellington flown by Sergeant Garrioch was engaged and, at 23.28 hours, shot down by *Hauptmann* Walter Ehle of *II./NJG 1*. The bomber crashed at Nunspeet, five men being taken prisoner. Next to fall was Pilot Officer Green's 49 Squadron Hampden, destroyed over Alkmaar by *Leutnant* Leopold Fellerer of *5./NJG 1*, and from which three men survived. The fighter was also hit.

Bomber Command Operations

Hannover 222 Rotterdam 43

Coastal Command Operations

Cherbourg, Ostend and Dortmund-Ems Canal 21

Luftwaffe Operations

Scattered raids and minelaying by 102 aircraft

One further bomber was lost, Flight Lieutenant McConnell's 21 Squadron crew were killed when their aircraft was shot down by *Flak* near Flushing. This was the first occasion that the new four-engined 'heavies' had operated, three Stirlings of 7 Squadron attacking the Rotterdam oil storage tanks. *Flak* gunners claimed two bombers over Boulogne and another at Le Havre. A 9 Squadron Wellington was hit by 'friendly' AA fire as

Left: Hauptmann Rolf Jung of I./NJG 2 (sitting on cockpit edge). The insignia of the 'Englandblitz' is still carried by combat aircraft of the new German Luftwaffe, but the outline of England no longer appears! Right: Paul Semrau of I./NJG 2 destroyed two Blenheims on 10/11th February.

it crossed the British coast and there were several incidents as the aircraft reached their bases, four bombers crash-landing. By far the greater danger however, was that of German night intruders; *I./NJG 2* had despatched several fighters from Gilze-Rijn and these soon began to make contact with the returning bomber force.

Oberleutnant Schulz of *2 Staffel* had lifted his Do17 from the runway at 23.50 hours, arriving in his patrol area seventy minutes later. He discovered an airfield with illuminated flarepath and soon sighted a British aircraft in the landing circuit. He attacked, reporting it as a Blenheim and claiming hits upon the port wing and engine before it fell out of sight. He was unable to observe the expected crash since he was at once attacked by either a Spitfire or Defiant, which made four unsuccessful attacks but drove him away after he had released his incendiaries. He had attacked Coltishall, where fighters from 222, 255 and 257 Squadrons were carrying out night flying practice. Sergeant Ramsay of 222 Squadron was attacked, but

125

his Spitfire was not hit. The Dornier was then attacked by Sergeant Marland of the same unit. Several 255 Squadron Hurricanes were also fired on, but none suffered damage. Sergeant Barnes of 257 Squadron also attacked Schulz, expending all his ammunition without effect.

Hauptmann Rolf Jung, also from *2 Staffel*, was the next pilot away, flying a Ju88. He arrived over East Anglia, where he first bombed an airfield and then he too proceeded to Coltishall. Here he attacked a 257 Squadron Hurricane which easily evaded him. Flying on to Marham he found Sergeant Rodger's 115 Squadron Wellington on final approach. Jung shot this down near Swaffham with one crewman being injured. Short of fuel, Jung turned for home and, almost immediately, his aircraft was hit and slightly damaged by AA fire. At 03.30 hours he sighted a Blenheim off Yarmouth and made a quick attack, but submitted no claim.

Leutnant Johannes Feuerbaum set off at 00.07 hours, this Dornier pilot returning claiming to have made a successful airfield strafe, including the destruction of a parked Wellington.

The Ju88 of *Oberleutnant* Semrau took off at 02.04 hours to catch the 'tail-enders'. Far out over the North Sea he found a lone 21 Squadron Blenheim, which he pursued back to England and shot down. Squadron Leader Sabine hurriedly crash-landed at Harford Bridges, near Bodney. Paul Semrau waited near Bodney where five minutes later he shot down Sergeant Chattaway's 21 Squadron Blenheim on final approach. Chattaway put the burning aircraft down on the runway, but he perished in the wreckage and his observer, severely injured, died later in the day.

Pilot Officer Hay of 144 Squadron had been briefed to attack Hannover. He reported:

"We attacked from 10,000 feet with 1 1,900lb G.P. bomb, but could not distinguish our burst from several other bombs which burst simultaneously. As we left there were at least five fires burning in the town, three of which were visible for 50 miles. In some cases we could see the framework of buildings which were being gutted. The rear gunner added his incendiaries. Nothing further of interest occurred until we neared base. We then saw a big flame shoot up about 10 miles east of Lincoln; it looked as though an aircraft had just crashed. Over Hemswell we met enemy aircraft. We saw two bursts of tracer, one of them quite close to us. We did not see the enemy aircraft itself."

Flying Officer B P Klee and Pilot Officer R G Marland of 222 Squadron. Marland was night-flying when the intruders struck. He attacked Albert Schulz but succeeded only in driving the Dornier away.

Hay had actually witnessed the destruction of Sergeant Bates' 49 Squadron Hampden, shot down at 06.49 hours by *Leutnant* Kurt Herrmann of *1./NJG 2*. Two members of the crew baled out before the bomber crashed near Scampton. Herrmann then visited Hemswell, to find a 144 Squadron Hampden in the circuit. Sergeant McVie, circling the base with navigation lights on, despite a warning of intruder activity, became an easy target. Herrmann's attack caused severe damage, but McVie dived away and eventually landed safely. Sergeant Dainty of the same squadron was refused permission to land and circled until his fuel was exhausted. This crew abandoned their bomber, which finally crashed near Newton.

Other intruders attacked bases in Cambridgeshire and in the Middlesborough area.

This was a marked success for the *Fernnachtjäger*; of their six claims, four bombers actually crashed, another was badly damaged. Only Schulz's 'Blenheim' was in error - plainly an unsuccessful attack upon a single engined fighter. Additionally, much damage and confusion had been caused, far out of proportion to the number of German fighters employed.

Two further combats took place over Britain, both near the Humber. Flight Lieutenant Trousdale of 255 Squadron claimed a Heinkel probably destroyed off Spurn Head, followed by a similar claim a short while later by Pilot Officer Hall of the same squadron. One He111 of *1./KG 4* crashed at Egmont-am-Zee following combat with a nightfighter. Another of *III./KG 27* force-landed at Primpel out of fuel, injuring one man.

Casualties 10/11th February 1941

Royal Air Force

7 Squadron Stirling N6002
Belly-landed at Oakington. Crew safe.

9 Squadron Wellington P1096
Hit by Royal Naval AA fire and crash-landed near Martlesham Heath. Sgt MacKay & crew safe.

15 Squadron Wellington T2702
Failed to return from sortie. Sgt Garrioch & crew lost.

21 Squadron Blenheim R3658
Shot down by intruder at Bodney. S/L Sabine & crew safe.

21 Squadron Blenheim Z5877
Shot down by intruder at Bodney. Sgt Chattaway & crew killed.

21 Squadron Blenheim T2232
Failed to return from sortie. P/O McConnell & crew lost.

29 Squadron Blenheim R2196
Belly-landed at Wellingore. P/O Braham & crew safe.

40 Squadron Wellington R1239
Hit Chance light landing. Crew safe.

49 Squadron Hampden X3001
Failed to return from sortie. P/O Green & crew lost.

49 Squadron Hampden AD719
Shot down near Lincoln by intruder. Sgt Bates & one man killed. Aircraft destroyed

61 Squadron Hampden P4405
Crashed near Oulton. F/L Frutiger & crew killed. Aircraft destroyed.

75 Squadron Wellington L7845
Crash-landed due to enemy action. Crew safe.

102 Squadron Whitley P5015
Belly-landed at Port Ballantyne. Sgt Sleath & crew safe.

107 Squadron Blenheim R3871
Crash-landed near Norwich. F/L Simmons & crew safe.

115 Squadron Wellington R1084
Shot down at Swaffham by intruder. One man from Sgt Rodgers' crew injured. Aircraft destroyed.

144 Squadron Hampden R1164
Damaged by intruder near Hemswell. Sgt McVie & crew safe.

144 Squadron Hampden X3007
Abandoned near Newton. Sgt Dainty & crew safe. Aircraft destroyed.

218 Squadron Wellington R9239
Overshot Stradishall. One man injured.

264 Squadron Defiant N3308
Damaged taxiing at Biggin Hill. P/O Grey & crew safe.

92 Squadron pilots at Manston, early 1941. Squadron Leader John Kent (left) with Flight Lieutenants Brian Kingcombe and Tony Bartley.

311 Squadron Wellington L7785
Damaged, cause not known.
604 Squadron Beaufighter R2159
Damaged landing at Middle Wallop. F/L Scott & crew safe.

Luftwaffe

I./KG 4 He111H5 3791
Crashed at Egmont-am-Zee after combat with fighter. Two men wounded. Aircraft 40% damaged.
III./KG 27 He111P2 2863
Force-landed at Primpel after combat sortie due to fuel shortage. Aircraft 80% damaged.
3./NJG 1 Bf110D1 3172
Shot down by German Flak at Wunstorf. Oblt W. Hansen (St.Kap) killed. Aircraft destroyed.
II./NJG 1 Bf110 ----
Damaged near Alkmaar. Lt L.Fellerer & crew safe. Aircraft 20% damaged.

11th February 1941

Isolated German aircraft were plotted over the Midlands and East Anglia during the day, but there were no interceptions. At 11.30 hours a lone Ju88 bombed St. Eval and was chased out to sea by Spitfires of 152 Squadron, which failed to catch it.

In the late afternoon a fighter sweep over northern France was carried out by Spitfires from Biggin Hill. 66 Squadron was bounced by five Bf109s from *I./LG 2* over Boulogne. Two Spitfires were at once shot down by *Leutnant* Geisshardt and

129

Oberleutnant Tismar. Pilot Officer Baker was killed and Pilot Officer Peter Mildren baled out into the sea. His body was later washed up on the French coast. The Spitfire pilots had no chance to react, for the '109s made only one devastating firing pass before diving away. *Flak* gunners 'double-claimed' both Spitfires.

Around the same time Flying Officer Mortimer-Rose of 234 Squadron attacked and claimed damage to a Ju88 near the Scilly Isles.

Casualties 11th February 1941

Royal Air Force

43 Squadron Hurricane P3809
Overshot Drem. P/O Doll safe.

66 Squadron Spitfire P7568
Failed to return from sortie. P/O Baker lost.

66 Squadron Spitfire P7520
Failed to return from sortie. P/O Mildren lost.

213 Squadron Hurricane V7006
Crashed landing at Driffield. Sub Lt Jeram safe.

257 Squadron Hurricane V6935
Belly-landed at Coltishall. P/O Johnson safe.

266 Squadron Spitfire R7020
Crashed landing at Wittering. P/O Ferris safe.

502 Squadron Whitley P5050
Damaged by gunfire from U-boat. F/O Walker & crew safe.

1 (RCAF) Squadron Hurricane P7528
Damaged landing at Castletown. F/O Napier safe.

2 (RCAF) Squadron Hurricane T2591
Crashed landing at Digby. F/O Walker safe.

Luftwaffe

III./JG 2 Bf109E7 4176
Crash-landed at Bernay. Aircraft 60% damaged.

5./JG 3 Bf109E4 0773
Crash-landed at Arques. Aircraft 10% damaged.

I./KG 26 He111H5 3577
Taxiing accident at Aalborg-West. Aircraft 25% damaged.

I./KG 26 He111H5 3781
Undercarriage collapsed at Stavanger/Sola. Aircraft 35% damaged.

III./KG 30 Ju88A5 3190 4D+CD
Crashed at Aulsmeer in fog. Ofw F. Funk & two crew killed. Aircraft 95% damaged.

III./KG 53 He111P2 2668
Crash-landed at Jüterbog. Aircraft 25% damaged.

11/12th February

That night Bomber Command despatched 98 aircraft to attack

The German daylight shipping defences were now becoming stronger with the provision of Flak-ships. Thus Coastal Command aircraft flew increasingly by night. Here, a Beaufort crew prepares for 'ops', posing with their mascot 'Pilot Officer Duck'.

Bremen, Hannover and Rotterdam. Coastal Command sent six Beauforts out on night shipping strikes in the Hubert Gat and several Hudsons patrolled along the French coastline on similar duties.

The scheduled sorties were accomplished, but there were several losses to Coastal Command. A 22 Squadron Beaufort flown by Pilot Officer Greenleas failed to return, crashing at Collieville. Three Hudsons of 206 Squadron were also lost. The aircraft flown by Pilot Officer Mason and Sergeants Bracker and Morris were all abandoned off the English coast due to fuel shortage caused by sudden gale force winds in the Western Approaches. German nightfighters were also airborne, but effected no interceptions. A Bf110 of *7./NJG 1* crashed near Duisberg out of fuel, killing the pilot, *Unteroffizier* Singler.

Over England the returning bomber crews now faced an even deadlier opponent than the intruders of the previous night - fog! In the normally reserved prose of the RAF 'It was a disaster'.

The 4 Group Whitleys suffered badly. Six were abandoned in the air, including three from 51 Squadron. Two Whitleys reached Scotland before the crews took to their parachutes. One more crashed attempting a landing. Another flew right across southern England, finally force-landing out of fuel near the River Severn. The Hampden force lost three, one being abandoned in mid-air, and five Wellington crews baled out.

Another ditched in the River Severn, while six more crashed landing. In total, seventeen aircraft were lost this night, with several more damaged

The Germans flew several minor raids against southeast England, notably a night attack against Chatham by six Ju87s of *5./St.G 1.* One Stuka, 'J9+DL' flown by *Feldwebel* Richard von Cramm, was shot down off Brightlingsea at 04.00 hours by HM drifter *Eager.*

Casualties 11/12th February 1941

Royal Air Force

22 Squadron Beaufort OA-N
Failed to return from sortie. P/O Greenleas & crew lost.

51 Squadron Whitley P4981
Force-landed near Barnsley. Sgt Boyer & crew safe.

51 Squadron Whitley P4974
Abandoned near Linton-on-Ouse. Sgt Fenton & crew safe. Aircraft destroyed.

51 Squadron Whitley P5013
Abandoned near Doncaster. Sgt Beddow & crew safe. Aircraft destroyed.

51 Squadron Whitley T4217
Abandoned. P/O Sharp and crew safe. Aircraft destroyed.

58 Squadron Whitley T4213
Abandoned at Westhope. Sgt Fullerton & crew safe. Aircraft destroyed.

58 Squadron Whitley P4974
Abandoned at Wishaw, Lanarks. Sgt Walters & crew safe. Aircraft destroyed.

78 Squadron Whitley N1490
Abandoned over Ayrshire. Sgt Quincey & crew safe. Aircraft destroyed.

83 Squadron Hampden X3119
Overshot Driffield. Sgt Jackson & crew safe.

83 Squadron Hampden AD722
Crashed near Finningley. Three of F/L Barker's crew killed. Aircraft destroyed.

83 Squadron Hampden AD734
Abandoned in fog. F/L Anderson & crew safe. Aircraft destroyed.

99 Squadron Wellington R2888
Abandoned (Sgt Robinson). One killed, two injured, one missing. Aircraft destroyed.

115 Squadron Wellington T2885
Force-landed. Crew unhurt.

115 Squadron Wellington R3238
Abandoned near Saffron Walden. W/C Edwards-Edwards & crew safe. Aircraft destroyed.

115 Squadron Wellington R1004
Abandoned; crashed on Newton Road, Cambridge. P/O Clarke & crew safe. Aircraft destroyed.

115 Squadron Wellington R1238
Undershot Finningley. Sgt Whittaker & crew safe.

149 Squadron Wellington L7811
Abandoned. Crew safe, aircraft destroyed.

149 Squadron Wellington P9247
Crashed near Digby, one man from Sgt Early's crew killed.

206 Squadron Hudson T9350
Failed to return from sortie. P/O Mason & crew lost.
206 Squadron Hudson T9289
Failed to return from sortie. Sgt Bracker & crew lost.
206 Squadron Hudson T9356
Failed to return from sortie. Sgt Morris & crew lost.
218 Squadron Wellington T2801
Crashed near Withernsea. P/O Smith & crew safe.
218 Squadron Wellington R1135
Belly-landed at Bassingbourn. F/O Agar & crew safe.
218 Squadron Wellington R1210
Abandoned near Tebay. F/O Anstey & crew safe. Aircraft destroyed.
218 Squadron Wellington T2885
Force-landed in River Severn near Frampton. Sgt Adams & crew safe.
Aircraft believed salvaged.
311 Squadron Wellington R1022
Belly-landed near Swinderby. Sgt Sedny & crew safe.

Luftwaffe

7./NJG 1 Bf110C 1396
Force-landed at Duisberg. Uffz K. Singler killed. Aircraft 95% damaged.
5./St.G 1 Ju87B2 0528 J9+DL
Failed to return from sortie. Fw R. von Cramm & crew killed.

12th February 1941

There was only slight activity. Coastal Command lost a Beaufort however, Flight Lieutenant Hunter's 217 Squadron crew being shot down by a German submarine-chaser off Brest. The Germans also lost an aircraft when 'A6+HH', a Ju88 of *1.(F)/120*, crashed into Pittairlie Wood, near Monifieth, Angus, while flying in low cloud on a reconnaissance sortie to Kinnaird Head. There were no survivors from *Feldwebel* Presia's crew.

Casualties 12th February 1941

Royal Air Force

217 Squadron Beaufort MW-
Failed to return from sortie. F/L Hunter & crew lost.

Luftwaffe

I./JG 3 FW58C2 0393
Rammed by landing Bf109 at Wizernes. Aircraft 40% damaged.
III./JG 51 Bf109F1 5664
Crashed into FW58 while landing at Wizernes. Aircraft 40% damaged.
E./JG 52 Bf109E4 0704
Crash-landed at Arques. Aircraft 50% damaged.
I./KG 1 He111H3 6892
Crashed landing at Quakenbrück. Fw E.Piep & crew killed. Aircraft destroyed.
2./KG 26 He111H5 3773
Crash-landed at Aalborg West. Aircraft 25% damaged.

1.(F)/120 Ju88A5 0482 A6+HH
Failed to return from sortie. Fw W.Presia & crew killed.
Wekusta O.b.d.L. He111H 2740
Crash-landed at Brest Sud. Fw G.Bodner & crew safe, aircraft 50% damaged.

13th February 1941

The previous night had seen isolated German raiders around the West Country and no activity by the RAF. In daylight the Luftwaffe sent cloud cover raiders in over Britain, but no interceptions were effected until the afternoon.

At 13.00 hours, a pair of Spitfires from 91 Squadron patrolling near Dover were alerted to the presence of Bf109s. These were from *JG 51*, the Spitfire pilots arriving to find them attacking the Dover balloon barrage. The Messerschmitts departed at high speed, leaving three balloons falling in flames. Flight Sergeant McKay claimed hits on one, but no damage was reported by the Germans.

At 1830 hours, a section from 111 Squadron intercepted an He111 off Aberdeen, where Pilot Officers Gage and Tucker claimed it damaged. One such machine, an aircraft from *3./KG 53*, force-landed at Sangatte with battle damage, possibly due to this encounter.

In the mid-afternoon, a lone Ju88 flew down the English coastline to Plymouth, where AA sites claimed hits upon it. It is probable that this aircraft then turned eastward and was intercepted at 17.05 hours by a pair of 609 Squadron Spitfires. Pilot Officer Nowierski delivered an attack, but his own aircraft was slightly damaged by return fire. The Junkers, an aircraft from *K.Gr.806*, struggled back to France, crash-landing at Caen with three of the crew wounded.

German naval *Flak* gunners made one claim off Norway, hitting a Hudson of 233 Squadron, which crashed at Leuchars on return from patrol.

Casualties 13th February 1941

Royal Air Force

1 Squadron Hurricane V7025
Overshot Kenley. F/L Clowes safe.
48 Squadron Anson N5236
Crashed landing at Port Ellen. F/O Morgan & crew safe.
48 Squadron Anson W1671
Undershot Stornoway. Sgt Rayner & crew safe.

53 Squadron Blenheim R3679
Damaged beyond repair, reason not known.
79 Squadron Hurricane P3100
Crashed landing at Pembrey. Sgt Bradley safe.
85 Squadron Havoc VY-
Crashed after take-off. F/L Allard DFC & crew unhurt.
218 Squadron Wellington R1210
Crashed at Morecambe, crew believed safe. Aircraft burnt.
229 Squadron Hurricane P3588
Crashed at Walkden due to engine failure. P/O Finnis safe.
233 Squadron Hudson N7372
Crashed at Leuchars on return from patrol. Sgt Wherrett & crew safe.
252 Squadron Blenheim Z6078
Belly-landed at Chivenor. P/O Davenport & crew safe.
263 Squadron Whirlwind P6976
Force-landed at Cannington, Soms. Sgt Skelton safe.
306 Squadron Hurricane V6946
Crashed. Sgt Jasinski injured.
311 Squadron Wellington P9226
Damaged on ground, cause not known.
312 Squadron Hurricane V6885
Crashed during dogfight practice. P/O Bartos killed. Aircraft destroyed.
502 Squadron Whitley T4276
Crashed at Port McCutcheon. F/L Foster & crew safe.
609 Squadron Spitfire PR-
Damaged by return fire from Ju88. P/O Nowierski safe.
1401 Flight Gladiator N5620
Overshot. P/O McDiermid safe.

Luftwaffe

3./KG 53 He111H5 3761
Force-landed at Sangatte due to enemy gunfire. Aircraft 50% damaged.
K.Gr.806 Ju88A1 4176
Landed damaged at Caen after combat with fighters. Three crew wounded.
Aircraft 60% damaged.
E./St.G.77 Ju87B1 5376
Force-landed at Freudenberg. Aircraft 65% damaged.
Stab./ZG 76 Bf110D3 4267
Taxiing accident at Stavanger. Aircraft 10% damaged.

13/14th February 1941

Once again Bomber Command was on 'stand down', but the Luftwaffe launched a sharp raid against London, employing about fifty aircraft. No claims were made by the defences, but a Ju87 Stuka of *9./St.G 1* flown by *Feldwebel* Fritz Lewandowski was reported missing from a sortie to the Thames estuary.

Casualties 13/14th February 1941

Royal Air Force
219 Squadron Beaufighter R2120
Abandoned at Partridge Green. Sgt Gee & crew safe.

306 Squadron Hurricane P3069
Crashed on training flight. P/O Bielkiewicz killed. Aircraft destroyed.

Luftwaffe

9./St.G 1 Ju87B1 0500 J9+LL
Failed to return from sortie. Fw F. Lewandowski & crew missing.

14th February 1941

Lone German bombers operated over northeast Scotland and over Kent and the *Luftwaffe* mounted a large-scale fighter sweep over the latter area in the mid-morning. Before this could be intercepted however, two Spitfires of 92 Squadron patrolling over Dover were bounced by a lone Bf109, which attacked Sergeant Don Kingaby. He out-turned the Messerschmitt and chased it back to France, claiming to have shot it down near Griz Nez.

In the meantime, the main force of Bf109s from *JG 52* and *I./LG 2* swept in over Southend at high level, where Spitfires of 64 Squadron were encountered. The British pilots were taken by surprise. No claims were made by the RAF, but the aircraft flown by Pilot Officer Lawson-Brown was shot down. He brought his crippled Spitfire back to Hornchurch, where he crash-landed, the fighter being 'written off'.

The Messerschmitts crossed the Thames, sweeping across north Kent to Maidstone, where ten 66 Squadron Spitfires were patrolling. Flight Lieutenant H R 'Dizzy' Allen put the squadron into a battle climb and they went up through the cloud. He recalled:

"The blinding glare of the sun hit us as we surged up from the grey of the cloud. Then someone screamed over the R.T. 'Break!'.

"'Jack it round, jack it round!' somebody said over the R.T. and I vaguely wondered who was supposed to jack it round.

"There was a very loud bang in my cockpit followed by the stink of explo-

Don Kingaby of 92 Squadron became known to the popular press as 'the '109 specialist' since at least seventeen of his 23 victories were claimed against this type. He is pictured here as CO of 122 Squadron in 1943

Left: Flight Lieutenant H R 'Dizzy' Allen of 66 squadron.
Right: Oberleutnant Johannes 'Macki' Steinhoff of 4. / JG 52

sives, my right arm hurtled into the air and my gauntleted hand hit the cockpit canopy with such force as to bruise the knuckles very severely, as I later discovered. I gave her full boost and transferred my left hand to the control column, as the right arm was hanging helplessly at my side and jacked her round as hard as I could turn. The Spitfire could out-turn the Me109 at medium altitudes and I got onto his tail. He had a big yellow nose and two 20 mm cannon in his wings. I closed to within 250 yards range and pressed the firing button. He was a dead duck. But nothing happened. I glanced at the pneumatic pressure gauge and saw it was reading empty. He had hit my air bottle. I half-rolled and escaped in cloud."

He force-landed at Biggin Hill and counted more than forty strikes in his aircraft. Sergeant Parsons was also wounded, his Spitfire 'Category B damaged' and those flown by Pilot Officers Peter Olver and 'Bogle' Bodie were also damaged. The fight continued down to the coast, where Pilot Officer Maxwell was shot down into the sea and killed.

Their opponents had claimed in total nine victories. *Major* Hans Trübenbach, *Kommodore* of *JG 52* claimed a Spitfire, as did *Oberleutnants* Johannes Steinhoff and Siegfried Simsch of *II Gruppe.* Similar claims were made by *Oberleutnant* Friedrich-Wilhelm Strakeljahn and *Oberfeldwebel* Schott of *I. / LG 2,* while 'doubles' were claimed by *Hauptmann* Herbert Ihlefeld and *Leutnant* Friedrich Geisshardt of the latter unit.

Apart from the casualties already mentioned, Pilot Officer Wilkinson of 3 PRU failed to return from a reconnaissance sortie to Gelsenkirchen. No trace of either Wilkinson or his Spitfire was ever found and it is possible that he too fell victim to the Messerschmitts as they re-crossed the Channel.

111 Squadron, patrolling off Scotland, had two fights. Yellow Section, operating off Montrose, intercepted an unidentified aircraft. Squadron Leader Maclean attacked and fired nearly 2,000 rounds without effect before it escaped. Shortly thereafter, Pilot Officer Kellett flew a convoy patrol off Aberdeen, finding and engaging a Ju88, which he claimed to have damaged. A Ju88 of *I./KG 30* crash-landed at Eindhoven with battle damage, obviously hit by either Maclean or Kellett.

Coastal Command Blenheims flew shipping strikes in the afternoon, operating in the Bergen area of Holland. Two machines of 235 Squadron, flown by Pilot Officers Davidson and Chamberlain, crashed on return. It is possible that one of these events was due to combat, since *Oberfeldwebel* Gerhardt of *1./JG 1* claimed a Blenheim destroyed off Den Helder during the afternoon.

Casualties 14th February 1941

Royal Air Force

54 Squadron Spitfire X4711
Crashed at Richmond, Yorks. P/O Coleman killed. Aircraft destroyed
56 Squadron Hurricane P3055
Crashed landing at North Weald. F/O Hime safe.
64 Squadron Spitfire P7751
Crashed after combat. P/O Lawson-Brown safe.
66 Squadron Spitfire P7451
Shot down by Bf109 off Dover. P/O Maxwell lost.
66 Squadron Spitfire P7504
Damaged by Bf109. F/L Allen wounded.
66 Squadron Spitfire P7522
Damaged by Bf109. Sgt Parsons wounded.
66 Squadron Spitfire P7602
Damaged by Bf109. P/O Olver safe.
66 Squadron Spitfire P7521
Damaged by Bf109. P/O Bodie safe.
235 Squadron Blenheim Z5970
Crashed at Great Croxton. P/O Davidson & crew killed. Aircraft destroyed.
235 Squadron Blenheim V5431
Crashed landing at Langham. P/O Chamberlain & crew safe.

257 Squadron Hurricane V6873
Crashed landing at Coltishall. P/O Blackburn safe.
302 Squadron Hurricane P3897
Hit by 610 Squadron Spitfire. Pilot believed safe.
308 Squadron Hurricane V7027
Crashed landing at Bramcote. P/O Wandzilak safe.
601 Squadron Hurricane V7416
Belly-landed at Northolt. Sgt Hulbert safe.
610 Squadron Spitfire KW-
Hit 302 Squadron Hurricane landing. Extent of damage not known.
Pilot believed safe.

Luftwaffe

1./JG1 Bf109E4 6073
Crashed near De Kooy. Uffz W.Schmidt killed. Aircraft destroyed.
III./JG27 Bf109E7 4184
Crash-landed at Wiener-Neustadt. Aircraft 15% damaged.
III./JG54 Bf109E4 0924 BJ+ST
Crashed near Waterloo, Belgium. Uffz Albrecht safe. Aircraft destroyed.
I./KG30 Ju88A5 0594
Crash-landed at Eindhoven. Aircraft 65% damaged.
SNF.Kdo 3 He59 2827
Taxiing accident at Boulogne. Aircraft 15% damaged.
Nach.Fl.St.LF 1 2 FW44 2513
Crashed at Grimbergen. Uffz Krüger injured. Aircraft 85% damaged.
Fl.Ber. I Fl.K Fi156C2 4430
Crash-landed at Criel. Aircraft 15% damaged.

14/15th February 1941

One loss was sustained by Bomber Command, when a Hampden of 50 Squadron was reported missing from the minelaying force. Pilot Officer Tunstall's aircraft was seen burning near Pointe de la Chambrette, northwest of Bordeaux, by several other crews. Coastal Command also participated in the night's operations by sending thirteen aircraft out to raid various coastal targets. No caualties were sustained.

> **Bomber Command Operations**
>
> Gelsenkirchen 44 Homburg 44
>
> Minelaying 11
>
> **Luftwaffe Operations**
>
> London, East Anglia, Humber 123

All the German aircraft involved in raids over Britain returned to their bases, but a Ju88C of *I. /NJG 2* crash-landed at Gilze-Rijn. This may be the aircraft claimed destroyed by Humber AA sites at 20.30 hours.

A remarkable incident took place at Debden, home of 85 Squadron. At 23.30 hours a twin-engined aircraft landed. Although no radio contact had been established, it was thought to be a Bomber Command aircraft. It taxied up to the control tower where Pilot Officer Hodgson, a Battle of Britain veteran, strolled out to meet it. A man jumped out and began to speak rapidly in a foreign language. At that instant Hodgson recognised the aircraft as an He111! Meanwhile several army officers had joined the young fighter pilot on the tarmac and Hodgson attempted to convey to them the fact that this was a German bomber. They failed to understand, due to the revving of the engines - perhaps fortunately, for Hodgson then realised that the rear gunner had his machine-gun trained on them.

The German crewman soon abandoned his attempts to communicate and climbed into the Heinkel, which rolled away into the darkness. With a blast of engines, it took off again and climbed away westwards. It is believed that this same aircraft subsequently proceeded to Feltwell, where it landed and immediately took off again. A third unauthorised landing also took place when a German aircraft was reported to have made a short stop at Tangmere, before taking off again. Truth can be stranger than fiction........[1]

Casualties 14/15th February 1941

Royal Air Force

50 Squadron Hampden X2983
Failed to return from sortie. P/O Tunstall & crew lost.

Luftwaffe

I./NJG 2 Ju88C2 0239 R4+FH
Force-landed at Gilze-Rijn due to enemy gunfire. Oblt H.Bönsch & crew safe. Aircraft 20% damaged.

---

[1]. One of these incidents could possibly have involved Hans Thurner, a pilot with *KG 55*, who is known to have inadvertently landed in England during this period. The story is related in *Kampffliegerasse 1939-45* by Georg Brütting

Chapter Five
'Cat and Mouse'

15th February 1941

The first incident of the day took place at dawn. *Feldwebel* Heinz Strüning of *I./NJG 2*, returning from an intruder sortie, engaged a 206 Squadron Hudson off Yarmouth. He claimed to have shot it down, but the British aircraft escaped undamaged. Squadron Leader Dias' crew claimed hits upon the German fighter.

In the morning, 615 Squadron was detailed to carry out its first *Rhubarb* operation. Squadron Leader Jocelyn Millard, then a Pilot Officer, remembers that day well:

Feldwebel Heinz Strüning of I./NJG 2

"The then recently appointed squadron CO, Wing Commander Holmwood, announced in the flight hut that the squadron had been detailed to carry out two sorties of a special nature that day, one in the morning and one in the afternoon, with three aircraft taking part in each.

"He began by giving a thorough briefing on the operations. The nature of the sorties was such that 10/10ths low cloud was a necessary condition for the raids involved, to minimise the risk of enemy detection. The weather on that particular day was bad, but it was 'ideal' for the occasion!

"Each sortie was to consist of a low level approach across the Channel (not forgetting partially submerged wrecks!) for low level attacks on enemy military targets in a coastal area, but Intelligence reports revealed that the ground defences along the French coast were too heavy to justify such raids.

"The reports also revealed that the ground defences along the coastline between Blankenberghe and Ostende were not as heavy, thus offering safer avenues of entry into occupied territory, hence the area was chosen for the

attacks.

"Whilst such a distant area was supposedly relatively light on ground defences, the time and fuel required to reach it allowed little of either for target searching and a return journey. With such a big disadvantage, the idea of such raids for our aircraft was nothing short of ill conceived.

"After the briefing came the question of pilots. . . who would go! The CO decided that the fairest way to decide was to to have a draw, and that all available pilots, including himself, would be included.

"There were two draws, one for each of the two sorties. The names drawn for the morning sortie (order unsure) were Flying Officer Stewart, Sergeant Pilots Waghorn and Fotheringham and, for the the afternoon, were the CO, myself and third whom I cannot now remember. After the draw there was a distinct air of calm and unease as the outcome of the draw began rapidly to sink in, then gradually everyone dispersed.

"I remained in the flight hut and sat by the old Tortoise stove for warmth and comfort, considering the real possibility of not having any more birthdays! Whilst lost in wondering, the CO came in and, seeing me by myself, came over and said, 'What's up Millie...scared?'

"I said, 'Yes, I am,' and he replied, 'Bloody hell, so am I!'

"He was an Australian and, from my experience of Australian pilots, I had somehow conceived the idea that they were anything but afraid of anyone or anything. One lives and learns.

"Now, realising (somewhat happily) that I was far from alone in being scared by the unknowns which lay ahead, I consoled myself with the thought that 'If a tough nut like him can be scared, then at least I shall have some good company on the way'.

"Shortly afterwards, the first three aircraft took off and headed for Manston, where they were to refuel to give the maximum flying time for the mission.

"As the hours passed, the weather began to improve a little. The cloud was slowly lifting and, by noon, small welcome breaks appeared. Although the change in weather conditions was slight, the improvement continued, so raising hopes that the afternoon raid might be cancelled.

"By about one o'clock none of the aircraft had returned to base and, being well overdue, the worst was feared. On the early afternoon news, 'Lord Haw-Haw' announced that three Hurricanes had been shot down off the coast of Belgium, but there was no mention of the pilots.

"With the failure of three aircraft to return and 'Haw-Haw's' knowledge of how many aircraft were on the raid, and their destination, it was evident that there was some truth in his announcment.

"Later that day it was learned that Flying Officer Stewart had been killed and Sergeant Fotheringham taken prisoner, but nothing was heard of Sergeant Waghorn. Unknown to us at the time, Sergeant Waghorn had in fact managed to return to the English coast and eventually to base.

"Despite some despondency over the morning's events, the afternoon brought some cheer in that the weather had improved considerably. There was a vast amount of broken cloud, a good deal of bright sunshine....but

Pilot Officer Jocelyn Millard of 615 Squadron. This photograph was taken in late 1940 by Pilot Officer Claude Strickland, who was later killed in a flying accident in the summer of 1941.
- S/L J.G.P.Millard

most heartening of all was the cancellation of the afternoon raid."

The cause of the losses is uncertain. Sergeant Fotheringham force-landed near Coxyde and Flying Officer Stewart crashed near Zeebrugge. 615 Squadron later flew a sweep but, apart from a snap shot by Pilot Officer Millard at a lone Bf109, no incidents were reported.

During the late morning, Luftwaffe fighters of *I./LG 2* flew a *Freijagd* across Kent and succeeded in bouncing 66 Squadron again near Maidstone. Sergeant Pearce was shot down, belly-landing wounded at Manston. Two RAF fighters were claimed, one by *Leutnant* Hahn.

All afternoon and into the evening Fighter Command patrols fought cloud cover raiders along the south and east coasts. 242 Squadron had two fights. Pilot Officer Kemp and Sergeant Pollard chased away a Bf110, while subsequently Pilot Officer Dennis Crowley-Milling attacked a Ju88 off Aldeburgh. He claimed this damaged, but his own aircraft was hit in the windscreen by return fire.

234 Squadron was more successful, Pilot Officer Boddington and Sergeant Armitage claimed to have damaged a Ju88 twenty miles south of Portsmouth at 17.05 hours. This would appear to have been an aircraft from *K.Gr.806*, which crash-landed at Caen after combat. Forty minutes later Squadron Leader Love and Pilot Officer Klee of 222 Squadron claimed an He111 destroyed off Corton.

One further claim was made off the east coast, time not known. Three Hurricanes of 71 Squadron led by Flight Lieutenant Vernon Keough intercepted a Do17. Keough, accompanied by Pilot Officers Kennerley and Morantz, attacked, claiming damage. Then Keough's aircraft, apparently hit by return fire, dived into the sea off Skegness, killing him.

During the day Flight Lieutenants Turner and Donaldson of 242 Squadron sighted an elusive reconnaissance aircraft, identified as a Bf109, over the Norfolk coast. They were unable to engage it.

A Bf110 of *2.(F)/122* force-landed at Sud Beveland after combat with 'friendly' fighters. It is possible that it was engaged either by 71 or 242 Squadrons (above). An He111 from *Stab./KG26* returned with *Feldwebel* Karl-Ernst Michelis and one of his crew wounded by AA fire near Peterhead.

Beauforts of Coastal Command were sent out to attack the U-boat installations at Brest and St. Nazaire. Three 217 Squadron machines, targetted to Brest, were jumped by Bf109s of *II./JG 77* some twelve miles north of the target. All three bombers, flown by Pilot Officers Tams, Williams and Flying Officer Gair, were shot down, the successful German pilots being *Hauptmann* Henz, *Unteroffizier* Schmidt and *Oberfeldwbel* Ertel.

Bomber Command also operated, five Blenheims from 114 Squadron patrolling along the coast of Holland in search of shipping. Sergeant Barnes' aircraft was intercepted and shot down near Vlissingen by *Feldwebel* Bachmann of *I./JG 52*; there were no survivors. Two more were claimed by *Flak* gunners in this area during the day.

Casualties 15th February 1941

Royal Air Force

57 Squadron Wellington T2962
Crashed on take-off from Wyton. P/O Bridger & crew safe.

66 Squadron Spitfire P7670
Crash-landed at Manston after combat. Sgt Pearce wounded.

71 Squadron Hurricane N7606
Crashed into sea following combat off Skegness. F/O Keough killed.

79 Squadron Hurricane P3035
Crashed landing at Pembrey. Sgt Gross safe.

114 Squadron Blenheim T2125
Failed to return from sortie. Sgt Barnes & crew lost.

217 Squadron Beaufort L9807
Failed to return from sortie. P/O Tams & crew lost.
217 Squadron Beaufort L9794
Failed to return from sortie. P/O Williams & crew lost.
217 Squadron Beaufort W6493
Failed to return from sortie. F/O Gair & crew lost.
219 Squadron Beaufighter R2150
Crashed at Scopwick, Lincs. P/O Buchanon & crew killed. Aircraft destroyed.
242 Squadron Hurricane LE-
Damaged by return fire from Do17. P/O Crowley-Milling safe.
256 Squadron Defiant N1741
Undercarriage collapsed landing. P/O McKinnon & crew safe.
256 Squadron Defiant N1645
Force-landed at Moreton-in-Marsh. Sgt Ellmers & crew safe.
615 Squadron Hurricane P3231
Failed to return from sortie. F/O Stewart lost.
615 Squadron Hurricane V7651
Failed to return from sortie. Sgt Fotheringham lost.
615 Squadron Hurricane V7316
Force-landed, cause not known. Sgt Waghorn safe.

Luftwaffe

5./JG 52 Bf109E1 3351
Crashed on take-off from Berck. Aircraft 50% damaged.
I.(Z)/JG 77 Bf110C4 3528
Hit obstruction at Sola. Aircraft 10% damaged.
II./KG 1 Ju88A5 8194
Force-landed near Münster, Oblt F.Zeitler & crew injured.
Aircraft 80% damaged.
Stab./KG 26 He111 ----
Damaged by AA fire. Fw K.E.Michelis & one man wounded.
Aircraft 20% damaged.
III./KG 27 He111P2 2463
Rammed by Ju88 at Leipzig-Hockau. Aircraft 60% damaged.
II./KG 76 Ju88A5 4109
Crashed in flames near Chateaudun. Hptm A.Fietz & crew killed.
Aircraft destroyed.
K.Gr.806 Ju88A5 6166
Crashed at Caen after combat with fighter. Aircraft 30% damaged.
2.(F)/122 Bf110C5 2184
Force-landed at Walphaartsdijk after attack by own fighters.
Aircraft 70% damaged.

15/16th February 1941

Bomber Command flew 143 sorties against targets in Germany, Holland and France, the main objectives being Hamburg and Sterkrade. Over occupied territory two losses were sustained. The first was Pilot Officer Dove's 15 Squadron Wellington, which was caught over Barchem at 23.05 hours by *Feldwebel* Kalinowski of *6./NJG 1*. It was shot down and two men were taken prisoner. Fourteen minutes later a 77 Squadron Whitley captained by Pilot Officer Hubbard met the same fate. It was shot down near Nijmegen by *Oberleutnant* Jüsgen of *I./NJG 3*. This crew was captured. *Flak* gunners claimed one more bomber. A Hampden crew reported an attack by a Bf109, which dived away after fire was returned. This may have been a Bf110 from *III./NJG 1*, which crash-landed at Deelen, hitting two parked Messerschmitts and 'writing-off' a Do215.

German bombers ranged over Britain, making scattered attacks and causing damage to London and Liverpool. Intruders were also in evidence, mainly seeking aircraft as they left their bases. At Waddington, a Hampden was attacked on take-off, but the German fighter made off after fire was returned. Two Oxfords were damaged in the Cranwell circuit by *Oberleutnant* Herbert Bönsch of *I./NJG 2*, who claimed an Oxford destroyed at 01.25 hours. Two Hampdens of 44 Squadron were also attacked and damaged by an intruder, possibly by *Feldwebel* Strüning of the same unit, who claimed a Wellington at 19.58 hours.

The first victory for the British came at 18.15 hours, when Flight Lieutenant John Cunningham of 604 Squadron patrolled over the Devon coastline and was given a 'customer' by their G.C.I. station. AI contact was quickly established and Sergeant Rawnsley guided his pilot to a visual sighting. It was a Heinkel about a thousand feet higher. The German bomber was circling, waiting for the full darkness. When it straightened out, Cunningham attacked, opening fire in a continuous burst that emptied the ammunition drums. The crippled bomber dropped away into the gathering gloom and there was a sudden explosion as *Leutnant* Eberhard Beckmann's '1G+FR' of *7./KG 27* exploded at Higher Luscombe Farm, Harberton, killing the crew.

A second Heinkel was lost this night when *Hauptmann* Heinrich Styrm's *6./KG 4* machine hit a balloon cable after being damaged by AA fire. '5J+GP' dived into the ground at Bent's Park, South Shields, where it exploded. Four of the crew died in the crash. The fifth man baled out, but was unlucky enough to fall on trolleybus wires and was electrocuted.

An unexpected windfall arrived at Steeple Morden at 04.30 hours, when *Leutnant* Herbert Florian force-landed his *8/KG1*

On the night of 15/16th February, John Cunningham of 604 Squadron (left) shot down this 7./KG 27 He111 flown by Leutnant Eberhard Beckmann.

Junkers cross-wind after becoming lost and running out of fuel. 'V4+GS' seemed intact, but was too badly damaged to be flown again.

Casualties 15/16th February 1941

Royal Air Force

9 Squadron Wellington T2900
Crashed at Honington. Sgt Stark & crew safe
10 Squadron Whitley T4234
Crash-landed at Dishforth. Sgt Towell & crew safe
15 Squadron Wellington T2847
Failed to return from sortie. P/O Dove & crew lost.
44 Squadron Hampden X3025
Damaged by intruder, hit 300 Squadron Wellington at Waddington.
S/L Smaills & crew safe.
44 Squadron Hampden X2917
Damaged by intruder. F/O Penman & crew safe.
77 Squadron Whitley T4164
Failed to return from sortie. P/O Hubbard & crew lost.
96 Squadron Hurricane P3833
Crashed at Cranage. P/O Lauder safe.
96 Squadron Hurricane V7591
Damaged landing at Cranage. Sgt Scott safe.
144 Squadron Hampden X3048
Belly-landed at Hemswell. S/L Lerwill & crew safe.
254 Squadron Blenheim Z6027
Damaged taxiing at Dyce. F/O Randall & crew safe.
255 Squadron Defiant N3340
Overshot, hit N1727. P/O Hall safe.

255 Squadron Defiant N1727
Hit by above. No casualty.
300 Squadron Wellington T2608
Hit by Hampden at Waddington. F/S Kaluga & crew safe.
307 Squadron Defiant N3402
Overshot Squires Gate. P/O Alexandrowicz & gunner safe.
2 FTS Oxford R6076
Damaged by intruder at Cranwell. F/O Hackney & crew safe.
2 FTS Oxford V3244
Damaged by intruder at Cranwell. F/O Blackstone & crew safe.

Luftwaffe

III./KG 1 Ju88A5 6214 V4+GS
Failed to return from sortie. Lt H.Florian & crew captured.
II./KG 4 He111P4 3085 5J+GP
Failed to return from sortie. Hptm H.Styrm & crew killed.
III./KG 27 He111P2 2911 1G+FR
Failed to return from sortie. Lt E.Beckmann & crew killed.
II./NJG 1 Bf110D3 3695
Hit two aircraft landing at Deelen. Aircraft 65% damaged.
II./NJG 1 Do215B5 0055
Hit by above at Deelen. Aircraft 30% damaged.
II./NJG 1 Bf110D3 3670
Hit by above at Deelen. Aircraft 80% damaged.

16th February 1941

Several engagements were reported by Fighter Command pilots against the few reported cloud-cover raiders. These interceptions were mostly notable for their lack of success. At 10.30 hours, Flight Lieutenant Colin MacFie and Sergeant Arnold of 616 Squadron had an encounter with a fast Ju88 off Donna Nook. The Junkers, almost certainly a reconnaissance aircraft, proved too fast to be caught and vanished into the clouds. An hour later Pilot Officers Kay and McIntyre of 257 Squadron took off for a fishery protection patrol. While over the trawlers, they saw a 'stick' of bombs explode in nearby Yarmouth. A Do17 appeared, heading towards them and they reefed their Hurricanes around to attack. The Dornier was faster, passing them some 400 yards to port and slipping straight into a cloudbank. Pilot Officer Bedford of the same unit was off at noon and had a similar experience. While orbiting Sheringham, he glanced in his rear-view mirror and was startled to find an He111 coming in very quickly behind him. As he turned steeply to engage, the German pilot banked and pulled away. Bedford attempted to follow, but the Heinkel escaped into cloud.

At 12.10 hours, two 302 Squadron Hurricanes patrolling over the south coast found a Ju88 near Bognor Regis. Pilot Officer Pilch and Sergeant Wedzik attacked, claiming that it had crashed into the sea. No Ju88 was lost, but a Junkers of *III./KG 77* was abandoned over Amiens and another from this *Gruppe* crash-landed at Juvincourt with tyre damage. A further Ju88, from *1.(F)/122* crash-landed at Melsbroek after combat with fighters - probably with MacFie and Arnold of 616 Squadron.

The *Luftwaffe* was successful at 16.40 hours, when a lone Spitfire from 1 PRU was intercepted over Calais by *Oberfeldwebel* Hübner of *II./JG 51*; Pilot Officer Chandler failed to return. Off Stavanger, *Leutnant* Dieter Uhlmann of *III./ZG 76* engaged Pilot Officer Holmes' 224 Squadron Hudson, which was damaged in this combat. The Bf110 later crashed into the sea. A pilot from an unidentified *Jagdgruppe* claimed a Blenheim destroyed off the Somme estuary.

Casualties 16th February 1941

Royal Air Force

224 Squadron Hudson T9344
Damaged in combat. P/O Holmes & crew safe.
504 Squadron Hurricane V6732
Hit car landing at Exeter. F/L Parsons safe.
603 Squadron Spitfire P7597
Hit by Hurricane on take-off. F/L Boulter injured, died 17.2.41.
1 (RCAF) Squadron Hurricane V6953
Crashed on take-off from Driffield. Pilot believed safe.
1 PRU Spitfire P9561
Failed to return from sortie. P/O Chandler lost.

Luftwaffe

Stab./JG 77 Bf109E7 0960
Crashed at Eisleben, Lt H.Hinrichs killed. Aircraft destroyed.
I./JG 77 Bf109E4 1633
Force-landed near Bergen. Aircraft 75% damaged.
I./KG 40 FW200 ----
Damaged by machine-gun fire near Ireland, one man killed. Aircraft 10% damaged.
II./KG 76 Ju88A5 3292
Belly-landed at Chateaudun. Aircraft 30% damaged.
III./KG 77 Ju88A5 5155
Abandoned near Amiens. Aircraft destroyed.
III./KG 77 Ju88A5 3236
Taxiing accident at Juvincourt, aircraft 30% damaged.
II./NJG 1 Bf110E1 3477
Taxiing accident at Deelen. Aircraft 25% damaged.

I/NJG2 Ju88C4 0538
Crash-landed at Gilze-Rijn, Aircraft 10% damaged.
Stab/StG.1 Bf110D3 3658
Taxiing accident at St Pol, aircraft 30% damaged.
III./ZG 76 Bf110D3 4265 2N+GS
Failed to return from sortie. Lt D.Uhlmann & crew killed.
4.(F)/122 Ju88A5 0528
Landed at Melsbroek after combat with fighters. Aircraft 65% damaged.
4.(H)/12 Hs126B1 3362 H1+FM
Damaged by storm at Landes de Barssac. Aircraft 5% damaged.
4.(H)/12 Fi156C1 0681
Damaged by storm at Landes de Barssac. Aircraft 5% damaged.

16/17th February 1941

No Bomber Command operations were scheduled, but around fifty *Luftwaffe* raiders attacked London, while minor incidents occurred over East Anglia. No combats or claims were reported.

Casualties 16/17th February 1941

Royal Air Force and Luftwaffe

- nil -

17th February 1941

The main areas of activity were north Scotland, East Anglia and the southwest of England.

The only fighter pilots to meet German raiders were from 222 Squadron. At 12.40 hours Squadron Leader Love and Sergeant Christie intercepted and claimed to have damaged a Do17 near Martham. Sergeants Ferraby and Davis patrolled over Cromer in the early afternoon and this pair were more fortunate. *Leutnant* Horst Dombrowski's *6./KG 76* crew had been briefed to attack West Raynham and were en route to their target when intercepted. The Spitfire pilots made no mistake, shooting Ju88 'F1+JP' down into the sea with the loss of the crew.

Squadron Leader Love was airborne again in the afternoon, accompanied by Sergeant Marland. They found another Junkers, 'V4+BS' of *8/.KG 1*, off Yarmouth at 13.15 hours. Both Spitfire pilots attacked and shot the bomber down. A radio message 'Ditching!' was received by the Germans before *Unteroffizier* Robert Stebetack put the bomber down on the sea, but no trace of the crew was ever found.

Further south, two Spitfires of 91 Squadron patrolled over the Dover Straits and were bounced by Bf109s. The aircraft flown by Flying Officer O'Meara was badly damaged and he crash-landed near Hawkinge with his fighter well peppered by cannon fire.

Bomber and Coastal Commands also operated, the former losing a 114 Squadron Blenheim, one of five engaged on cloud cover raids. This aircraft, piloted by Flight Lieutenant Marks, was shot down off Brunsbüttel by *Flak*.

The final engagement took place off Norway, when Flight Lieutenant Leach's 224 Squadron Hudson was intercepted and damaged by Bf110s of *III./ZG 76* protecting a convoy.

Casualties 17th February 1941

Royal Air Force

51 Squadron Whitley Z6488
Crashed into Hucknall village. Sgt Wilson & crew safe.
78 Squadron Whitley T4215
Belly-landed near Billingford, Norfolk. Sub Lt Hoad & crew safe.
91 Squadron Spitfire DL-P
Crash-landed after combat. F/L O'Meara safe.
114 Squadron Blenheim Z5902
Failed to return from sortie. F/L Marks & crew lost.
224 Squadron Hudson N7315
Damaged in combat. F/L Leach & crew safe.
240 Squadron Stranraer K7293
Sank in gale at Stranraer.
307 Squadron Defiant N3310
Crashed at Wrea Green. Sgt Bochanski & crew injured.
502 Squadron Whitley P5107
Crashed on take-off from Limavady. Sgt Wilkinson & crew safe.
612 Squadron Whitley T4291
Damaged landing at Sumburgh. P/O Downey & crew safe.
612 Squadron Whitley T4275
Force-landed near Northallerton, Yorks. Sgt Walley & crew safe.

Luftwaffe

III./JG 2 Bf109E4 0978
Crashed at Octeville. Gfr K.Fahrnow killed. Aircraft destroyed.
E./JG 27 Bf109E4 1075
Belly-landed at Roth. Aircraft 30% damaged.
I./JG 51 Bf109E1 3409
Crash-landed at Abbeville. Aircraft 20% damaged.
IV./JG 51 Bf109E3 1280
Crash-landed at Wizernes. Aircraft 25% damaged.
I./JG 52 Bf109E4 1095
Taxiing accident at Vlissingen, aircraft 5% damaged.

III./KG 1 He111H2 2218 V4+BS
Failed to return from sortie. Uffz R.Stebetack & crew missing.

E./KG 1 He111H2 3146
Crash-landed at Salzwedel. Aircraft 40% damaged.

I./KG 76 Ju88A5 7179 F1+GL
Crash-landed at Giebelstadt. Aircraft 5% damaged.

I./KG 76 Ju88A5 5192
Crash-landed at Giebelstadt. Aircraft 10% damaged.

II./KG 76 Ju88A5 4170 F1+JP
Failed to return from sortie. Lt H.Dombrowski & crew missing.

E./KG 76 Ju88A5 8060
Crash-landed at Illesheim. Aircraft 10% damaged.

I./KG 77 Ju88A5 2141
Crashed at Beauvais-Tille. Fw E.Rosner & one crewman killed, two injured. Aircraft destroyed.

E./KG 77 Ju88A1 5024
Crashed near Ludes. Uffz J.Krauss & crew killed. Aircraft destroyed.

I./NJG.2 Ju88C4 0361
Crash-landed at Gilze-Rijn. Aircraft 40% damaged.

I./NJG.2 Ju88C2 0230
Crashed at Gilze-Rijn. Ofhr H.Klarhöfer & crew killed. Aircraft destroyed.

L.Fl.Res 3 He111P2 2680
Belly-landed at Romilly. Aircraft 40% damaged.

Korps.Aufkl.Staffel Fi156C2 4286
Crashed at Seesen. Aircraft 40% damaged.

17/18th February 1941

No RAF bombing raids were scheduled, but a lone Whitley of 1419 Flight, flown by Squadron Leader Keost, failed to return. This aircraft, engaged upon monitoring German radar and blind-bombing 'beam' transmissions, was force-landed after engine failure, the crew being captured.

Around fifty Luftwaffe raiders attacked London, while minor incidents occurred over East Anglia. Only one combat took place when Squadron Leader Little, flying a 219 Squadron Beaufighter, intercepted and destroyed a Do17 of *3./K.Gr.606* over Windsor at 20.30 hours. All four men from *Leutnant* Günther Hübner's crew took to their parachutes before '7T+JL' exploded at Oakley Court, Bray.

Casualties 17/18th February 1941

Royal Air Force

236 Squadron Blenheim ND-
Damaged in raid on St Eval.

248 Squadron Blenheim Z5974
Force-landed near Newburgh. F/O Atkinson & crew safe.

254 Squadron Blenheim V5429
Overshot Dyce. P/O Wright & crew safe.

One of the few victims to the Parachute and Cable weapon, the 4./KG 53 Heinkel of Feldwebel Erich Busch lies forlornly in a field near Watton.

1419 Flight Whitley T4264
Failed to return from sortie. S/L Keost & crew lost.

Luftwaffe
3./K.Gr.606 Do17Z3 3472 7T+JL
Failed to return from sortie. Lt G.Hubner & crew captured.

18th February 1941

Weather conditions remained bad. Hurricanes of 242 Squadron flew a *Rhubarb* during which Sergeant Brzeski claimed to have strafed a Bf109 on the ground. Over England however, a German aircraft was brought down by an unusual method. At 07.55 hours, an He111 of *4./KG 53* was flying fast and low over Norfolk, heading for Watton, having previously attacked East Wretham and Honington. As it approached the airfield the defences opened fire and the Heinkel was hit by a Parachute and Cable weapon, which caused severe wing damage. *Feldwebel* Erich Busch belly-landed 'A1+CM' at Ovington with two of his crew slightly hurt.

Casualties 18th February 1941

Royal Air Force
3 Squadron Hurricane P3607
Crashed landing at Castletown. Sgt Lilburn injured.
236 Squadron Blenheim V5450
Damaged in action. Sgt Lindley & crew safe.
612 Squadron Whitley P5071
Crashed landing at Dyce. Sgt Beare & crew safe.
1 (RCAF) Squadron Hurricane V7026
Crashed on Bridlington Golf Course. F/L Reynolds killed.

Luftwaffe

III./JG 77 Bf109E7 6433
Crashed landing at Morlaix. Aircraft 70% damaged.

4./KG 30 Ju88 2327
Crashed at Havelberg. Aircraft destroyed.

E./KG 51 Ju88A1 8026
Belly-landed at Kaufering. Aircraft 15% damaged.

4./KG 53 He111H3 3349 A1+CH
Failed to return from sortie. Fw H.Busch & crew captured.

E./KG 55 He111P4 2975
Crash-landed at Landsberg. Aircraft 30% damaged.

E./KG 55 He111P2 1669
Crash-landed at Nancy. Aircraft 30% damaged.

I./KG 77 Ju88A5 3303
Crash-landed at Juvincourt. Aircraft 30% damaged.

E./K.Gr.100 He111H3 5616
Crash-landed at Hagenau. Aircraft 40% damaged.

II./NJG 1 Bf110D3 4227
Crashed on take-off from Deelen. Lt H.Matthes killed. Aircraft destroyed.

18/19th February 1941

The quiet phase continued for the RAF, but scattered German raids were carried out against east coast towns. One Ju88 of *5./KG 30* belly-landed at Gilze-Rijn on return, possibly due to damage caused by AA fire at Harwich.

Casualties 18/19th February 1941

Royal Air Force

- nil -

Luftwaffe

5./KG 30 Ju88A5 3268
Belly-landed at Gilze-Rijn due to enemy gunfire. Aircraft 20% damaged.

19th February 1941

No RAF fighters encountered the few German aircraft reported. One He111 of *I./KG 26* was shot down by AA fire, *Leutnant* Erwin Hoffmann and his crew being lost in the North Sea after their aircraft was set on fire off Scotland. This may have been the bomber claimed by gunners aboard HM trawler *Stella Rigel*. Over one hundred casualties were sustained in Newmarket town, when a lone Dornier, obviously trying for the airfield, was engaged by ground defences and allowed its bomb-load to undershoot.

Casualties 19th February 1941

Royal Air Force

611 Squadron Spitfire R6759
Damaged landing at Hornchurch. Sgt Smith safe.

Luftwaffe

II./JG 51 Bf109E7 4201
Crashed on take-off from Mardyck. Aircraft 40% damaged.

E./JG 51 Bf109E3 5102
Crash-landed at Cazaux. Aircraft 80% damaged.

I./KG 26 He111H5 3684
Failed to return from sortie. Lt E.Hoffmann & crew missing.

III./KG 53 He111H2 6812
Crashed near Posen. Lt W.Fischer & two crew killed, one injured. Aircraft destroyed.

E./KG 54 Ju88A1 6044
Crash-landed at Lechfeld. Aircraft 25% damaged.

E./KG 55 He111H2 5277
Crash-landed at Landsberg. Aircraft 15% damaged.

K.Gr.100 He111H5 5631
Crash-landed at Dinard. Aircraft 55% damaged.

K.Gr.100 He111H3 3352 6N+AH
Taxiing accident at Dinard. Aircraft 15% damaged.

K.Gr.606 Do17Z3 3485
Crash-landed at Brest. Aircraft 60% damaged.

3.(F)/123 Do17P1 4175
Crash-landed on Jersey. Aircraft 30% damaged.

2.(H)/12 Hs126B1 3485
Taxiing accident at Biarritz. Aircraft 60% damaged.

2.(H)/41 Hs126B1 4055
Force-landed at Steinau. Aircraft 50% damaged.

19/20th February 1941

As darkness fell, five Blenheims of 53 Squadron set out to raid Brest. The *Luftwaffe* responded by attacking Swansea and London, with minor 'nuisance' raids on Scotland and Kent. An He111 of *III./KG 27* crashed in flames at Avord on return, all four men from *Oberfeldwbel* Hans Moritz's crew perishing.

Casualties 19/20th February 1941

Royal Air Force

- nil -

Luftwaffe

III./KG 27 He111P2 1590
Crashed landing at Avord. Ofw H.Moritz & crew killed. Aircraft destroyed.

20th February 1941

Only a few German aircraft were reported over Britain, mostly around East Anglia, where a few bombs fell.

Two 611 Squadron Spitfires flew a morning *Rhubarb* over France and a Bf109 of *I./LG 2* was sighted over Wissant. This was attacked and claimed damaged by Sergeant Townsend. The Messerschmitt subsequently crash-landed at Calais. Another aircraft from this unit was lost when *Feldwebel* Heinz Pohland's fighter blew up over Offerquerque without visible cause. The pilot was killed.

One German aircraft attempted to bomb Wattisham in the late morning, where the AA defences claimed a 'Do215' probably destroyed. This was a Do17 from *9./KG 3* flown by *Oberleutnant* Willi Deuss, which returned with two crewmen wounded. HMS *Bramble* was also attacked, but its gunners shot down a Bf110 'S9+FK' of *3./E.Gr.210* into the North Sea, killing *Leutnant* Friedrich Heunisch and his crew.

At 12.10 hours, Coltishall was strafed by a Ju88. Although one fighter was scrambled the pilot was unable to find his elusive quarry.

In the early afternoon five Spitfires of 41 Squadron took off to patrol along the south coast. Conditions were not good, developing into a snowstorm as they crossed Dungeness. It was here, at 15.54 hours, that the Bf109s of *Stab./JG 51* bounced them, ripping the British formation to shreds. Sergeant Angus was at once shot down by *Major* Mölders and baled out into the sea. Wasting no time, Werner Mölders then attacked and shot down Sergeant McAdam, who also took to his parachute. This latter event was witnessed by Pilot Officer Brown, who was horrified to see the pilot, hanging in his harness, hit by incendiary ammunition that set his clothing alight. Brown was then attacked from astern and took violent evasive action. At length the '109s broke off the action and departed. Brown attempted to pursue them, but his Spitfire was not fast enough. He later said that the Messerschmitts worked very cleverly in pairs, one pair attacking while the others guarded them.

McAdam was later picked up dead; he had been hit in the back by a cannon shell. There was always a great deal of stray ammunition flying about in a dogfight and parachuting airmen

The fight in the snowstorm on 20th February. Major Werner Mölders (above left), leading his Stab./JG 51, bounced 41 Squadron and shot down both John McAdam (top right) and Robert Angus. Neither survived the encounter.

were often at risk from this. In this case it seems probable that Brown, flying towards the parachute, had himself been the target. Mölders, a man repected on both sides of the Channel, would almost certainly have court-martialled any of his pilots seen strafing a parachuting airman. His views on the subject were well known.

Several further losses were sustained by the Luftwaffe. *Feldwebel* Bouillon and *Unteroffizier* Pichler of 7./JG 77 had been ordered to investigate an unidentified aircraft near Morlaix. They sighted a twin-engined bomber and dived to identify it. Suddenly the wings of Helmut Bouillon's Messerschmitt broke off and he plunged into the sea. Johann Pichler,

157

evidently believing that his companion had been shot down, opened fire. The bomber, a Ju88 of *3.(F)/121*, turned away and went down to crash-land with two wounded crewmen aboard. Another reconnaissance Junkers of *5.(F)/122* crash-landed at Jersey, reportedly due to combat with a Spitfire.

Casualties 20th February 1941

Royal Air Force

19 Squadron Spitfire P7430
Crashed on take-off from Fowlmere. Sgt Charnock safe.

41 Squadron Spitfire P7302
Shot down by Bf109. Sgt McAdam killed.

41 Squadron Spitfire P7322
Shot down by Bf109. Sgt Angus killed.

257 Squadron Hurricane W9306
Damaged in strafe at Coltishall.

302 Squadron Hurricane R2687
Crashed during dogfight practice near Arundel. P/O Pilch killed.

1 PRU Spitfire X4674
Stalled landing at Benson. P/O Flynn safe.

Luftwaffe

3./EGr.210 Bf110E1 3474 S9+PK
Failed to return from sortie. Lt F.Heunisch & crew missing.

III./JG 77 Bf 109E7 4939
Crashed while attacking Ju88 of 3(F)/121 near Morlaix. Fw H.Bouillon killed. Aircraft destroyed

E./JG 77 Bf109E3 ----
Crashed on take-off from La Rochelle. Aircraft 70% damaged.

8./KG 3 Do17Z ----
Damaged by enemy gunfire. Oblt W.Deuss & one crewman wounded. Aircraft 20% damaged.

Stab./KG 27 He111P2 1694
Force-landed near Vannes. Aircraft 25% damaged.

E./KG 51 Ju88A1 6003
Crash-landed at Lechfeld. Aircraft 35% damaged.

E./KG 51 Ju88A1 6014
Crash-landed at Lechfeld. Aircraft 15% damaged.

E./KG 54 Ju88A1 4069
Belly-landed at Lechfeld. Aircraft 30% damaged.

E./K.Gr.100 He111H1 5101
Undercarriage damage at Lüneburg. Aircraft 15% damaged.

I./LG 2 Bf109E4 2033
Belly-landed at Calais. Aircraft 35% damaged.

I./LG 2 Bf109E4 5791
Exploded over Offerquerque. Fw H.Pohland killed. Aircraft destroyed.

I./NJG 3 Bf110C4 3586
Crash-landed at Vechta. Aircraft 10% damaged.

2.(F)/22 Ju88A5 0651
Crashed landing at Sola. Aircraft 50% damaged.

3.(F)/121 Ju88A5 0665 7A+CL
Damaged by Bf109s. Two men wounded. AircraftL 50% damaged.
5.(F)/122 Ju88A5 0466
Force-landed on Jersey due to enemy gunfire. One man wounded.
Aircraft 25% damaged.
2.(H)/12 Hs126B1 3410
Force-landed near Lamotte Achard. Aircraft 50% damaged.
K.Gr.z.b.V.102 Ju52/3m 6276
Crashed at Crailsheim. Hptm W.Lessau & crew killed. Aircraft destroyed.

20/21st February 1941

Bomber Command was 'stood down', but there was no peace for either the *Luftwaffe* or Swansea, which was attacked by around fifty bombers, led by the Heinkels of *K.Gr.100* and *II./KG 27*. Thousands of incendiaries fell, causing considerable damage. London was also bombed on a smaller scale and there were scattered attacks elsewhere. No claims were made by the defences. Several German aircraft crashed on return.

Casualties 20/21st February 1941

Royal Air Force
256 Squadron Defiant N3446
Crashed on training flight. Sgt Rees' gunner killed.
Fighter Interception Unit Beaufighter R2201
Belly-landed at Ford. P/O Ryalls & crew safe.

Luftwaffe
III./KG 1 Ju88A5 3203
Crash-landed at Gevilliers. Aircraft 90% damaged.
3./KG 26 He111H5 3589
Ditched in Skaggerak, two crew injured. Aircraft destroyed.
I./KG 27 He111H5 3689
Abandoned near Romans. Aircraft destroyed.
I./KG 77 Ju88A5 3163
Crash-landed at Juvincourt. Aircraft 50% damaged.
I./KG 77 Ju88A5 4171
Crashed at Juvincourt. Fw S.Wolf & crew killed. Aircraft destroyed.

21st February 1941

There were a few German aircraft over eastern England and Scotland. At 11.43 hours two Hurricanes of 111 Squadron engaged a Ju88 off Dyce. Flying Officer Kellett and Sergeant Hruby attacked, expending all their ammunition and claiming it damaged. Their opponent could possibly have been a He115 from *1./K.Fl.Gr.106*, that subsequently crashed at Nord-Wickerhout, killing the crew.

An uneventful fighter sweep was flown between Boulogne and Calais by the Biggin Hill Spitfires, while a Blenheim raid upon Ghent was aborted due to weather conditions.

Casualties 21st February 1941

Royal Air Force

32 Squadron Hurricane V6988
Crashed at Bournemouth. Sgt Skrivanek killed. Aircraft destroyed.

41 Squadron Spitfire P7816
Crashed at Bodel Street, near Chilham. Sgt J S Gilders killed.

86 Squadron Blenheim L9273
Damaged landing at Leuchars. P/O Bleby & crew safe.

93 Squadron Havoc AX915
Hit balloon cable at Crewe and crashed. P/O Hyett & crew killed. Aircraft destroyed.

224 Squadron Hudson T9351
Overshot Leuchars. P/O Gould & crew safe.

236 Squadron Blenheim R2799
Crashed on take-off. P/O Lumsden & crew safe.

242 Squadron Hurricane N2476
Crashed at Grange Farm, Alderton. P/O Brown killed. Aircraft destroyed.

501 Squadron Hurricane P3653
Hit balloon cable at Bristol and crashed. Sgt Grimmett killed.

615 Squadron Hurricane Z2637
Overshot Kenley. Pilot safe.

Luftwaffe

E./JG 3 Bf109E4 1155
Force-landed at Tours. Aircraft 60% damaged.

1./K.Fl.Gr.106 Ju88A5 6184
Crashed at Nord-Wickhout. Hptm W Holle & crew killed. Aircraft destroyed.

I./NJG.3 Bf110C4 3523
Belly-landed at Vechta. Fw R.Scherbaum killed. Aircraft destroyed.

I./St.G.1 Ju87B1 0483
Crash-landed at Bonn-Hangelar. Aircraft 25% damaged.

21/22nd February 1941

Bomber Command Operations
Wilhelmshaven 34 Boulogne 3
Düsseldorf 7 Airfields 7 Minelaying 32
Coastal Command Operations
Brest 12
Luftwaffe Operationss
Swansea 68
Minor raids elsewhere

One Wellington of 75 Squadron failed to return from Wilhelmshaven, Pilot Officer Falconer's crew being shot down over the target by heavy *Flak*. A 149 Squadron machine piloted by Flying Officer Henderson went into the Channel returning from Boulogne. The crew were lost. One of the minelaying Hampdens was intercepted by a fighter, but escaped undamaged. Another crashed on return. *Flak* claimed two bombers.

Much damage was caused in Swansea. Despite two claims by defending gunners all returned, although two Heinkels of *II./KG 27* crashed near their base, one crew baling out.

Casualties 21/22nd February 1941

Royal Air Force

61 Squadron Hampden L4108
Overshot St Eval. Sgt Cooper & crew safe.
75 Squadron Wellington T2503
Failed to return from sortie. P/O Falconer & crew lost.
75 Squadron Wellington T2547
Overshot Feltwell. P/O Hewitt & crew safe.
82 Squadron Blenheim T2033
Damaged landing at Bodney. S/L Burt & crew safe.
149 Squadron Wellington R1045
Crashed into Channel. P/O Henderson & crew lost.
256 Squadron Defiant N1697
Overshot Colerne. F/S Stenton & crew safe.

Luftwaffe

II./KG 27 He111P2 2798 1G+CP
Abandoned at Monteburg on combat sortie. Ofw K. Riemenschneider injured. Aircraft destroyed.
II./KG 27 He111P2 2611 1G+FP
Force-landed near Caen, Lt C.Fritsche & one crewman killed, three injured. Aircraft destroyed.

Chapter Six
The Mounting Cost

22nd February 1941

The first combat occurred at 10.25 hours when two 74 Squadron Spitfires patrolled over a convoy off Kent. Two Bf110s were sighted, reconnaissance aircraft from *2.(F)/122*. Pilot Officer Churches and Sergeant Morrison attacked from above and, although one Messerschmitt managed to escape at low level, the two fighter pilots harried *Oberfeldwebel* Gottfried Bodenschatz's aircraft down to 400 ft before delivering the coup de grâce. 'F6+WK' plunged into the sea northeast of Whitstable. Another Bf110 was sighted later when 266 and 616 Squadrons flew a fighter sweep, but although Pilot Officer Johnson of the latter unit broke formation to shoot at it, no hits were seen and it escaped in cloud.

The *Luftwaffe* sent five high level sweeps in over Kent in the afternoon, involving around 200 fighters in total. They drew RAF fighters up, but no combats resulted. They also decoyed the defenders away from a *Jabo* attack on Manston. One British fighter was lost when 605 Squadron patrolled over the south coast. Pilot Officer Rothwell's Hurricane suddenly dropped out of formation at 30,000 ft and spun into the ground, probably due to oxygen failure.

At 14.04 hours a Heinkel was sighted near Bristol. AA gunners at Portishead put up a six-minute barrage, shooting down '1G+GM' of *4./KG 27*, which crashed at the water's edge between Avonmouth and St. George's Wharf, Portbury. Only the pilot, *Leutnant* Bernhard Rusche, succeeded in baling out. Falmouth gunners scored two hours later, claiming a bomber damaged. This appears to have been an He111 of *I./KG 28*, which later belly-landed at Nantes.

In the early evening, two Hurricane pilots of 111 Squadron patrolling off Peterhead sighted an He115 of *1./K.Fl.Gr.106* just

The harsh winter conditions did not make the lives of the Blenheim crews any easier. Here, a crew from 139 Squadron prepares to board their Blenheim IV for another operation.

above the sea. Pilot Officers Bain and Gregory came in fast, under heavy return fire, claiming a 'probable'. Gregory's fighter was hit in the windscreen by return fire. The floatplane later crashed attempting to force-land on the sea and all three crew members were lost. A second floatplane from this unit was lost while searching for *Leutnant zur See* Theodor Koch and his crew.

Coastal Command Blenheims patrolled over the North Sea during the day, three aircraft of 235 Squadron intercepting an He111 of *Wekusta O.b.d.L.* The Heinkel put up a stiff fight, shooting down Sergeant Wallis' aircraft, but concerted attacks by Flying Officer Jackson-Smith and Sergeant Hall resulted in the bomber escaping with no reported damage. One bomber was lost, however, when an He111 - '1H+KL' of *3./KG 26* - crashed near the Faeroes with the loss of *Feldwebel* Helmut Much and his crew. On 9th March the wreckage was recovered by a naval vessel and brought into Leith.

Casualties 22nd February 1941

Royal Air Force

19 Squadron Spitfire P7535
Crashed on take-off from Duxford. Sgt Johnson killed. Aircraft destroyed.

41 Squadron Spitfire P7816
Crashed near Ashford. Fate of pilot not known.

46 Squadron Hurricane R4191
Crashed at Asterby, Lincs. F/O Morgan-Grey killed. Aircraft destroyed.

46 Squadron Hurricane V7074
Crashed at Asterby, Lincs. Sgt Hudson killed. Aircraft destroyed.

64 Squadron Spitfire P7678
Crashed landing at Rochford. Sgt Stone safe.

64 Squadron Spitfire R6769
Crashed landing at Rochford. P/O Brown safe.

71 Squadron Hurricane P3351
Crashed landing at Kirton-in-Lindsay. P/O Petersen safe.

111 Squadron Hurricane P2979
Damaged by return fire from He115. P/O Gregory safe.

111 Squadron Hurricane V7400
Crashed landing at Dyce. P/O Skelly safe.

224 Squadron Hudson T9315
Crashed landing at Leuchars. P/O Wright & crew safe.

235 Squadron Blenheim T1803
Failed to return from sortie. Sgt Wallis & crew lost.

252 Squadron Beaufighter R2153
Damaged landing at Chivenor. F/O MacDonald & crew safe.

312 Squadron Hurricane P3512
Crashed after take-off from Penrhos. Sgt Kruta safe.

600 Squadron Blenheim Z5722
Damaged landing at Catterick. P/O Schumer safe.

602 Squadron Spitfire LO-
Belly-landed due to jammed undercarriage. P/O Francis safe.

605 Squadron Hurricane Z2347
Spun into ground near Littlehampton. P/O Rothwell killed. Aircraft destroyed.

Luftwaffe

E./JG 53 Bf109E4 1352
Hit ground at Poursay. Aircraft 80% damaged.

I./JG 77 Bf109E3 1534
Crashed at Herdla. Aircraft 5% damaged.

I./KG 26 He111H5 3737 1H+KL
Failed to return from sortie. Fw H.Much & crew missing.

II./KG 27 He111H3 3247 1G+GM
Failed to return from sortie. Lt B.Rusche captured, four crew killed.

I./KG 28 He111H4 6976
Belly-landed at Nantes due to enemy gunfire. Aircraft 20% damaged.

9./LG 2 Hs126B1 3103
Crash-landed at Metz. Uffz L.Aigner killed. Aircraft 90% damaged.

1./K.Fl.Gr.106 He115C1 2750 M2+JH
Force-landed 80m NW Hourtin. Lt.z.S. T.Koch & crew missing.

I./KFlGr.106 He115C1 M2+AH
3249 Crashed into sea. Hptm G.Gritzmacher & crew missing.
2.(F)/122 Bf110C5 2260 F6+WK
Failed to return from sortie. Ofw G.Bodenschatz & crew missing.
K.Gr.z.b.V.101 Ju52/3m 6509
Crashed at Rottach-Egern. Fw H.Laars and three crew killed, two injured. Aircraft destroyed
K.Gr.z.b.V.102 Ju52/3m 6847
Force-landed on frozen lake near Brenner, Oblt A.Hane & crew injured. Aircraft 90% damaged.

22/23rd February 1941

Twenty-nine Wellingtons of 3 Group set out to bomb Brest. Sergeant Bright's 115 Squadron aircraft was near Morlaix when a Bf110 was sighted 500 yards below. The Wellington rear-gunner opened fire directly into the cockpit area as Bright threw the bomber into a steep climb, stall-turning to allow his gunner another burst. The Messerschmitt was seen to lose its port fin and rudder, stalled and spun down into the clouds. The fighter was claimed destroyed. Five bombers crashed on return. Flak claimed one Wellington.

One German loss was reported when an He115 from *3 Staffel, K.Fl.Gr.506* failed to return, presumably from a minelaying sortie. No trace was found of *Leutnant zur See* Buchmann's crew.

Casualties 22/23rd February 1941

Royal Air Force
25 Squadron Beaufighter R2191
Overshot Wittering. W/C Atcherley & crew safe.
40 Squadron Wellington T2986
Overshot Alconbury. P/O Greer & crew safe.
115 Squadron Wellington T2887
Belly-landed at Marham. Crew safe.
115 Squadron Wellington R1221
Crashed at East Winch, near Marham, in fog. Sgt Milton & crew killed. Aircraft destroyed.
115 Squadron Wellington T2511
Overshot Marham. P/O Clarke & crew safe.
612 Squadron Whitley T4294
Crashed on Trannach Hill. P/O Hatchwell & crew injured.

Luftwaffe
2./K.Fl.Gr.506 He115 3254 S4+KK
Force-landed near Perros-Guirec. Aircraft 90% damaged.
3/K.Fl.Gr.506 He115 2774 SS4+HL
Failed to return from sortie. Lt zur See H.Buchmann & crew missing.

23rd February 1941

No fighter combats took place during the day, but 64 Squadron recorded the loss of two pilots from an operational sortie. Pilot Officers Gray, Pippett and Hawkins set off for a convoy patrol at 08.00 hours, but Gray returned alone. It is presumed that his companions collided in midair over the sea.

Bomber Command sent three Blenheims of 110 Squadron to raid Boulogne. Sergeant Stone's aircraft was attacked east of Orfordness by a Bf109. The bomber was not hit and the gunner claimed that the Messerschmitt dived away after taking hits.

Another loss was sustained by the RAF when a Spitfire of 1 PRU piloted by Flight Lieutenant Lockyer failed to return from a sortie to Antwerp. It was shot down off the French coast by a Bf109 pilot from an unidentified *Gruppe*.

Anti-shipping strikes by German bombers led to a further loss when '1G+LS', an He111 from *8./KG 27* flown by *Feldwebel* Arnold Pütz, attacked fishing vessels near the Fastnet Rock. Gunners aboard HM trawlers *Grackle* and *Dandara* shot the Heinkel down into the sea. There were no survivors.

Casualties 23rd February 1941

Royal Air Force

64 Squadron Spitfire P7778
Failed to return; believed collided. P/O Hawkins lost.

64 Squadron Spitfire P7852
Failed to return; believed collided. P/O Pippett lost.

86 Squadron Blenheim V5626
Crashed landing at Leuchars. Sgt Boyce & crew safe.

232 Squadron Hurricane V7156
Crashed landing at Elgin. F/S Brandt safe.

233 Squadron Hudson N7269
Crashed on take-off from Aldergrove. Sgt Ballantyne & crew safe.

306 Squadron Hurricane P3069
Crashed at Buntingdale on final approach. Pilot believed safe.

307 Squadron Defiant N3339
Fin cut off in landing collision. F/L Lumsden & crew safe.

500 Squadron Anson R9698
Crashed landing at Detling. P/O Armstrong & crew safe.

1 PRU Spitfire P9315
Failed to return from sortie. F/L Lockyer lost.

Luftwaffe

I./JG 1 Bf109E4 5337
Crashed at De Kooy. Fw A.Hofer killed. Aircraft destroyed.

A Do17 of KG 3 at dispersal, awaiting darkness.

II./KG 1 Ju88A5 4195
  Crashed on take-off from Münster-Handorf. Uffz L.Kowalski & crew killed.
  Aircraft 95% damaged.
III./KG 27 He111P2 1605 1G+LS
  Failed to return from sortie. Fw A.Pütz & crew lost.
II./KG 76 Ju88A5 7192
  Crash-landed at Dessau. Aircraft 30% damaged.
II./NJG 1 Bf110C4 3273
  Crash-landed at Bergen. Aircraft 20% damaged.
Fl.Ber. II Fl.K, Fi156C2 4276
  Crash-landed at Amiens. Aircraft 80% damaged.

23/24th February 1941

Bomber Command carried out small-scale raids after nightfall. Seventy-two sorties (seventeen recalled) were directed against coastal targets plus six leaflet-droppers over Paris. There were two losses. Sergeant Lloyd's 115 Squadron Wellington and a 51 Squadron Whitley flown by Sergeant Fenton were both reported missing. Lloyd's aircraft was seen to be shot down by *Flak* over Calais.

A few German aircraft crossed the English coast, heading for the Midlands, but there were no interceptions or claims. A Do17 of *8./KG 3* was hit by gunfire near Norwich and returned with two men wounded, while an He111 of *III./KG 27* crash-landed at Rennes. A British nightfighter was lost when Sergeant Hopewell of 151 Squadron abandoned his Defiant due to fuel shortage. His gunner was not so lucky. His parachute snagged on the tail unit and he crashed to his death.

Casualties 23/24th February 1941

Royal Air Force

9 Squadron Wellington R1297
Damaged by Flak. F/L Shaw & crew safe.

10 Squadron Whitley T4231
Crashed landing at Dishforth. Sgt Hayward & crew saf.

51 Squadron Whitley P4934
Failed to return from sortie. Sgt Fenton & crew lost.

59 Squadron Blenheim V5394
Crashed landing at St Eval. P/O Wightman & crew safe.

59 Squadron Blenheim T2040
Abandoned near Tavistock. P/O Scarfe & crew safe.

59 Squadron Blenheim R3631
Overshot St Eval. P/O Kennedy & crew safe.

78 Squadron Whitley P5105
Overshot Wellingore. Sgt Cope & crew safe.

96 Squadron Hurricane V6886
Crashed landing at Cranage. F/O Vesely safe.

107 Squadron Blenheim T2138
Crashed landing at Swanton Morley. S/L Kemp & crew safe.

107 Squadron Blenheim T2141
Crashed landing at Swanton Morley. Sgt Ralston & crew safe.

115 Squadron Wellington L7810
Failed to return from sortie. Sgt Lloyd & crew lost.

151 Squadron Defiant N3388
Abandoned near Watton. Sgt Hopewell's gunner killed. Aircraft destroyed.

217 Squadron Beaufort L9805
Damaged taxiing at St Eval. P/O Kenny & crew safe.

Luftwaffe

III./KG 3 Do17 ----
Hit by gunfire near Norwich. One man killed, one wounded. Aircraft 35% damaged.

III./KG 27 He111P2 1405
Crash-landed near Rennes. Aircraft 25% damaged.

I./NJG 2 Ju88C4 0544
Crashed at Gilze-Rijn. Fw J.Schüster & crew killed. Aircraft destroyed.

24th February 1941

The sole RAF fighter combat of the day occurred at 10.41 hours, when Pilot Officers Johnson and Atkins of 257 Squadron intercepted a convoy-raiding Ju88 off Happisburgh. As the Junkers passed below and behind them, Atkins gave a 'Tally-Ho!', diving to make a rear-quarter attack from the port side. Both he and the German aircraft vanished into cloud, but he then reported being hit by return fire before contact was lost. Johnson searched for 45 minutes, but Atkins was not found.

Hurricane P8810, the last 'fabric wing' machine, came to grief when Sgt F.Margarson of 232 Squadron landed in a blizzard following a scramble.
- F.Margarson via Brian Cull

Many Coastal Command aircraft were ranging along the French coastline. Pilot Officer Welch of 217 Squadron was ordered to seek German destroyers near Ushant. He found the warships, but soon after attacking he was jumped by a Bf109 of *III./JG 77* and his Beaufort was badly shot about. The German pilot, *Feldwebel* Blaurock, claimed a 'Blenheim' shot down, but Welch managed to bring his aircraft back. The German pilot broke off his attack when three Coastal Command Blenheims appeared. The Coastal forces lost two aircraft however. A 236 Squadron Blenheim flown by Pilot Officer Walters crashed and 209 Squadron lost its Commanding Officer, Wing Commander Bainbridge, when his Lerwick failed to return from patrol.

74 Squadron sustained two losses, Sergeant Morrison failing to return, while Pilot Officer Rogowski crash-landed near Eastbourne, injured. No reason for these casualties has yet been discovered.

Casualties 24th February 1941

Royal Air Force
23 Squadron Blenheim L1340
Damaged beyond repair. No details.
48 Squadron Anson W1652
Crashed on take-off from Hooten Park. F/L Brass & crew safe.
74 Squadron Spitfire P7618
Failed to return from sortie. Sgt Morrison lost.
74 Squadron Spitfire P7559
Crash-landed at Eastbourne. P/O Rogowski wounded.
79 Squadron Hurricane P3122
Crash-landed on Pembrey Range. Sgt Venba killed. Aircraft damaged.
86 Squadron Blenheim V5561
Crashed landing at Leuchars. P/O Elliott & crew safe.
209 Squadron Lerwick L7263
Failed to return from sortie. W/C Bainbridge & crew lost.

217 Squadron Beaufort L9861
Damaged by Bf109. P/O Welsh & crew safe.

232 Squadron Hurricane P8810
Crashed landing at Elgin. Sgt Margarson injured.

236 Squadron Blenheim T1942
Overshot St Eval. P/O Wathers & crew safe.

247 Squadron Hurricane V9190
Crashed on take-off from Roborough. Sgt Deuntzer safe.

257 Squadron Hurricane P5182
Failed to return from sortie. P/O Atkins lost.

303 Squadron Spitfire R6977
Crash-landed at London Colney. P/O Zumbach safe.

Luftwaffe

III./KG 26 He111H3 6825
Crashed at Le Bourget. Ofw W.Hasenbein & crew injured. Aircraft destroyed.

K.Fl.Gr.606 Do17Z3 2805
Taxiing accident at Ansbach, aircraft 5% damaged.

I./ZG 26 Bf110E1 3867
Force-landed at Schleissheim. Gfr A.Herrman & crew safe.
Aircraft 65% damaged.

Kur.St. OKM Ju W34 1487
Crash-landed at Le Bourget. Uffz Bernhard Schneegold and two men injured, one killed. Aircraft destroyed.

24/25th February 1941

The principal night objective for Bomber Command was Brest, which was attacked by 57 bombers. These included Manchesters of 207 Squadron, making their operational debut. Despite a claim for a Wellington by *Flak* gunners, all aircraft returned safely.

Luftwaffe bombers were reported over East Anglia, Merseyside and the Home Counties. Except for a sharp attack on Cambridge, damage was slight and there were no claims or aircraft casualties

Casualties 24/25th February 1941

Royal Air Force

106 Squadron Hampden AD790
Force-landed. F/O Price & crew safe.

207 Squadron Manchester L7284
Crash-landed at Waddington. F/O Burton-Gyles & crew safe.

247 Squadron Hurricane P3041
Crashed near St Dennis, Cornwall. Sgt McEwan killed. Aircraft damaged.

256 Squadron Defiant N1755
Overshot Middle Wallop. P/O Johnson & crew safe.

307 Squadron Defiant N3375
Crashed on take-off from Squires Gate. F/L Antonowicz & gunner safe.

German ground crews labour to clear snow from these Bf109s of JG 77 in Norway

600 Squadron Blenheim L1326
Crashed on take-off from Prestwick. P/O Schumer & crew safe.
604 Squadron Blenheim L8681
Damaged landing at Middle Wallop. S/L Kelly & crew safe.

Luftwaffe

- nil -

25th February 1941

A few German reconnaissance aircraft were reported around the British coastline. Six Hurricanes of 242 Squadron met an unidentified aircraft near Martlesham, which escaped unscathed. One Hurricane was damaged.

In the early afternoon six Coastal Command Blenheims attacked Dunkirk, escorted by three fighter squadrons, with five more units in support. *JG 51* rose to intercept over the target where 54 Squadron were engaged, making no claims but having one Spitfire badly damaged. Sergeant Burtonshaw force-landed at West Malling. One Spitfire of 303 Squadron was also shot-up. 611 Squadron fared better. Ably led by the Hornchurch Station Commander, Group Captain Harry Broadhurst, and by their CO Squadron Leader Bitmead, they engaged several Staffeln of *II Gruppe* and made four claims. Broadhurst, Bitmead and Flight Lieutenant Watkins each claimed a Bf109 destroyed, the former also claiming a 'probable'. Two Messerschmitts were lost, both from *6 Staffel. Unteroffizier* Wilhelm Topp was killed when his fighter crashed near Oye Plage, while *Fähnrich* Günter Rübell was wounded, crash-landing at Mardyck. A third Bf109 was lightly damaged, force-landing at Mardyck also. One Spitfire

Group Captain Harry Broadhurst was one of the few senior officers allowed to fly regularly on operations. He later commanded the Second Tactical Air Force.

- ACM Sir Harry Broadhurst

failed to return. Pilot Officer Stanley was shot down into the sea off Gravelines by *Major* Mölders.

After the Dunkirk attackers had returned, Messerschmitts of *I./LG 2* flew a Channel patrol and jumped a 91 Squadron Spitfire near Hawkinge. This was flown by Sergeant Gillies, who was shot down by *Leutnant* Geisshardt, crash-landing on the airfield uninjured.

One further claim was made by the Luftwaffe, *Unteroffizier* Esser of *III./JG 77* reporting the destruction of a Blenheim. This was possibly Pilot Officer Alexander's 236 Squadron aircraft, which failed to return on this date.

Casualties 25th February 1941

Royal Air Force

12 Squadron Wellington W5365
Crashed at Tollerton. S/L Lawrence & crew safe.

19 Squadron Spitfire P7421
Force-landed after sweep. Sgt Brown safe.

54 Squadron Spitfire P7739
Force-landed at West Malling. Sgt Burtonshaw safe.

68 Squadron Blenheim L1178
Damaged beyond repair. Cause not known.

91 Squadron Spitfire P7675
Damaged by Bf109. Sgt Gillies safe.

96 Squadron Defiant N3433
Crashed at Sealand. Sgt Stones' gunner injured.

236 Squadron Blenheim ND-
Failed to return from sortie. P/O Alexander & crew lost.

238 Squadron Hurricane V7021
Damaged landing at Chilbolton. P/O Remy safe.

242 Squadron Hurricane -----
Damaged in combat near Martlesham Heath. Pilot unhurt.
303 Squadron Spitfire N3108
Damaged by Bf109. Pilot safe.
320 Squadron Hudson TD-
Crashed on take-off from Carew Cheriton. 2/Lt Van Kooy & crew safe.
605 Squadron Hurricane Z2321
Force-landed near Littleport. Sgt Jenning safe.
611 Squadron Spitfire X4592
Failed to return from sortie. P/O Stanley lost.
2 (RCAF) Squadron Hurricane V7722
Force-landed near Fosdyke. Sgt Carless safe.
2 (RCAF) Squadron Hurricane V7745
Broke up in dive. P/O Russell believed safe. Aircraft destroyed.

Luftwaffe

II./JG 51 Bf109E7 4962
Undercarriage damage at Mardyck. Aircraft 20% damaged.
II./JG 51 Bf109E7 6468
Crashed near Oyeplage after combat. Uffz W.Topp killed. Aircraft destroyed.
II./JG 51 Bf109E7 4216
Damaged in combat and landed at Mardyck, Fhr G.Rübell wounded.
Aircraft 60% damaged.
E./KG 51 Ju88A5 5006
Taxiing accident at Lechfeld. Aircraft 35% damaged.
II./KG 53 He111H2 5493
Crashed near Harderwijk, Lt P.Ficker & crew killed. Aircraft destroyed.

25/26th February 1941

The RAF despatched 80 bombers to attack Düsseldorf. Twenty-three further sorties were made on Boulogne and also upon airfields in France and Holland. There was one loss. Sergeant Ralston's 103 Squadron Wellington, hit by *Flak* at Duisburg, crashed into the Rhine, near Kleve. The crew were taken prisoner after baling out. Another 103 Squadron aircraft was chased for several minutes by a fighter, but escaped undamaged. Blenheim fighter intruders of 23 Squadron were also operating over the Continent and Pilot Officer Brown claimed an He111 destroyed near Merwe. This could possibly have been a Ju88 of *5.(F)/121*, which crashed at Guerand with two of the crew wounded. The main raid, carried out through complete overcast, was a failure. Only seventy-six crews located the target.

Several small-scale raids were undertaken by the *Luftwaffe*, attacking targets in the northeast, southeast and also East Anglia, where the intruders of *I./NJG 2* also patrolled. London was also attacked. It was a bomber targeted to the capital that became the sole casualty when, at 21.25 hours, Squadron Leader Peter Townsend of 85 Squadron sighted a Do17 illuminated in a searchlight beam. He closed in, opening fire with a two-second burst from close range. The Dornier, 'U5+FM' of *4./KG 2*, went into a dive, leaving a white vapour trail. The rear-gunner fired wildly as the Hurricane pilot delivered a second attack, after which the bomber went down in a tight spiral dive. *Leutnant* Heinz Patscheider and his crew baled out, but one man was killed when his parachute failed. The all-black bomber then crashed into the ground at Little Waldingfield, near Lavenham, Suffolk, where it blew up. Fittingly, the squadron's first night victory had fallen to its Commanding Officer. One other visual contact was gained when Sergeant Copeland of 151 Squadron found a Ju88, but the guns of his Defiant failed to fire.

Over East Anglia, *Feldwebel* Ziebarth of *I./NJG 2* evened the score by catching a 218 Squadron Wellington on approach to Marham and shot it down. One man from Sergeant Hoos' crew was killed.

Casualties 25/26th February 1941

Royal Air Force

25 Squadron Beaufighter R2156
Undershot Wittering. Sgt Hollowell & crew safe.
29 Squadron Beaufighter R2193
Belly-landed at Digby satellite. P/O Lovell & crew safe.
103 Squadron Wellington T2621
Failed to return from sortie. P/O Ralston & crew lost.
105 Squadron Blenheim T1989
Overshot Swanton Morley. P/O Dore & crew safe.
149 Squadron Wellington R3206
Damaged landing at Aston Down. F/O Thorne & crew safe.
218 Squadron Wellington R1009
Damaged by intruder and force-landed near Marham. Sgt Hoos & crew safe.
218 Squadron Wellington L7859
Crashed at Stradishall. P/O Hordern & crew injured.
221 Squadron Wellington T2557
Overshot Bircham Newton. F/O Cattley & crew safe.

Luftwaffe

II./KG 2 Do17Z2 1134 U5+PH
Failed to return from sortie. Lt H.E.Patscheider & crew lost.
3.(F)/121 Ju88A5 0534
Crashed at Guerand. Two crew injured. Aircraft destroyed.

Howard Squire, with Herbert Ihlefeld at his shoulder, beside the belly-landed P7443 KL-E. Squire was allowed to write a note 'I have been shot down in France and I am safe', which was subsequently dropped near Croydon by Ihlefeld personally. Unfortunately, the message was never found.

26th February 1941

German aircraft operated over Kent and East Anglia, where a few bombs fell. The main events of the day, however, centred upon the southeast, where several vicious fighter combats took place.

In the mid-morning, six Hurricanes of 56 Squadron patrolled Dover and were bounced by *Stab IV./JG 51*. One Hurricane was lost. Sergeant Turner was shot down into the Channel by *Oberleutnant* Keitel, the *Gruppenkommandeur*.

Circus No.5 was carried out at midday, twelve Blenheims of 139 Squadron escorted by sixty-four fighters setting out to bomb Calais. The raid was carried out without interference, apart from heavy Flak, but as the force turned for home, Sergeant Squire of 54 Squadron followed his leader to seek a lone '109, then lost him, only to be caught by *Hauptmann* Herbert Ihlefeld of I./LG 2, who shot him down near Calais, where Howard Squire force-landed without injury. Ihlefeld later took him to the *I. /LG 2* mess, where he was entertained before going to prison camp.

A little later three 242 Squadron Hurricane pilots managed to find a Bf110 off Orfordness, which was attacked and claimed damaged by Sergeant Redfern. Following this, Flight Lieutenant Hanks and Pilot Officer Mason of 257 Squadron found an aircraft identified as a Do17 off the coast. Although Hanks fired several bursts from dead astern, no hits were seen. The enemy aircraft - probably another Bf110 - escaped.

In the early evening, Bf109s were again in action, *JG 51* flying a *Freijagd* over Kent and the south coast. Near Maidstone the Messerschmitts engaged 615 Squadron Hurricanes. One of the British pilots, Flying Officer Christopher Foxley-Norris recalled what happened:

> "Six Hurricane Mk.II of 615 Squadron took off from Kenley, flying in two 'vics' of three aircraft. I was flying in the rear 'vic' with Wing Commander Holmwood, our Australian CO, leading and Pilot Officer 'Alfie' Hone weaving as rear cover. We never saw or heard anything of the latter after take-off, which accounted for our later vulnerability.
>
> "We were controlled to over 30,000 feet over Kent, heading west and were vectored onto a formation of German fighters alleged to be quite close dead ahead of us and encouraged to 'buster' (full throttle) to overhaul them. 'You must be able to see them now!'. I have always suspected that the two plots were confused by control, because at that moment we were jumped by numerous Me109s from behind. My attacker shot off my propeller at the hub, which was unusual and did a lot of other damage. I baled out at great height, probably over 25,000 feet, with some initial trouble disentangling my oxygen and radio leads. I finally landed heavily in a field near Ashford, where I received a mistakenly hostile reception from some of the local worthies (I was wearing a black flying suit)."

He was slightly injured, but Wing Commander Holmwood, who also took to his parachute, fell to his death when his parachute caught fire. Pilot Officer Hone, the first to be attacked, crashed inverted. Badly concussed, he scrambled clear and drew his service revolver, firing wildly at people who rushed to his aid. When his ammunition was expended, he was overpowered and rushed to hospital. Meanwhile the remaining three Hurricane pilots fought the '109s as far as Dungeness, where one was claimed destroyed by Adjutant Lafont, who shot down *Oberleutnant* Keitel, *Kommandeur* of *IV/JG51*, whose fighter crashed into the Channel with the loss of the pilot. The successful *Luftwaffe* pilots had been *Hauptmann* Hermann-

Left: Hermann-Friedrich Joppien, Kommandeur of I./JG 51. He was killed in action in Russia on 25th August 1941 with a total of 70 victories to his credit.
Rght: Christopher Foxley-Norris relaxes with his pipe by the dispersal hut at Kenley. He is wearing the black flying suit that nearly caused him further grief on 26th February   - S/L J.G.P.Millard

Friedrich Joppien of I/JG51, who claimed two Hurricanes while *Oberleutnant* Horst Geyer of the *Geschwaderstab* claimed the third.

At the same time more RAF fighters arrived on the scene. 610 Squadron reached Dungeness in time to meet the departing Bf109s. Pilot Officer Grey was attacked and shot down by *Major* Mölders, the Spitfire pilot force-landing near Rye. Sergeant Horner managed to get a Messerschmitt in his gunsight and opened fire, claiming it probably destroyed. *JG 51* sustained two further losses when *Oberleutnant* Giselbert Pirkner and *Feldwebel* Willi Gasthaus, both from *4 Staffel*, collided at Mardyck. Both pilots lost their lives.

Mölders' claim brought his victory tally to sixty in World War Two and, with his fourteen successes in Spain, his overall score was fast approaching *Freiherr* Manfred von Richthofen's First War tally of eighty.

One further combat was reported by the RAF when Pilot Officer Gage of 91 Squadron was attacked by Messerschmitts near Dover. His Spitfire was slightly damaged.

Casualties 26th February 1941

Royal Air Force

21 Squadron Blenheim N4618
Damaged beyond repair. Cause not known.

54 Squadron Spitfire P7443
Failed to return from sortie. Sgt Squire lost.

56 Squadron Hurricane Z2755
Failed to return from sortie. Sgt Turner lost.

91 Squadron Spitfire P7676
Damaged by Bf109. P/O Gage safe.

141 Squadron Defiant N1706
Crashed landing. F/O Constantine & crew safe.

229 Squadron Hurricane V7245
Damaged landing at Speke. Sgt Smith safe.

232 Squadron Hurricane P3928
Crashed on take-off from Elgin. Sgt Hitching safe.

240 Squadron Stranraer K7299
Ditched and sank near Campbeltown, Argyll. F/L Furlong & crew believed safe.

308 Squadron Hurricane V7073
Crashed near Guisborough. Sgt Parafinski unhurt.

608 Squadron Blenheim L1430
Damaged landing at Thornaby. P/O Rose & crew safe.

610 Squadron Spitfire DW-
Damaged by Bf109. P/O Grey safe.

615 Squadron Hurricane Z2354
Shot down by Bf109. W/C Holmwood killed.

615 Squadron Hurricane Z2698
Shot down by Bf109 and crash-landed. P/O Hone injured.

615 Squadron Hurricane Z2754
Shot down by Bf109 and baled out. F/O Foxley-Norris safe.

Luftwaffe

I./JG 1 Bf109E4 1789
Taxiing accident at Schipol. Aircraft 20% damaged.

E./JG 26 Bf109E4 0702
Force-landed at Eindhoven. Aircraft 20% damaged.

E./JG 26 Bf109E4 1581
Force-landed at Eindhoven. Aircraft 12% damaged.

E./JG 26 Bf109E7 4069
Force-landed at Eindhoven. Aircraft 10% damaged.

E./JG 26 Bf109E7 6033
Force-landed at Eindhoven. Aircraft 10% damaged.

E./JG 26 Bf109E7 6355
Force-landed at Eindhoven. Aircraft 10% damaged.

E./JG 26 Bf109E7 0806
Force-landed at Eindhoven. Aircraft 20% damaged.

E./JG 26 Bf109E4 2667
Force-landed at Eindhoven. Aircraft 20% damaged.
E./JG 26 Bf109E3 2745
Force-landed at Eindhoven. Aircraft 15% damaged.
E./JG 26 Bf109E4 3236
Force-landed at Eindhoven. Aircraft 25% damaged.
II./JG 51 Bf109E7 6455
Collided over Mardyck. Fw G.Pirkner killed. Aircraft destroyed.
II./JG 51 Bf109E7 5456
Collided over Mardyck. Fw W.Gasthaus killed. Aircraft destroyed.
IV./JG 51 Bf109E4 3753 Black <
Failed to return from sortie. Oblt H.Keitel lost.
I./KG 3 Do17Z3 3824
Taxiing accident at Schipol. Aircraft 15% damaged.
II./KG 30 Ju88A5 3310
Taxiing accident at Gilze-Rijn. Aircraft 45% damaged.
IV./KG 30 Ju88A5 0586
Undercarriage damage at Ludwigslust. Aircraft 45% damaged.
I./LG 1 Ju88A5 6257
Crash-landed at Frankfurt-Rhein-Main. Aircraft 15% damaged.
III./ZG 76 Bf110D3 4269
Crash-landed at Sandnes. Uffz H.Lambrecht and one crewman killed.
Aircraft destroyed.

26/27th February 1941

Köln was the objective for 126 of the 140 Bomber Command aircraft despatched, while others hit Boulogne and mined the Elbe estuary. Slight damage was reported to the western edge of the city. One 82 Squadron Blenheim flown by Sergeant Dalton was reported missing.

Swordfish of 812 Squadron Coastal Command also undertook minelaying sorties. One aircraft failed to return. This aircraft ditched near Cromer with the loss of the crew. Six further bombers were lost in accidents on return. The intruders of *I./NJG 2* were lurking over East Anglia again and two claims were made. *Oberleutnant* Herbert Bönsch claimed a Blenheim destroyed near Scampton at 00.10 hours, while *Oberleutnant* Kurt Hermann claimed an Oxford thirty minutes later at Waddington. One of these pilots actually shot down an Oxford of 2 CFS which was in the Cranwell circuit. Flight Lieutenant Trench was flying solo and was killed. One German intruder, a Ju88 from *3 Staffel*, crash-landed at Gilze-Rijn on return with battle damage.

British intruders were also abroad. Pilot Officer Love of 23 Squadron patrolled the area Merville-Bethune-Cambrai and found two bombers, both of which he claimed to have damaged.

179

Kurt Hermann of I./NJG 2. The fin of his Ju88C has clearly been over-painted black, obscuring the swastika. At this time, he had been credited with seven victories.

The Luftwaffe was also very active, *KG 1* and *K.Gr.100* leading an attack against Cardiff, which was considerably damaged. Widespread attacks were carried out against other targets in the south of England.

At around 20.00 hours, Pilot Officer Hodgkinson, flying a 219 Squadron Beaufighter, intercepted and claimed to have damaged an He 111 over Tangmere. Thirty minutes later Squadron Leader Michael Anderson of 604 Squadron claimed a Ju88 damaged in the Middle Wallop area. Almost simultaneously, AA gunners at Newport caught *Leutnant* Helmut Schmidt's Ju88 of *3.(F)/121* in a withering barrage, blasting '7A+AL' into the Bristol Channel with the loss of the crew.

Casualties 26/27th February 1941

Royal Air Force

10 Squadron Whitley ZA-
Crashed. Three crew killed. Aircraft destroyed.

51 Squadron Whitley T4148
Crashed at Sutton Bank, Yorks. Sgt Wall safe.

57 Squadron Wellington R3195
Undershot Feltwell. P/O Hutchings & crew safe.

59 Squadron Blenheim R3833
Hit balloon cable at Dover. P/O Collier & crew believed killed.

78 Squadron Whitley P4996
Crashed at Achnashellach. W/C Toland & crew killed. Aircraft destroyed.

82 Squadron Blenheim T2031
Failed to return from sortie. P/O Dalton & crew lost.

83 Squadron Hampden X3134
Crashed at Durrington Cross. W/C Stanhope & crew killed. Aircraft destroyed.

141 Squadron Defiant N1706
Undershot Gravesend. F/O Constantine & crew safe.
256 Squadron Defiant N3520
Crashed near Upavon. F/O Johnson killed. Aircraft destroyed.
812 Squadron Swordfish -----
Ditched off Cromer. Crew killed.
2 CFS Oxford R6107
Shot down by intruder at Cranwell. F/L Trench killed. Aircraft destroyed.

Luftwaffe

3./NJG 2 Ju88C4 0371
Force-landed at Gilze-Rijn due to enemy gunfire. Aircraft 15% damaged.
3.(F)/121 Ju88A5 0667 7A+AL
Failed to return from sortie. Lt H.Schmidt & crew missing.

27th February 1941

Although the Germans made many isolated attacks under cover of cloud during the day, Fighter Command was unable to claim any successes. AA gunners at Bircham Newton claimed a 'Do215' damaged at 12.14 hours, which was undoubtedly a Do17 of *8/KG2*, in which one man was wounded.

At 13.30 hours, a Ju88 attacked Benson, dropping a stick of bombs, which destroyed a Wellington and damaged six more.

Casualties 27th February 1941

Royal Air Force
One Wellington destroyed and six training damaged during raid on Benson.

Luftwaffe

III./JG 2 FW56A1 2364
Crashed on take-off from St Martin. Aircraft 20% damaged.
II./KG 1 Ju88A5 5180
Undercarriage damage at Münster-Handorf. Aircraft 10% damaged.
E./KG 1 He111H2 5431
Crashed at Brandenburg. Aircraft 45% damaged.
III./KG 2 Do17 ----
One man wounded by AA fire. Aircaft 35% damaged.
E./KG 51 Ju88A1 7007
Crashed at Epfenhausen after take-off. Fw L.Weichseldorfer & crew killed. Aicraft destroyed.
II./ZG 76 Bf110D3 3720
Belly-landed at Stavanger. Aircraft 10% damaged.
4.(F)/ 14 Ju88A5 0579
Taxiing accident at Herzogenaurach. Aircraft 30% damaged.
2.(H)/ 12 Hs126B1 4024
Force-landed at Royan. Aircraft 25% damaged.
2.(H)/ 12 Kl35 4616
Crashed at Royan, Ofw W.Metz and passenger injured. Aircraft 95% damaged.
L.Fl.Res 3 Ju88A5 6264
Crash-landed at Weisbaden-Erbenheim. Aircraft 35% damaged.

27/28th February 1941

Bomber Command was placed on 'stand down', but a few German raiders were out over Britain. No successes were claimed, but an He111 from *3./KG 53* failed to return. 'A1+AL', flown by *Oberleutnant* Hans Zeigler, disappeared without trace.

Casualties 27/28th February 1941

Royal Air Force

- nil -

Luftwaffe

3./KG 53 He111H5 3563 A1+AL
Failed to return from sortie. Oblt H.Ziegler & crew missing.

28th February 1941

During the day a lone German bomber raided Dover. This was the only attack made by the several bombers reported around the coast. At 12.30 hours Blue Section of 611 Squadron stalked a bomber east of the Crouch estuary. The aircraft was attacked and claimed damaged by Squadron Leader Bitmead, Pilot Officer Sutton and Sergeant Smith.

Bomber Command sent eight Blenheims of 139 Squadron to raid coastal targets. Seven delivered attacks and three crashed on return.

Casualties 28th February 1941

Royal Air Force

19 Squadron Spitfire P7379
Damaged in mid-air, force-landed at Fowlmere. Sgt Charnock safe.

61 Squadron Hampden X2906
Crashed on take-off from Hemswell. P/O Adshead & crew safe.

71 Squadron Hurricane X7435
Crashed landing at Coltishall. F/L Trousdale safe.

91 Squadron Spitfire P7674
Crash-landed at Lympne. Sgt Forrest safe.

139 Squadron Blenheim L9420
Crashed on return from sortie. Hit T1799. F/S Bennett & crew safe.

139 Squadron Blenheim T1799
Hit by above after landing. Sgt Vivian & crew safe.

139 Squadron Blenheim R3903
Crashed on return. F/L Edwards & crew safe.

139 Squadron Blenheim R3907
Damaged landing at Swanton Morley. Sgt McPhee & crew safe.

The wreckage of Blenheim T1859 of 105 Squadron lies in a field near Gröningen, another victim to Paul Gildner of 4 Staffel NJG 1.

610 Squadron Spitfire P7777
Crashed landing at Westhampnett. P/O Scott safe.

Luftwaffe

II./JG 51 Bf109E1 4855
Force-landed at Boulogne. Aircraft 30% damaged.
E./KG 28 He111H2 2334 1T+EU
Crashed at Bad Zwischenahn. Ofw W.Ernst and one man killed.
Aircraft destroyed.
I./NJG 2 Ju88C4 0660
Crashed on take-off from Gilze-Rijn. Aircraft 35% damaged.

28th February/1st March 1941

122 British bombers set forth, most of these attacking the battleship *Tirpitz* at Wilhelmshaven, the remaining six bombing Boulogne. One Blenheim was lost. Sergeant Heape and his 105 Squadron crew were shot down by *Oberfeldwebel* Paul Gildner of *4./NJG 1* near Gröningen at 02.58 hours.

The German bomber forces switched their attentions to London, where many residential buildings were damaged. No claims were made by the defences.

Casualties 28th February/1st March 1941

Royal Air Force

105 Squadron Blenheim T1859
Failed to return from Sortie. Sgt Heape & crew lost.
207 Squadron Manchester L7312
Crashed landing at Waddington. Sgt Harwood & crew safe.

Luftwaffe

- nil -

March 1941 - Overview

Royal Air Force

Fighter Command

There were few major movements. On the 3rd, 312 Squadron moved from Cranage and Squires Gate to Valley. 600 Squadron, now fully operational on Beaufighters, left Catterick and moved north to Drem on the 14th. They would remain there for only two weeks, for on 28th March they moved on to Colerne. Meanwhile, on the 26th, 256 Squadron moved from Colerne and Middle Wallop to Squires Gate, changing places with 307 Squadron which joined 600 Squadron at Colerne. Finally, 605 Squadron moved north to Ternhill on the 31st and were replaced at Martlesham Heath by 17 Squadron from Croydon. Less significant changes during March were:

1st	43 Squadron	Crail to Drem.
	46 Squadron	Church Fenton and Wellingore to Sherburn-in-Elmet.
2nd	607 Squadron	Macmerry to Drem.
13th	315 Squadron	Acklington to Speke.
18th	263 Squadron	St. Eval to Portreath.
29th	3 Squadron	Detachment sent from Sumburgh to Castletown.
31st	54 Squadron	Hornchurch to Rochford.
	64 Squadron	Rochford to Hornchurch

The process of modernisation continued. Variants of Spitfire II were received by 65, 118, 222 and 266 Squadrons, while the 'Jim Crows' of 91 (shipping reconnaissance) Squadron began to replace their fairly new Spitfire IIs with the coveted Spitfire Vb. Hurricane IIs went to 111, 302, 310 and 601 Squadrons. 255 Squadron supplemented their Defiant Is with a few Hurricane Is and 23 Squadron became the second unit to begin re-equipment with Havoc I nightfighters.

Only one new unit was formed when 485 (RNZAF) Squadron came into being at Driffield on the 1st, equipped with Spitfire Is. Also on this date Nos. 1 and 2 (RCAF) Squadron were renumber 401 and 402 Squadrons respectively.

On 19th March an important development took place which was to alter the whole complexion of RAF fighter operations for the remainder of the war. During the latter part of the Battle of Britain, controversy had surrounded the 'Big Wing' concept, as postulated by Squadron Leader Douglas Bader and Air Marshal Trafford Leigh-Mallory. While there is now little doubt that this tactic, as employed in 1940, was at best ill-founded, the idea had not been forgotten. Problems with the early Circus operations had now brought the plan into sharp focus again. It had become vital to devise a method of controlling large numbers of escort fighters in cross-Channel operations. Accordingly, the post of Wing Commander (Flying) was introduced. A Wing of usually three squadrons was now to be commanded and led into battle by the Wing Leader. This post therefore was essentially operational rather than administrative. Initially, the new Wing Leaders in the south and the units under their command were as follows:

Biggin Hill Wing
Wing Commander A G Malan DFC

74 Squadron	Squadron Leader J C Mungo-Park DFC
92 Squadron	Squadron Leader J A Rankin DFC
609 Squadron	Squadron Leader M Lister-Robinson DFC

Kenley Wing
Wing Commander J R A Peel

1 Squadron	Squadron Leader R E P Brooker DFC
615 Squadron	Squadron Leader E Eyre

Hornchurch Wing
Wing Commander A D Farquhar

54 Squadron	Squadron Leader R F Boyd DFC*
64 Squadron	Squadron Leader B Heath DFC
611 Squadron	Squadron Leader E R Bitmead

Tangmere Wing

Wing Commander D R S Bader DSO DFC

145 Squadron   Squadron Leader W J Leather DFC
610 Squadron   Squadron Leader J Ellis DFC
616 Squadron   Squadron Leader H F Burton DFC

North Weald Wing

Wing Commander R G Kellett DSO DFC VM

56 Squadron   Squadron Leader E N Ryder DFC
242 Squadron   Squadron Leader W P Treacey
249 Squadron   Squadron Leader R A Barton DFC

Northolt Wing (Polish)

Wing Commander G A Manton
and Wing Commander W Urbanowicz (joint command)

303 Squadron   Squadron Leader Z Henneberg
601 Squadron   Squadron Leader J O'Neill DFC

Duxford Wing (Tactical Reserve)

Wing Commander M N Crossley DFC

19 Squadron   Squadron Leader B J Lane DFC
310 Squadron   Squadron Leader J Jeffries DFC

Bomber Command

The pressing needs of Coastal Command operations over the North Sea, particularly against Scandinavian coastal shipping, forced the release of Blenheim units for this purpose. 114 Squadron moved to Thornaby-on-Tees on the 2nd and was followed next day by 107 Squadron, which went to Leuchars, both units coming under control of No.18 Group.

Elsewhere, 97 Squadron transferred to Coningsby on the 10th and five days later a detachment of 110 Squadron Blenheims arrived at Wattisham. 99 Squadron moved to Waterbeach on 18th and 'A' Flight of 7 Squadron set up home at Newmarket on 20th. 218 Squadron began to re-equip with Wellington II aircraft.

During March, the Prime Minister ruled that the Battle of the Atlantic should be given top priority for the next four months.

Squadron Leader Adolph Gysbert Malan DFC, one of the best-known fighter pilots and leaders during 1941, was an obvious choice to become one of the first Wing Leaders in March.
- Andy Saunders

In a letter to the Secretary of State for Air, he wrote,

"We must take the offensive against the U-boat and the Focke-Wulf wherever and whenever we can. The U-boats at sea must be hunted, the U-boat in the building yard or in dock must be bombed. The Focke-Wulf and other bombers employed against our shipping must be attacked in the air and in their nests."

As a corollory to this, it was decided that an all-out attempt at coastal blockade should be commenced by the 2 Group Blenheim force. A directive outlining this was issued by the Secretary of State for Air to HQ Bomber Command on 9th March. Accordingly, Air Vice Marshal Saundby wrote to Air Vice-Marshal D F Stevenson (AOC 2 Group),

"Your primary objective is to be enemy coastwise shipping between Denmark and Ushant."

Stevenson replied on 10th March, giving details of the main areas of operations:

(1) Off Horns Reef.

(2) Between the Ems estuary and Texel.

(3) From Texel to Ostend.

(4) From Ushant to Cherbourg.

He also suggested the areas between Cherbourg and Dieppe and the coastline off the Pas de Calais might also be of interest, but added, '...but this is likely to be a bit warm.' He also gave tactical guidelines for shipping attacks:

"We are in favour of a low approach over the sea and, on sighting, pull up to 1,500 feet with either a level or glide attack from 1,000 feet."

These tactics were to prove unsound. A formation of Blenheims flying over a convoy where Flak-ships and fighters could be expected gave the defenders a definite advantage. Many Blenheim crews would be lost before a more radical method was eveolved:

> "We would form up in a tight formation at around 1,000 feet near the areodrome but descended to less than 100 feet as soon as we crossed the English coast. When the target was sighted, we opened up the formation so that each pilot could take his own evasive action on the approach to the convoy. We skimmed the wave-tops in the hope that the anti-aircraft gunners on the ships would not be able to depress their guns sufficiently to fire at us. Just before pulling up over the masts of the ship, we would aim to toss our bombs into the side of the ship. As soon as we cleared the masts we quickly descended again to fifty feet or so above the sea. The crews were at their most vulnerable when they flew through the cross-fire of the supporting ships."
>
> Air Marshal Sir Ivor Broom
> (Sergeant Pilot 114 Squadron)[1]

Coastal Command

On 1st March, there were several unit changes. 42 Squadron moved from Wick to Leuchars, a detachment from 220 Squadron went from Thornaby-on-Tees to Wick and a detachment of 59 Squadron Blenheims transferred from Manston to Bircham Newton, the remainder of the unit moving to Thorney Island on the 15th. On the 3rd, 86 Squadron moved from Wattisham to North Coates and 236 from went from St. Eval to Carew Cheriton on 21st March.

There were three important changes affecting flying-boat units. 119 Squadron was formed at Bowmore on 13th from the original 'G' Flight, which had seen service in Norway in 1940. This unit was equipped with Short S.26/M aircraft (converted civil passenger flying-boats). At the end of the month two squadrons left Stranraer. The Lerwicks of 209 Squadron went to Castle Archdale on 26th, while 240 Squadron moved to Killadeas in Northern Ireland two day later, where it gave up

---

1. Attrition among Blenheim crews was severe during the anti-shipping campaign. Survivors of that period are difficult to find. Sir Ivor Broom actually commenced operations in July 1941, but his comments apply equally well to the period under review.

its obsolete Stranraers in favour of Catalina Is. The Swordfish of 812 (Fleet Air Arm) Squadron arrived at RNAS Campbelltown on 20th. Two further units received improved aircraft during March, 269 Squadron getting Hudson IIIs, while the out-dated Ansons of 608 Squadron were replaced by Blenheim IVs.

The Luftwaffe

Fighter Forces

II./JG 52 moved from Maldeghem to Raversyde on the 6th and four days later *JG 53* arrived from Germany to replace *JG 26*. This unit settled in at Wizernes, Crécy, St. Omer and Berck-sur-Mer (see text), but *III Gruppe* moved on to St. Brieuc on the 30th. Meanwhile *II./JG 54* tansferred from St. André to Evreux on the 21st, *IV./JG 51* from Etaples to Le Touquet in mid-March and *II./JG 2* from Beaumont-le-Roger to Brest on 29th March. A new unit was established on this latter date with the formation of *Stab./NJG 3*.

Bomber Forces

Their were many airfield changes and arrivals. In the early part of the month *II./KG 27* moved from Dinard to Bourges, on 3rd *March III./KG 26* went from Achiet to Le Bourget and five days later the Bf110s of *E.Gr.210*, training now complete, transferred from Ursel to Wevelghem. Next day *Stab* and *II./KG 77* left Rheims, moving to Juvincourt and Beauvais respectively. On the 12th *II./KG 4* transferred from Eindhoven to Soesterberg, while *III Gruppe* from Schipol moved into Eindhoven. *I./KG 30* at Gilze-Rijn changed places with *II Gruppe* from Eindhoven in the middle of march, possibly on the 16th, when *I./KG 1* transferred from Clairmont to Rosiéres-en-Santerre. *I./KG 77* left Rheims on the 22nd to join the Geschwaderstab at Juvincourt and finally *Stab./KG 1* arrived at Rosiéres-en-Santerre from Amiens/Glisy in late March, when *III Gruppe* moved from Achiet to Royé.

New arrivals in the west were *Stab, I* and *III./KG 76. III Gruppe* went to Gilze-Rijn on the 6th, *I Gruppe* to Chateaudun three days later and the *Stab* flew in to Criel on the 16th.

There was a continuation of the movement of *Luftwaffe* units away from the Channel Front however. *III./KG 3* departed for the Balkan area on the 16th, while the remainder of the *Geschwader* began moving to Germany to re-equip with Ju88s. *I./KG 2* transferred from Cambrai to Merville on 21st March, but by the end of the month they too were en route for the Balkans. JG 54 left on the 29th and *Hauptmann* Ihlefeld's *I./LG 2* also left on this date, as did *Stab, II* and *III./JG 77*. The following day *KG 51* headed east and, by the end of the month, *Stab* and *III./KG 2, II./LG 2, 4.(F)/121, 2.(F)/123* and *1.(F)/22* had all gone to the Balkan area.

Naval Developments

The battlecruisers *Scharnhorst* and *Gneisenau* were now nearing the end of their successful raiding cruise. On 8th March they found a convoy escorted by the battleship HMS *Malaya* and again avoided contact. Luck was with them on the 15th however. A two-day foray against a British convoy sent twelve merchant vessels to the bottom. Six days later they arrived at Brest harbour, which had been vacated by the cruiser *Hipper* on 15th. This warship had moved into the North Atlantic, passed through the Denmark Strait and arrived at Kiel on 28th. Shortly afterwards, the *Admiral Scheer* made the same passage, joining *Hipper* at Kiel on 1st April. Both vessels then commenced a complete refit.

The presence of of the two battlecruisers at Brest was immediately reported by Coastal Command reconnaissance Spitfires. They now posed a threat that could not safely be ignored. During the next months both Bomber and Coastal Commands were to expend considerable effort in attempts to destroy these vessels in accordance with the Prime Minister's orders.

Chapter Seven
The Luftwaffe Returns

1st March 1941

In the morning, two 263 Squadron Whirlwinds patrolled near The Scilly Isles, where at 11.05 hours a Ju88 was attacked and claimed damaged by Pilot Officer Thornton-Brown.

There was no further action until 15.30 hours, when Squadron Leader Wood led six 74 Squadron Spitfires to patrol over the Gravelines area. It was twenty minutes before the Germans reacted. Without warning, three Bf109s hurtled over the Spitfires, then seven more appeared, closing fast. Pilot Officer Spurdle broke into the attack, claiming a Messerschmitt

A 263 Squadron Whirlwind rolls in for a practice attack. It was a remarkably agile fighter for its size and carried a heavy punch with its four 20mm nose-mounted cannon. Like all 'twins', however, it was inferior to single-engined fighters and was more suitable for bomber interception and ground attack duties. - British Official

shot down, but then saw another dive onto Wood's tail and open fire, damaging the Spitfire and wounding the pilot. Wood turned for home, his fighter trailing smoke as the Bf109 went into a climbing turn to port preparatory to making a second pass. Spurdle then intervened, his gunfire apparently hitting the German fighter in the fuselage, which he said had 'black numerals and a bright green nose'. This aircraft was also claimed destroyed and would appear to have been that flown by *Hauptmann* Ihlefeld of *I./LG 2*, who claimed a Spitfire destroyed in this action. Wood managed to crash-land on the English coast, while Ihlefeld actually escaped undamaged. One further Messerschmitt was claimed destroyed by Sergeant Glendinning. Either he or Spurdle had hit a machine from *10./JG 51*, *Feldwebel* Jennewein who force-landed at Caffiers wounded.

Three Spitfires of 145 Squadron patrolled off the Isle of Wight at 19.15 hours, intercepting a Ju88 from *III./KG 77* which had been targeted to Cardiff. Flying Officers Newling, Clarke and Sergeant Twitchett combined their fire to shoot '3Z+DR' down into the sea off St. Catherine's Point; *Oberleutnant* Walter Fick and his crew were lost.

Finally at 19.57 hours AA gun-sites at Banff engaged and shot down an He111 of *2./KG 26* flown by *Oberleutnant* Hatto Kuhn, which crashed into the sea off Melrose Head with the loss of the crew.

Two RAF fighter pilots were lost during the day. Sergeant Bell of 234 Squadron was reported missing from a convoy patrol, while Pilot Officer Brennan of 3 Squadron crashed into the sea following a mid-air collision with Sergeant Joyce, who force-landed safely.

Coastal Command reported Flight Lieutenant Buckley's 221 Squadron Wellington crew missing from patrol.

Casualties 1st March 1941

Royal Air Force

3 Squadron Hurricane P3255
Collided, P/O Brennan missing. Aircraft lost.
3 Squadron Hurricane OP-
Collided, Sgt Joyce safe. Aircraft damaged.
19 Squadron Spitfire P7421
Belly-landed at Fowlmere. Sgt Denston safe.

19 Squadron Spitfire P7547
Crash-landed at Fowlmere. Sgt Scott safe.
29 Squadron Beaufighter R2128
Crashed landing at Cranwell. P/O Davison & crew safe.
74 Squadron Spitfire JH-
Damaged by Bf109. S/L Wood wounded.
106 Squadron Hampden AD763
Crashed at Coningsby. P/O Brown & crew safe.
221 Squadron Wellington L4261
Failed to return from sortie. F/L Buckley & crew lost.
234 Squadron Spitfire N3101
Failed to return from sortie. Sgt Bell lost.
247 Squadron Hurricane P3597
Damaged landing at Roborough. P/O Varley safe.
312 Squadron Hurricane P3934
Belly-landed at Penrhos. F/O Cruml safe.

Luftwaffe

E./JG3 Bf109E4 2744
Exploded on ground Fontenet. Aircraft destroyed.
10./JG 51 Bf109E4 2056
Force-landed at Caffiers due to enemy gunfire. Fw G.Jennewein wounded.
Aircraft 80% damaged.
5./JG 53 Bf108 1113
Force-landed at Lumbres, lost. Aircraft 45% damaged.
2./KG 26 He111H5 3774 1H+BK
Failed to return from sortie. Oblt H.Kuhn & crew lost.
III./KG 77 Ju88A5 5147 3Z+DR
Failed to return from sortie. Oblt W.Fick & crew lost.
2.(F)/22 Do17M 2163
Crashed near Mandal. Lt zur See S.Wickert and one crewman killed.
Aircraft lost.
Wekusta 1 He111H2 5590
Crashed landing at Lauenburg. Fw O.Fiedler & crew injured.
Aircraft 80% damaged.
Kur.St.110 Ju52 6670
Crashed at Brunnenberg. Fw F.Hilbig & crew killed. Aircraft destroyed.

1/2nd March 1941

Bomber Command Operations
Köln 131 Boulogne 3
Luftwaffe Operations
Cardiff 37 Hull 24 Minor raids elswhere

Losses from the Köln raid were relatively high, mainly due to bad weather. Flight Lieutenant Lawson's 9 Squadron Wellington was ditched off Spurn Head with the loss of the crew, but three Whitleys of 51 Squadron (flown by Sergeants Beddow, Bruce and Smith) together with three from 10,

78 and 102 Squadrons (piloted by Sergeants Woodbridge, Quincy and Squadron Leader Florigny), all failed to return. These six bombers are believed to have been lost at sea. Florigny had become lost and had landed on a coastal airfield to discover that it was actually Haamstede, in Holland. He took off again before the startled Germans could react, but was forced to ditch the Whitley in the North Sea. Four of the crew reached the dinghy, but the securing rope then came undone; the dinghy was whisked away leaving the pilot standing on the wing of the sinking Whitley. Florigny was not found. By terrible coincidence his brother was aboard Sergeant Woodbridge's Whitley, also lost in the North Sea this night. A further five bombers crashed in England.

The *Luftwaffe* was active along the south coast, where many bombs fell. Intruder activity was reported over East Anglia, *Oberleutnant* Bönsch of *1./NJG 2* claiming a Hampden destroyed near Scampton, possibly a loss to the 5 Group force. Two Ju88Cs from *I./NJG 2* crash-landed at Gilze-Rijn on return.

Casualties 1/2nd March 1941

Royal Air Force

9 Squadron Wellington R1288
Ditched off Spurn Head. F/L Lawson & crew killed.

10 Squadron Whitley T4265
Failed to return. Sgt Woodbridge & crew lost.

50 Squadron Hampden X2984
Crashed near Bridlington, one man from P/O Pexton's crew killed.

51 Squadron Whitley N1481
Failed to return. Sgt Beddow & crew lost.

51 Squadron Whitley P5108
Failed to return. Sgt Bruce & crew lost.

51 Squadron Whitley -----
Failed to return. Sgt Smith & crew lost.

61 Squadron Hampden AD723
Crashed at Caistor, Lincs. Sgt Cooper & crew killed.

61 Squadron Hampden X3147
Crashed at Bircham Newton. Sgt Clarke & crew killed.

61 Squadron Hampden P1253
Crashed near Haverhill. Two men from P/O Noble's crew killed.

78 Squadron Whitley N1525
Failed to return. Sgt Quincey & crew lost.

78 Squadron Whitley T4235
Crash-landed at Schole. Sgt Marshall & crew safe.

99 Squadron Wellington T2957
Hit P9248 of 149 Squadron landing. Crew safe

The Armstrong-Whitworth Whitley proved slow and vulnerable to Flak and fighters, but its long range gave it a certain advantage over the Wellington and Hampden. Here, two aircraft of 77 Squadron formate on a practice flight.

102 Squadron Whitley DY-S
Ditched in North Sea, S/L Florigny lost, four rescued.
106 Squadron Hampden AD735
Damaged taxiing at Coningsby. S/L Parker & crew safe.
109 Squadron Wellington T2556
Crashed landing at Boscombe Down. F/O Somerville & crew safe.
144 Squadron Hampden P4394
Crashed at Wainfleet St.Marys. Three men from P/O Skinner's crew killed. Aircraft destroyed.
144 Squadron Hampden AD737
Force-landed near Hemswell. P/O McVie & crew safe.
149 Squadron Wellington P9248
Hit by T2957 of 9 Squadron while parked.

Luftwaffe

I./NJG 2 Ju88C4 0377
Crash-landed at Gilze-Rijn. Aircraft 15% damaged.
I./NJG 2 Ju88C4 0375
Crash-landed at Gilze-Rijn. Aircraft 15% damaged.

2nd March 1941

In the morning AA sites at Lerwick fired on two German aircraft, gunners claiming both damaged. It is possible that one was an He59 of *Seenotflugkommando 4* that subsequently crashed into the North Sea. *Unteroffizier* Raab and his crew were rescued.

In the afternoon a raider was reported approaching Sumburgh. Two patrolling Hurricane pilots from 3 Squadron sighted it at 14.35 hours. Pilot Officers Robertson and Gabb intercepted, finding a FW200 of *I./KG 40* flying at low level some five miles ahead. Both pilots attacked under intense return fire, Robertson making dummy passes after expending his ammunition. The Focke-Wulf was last seen heading east trailing smoke and was claimed damaged. It later crashed at Stavanger with one badly wounded crewman aboard, the crew claiming a Spitfire destroyed.

Two hours later Squadron Leader Stanford-Tuck of 257 Squadron flew a solo patrol, engaging a Dornier off Cromer. His aircraft received a few bullets through the cockpit canopy, but he claimed the 'Do17' destroyed. This was not so, but a Do215 of *2.(F)/O.b.d.L.* crashed at Evreux after a sortie, with *Leutnant* Dietrich Albrecht and his crew injured.

Coastal Command aircraft attacked Haamstede, Lister, Borkum and Harlingen, besides making several convoy strikes during which a vessel was claimed torpedoed by Beauforts. All aircraft returned safely.

Casualties 2nd March 1941

Royal Air Force

105 Squadron Blenheim R3703
Damaged in crosswind landing at Swanton Morley. Sgt Sarjeant & crew safe.
214 Squadron Wellington T2469
Crash-landed at Marham. F/O Burberry & crew safe.
257 Squadron Hurricane DT-A
Damaged by return fire from Do17. S/L Stanford-Tuck safe.
266 Squadron Spitfire X4613
Crashed at Gedney Hill, Lincs. F/L Bazley safe.
303 Squadron Spitfire P9519
Crashed landing at Northolt. F/O Kolaczkowski safe.

Luftwaffe

III./JG 2 Bf109E7 4174
Crash-landed near St.Martin. Aircraft 10% damaged.
E./JG 52 Bf109D1 3197
Force-landed at le Chantenault. Ofhr B.Leonhardy injured.
Aircraft 70% damaged.

Unsung Heroes. The Sunderland crews of coastal Command ably protected convoys in the Western Approaches from U-boats and Luftwaffe bombers.

E./KG 1 Ju88A5 3358
Crash-landed at Hannover. Aircraft 20% damaged.
III./KG 26 He111H4 3220
Hit obstruction at Amiens. Aircraft 50% damaged.
I./KG 40 FW200B3 0031
Force-landed at Stavanger due to enemy gunfire. One man wounded.
Aircraft 60% damaged
2.(F)/O.b.d.L Do215 0082
Force-landed near Evreux. Lt D.Albrecht & crew all injured.
Aircraft 90% damaged
SNF.Kdo.4. He59E 1826
Ditched in North Sea. Uffz Raab injured. Aircraft lost.

2/3rd March 1941

Fifty-four bombers attacked Brest, the main objective being the cruiser *Hipper*. A further 15 aircraft bombed Rotterdam docks and strafed airfields. A Wellington of 115 Squadron flown by Sergeant Elliott was shot down by *Flak* over Brest, while Sergeant Warcup's 21 Squadron Blenheim was shot down by naval *Flak* off Holland.

A few German raiders attacked coastal targets in the southwest of England, but the defences reported no successes.

Casualties 2/3rd March 1941

Royal Air Force

21 Squadron Blenheim Z5901
Failed to return from sortie. Sgt Warcup & crew lost.
25 Squadron Beaufighter R2069
Crashed landing at Cottesmore. P/O Herrick & crew safe.
44 Squadron Hampden X3026
Crashed on take-off from Waddington. P/O Smith & crew safe.
44 Squadron Hampden X3142
Overshot Waddington. P/O Ross & crew safe.
58 Squadron Whitley Z6465
Crashed near Ternhill. Sgt Bunn & crew killed.

82 Squadron Blenheim T1862
Hit balloon cable at Church Fenton. S/L Barker & crew believed safe.
102 Squadron Whitley Z6467
Force-landed at Sedgefield. Sgt Sleath & crew safe.
115 Squadron Wellington R3279
Failed to return from sortie. Sgt Elliott & crew lost.
218 Squadron Wellington T2469
Belly-landed. Crew safe.

Luftwaffe

- nil -

3rd March 1941

Six Spitfires of 54 Squadron took off at 14.35 hours and flew to Dungeness, sighting about twenty contrails above. These were Bf109s of *I./JG 51*, covering a *Jabo* attack against Manston. A *Schwarm* of Messerschmitts attacked the Spitfires from astern, one coming in astern of Pilot Officer Campbell, who throttled back causing the German to overshoot. Campbell fired three close-range bursts and *Leutnant* Manfred Ottmer baled out, but died when his parachute failed to open. His fighter, bearing the code 'TG+GW', crashed at Brenzett and was later inspected by 54 Squadron aircrew. Pilot Officer Lockwood was shot down and killed by *Hauptmann* Joppien, who claimed two Spitfires destroyed during this engagement, one south of Ashford and the other near Folkestone ten minutes later.

Meanwhile Heinkels from *I./KG 27* flying anti-shipping sorties in the Western Approaches sustained two losses. *Feldwebel* Heinrich Schaarschuch radioed 'Damaged by Flak, landing Scilly Isles', but was not where he supposed. At 15.20 hours he put '1G+AL' neatly down on Lundy Island, his crew reputedly holding local inhabitants at gunpoint until they had set fire to the aircraft. A second aircraft, '1G+HL' flown by *Leutnant* Alfred Heinzl, sent the message 'Damaged by fighter. Force-landing in Eire!' and subsequently force-landed at Lackenshane, Eire, where the crew were interned. One fighter engagement occurred off Lyme Regis when Yellow Section of 234 Squadron found a Bf110, which proved too fast for Sergeants Shepherd, Harker and Martin to catch.

Casualties 3rd March 1941

Royal Air Force

41 Squadron Spitfire X4774
Overshot Catterick. S/L Finlay safe.

42 Squadron Beaufort W6499
Crashed landing at Dumfries. F/O Garbett & crew safe.

43 Squadron Hurricane P3466
Crashed landing. Sgt Richardson safe.

43 Squadron Hurricane V6994
Crashed at Clifton, Yorks. P/O Lloyd safe.

54 Squadron Spitfire P7300
Shot down by Bf109 near Maidstone. P/O Lockwood killed.

65 Squadron Spitfire R6691
Damaged landing at Wittering. Sgt Rose safe.

233 Squadron Hudson N7296
Crashed landing at Leuchars. Sgt Green & crew safe.

247 Squadron Hurricane P3580
Crashed landing at Roborough. F/L Fordham died 5.3.41.

247 Squadron Hurricane P2833
Crashed landing at Roborough. Sgt Blight safe.

254 Squadron Blenheim V5734
Overshot Wick. P/O Parry & crew safe.

308 Squadron Hurricane V7053
Crashed on take-off from Hawarden. F/L Younghusband safe.

310 Squadron Hurricane V6797
Belly-landed at Little Downham, Ely. F/O Zadoral safe.

603 Squadron Spitfire P7683
Overshot Turnhouse. F/L Berry safe.

Luftwaffe

II./JG 2 Bf109E4 5120
Collided near Liseux. Pilot baled out. Aircraft destroyed.

II./JG 2 Bf109E7 1530
Collided near Liseux. Pilot baled out. Aircraft destroyed.

3./JG 51 Bf109E 2075 TG+GW
Failed to return. Lt M.Ottmer lost.

E./JG 52 Bf109E4 1158
Force-landed at Tours. Aircraft 25% damaged.

III./KG 4 He111H4 3271
Crashed-landed near Leeuwarden. Aircraft 80% damaged.

I./KG 27 He111H5 3664 1G+HL
Failed to return from sortie. Lt A.Heinzl & crew lost.

I./KG 27 He111H5 3911 1G+AL
Failed to return. Fw H.Schaarschuch & crew lost.

III./KG 53 He111H5 3832
Crash-landed at Vendeville. Aircraft 35% damaged.

II./KG 76 Ju88A5 8073
Crash-landed at Caen. Aircraft 40% damaged.

K.Gr.z.b.V.108 Do17P1 1106
Crash-landed at Gardermoen, one man injured. Aircraft 35% damaged.

I./LG 2 Bf109E4 3749
Force-landed at La Portel due to enemy gunfire. Aircraft 35% damaged.
2./E.Gr.210 Bf110E1 3824
Crash-landed at Ursel. Aircraft 15% damaged.

3/4th March 1941

Two losses were sustained from the raids. Sergeant Good's 106 Squadron Hampden fell to *Flak* near Antwerp while Squadron Leader Griffiths-Jones' 7 Squadron Stirling was lost at sea on return from Brest. It was brought down by *Flak* and was the first Stirling to be lost on operations.

Bomber Command Operations

Köln 71 Boulogne 8 Brest 7

Luftwaffe Operations

Cardiff 47 Southampton 14 Tyneside 22.
Minor raids elsewhere

Intruders from 23 Squadron were also operating. Pilot Officer Ensor discovered an He111 over Merville, closed to minimum range and claimed the bomber shot down in flames after his gunner had also fired on it. Flight Lieutenant Hoare claimed a Heinkel probably destroyed near Lille, but Sergeant Rose failed to return. His aircraft crashed near Guines, possibly victim to *Flak* gunners, who claimed a Blenheim destroyed at Antwerp.

One He111 of *III./KG 26* failed to return from Cardiff. It is believed that '1H+GR' was brought down by AA fire off the Welsh coast at 22.08 hours, *Feldwebel* Wilhelm Rudiger's crew being lost. A Heinkel from *KG 53* was damaged by AA fire and a Ju88 of *2./KG 30* was abandoned on return.

Casualties 3/4th March 1941

Royal Air Force

7 Squadron Stirling N3653
Failed to return. S/L Griffiths-Jones & crew lost.
10 Squadron Whitley T4202
Damaged by Flak. S/L Tomlinson & crew safe.
15 Squadron Wellington R1240
Crashed landing at Wyton. P/O Sands & crew safe.
23 Squadron Blenheim L1453
Failed to return from sortie. Sgt Rose & crew lost.
77 Squadron Whitley Z6463
Crashed force-landing near Catterick. One man from P/O Rogers' crew killed.
102 Squadron Whitley T4214
Overshot Topcliffe. Sgt Wragg & crew safe.
106 Squadron Hampden X3002
Failed to return from sortie. Sgt Good & crew lost.

Birds scatter as a section of Hurricanes from 310 Squadron scrambles.

- British Offcial

247 Squadron Hurricane Z2640
Crashed landing at Roborough. P/O Crossey safe.
311 Squadron Wellington P9235
Overshot East Wretham. P/O Sejbl & crew safe.

Luftwaffe

III./KG 26 He111H5 3601 1H+GR
Failed to return. Fw W.Rudiger & crew lost.
2./KG 30 Ju88A5 4213
Abandoned near Eindhoven. One man injured. Aircraft destroyed.
I./KG 53 He111H5 3817
Damaged by gunfire on sortie to Newcastle. Aircraft 10% damaged.

4th March 1941

Early in the morning, fighters were scrambled to intercept *Luftwaffe* reconnaissance machines. At 07.00 a Do215 was encountered off Dunkirk and was claimed damaged by Flight Lieutenant Freeborn and Pilot Officer Poulton of 74 Squadron. Four hours later three 152 Squadron Spitfires, patrolling over the Isle of Wight, sighted a Ju88 of *3.(F)/121* just below them. Pilot Officers Rowlands, Miller and Sergeant Short dived to attack, and were quickly joined by 302 Squadron Hurricanes flown by Pilot Officers Krol, Neyda and Sergeant Beda. The German aircraft took evasive action and escaped after taking several hits, finally crash-landing at Dinard. The six fighter pilots were credited with a 'shared damaged'.

Later in the day a lone Ju88 from *1.(F)/120* attempted to penetrate the Scapa Flow defence, but was engaged and shot down off Westray Island by Hurricanes of 253 Squadron flown by Flying Officer Corkett and Pilot Officers Crowther and Yapp; *Feldwebel* Johannes Mischke's crew were killed.

Fighter Command flew two unopposed sweeps over northern France during the day, but Flight Lieutenant Taylor of 1 PRU found a Bf109 over Guipavas airfield, which he claimed to have shot down. The Spitfire pilot then strafed twelve parked Messerschmitts, claiming damage to at least one. Meanwhile Flying Officer Lewis of 235 Squadron intercepted a Ju88, but abandoned the chase when his guns failed.

Casualties 4th March 1941

Royal Air Force

1 Squadron Hurricane V7258
Force-landed near Keswick. Sergeant Wood safe.
54 Squadron Spitfire P7299
Crashed on take-off. S/L Lawrence safe.
74 Squadron Spitfire P8016
Crashed near Sutton, Surrey. Fate of pilot not known.
141 Squadron Defiant N1795
Crashed at Watling Street. P/O Williams & crew believed safe.
151 Squadron Defiant N1749
Crashed near Stamford. F/O Williams & crew killed.
151 Squadron Defiant N3400
Lost wing covering and crashed. Fate of crew not known.
224 Squadron Hudson N9235
Crashed at Lochbraden. W/C Clarke & crew believed safe.
248 Squadron Blenheim L9450
Lost: no details available.
254 Squadron Blenheim R3827
Crashed on take-off. One man from P/O Webb's crew killed.

Luftwaffe

1.(F)/120 Ju88 0683 A6+LH
Failed to return from sortie. Fw J.Mischke & crew lost.
3.(F)/121 Ju88A5 0520
Crashed at Dinard on return from sortie. Aircraft 30% damaged.
K.Gr.z.b.V.101 Ju52 6878
Crashed at Parchim. Flg K.Bedecker and one crewman killed. Aircraft destroyed.
K.Gr.z.b.V.108 Ju52 5945
Crashed at Gardermoen. Fw P.Adam & crew lost. Aircraft destroyed.
E.Gr.See He115C1 2723
Missing, believed east of the Shetland islands. Uffz E.Hary & crew lost.

4/5th March 1941

Coastal Command raided Calais without loss. The *Luftwaffe* again bombed Cardiff, while several smaller attacks were reported elsewhere. Cardiff AA defences brought down an He111 of *1./KG 28*, which fell into the Bristol Channel off Llantwit Major at 19.01 hours, killing *Major* Roman von Auernig and his crew.

One nightfighter interception took place when Squadron Leader Anderson of 604 Squadron stalked another *I./KG 28* Heinkel south of the Devon coast. This was '1T+BH' flown by *Leutnant zur See* Otto Hanffstengel, which was shot down into the Channel off Beer Head at 21.58 hours.

One further Luftwaffe aircraft failed to return. *Leutnant* Christian Thony's Ju88 '3Z+GS' from *III./KG 77* disappeared without trace and is believed to have been another victim of the Cardiff AA defences, which made a total of three claims.

Casualties 4/5th March 1941

Royal Air Force

82 Squadron Blenheim R3812
Damaged landing at Bodney. Sergeant Harrison & crew safe.
502 Squadron Whitley P5010
Force-landed near Limavady. F/O Paterson & crew safe.

Luftwaffe

1./KG 28 He111H4 3293 1T+AH
Failed to return. Maj R.von Auernig & crew lost.
1./KG 28 He111H5 3561 1T+BH
Failed to return. Lt zur See O.Hanffstengel & crew lost.
III./KG 77 Ju88A5 0554 3Z+GS
Failed to return. Lt C.Thony & crew lost.

Pilots of 263 Squadron pose in front of 'HE-P' at St.Eval
- British Official

5th March 1941

263 Squadron despatched several sections of Whirlwinds to patrol the Western Approaches. At 09.54 hours a Ju88 was sighted off Lands End. It was attacked and claimed damaged by Pilot Officer Kitchener. *I./KG 27* had sent several He111s out on anti-shipping strikes in this area and two hours later two of these bombers engaged a Sunderland of 10 (RAAF) Squadron to the south of Eire. Squadron Leader Birch's crew succeeded in shooting down *Leutnant* Heinz Brodowski's '1G+EK', which crashed into sea off Stone Head with the loss of the crew. The Sunderland crew claimed damage to the second Heinkel, which made off with its starboard engine trailing smoke.

Coastal Command reported another engagement when Flight Lieutenant McArthur of 236 Squadron fought another He111. No claim was made and the Blenheim was badly hit by return fire. All three of the crew were wounded. His opponent is believed to have been an aircraft of *I./KG 27*. *Oberfeldwebel* Kurt Brosch and one other crewman were wounded following a combat with a 'Beaufighter' off Eire.

Circus No 6 was flown in the afternoon when six Blenheims of 139 Squadron attacked Boulogne docks. Bf109s of *JG 51* were scrambled and elements of *II Gruppe* engaged the Hornchurch Wing, operating as Target Support, some ten miles east of Le Touquet. Group Captain Harry Broadhurst, leading 611 Squadron, claimed one destroyed and a second damaged, while another 'probable' was claimed by Sergeant Townsend. 54 Squadron pilots made three claims; a Bf109 destroyed by Pilot Officer Stokoe, who claimed to have forced his opponent to crash without firing a shot, and two 'probables' by Pilot Officers Bailey and Colebrook. *II./JG 51* lost no aircraft and Spitfires were claimed by *Leutnant* Steffens and *Unteroffizier* Tange.

The Tangmere Spitfires, supposed to be flying as Close Escort, had missed their rendezvous with the bombers and were ordered to proceed independently. As they neared Boulogne at 27,000 feet came the warning 'Bandits approaching from the southeast!' Flight Lieutenant Norris then saw four '109s crossing the coast and flying up-sun of the Wing. As the Spitfires turned, four more Messerschmitts came in fast from the port quarter and the Wing turned to meet them head-on.

610 Squadron, pictured in late 1940. Top row (l to r) Sgt Richardson, Plt Off Grey, Sgt Warden, Plt Off Fenwick, Plt Off Douglas, Flg Off Ross. Bottom row, Sgt Page, Plt Off Drever (MIA 5.3.41) Sgt Raine, Sgt Horner, Sgt Hamlyn, Sqn Ldr Ellis, Flt Lt Norris, Sgt Ballard, Sgt Denchfield (PoW 5.2.41) Sgt Ward-Smith. - H D Denchfield

The '109s flicked over them and steep-turned to come in from astern. The sparring was over.

Two Messerschmitts attacked from astern, shooting at Blue Section of 610 Squadron. The Spitfires broke hard and Sergeant Page saw a diving '109 below. He followed it down, seeing his ammunition scoring hits before pulling up to avoid collision. This was claimed as probably destroyed. Sergeant Morgan attacked another below and to port, then climbed to engage two more above without result. Sergeant Horner saw Morgan's fruitless pass on the first and, when the former climbed away, he took up the chase, claiming to have caught it before it outdistanced him in a near-vertical dive. This was claimed as damaged. Then the German fighters were gone.

When the Wing reformed it was discovered that four Spitfires of 610 Squadron were missing. Sergeant Hamer's fighter had been badly hit and he struggled back to England alone. He was killed attempting to crash-land near Wilmington. From the other three pilots there was no word. Pilot Officers Ormond, Owen and Drever had all been shot down.

Claims for Spitfires were submitted by *Major* Beckh, *Oberfeldwebels* Borchers and Schweikart and *Feldwebel* Moller of *IV./JG 51*, while *Unteroffizier* A.Lesch of *2 Staffel* was shot down and killed, while *Leutnant* Georg Seelmann of *IV./JG 51* crash-landed unhurt and a third Bf109, of *I./LG 2*, crash-landed at La Portel after combat.

No night raids were undertaken by the RAF and no *Luftwaffe* attacks of any appreciable size were reported.

Casualties 5th March 1941

Royal Air Force

26 Squadron Lysander R9060
Crashed at Eastleigh. Aircraft destroyed.

46 Squadron Hurricane V3706
Damaged on take-off from Sherburn-in-Elmet. Sgt Simpson safe.

56 Squadron Hurricane Z2355
Belly-landed at North Weald. Sgt Vardy safe.

85 Squadron Havoc BJ402
Crashed landing at Debden. F/O Carnaby & crew safe.

224 Squadron Hudson N7325
Crashed at Wick. F/L Selley & crew killed.

235 Squadron Blenheim QY-
Force-landed at St.Eval. P/O Eyre & crew safe.

252 Squadron Beaufighter R2198
Damaged landing at Chivenor. P/O Lingard & crew safe.

315 Squadron Hurricane V9188
Crashed landing at Acklington. Sgt Slonski safe.

402 Squadron Hurricane W9135
Crashed on take-off from Digby. P/O Foster injured.

610 Squadron Spitfire P7501
Crashed at Wilmington after combat. Sgt Hamer killed.

610 Squadron Spitfire P7596
Failed to return from Circus. P/O Ormond lost.

610 Squadron Spitfire P7752
Failed to return from Circus. P/O Owen lost.

610 Squadron Spitfire P8027
Failed to return from Circus. Sgt Drever lost.

616 Squadron Spitfire P7841
Crashed: no details available.

1 PRU Spitfire L1055
Crashed on take-off from Benson. P/O Kowalski safe.

Luftwaffe

2./JG 51 Bf109E 6602
Shot down in combat. Uffz A.Lesch killed. Aircraft destroyed.

III./JG 51 Bf109E8 4894
Belly-landed at Wizernes, technical failure. Pilot unhurt. Aircraft 70% damaged.
III./JG 51 Bf109E7 2037
Crashed on take-off from Wizernes, pilot unhurt. Aircraft 20% damaged.
IV./JG 51 Bf109E4 5255
Crashed near Le Touquet following combat. Lt G.Seelmann unhurt.
Aircraft 90% damaged.
I./KG 27 He111H5 3734 1G+EK
Failed to return. Lt H.Brodowski & crew lost.
I./KG 27 He111 ----
Damaged in combat southeast of Eire. Ofw K.Brosch and one crewman wounded.
Aircraft 40% damaged.
I./KG 76 Ju88A5 7214
Crash-landed at Giebelstadt, crew unhurt. Aircraft 35% damaged.
I./LG 2 Bf109E7 2749
Force-landed at La Portel after combat pilot unhurt. Aircraft 35% damaged.
Stab./ZG 26 Bü131D1 6181
Force-landed at Leutkirch. Uffz H.Rohde and one crew injured.
Aircraft 50% damaged.
3.(F)/122 Ju88A5 0452
Force-Landed at Haute Fontaine, crew unhurt. Aircraft 5% damaged.

Casualties 5/6th March 1941

Royal Air Force

248 Squadron Blenheim Z5904
Overshot Dyce. P/O Arnold & crew safe.

Luftwaffe

- nil -

6th March 1941

There was little action due to the weather. 91 Squadron had two
fights. Flight Lieutenant Lee-Knight claimed a Do17 probably
destroyed near Dover at 11.30 hours and Flight Sergeant
McKay claimed another shot down off Folkestone in the
afternoon. One Dornier of *III./KG 3* was hit, almost certainly by
McKay, but escaped with a crewman killed. The night brought a
small raid against Tyneside, during which one attacker was
claimed damaged by AA batteries.

Casualties 6th March 1941

Royal Air Force

29 Squadron Beaufighter R2182
Crashed landing at Wellingore. F/O Humphreys & crew safe.
64 Squadron Spitfire P7582
Crashed landing. P/O Tidman safe.

93 Squadron Havoc BJ460
Crashed landing at Middle Wallop. P/O Poulton & crew safe.
220 Squadron Hudson T9354
Hit by AA fire near Watton. P/O Collins & crew safe.
222 Squadron Spitfire N3246
Damaged landing at Coltishall. Sgt Chipping safe.
308 Squadron Hurricane ZF-
Force-landed near Lavington. P/O Wandziliak safe.
308 Squadron Hurricane ZF-
Crashed in force-landing. S/L Morris injured.
320 Squadron Anson N5202
Damaged taxiing at Carew Cheriton. Capt Otten & crew safe.

Luftwaffe

1./JG 1 Bf109E4 5361
Crashed landing at Schipol. Aircraft 10% damaged.
E./JG 2 Bf109E1 3218
Crashed on take-off from Le Havre, pilot unhurt. Aircraft 20% damaged.
E./KG 1 Ju88A5 3337
Crash-landed at Cambrai, crew unhurt. Aircraft 35% damaged.
III./KG 3 Do17Z ----
Damaged by gunfire over England. One man killed. Extent of damage not known.
E./KG51 Ju88A1 5007
Crash-landed at Lechfeld, crew unhurt. Aircraft 10% damaged.
E./St.G.1 Ju87B1 0452
Force-landed at Stenay in bad weather, crew unhurt.
Aircraft 40% damaged.
E./ZG 26 Bf110C1 1347
Force-landed at Ingolstadt, crew unhurt. Aircraft 10% damaged.
I./ZG 76 Bf110C1 2825
Crashed at Wittmund. Lt E.Nelson & crew killed. Aircraft destroyed.
1./196 Ar196A2 0109
Crashed taking off from battlecruiser Scharnhorst 350 sea miles northeast of
Kapverden. Aircraft 80% damaged.

Casualties 6/7th March 1941

Royal Air Force & Luftwaffe

- nil -

7th March 1941

During the afternoon, Flight Lieutenant Ballantyne of 255
Squadron claimed a Heinkel damaged near Kirton-in-Lindsay.
The Royal Navy enjoyed more success however. A Bf110 of
2./E.Gr.210, briefed to attack targets near Harwich, was
engaged by gunners aboard HMS *Guillemot*. The Messerschmitt,
'S9+IK' flown by *Feldwebel* Konrad Fleischmann, took direct
hits and crashed into the sea. A similar fate befell the *2./KG 3*
Do17 of *Oberleutnant* Kunst, which was engaged by AA gunners

Ground crew service a 91 Squadron Spitfire VB at Hawkinge.

near Gorleston at 07.35 hours and shot down into the sea. One man was killed and the others were captured.

Only Coastal Command flew offensive operations in daylight, attacking Den Helder and Ockenburg and claiming a ship sunk off Holland. One Beaufort crashed on return, while a 608 Squadron Anson was ditched on convoy patrol.

Casualties 7th March 1941

Royal Air Force

22 Squadron Beaufort L9854
Crash-landed at North Coates. F/O Campbell & crew safe.
106 Squadron Hampden AD768
Crashed landing at Coningsby. Sgt Haggar & crew safe.
139 Squadron Blenheim T1922
Crashed on take-off. S/L Birch & crew killed.
229 Squadron Hurricane V7072
Crashed near Penrhos. P/O Stegman safe.
236 Squadron Blenheim T1812
Force-landed at Truro. P/O Robb & crew safe.
256 Squadron Defiant N1694
Abandoned near Southport, lost. Crew safe.
264 Squadron Defiant N3478
Crashed after collision. Fate of crew not known.
264 Squadron Defiant N3332
Collided with above. Fate of crew not known.
266 Squadron Spitfire X4254
Crashed landing at Wittering. F/O Mitchell safe.
502 Squadron Whitley P5050
Force-landed at Limavady. P/O Wilkinson & crew safe.
608 Squadron Anson R9817
Crashed off Collieston. Two men from Sgt Cutting's crew killed.

Luftwaffe

4./JG 51 Bf109E4 3824
Belly-landed at Mardyck. Aircraft 10% damaged.

II./JG 26 Bf109E7 3711 Black 6
Crash-landed at Detmold. Gfr Korthaus injured. Aircraft 15% damaged.

E./JG 53 Bf109E7 3522
Crash.landed at Berck-sur-Mer, pilot unhurt. Aircraft 85% damaged.

E./JG 53 Bf109E7 6416
Crash.landed at Berck-sur-Mer, Lt W.Schaller injured. Aircraft 80% damaged

2./KG 3 Do17Z2 3391 5K+MK
Failed to return. Oblt E.Kunst & crew lost.

10./KG 3 Do17Z3 4239
Crashed at Tirlemont. Uffz H.Peter and two crew killed, one injured. Aircraft destroyed.

I./KG 76 Ju88A5 515 F1+GH
Belly-landed at Giebelstadt, crew unhurt. Aircraft 20% damaged.

III./KG 76 Ju88A5 4244
Crash-landed at Illesheim, crew unhurt. Aircraft 30% damaged.

1./E.Gr.210 Bf110E1 3827 S9+JK
Failed to return. Fw K.Fleischmann & crew lost.

7/8th March 1941

The RAF was again on 'stand down', but around fifty German bombers made small attacks upon targets along the east coast of England and Scotland. No claims were made by the defences, but two bombers were lost. An He111 of *1./KG 26* attacked shipping off Buddon, Perthshire, where *Unteroffizier* Kurt Seeland brought '1H+HH' in low, misjudged his height and hit the mast of his target. The bomber crashed into the River Tay at 20.06 hours. The second loss was a Ju88 '4D+DN' of *5./KG 30*, which is believed lost to AA fire off Dover. No trace was found of *Feldwebel* Hans Steinacker and his crew.

Casualties 7/8th March 1941

Royal Air Force

- nil -

Luftwaffe

I./KG 26 He111H5 3650 1H+HH
Failed to return. Uffz K.Seeland & crew lost.

5./KG 30 Ju88A5 3198 4D+DN
Failed to return. Fw H.Steinacker & crew lost.

8th March 1941

One fighter engagement took place when two Spitfires of 266 Squadron patrolled off Skegness and intercepted a Ju88 from

4.(F)/122, flown by *Oberfeldwebel* Beuker. Flying Officer Ferris and Sergeant Van Schaick pursued it out to sea under heavy return fire. At 10.13 hours 'F6+BM' crashed into the sea. The last burst from the rear gunner hit Ferris' Spitfire, which also fell into the sea killing the pilot.

Coastal Command lost an aircraft when Sergeant Childe's 269 Squadron Hudson was ditched with the loss of two crewmen. A Ju88 of *II./KG 30* was also reported missing; *Hauptmann* Karl-Ferdinand Schneider's crew disappeared without trace.

Casualties 8th March 1941

Royal Air Force

64 Squadron Spitfire P7663
Crashed landing at Rochford. F/S Choron safe.

151 Squadron Hurricane V7234
Force-landed near Stamford. Sgt Bodien safe.

235 Squadron Blenheim V5896
Crash-landed near Bircham Newton. F/O MacKay & crew safe.

266 Squadron Spitfire X4594
Shot down into sea by Ju88. F/O Ferris lost.

269 Squadron Hudson T9334
Crashed in sea. Two men from Sgt Childe's crew killed.

302 Squadron Hurricane Z2499
Belly-landed at Wroybourne. P/O Narucki safe.

320 Squadron Hudson T9356
Crashed landing at Carew Cheriton. F/O Prager & crew safe.

601 Squadron Hurricane Z2581
Belly-landed at Denham due to engine failure. P/O Manak safe.

601 Squadron Hurricane Z2817
Overshot Northolt. Sgt Hurst safe.

Luftwaffe

IV./JG 51 Bf109E4 2053
Crashed on take-off from Etaples. Aircraft 20% damaged

I./JG 54 Bf109E1 4843
Crashed and wrecked at Wesermünde. Fw P.Ponzet killed.

E./JG 77 Bf109E1 3640
Crashed on take-off from Aachen, pilot unhurt. Aircraft 90% damaged.

I./KG 30 Ju88A5 4213
Crashed and wrecked, crew unhurt.

4./KG 30 Ju88A5 2220 4D+FM
Failed to return. Hptm K-F.Schneider & crew lost

I./KG 40 FW200C3 0040
Crashed after take-off. Oblt W.Clausen & two crew injured, one killed. Aircraft 40% damaged.

E./KG 51 Ju88A1 2052
Hit Ju88 while landing at Lechfeld. Crew unhurt. Aircraft 10% damaged.

E./KG 51 Ju88A5 6002
Hit by above at Lechfeld. No casualties. Aircraft 35% damaged.

II./KG 77 Ju88A5 -----
One man wounded by gunfire, Fw H.Kirsch wounded. Aircraft 25% damaged.
K.Gr.z.b.V.9 Ju52 2984
Crashed at wrecked at Ripont. No casualties.
E.Gr.210 Bf110E1 3475
Damaged taxiing at Ursel, crew unhurt. Aircraft 10% damaged.
4.(F)/122 Ju88A5 0404 F6+BM
Failed to return. Ofw F.Beuker & crew lost.
7.(H)/13 Hs126B1 ----
Force-landed in Luxembourg, lost. Crew unhurt. Aircraft 40% damaged.
Fl.Ber. I Fl.K. Fi156C2 4239
Crash-landed at Criel, crew unhurt. Aircraft 25% damaged.

8/9th March 1941

No raids were undertaken by the RAF, but an intruder crew from 23 Squadron claimed a success over France. Pilot Officer Gawith claimed to have attacked and damaged an He111 and a Do17 in the Beauvais area.

One hundred and twenty-five Luftwaffe bombers attacked London, causing heavy casualties and damage. AA sites claimed a 'probable' and two damaged. *Leutnant* Otto Kirch and his crew from *II./KG 27* perished when their Heinkel crashed on return near Chartres, probably due to Portsmouth gun-sites. A *6./KG 30* Ju88 crash-landed at Gilze-Rijn, another Junkers from *II./KG 76* sustained a man wounded in action, and a Heinkel from *I./KG 1* force-landed at Amiens. It is possible that one of these casualties involved the 23 Squadron intruder.

Casualties 8/9th March 1941

Royal Air Force
23 Squadron Blenheim L6730
Undershot Manston. P/O Pushman & crew safe.

Luftwaffe
I./KG 1 He111H3 5677
Crash-landed at Amiens/Glisy. Aircraft 10% damaged.
II./KG 27 He111H3 3166 1G+FN
Crashed near Chartres. Lt O.Kirch & crew killed. Aircraft destroyed
6./KG 30 Ju88A5 6057
Crash-landed at Gilze-Rijn. Aircraft 35% damaged.
II./KG 76 Ju88A5 3290
Crash-landed at Evreux. Aircraft 10% damaged.
II./KG 76 Ju88A5 7174
Force-landed at Chateaudun due to enemy gunfire. Aircraft 25% damaged.

9th March 1941

Weather conditions prevented all but a few Coastal Command

sorties by the RAF and a *Jabo* attack upon Manston by the Germans. The night brought another raid against London, 94 *Luftwaffe* bombers adding further damage to the still smouldering results of the previous evening's foray. One Ju88 was claimed damaged by AA batteries.

Casualties 9th March 1941

Royal Air Force
32 Squadron Hurricane V7057
Spun into ground on aerobatics practice. Sgt Kyselo killed.
607 Squadron Hurricane V6962
Belly-landed at Drem. P/O Nartowicz safe.

Luftwaffe
E./JG 2 Bf109E4 1341
Crashed at Le Havre, Gfr G.Bartzik killed. Aircraft destroyed.
1./JG 52 Bf109E4 5812
Crash-landed at Woensdrecht. Aircraft 35% damaged.
II./JG 51 Bf109E4 6464
Crashed landing at Mardyck. Aircraft 30% damaged.
III./KG 2 Do17Z3 2835
Damaged taxiing at Cambrai, crew unhurt. Aircraft 10% damaged.
4./KG 30 Ju88A1 4174
Crash-landed at Abbeville. Aircraft 45% damaged.
II./KG 30 Ju88A5 6057
Crash-landed at Gilze-Rijn, crew unhurt. Aircraft 35% damaged.
II./LG 2 Bf109E7 6425
Blown up by own bomb at Calais/Marck. Aircraft destroyed.
II./St.G.77 Ju87B1 5087
Crashed landing at Toussous-le-Noble, Oblt H.Pabst and gunner injured.
Aircraft 50% damaged.

Casualties 9/10th March 1941

Royal Air Force
502 Squadron Whitley P5059
Damaged by gunfire from British convoy. P/O Wilkinson & crew safe.

Luftwaffe
- nil -

10th March 1941

With clearing weather, Luftwaffe *Jabos* were out early attacking Hawkinge. At 11.15 hours three 145 Squadron Spitfire pilots discovered a Ju88 of *K.Gr.806* over the Channel. Flight Lieutenant Bungey led Flying Officer De Hemptinne and Pilot Officer Gundrey in to attack and the Junkers was claimed damaged. It later crash-landed at Caen. The *Luftwaffe* sustained another loss when a Bf110 from *3.(F)/123* was reported missing south of Portsmouth. 54 Squadron flew a sweep over France at 15.35 hours. The Spitfires were patrolling alone the French coastline when Bf109s from *IV./JG 51* bounced Sergeant Cooper, who was shot down into the sea off Le Treport by *Major* Beckh, who power-dived away. The attack had been so swift that no British fighter pilot witnessed this event.

Major Friedrich Beckh of IV./JG 51, 48 victories († 21.6.42)

Coastal Command lost two 272 Squadron Blenheims, one force-landing in Eire and the other ditching.

The Luftwaffe fighter force was further strengthened by the arrival of *Major* Günther von Maltzahn's *JG 53 Pik As* from Germany. The *Stab* went to Wizernes, *I Gruppe* to Crecy, *II Gruppe* to St. Omer and *III./JG 53* arrived at Berck-sur-Mer. *JG 53* had been involved in action since the 'Phoney War' of 1939, and had earned the reputation of being a tough and aggressive unit.

Casualties 10th March 1941

Royal Air Force

54 Squadron Spitfire P7381
Failed to return from sweep. Sgt Cooper lost.

115 Squadron Wellington KO-
Crashed landing at Marham. F/L Clyde-Smith & crew safe.

221 Squadron Wellington P9223
Damaged landing at Limavady. S/L Dev & crew safe.

272 Squadron Blenheim Z5733
Missing. P/O Van Waeyenberghe & crew lost.

272 Squadron Blenheim Z5752
Missing. Sgt Chanler & crew lost.

303 Squadron Spitfire P8040
Damaged landing at Hawkinge. Sgt Popek safe.

303 Squadron Spitfire P7821
Crashed on take-off from Hawkinge. S/L Henneberg safe.

607 Squadron Hurricane V6687
Crashed near Harper Rigg Loch. F/O Pollitt killed.

616 Squadron Spitfire P7662
Crashed at Worthing. Sgt Bingley killed.
1 PRU Spitfire R7114
Crashed landing at Benson. F/O Carthew safe.

Luftwaffe

1./JG 51 Bf109F2 5405
Crash-landed at Coquelles. Aircraft 20% damaged.
1./JG 51 Bf109F2 4825
Crash-landed at Mardyck. Aircraft 25% damaged.
4./JG 51 Bf109E1 6668
Crash-landed at Coquelles. Aircraft 15% damaged.
I./JG 54 Bf109E4 1434
Crash-landed at Leeuwarden. Aircraft 65% damaged.
III./JG 54 Bf109E1 6349
Crashed on take-off from Dinan, pilot unhurt. Aircraft 80% damaged.
Z./JG 77 Bf110C4 2275
Crash-landed at Sola, crew unhurt. Aircraft 60% damaged.
I./KG 27 He111----
Damaged by AA gunfire PQ 5240/15 West, two men wounded.
Aircraft 10% damaged.
III./KG 53 He111H2 2328
Crashed 1km northeast of Lüben. Hptm H.Giersch and one crewman killed, two injured. Aircraft 90% damaged.
E./KG 77 Ju88A1 3155
Crashed landing at Laon. Aircraft 40% damaged.
K.Gr.806 Ju88A5 4157
Damaged in combat over Channel. Aircraft 40% damaged.
5.(F)/122 Ju88A5 0390
Crashed landing at Jersey. Aircraft 50% damaged.
5.(F)/122 Ju88A5 0461
Hit by above. Aircraft 80% damaged.
3.(F)/123 Bf110E3 2316 4U+XL
Failed to return. Stfw H.Zeigenbalg & crew lost.
1.(H)/10 FW189 0059
Crashed at La Valle. Uffz B.Matschke & crew killed. Aircraft destroyed.
2.(F)/O.b.d.L. Do215B 0083
Collided on take-off at Le Bourget. Three men from Fw R Gross' crew injured.
Aircraft 60% damaged.
Wekusta 51 He111H2 2431
Collided with above. Uffz K.Tschersich & two crew killed, one injured.
Aircraft 30% damaged.

10/11th March 1941

| Bomber Command Operations |
| Köln 19 Le Havre 14 St. Nazaire 14 |
| **Luftwaffe Operations** |
| Portsmouth 244 |

There was one aircraft reported missing from these mainly short-range operations. A Hampden of 44 Squadron flown by Pilot Officer Stockings DFC was approaching the Ruhr when it was intercepted by *Hauptmann* Streib of *I./NJG 1* at 22.18 hours and shot down near Venlo for his tenth victory. A Whitley was claimed destroyed by *Flak* gunners at Boulogne.

23 Squadron Blenheims were again operating, but sustained a loss when Sergeant Skillen's aircraft failed to return. After bombing a Heinkel of *I./KG 1* at Amiens/Glisy, he attempted to attack another in the circuit. He misjudged his pass however and collided with *Feldwebel* Walter Schlagregen's aircraft, both machines crashing in flames on the airfield.

Over southwest England many fighters had been scrambled to meet the threat against Portsmouth. 219 Squadron Beaufighters were airborne, two pilots reporting success. Wing Commander Tom Pike claimed a Heinkel destroyed between Guildford and Horsham at around 20.00 hours while Sergeant Sargent claimed another near Newhaven. Neither can be confirmed from German records, but a 35 Squadron Halifax was shot down by a British nightfighter, apparently one of these Beaufighter pilots. It crashed at Normandy, Surrey, only Squadron Leader Gilchrist and his flight engineer surviving. AA gunners in the target area claimed four bombers destroyed and one was actually lost, *Unteroffizier* Werner Benne's Ju88 'V4+JT' of *III./KG 1* failed to return.

Intruders of *I./NJG 2* were lurking over East Anglia. A 78 Squadron Whitley was attacked and damaged, but landed safely. RAF fighters were also in the area, Flight Lieutenant Denison of 79 Squadron engaging a Ju88 intruder at 23.30 hours. After a few bursts of fire the crippled Junkers was force-landed at Hay Green, Terrington St. Clement. 'R4+CH' was the first example of a Ju88C to fall into British hands. The pilot was *Oberleutnant* Kurt Hermann, who was then a leading intruder *Experte* with eight victories confirmed. His Bordfunker, *Unteroffizier* Engelbert Böttner, always believed that they had been hit by ground fire:

> "The night sky was clear and bright during our time over the mainland and we could see the Flak firing at us. We were still trying to find a target when our right motor was hit by Flak. Despite jettisoning the bombs, we lost height and had to make a crash-landing near Kings Lynn. I was seriously injured in the landing and was taken to hospital for treatment."

Denison's claim was the only one in the area and it must be assumed that he attacked unseen. The Ju88 was later inspected

Above: *The wreckage of a 44 Squadron Hampden, down in Holland.*
- *G.J.Zwanenberg MBE*
Right: *The night brought a two-fold success for the British, when Kurt Hermann was captured together with his Ju88C4 long-range fighter.*
- *via Simon Parry*

and evaluated at the RAE Farnborough.

One abortive fight occurred when Wing Commander Appleton of 604 Squadron engaged an alert German crew. Violent evasive action allowed the *Luftwaffe* machine to escape before a shot could be fired.

Casualties 10/11th March 1941

Royal Air Force

23 Squadron Blenheim YP-X
Failed to return. Sgt Skillen & crew lost.

35 Squadron Halifax L9489
Shot down by RAF fighter at Normandy, Surrey.
S/L Gilchrist and one crewman safe.

44 Squadron Hampden X2918
Failed to return from sortie. P/O Stockings DFC & crew lost.

77 Squadron Whitley P4985
Crashed at Abingdon after abort. Sgt Taylor & crew safe.

78 Squadron Whitley EY-
Damaged by intruder. Two crew killed.

110 Squadron Blenheim L9305
Crashed landing at Horsham-St-Faith. Sgt Henry & crew safe.

144 Squadron Hampden AD720
Crashed on take-off from Hemswell. Sgt Leitch & crew killed.

247 Squadron Hurricane P3777
Crashed landing at St.Eval. P/O Waechter safe.

402 Squadron Hurricane P3273
Damaged landing at Digby. Sgt Carless safe.

Luftwaffe

I./NJG 2 Ju88C4 0343 R4+CM
Failed to return. Oblt K.Herrmann & crew lost.

Stab./KG 1 He111H3 3251
Collided with British intruder at Amiens/Glisy. Fw W.Schlagregen & crew killed.
Aircraft destroyed.

I./KG 1 He111H3 5641
Bombed at Amiens/Glisy. Aircraft destroyed.

III./KG 1 Ju88A5 3354 V4+JT
Failed to return. Uffz W.Benne & crew lost.

11th March 1941

During the morning a formation of nine Hurricanes from 615 Squadron patrolled the over Thames estuary, sighting a dozen Bf109s above them. Without orders, Adjutant Bourquillard broke formation and climbed towards them, to be quickly bounced and shot down by *Leutnant* Huppertz of *IV./JG 51*. The Hurricane dived into the ground at Tilbury and the pilot was killed.

To the southwest, a section of 263 Squadron Whirlwinds encountered a Ju88 off Cornwall at 17.07 hours. Pilot Officer Kitchener delivered an attack that resulted in a 'damaged' claim being submitted, but Pilot Officer Hitchen's aircraft was badly hit by return fire and he was wounded. He crash-landed safely, escaping before his aircraft caught fire. Thirty minutes later three 234 Squadron Spitfires intercepted a Bf110 '4U+SL' of *1.(F)/123* southwest of Portland. Squadron Leader Blake, Flight Lieutenant Mortimer-Rose and Pilot Officer Wootton attacked, shooting the aircraft down into the Channel. *Leutnant* Wilhelm Gössmann and his *Bordfunker* were killed.

Coastal Command aircraft were very active. Two Blenheim crews had inconclusive engagements with Bf109s in the Channel area, but a 220 Squadron Hudson flown by Pilot Officer Simpson fought and shot down an He59 seaplane of *Seenotflug Kommando 5* near Horn's Reef. The crew were later rescued. Two losses were recorded, a 502 Squadron Whitley flown by Pilot Officer Preston was ditched, while Pilot Officer Plumb's 53 Squadron Blenheim failed to return.

A 234 Squadron Spitfire at readiness, St. Eval Spring 1941.

One bomber was lost by the Germans when *Oberleutnant* Rolf Alander's He111 from *Stab./KG 26* failed to return from a sortie to Scotland.

Casualties 11th March 1941

Royal Air Force

53 Squadron Blenheim P4850
Failed to return. P/O Plumb & crew lost.

77 Squadron Whitley T4337
Damaged by RAF fighter near Abingdon. Sgt James & crew safe.

152 Squadron Spitfire P7910
Force-landed at Aylsbere, Exeter. Sgt Harrison safe.

209 Squadron Lerwick L7265
Crashed force-landing at Lough Erne. F/L Flint & crew safe.

263 Squadron Whirlwind HE-
Crashed after combat. P/O Hitchen wounded.

502 Squadron Whitley T4222
Crashed into sea. P/O Preston & crew rescued. unhurt.

615 Squadron Hurricane Z2757
Shot down by Bf109 over Tilbury. Adj Bouquillard killed.

Luftwaffe

Stab./JG 2 Fi156A0 0610
Crashed at Brianne, crew unhurt. Aircraft 55% damaged.

E./JG 3 Bf109E 3395
Crash-landed at Rue. Gfr R.Fink injured. Aircraft 90% damaged.

I./JG 26 Bf109E7 6485
Crashed on take-off from Dortmund, pilot unhurt.
Aircraft 30% damaged.

III./JG 51 Bf109E 3781
Crash-landed at Wizernes. Aircraft 20% damaged.
E./JG 51 Bf109E7 5615
Crash-landed at Cazaux, pilot unhurt. Aircraft 45% damaged.
E./JG 51 Bf109D1 2256
Crashed landing at Wesendorf, Fhr J.Arlt killed. Aircraft 90% damaged.
II./JG 54 Bf109E4 3911 White 8
Crashed in sea after take-off from Cherbourg. Uffz S.Heinberger killed.
Stab./KG 26 He111H5 3655 1H+AA
Failed to return. Oblt R.Alander & crew lost.
III./KG 26 He111H5 3609
Crashed near Amiens, one crewman killed, two injured. Aircraft 70% damaged.
E./KG 54 Ju88A1 3354 B3+NX
Crashed at Lechfeld. Uffz H.Spahn and two crew killed. Aircraft destroyed.
III./KG 55 He111P2 1496
Crashed landing at Villacoublay. Aircraft 60% damaged.
II./KG 77 Ju88A5 8134
Crashed landing at Beauvais. Aircraft 30% damaged.
E.Gr.210 Bf110E1 3959
Crash-landed at Merville. Lt E.Dipser and gunner injured.
Aircraft 45% damaged.
1.(F)/123 Bf110C5 2309 4U+SL
Failed to return. Lt W.Gössmann & crew lost.
SNF.Kdo.5 He59 2793
Shot down by Hudson west of Esbjerg. Ofw Schneider & crew rescued.
Aircraft sank.

11/12th March 1941

27 Wellingtons raided the Kiel U-boat pens, while five Coastal Command Blenheims attacked Brest. All returned safely. Intruders from 23 Squadron were also abroad and Pilot Officer Ensor strafed Amiens/Glisy airfield.

Birmingham was attacked by 125 *Luftwaffe* bombers, while small raids were carried out in the southwest and against Liverpool. Three bombers were claimed shot down by AA defences. A Heinkel was intercepted off Selsey Bill by Squadron Leader Ellis of 610 Squadron, this Spitfire pilot claiming it destroyed at 00.30 hours. Two Heinkels were actually hit, but none were lost.

Casualties 11/12th March 1941

Royal Air Force
201 Squadron Sunderland L2168
Overshot Sullom Voe. F/L Fletcher & crew safe.

Luftwaffe
III./KG 77 Ju88A5 4214
Crash-landed at Juvincourt, crew unhurt. Aircraft 60% damaged.

The fiercely aggressive Edward Mortimer-Rose of 234 Squadron (centre). He later flew in Malta and was killed in a mid-air collision in North Africa, having been credited with at least ten victories. He is pictured here with Flg Off C C H Davies (left) and Flt Lt H.J.S.Beazley.

K.Gr.100 He111H3 5693
Crash-landed at Vannes. Aircraft 15% damaged.
K.Gr.100 He111H3 3212 6N+HH
Damaged by AA fire over Plymouth. Aircraft 15% damaged.

12th March 1941

The *Luftwaffe* sent two small fighter sweeps over Kent during the afternoon and early evening. The first occurred at around 17.30 hours when two Spitfires of 91 Squadron engaged a *Staffel* near Dungeness. The Germans were chased out to sea, where Pilot Officer Fisher claimed one destroyed and another damaged. An hour later two more 91 Squadron Spitfires engaged Bf109s from *Stab./JG 51* over Dungeness and were shortly joined by 74 Squadron at full strength. The resulting dogfight was short. No claims were made by RAF pilots, but Sergeant Glendinning of 74 Squadron was shot down and killed and Sergeant Mann of 91 Squadron was wounded, but managed to crash-land his crippled fighter. *Major* Mölders claimed a Spitfire in this area as did *Hauptmann* Geyer. A claim by *Hauptmann* Joppien of *I./JG 51* possibly relates to the loss of Sergeant Burtonshaw of 54 Squadron, who crashed and died near Maidstone due to unknown causes.

Further west, three Spitfires from 234 Squadron engaged a Bf110 of *5.(F)/122* near Portsmouth. Flight Lieutenant Mortimer-Rose led Pilot Officer Masters and Sergeant Shepherd into the attack, but the Messerschmitt disappeared into cloud with no sign of damage and no claim was submitted. In fact 'F6+FN' flown by *Leutnant* Dr. Manfred Vukitz was reported missing in this area.

A Coastal Command Blenheim fighter crew reported an engagement, Squadron Leader Bocock of 235 Squadron engaging a Ju88 off Kristiansand. One pass was made and the Junkers was claimed damaged. It is likely to have been an aircraft from *2.(F)/22* that later crashed at Sola. The Command lost another 502 Squadron Whitley which was ditched in Galway Bay. Two men from Pilot Officer Deer's crew were interned. Three were killed.

Casualties 12th March 1941

Royal Air Force

54 Squadron Spitfire P7689
Crashed at Maidstone. Sgt Burtonshaw killed.

74 Squadron Spitfire P7506
Shot down by Bf109 over Dungeness. Sgt Glendinning killed.

91 Squadron Spitfire P7693
Shot down by Bf109. Sgt Mann crash-landed at Dungeness wounded.

256 Squadron Defiant N3451
Crashed at Imber, Wilts. Sgt Hocknell & crew killed.

260 Squadron Hurricane V7124
Crashed landing at Skitten. P/O Allen-White safe.

502 Squadron Whitley P5045
Crashed into Galway Bay. P/O Deer and one crew interned in Eire, three killed.

502 Squadron Whitley T4278
Force-landed at Limavady. F/L Foster & crew safe.

600 Squadron Blenheim T2136
Belly-landed at Thirsk. P/O Coombs & crew safe.

Luftwaffe

I./KG 3 Do17Z2 2546
Belly-landed at Ottenheim. Aircraft 60% damaged.

E./KG 54 Go145A1 1043
Force-landed at St. Pierre-au-Bois, crew unhurt. Aircraft 25% damaged.

III./KG 55 He111P2 2802
Damaged taxiing at Villacoublay. Aircraft 70% damaged.

E./St.G.1 Ju87B-1 5228
Crashed at Asch, Oblt K.Torpier and gunner killed. Aircraft destroyed.

2.(F)/22 Ju88A5 0675
Force-landed at Sola. Aircraft 85% damaged.
5.(F)/122 Bf110 2289 F6+FN
Failed to return. Lt Dr. M.Vukitz & crew lost.
7.(H)/12 H2126B1 4126
Crash-landed at Schwabisch Hall, Fw A.Hartig injured. Aircraft 80% damaged.

12/13th March 1941

Bomber Command Operations
Hamburg 88 Bremen 86 Berlin 72 Boulogne & Calais 8 Minelaying 1 OTU 1
Luftwaffe Operations
Liverpool 316 Many further widespread attacks

The raids, announced as, 'The heaviest of the war', caused substantial damage to the Blohm und Voss Works at Hamburg and to the Bremen Focke-Wulf factory, but cost Bomber Command seven aircraft. At 22.46 hours Sergeant Hall's 9 Squadron Wellington was intercepted by *Feldwebel* Rasper of *4. Staffel, NJG 1* and was shot down into the Ijsselmeer near Medemblik. Shortly after midnight *Oberleutnant* Wohlers of *8 Staffel* destroyed a 50 Squadron Hampden flown by Flight Lieutenant Johnson, this crashing near Nordhorn. 40 Squadron lost two Wellingtons, Sergeant Gough's machine crashing near Boulogne, while that flown by Squadron Leader Lynch-Blosse fell at Bethem, near Cloppenburg. This crew were captured and were possibly shot

Fw Hans Rasper (left) with his Bordfunker Uffz Erich Schreiber of 4./NJG 1, standing in front of their Bf110 G9+BM.
- Hans Rasper via Simon Parry

down by *Unteroffizier* Kupfer of *I./NJG 3*. Hamburg *Flak* defences brought down Sergeant Stewart's 82 Squadron Blenheim. A 102 Squadron Whitley, flown by Flight Lieutenant Long DFC, crashed at Denekamp, in Holland, while a 218 Squadron Wellington, piloted by Flying Officer Crosse, crashed at Opperdoes. During the raid a 103 Squadron Wellington was chased by a Bf109, but evaded undamaged. Another RAF crew succeeded in shooting down a Bf110 of *II./NJG 1*; *Oberleutnant* Zur Lippe Weissenfeld and his gunner were wounded, but their machine was force-landed safely. A Bf110 from *III Gruppe* force-landed at Rheine, having been attacked in error by another German nightfighter crew. Five bombers were claimed by *Flak* batteries.

Pilot Officer Hartop's 144 Squadron crew had been briefed to bomb Berlin:

> "We arrived over Berlin without difficulty, and visibility was excellent with slight industrial haze. We definitely identified the Alexanderplatz station, but owing to intense AA our bombs dropped a half-mile beyond the aiming point. We were badly shot-up over Berlin with at least 50 holes in the aircraft, in the engine, two big holes in the starboard wing through the engine nacelle, tank and front perspex. As a result of this we decided to come home the shortest way, heading for the British coast. The port engine cut, and we flew the last 40 minutes on one engine.....while making our approach the starboard engine cut, and we scraped over trees and managed to make a crash-landing with the undercarriage up in the field adjoining the dispersal field, about 300 yards short of the flare path."

The docks at Liverpool and Birkenhead were the main targets for 316 German aircraft. The first bomber to come to grief did so under strange circumstance. At 21.24 hours *Feldwebel* Günther Unger steadied his *9./KG 76* Junkers for the bombing run over the already-burning target. As the bombs dropped, 'F1+BT' took a direct AA hit, the port engine burst into flames and Unger ordered his crew bale to out. He then headed the aircraft towards the Irish sea before he himself abandoned the aircraft:

> "I saw the plane was burning and thought we would drop into the sea. It started to fly very quietly. I knew I had no time left; I must jump. I was the last.
>
> "I landed in the sea. My fingers were so cold I could not move them. I could not get the parachute off. It threw me back into the water when I tried to stand up."

Unger fought the cold and the tide for nearly two hours before finally struggling ashore on the beach.

The Defiant usually flown by Flt Lt
F.D.Hughes of 264 Squadron. He and his
gunner, Sgt Fred Gash, brought down Karl
Brüning's KG 55 Heinkel at Ockley. Note the
badge of Ulster on the nose of 'Coimbatore II'

Karl Brüning.

"I walked along a street and nobody was to be seen. Suddenly I saw a Home
Guardsman approaching me. He kept shouting 'Go back'. I had a pistol in
my pocket all the time. He did not want to be bothered."

An officer then appeared. He offered Unger a cigarette, relieved
him of his pistol and took him prisoner. All four crewmen had
landed safely in the northwest corner of the Wirral. Here, for
the moment, we will leave this incident.

A few minutes earlier Flying Officer Hughes of 264 Squadron
found a *5./KG 55* Heinkel over Beachy Head. After a long chase
to Surrey, Hughes' gunner delivered a killing burst and
Stabsfeldwebel Karl Brüning baled out before 'G1+GN' crashed
at Ockley, where it exploded. Almost simultaneously, Flying
Officer Geddes of 604 Squadron intercepted a Ju88 of *6./KG 76*
over Warminster. After a burst of fire *Feldwebel* Jakob
Herrmann's 'F1+OP' heeled over, one man baled out and the
Junkers dived into the ground. At this time another 604
Squadron Beaufighter pilot, Sergeant Wright, claimed a bomber
damaged over southern England.

Thirty minutes later a Defiant of 307 Squadron flown by
Sergeant Jankowiak patrolled near Ruthin and intercepted a
bomber that he identified as an He111 and engaged with a
three-second burst, claiming it damaged. Available evidence
suggests that this was no Heinkel, but actually Unger's Ju88,
which had turned around and was now heading southeast.
Although Jankowiak's fire certainly hit it, stubbornly it refused
to die.

At 22.10 hours another Defiant pilot, Sergeant McNair of 151 Squadron, found an He111 of *6./KG 55* over Widnes - 'G1+OP' flown by *Oberfeldwebel* Karl Singler. McNair shot the bomber down, the pilot and several crewmen parachuting before the bomber crashed. Then, fifteen minutes later, AA gunners at Birmingham claimed a bomber destroyed, and down came a Ju88, narrowly missing the radio transmitting masts at Droitwich before crashing at Wychbold. Unger's Ju88 had finally come down. Forty years later he was to say:

"When I first heard about it I could not believe my plane had come so far. It seemed to me incredible because when I baled out, my Ju88 was flying towards the Irish Sea. The autopilot was working correctly, but it is possible that the fire in the left engine destroyed the autopilot and that the plane made a slow left turn and crashed near Wychbold."

At 23.05 came the next combat, when Flight Lieutenant Cunningham of 604 Squadron claimed a Junkers damaged near Middle Wallop. Five minutes later Flying Officer Vesely of 96 Squadron attempted to engage a bomber over Liverpool, but his armament failed. At point-blank range the German *Bordschütze* put a burst into the Hurricane, wounding the pilot.

The third success for the Defiant units occurred at 23.45 hours. Flying Officer Welsh of 264 Squadron stalked '1G+DM', a Heinkel of *4/KG27*, and shot it down into the sea off Hastings with the loss of *Leutnant* Helmuth Robrahn and his crew. A minute later John Cunningham claimed an He111 probably destroyed near Middle Wallop. It was possibly an aircraft from *III./KG 26*, which compensated for an earlier inconclusive encounter with a Dornier. Then there was a pause in fighter interceptions until 00.46 hours, when Flight Lieutenant Sanders of 255 Squadron claimed another He111 probably destroyed near Kirton-in-Lindsay.

Finally at 01.50 hours Pilot Officer Stevens of 151 Squadron engaged a Ju88, claiming it probably destroyed off Orfordness. His opponent was probably *Leutnant* Arno Kick's machine from *II./KG 30*, which crash-landed at Gilze-Rijn with the pilot wounded.

In addition to the losses noted above one further Heinkel was lost, two more went into the sea off France, and a Ju88 crashed on return at Juvincourt.

Ofw Karl Singler's G1+OP down at Widnes following an attack by Sgt McNair of 151 Squadron.

Intruders of *I./NJG 2* were again hunting over East Anglia. A 54 OTU Blenheim flown by Pilot Officer Calvert was attacked and belly-landed on fire at Church Fenton. The intruder was driven off by Pilot Officer Babbington. Another Blenheim, flown by Squadron Leader Allen of 21 Squadron, was attacked and damaged as was a 311 Squadron Wellington flown by Pilot Officer Bala. Claims were submitted by *Feldwebel* Mittelstädt of *3 Staffel*, for a Blenheim at 22.10 hours and by *Feldwebel* Hahn of the same unit for a Blenheim.

Casualties 12/13th March 1941

Royal Air Force

9 Squadron Wellington N2744
Failed to return. Sgt Hall & crew lost.
10 Squadron Whitley T4263
Damaged by Flak. P/O Humby & crew safe.
21 Squadron Blenheim R3758
Damaged by intruder. S/L Allen & crew safe.
40 Squadron Wellington R1013
Failed to return. S/L Lynch-Blosse & crew lost.
40 Squadron Wellington T2515
Failed to return. Sgt Gough & crew lost.

227

40 Squadron Wellington BL-
Damaged landing. Crew unhurt.
50 Squadron Hampden AD721
Failed to return. F/L Johnson & crew lost.
64 Squadron Spitfire P7811
Crashed landing. P/O Watson safe.
75 Squadron Wellington AA-
Damaged landing. Crew safe.
82 Squadron Blenheim V5397
Failed to return. Sgt Stewart & crew lost.
96 Squadron Hurricane ZJ-
Damaged by He111. Sgt Vesely wounded.
102 Squadron Whitley T4236
Failed to return. F/L Long DFC & crew lost.
102 Squadron Whitley T4140
Crashed at Bircham Newton. P/O Malin & crew safe.
102 Squadron Whitley DY-C
Crashed landing. P/O Pitt & crew safe.
218 Squadron Wellington R1326
Failed to return. F/O Crosse & crew lost.
255 Squadron Defiant N1770
Force-landed. P/O Wright & crew safe.
311 Squadron Wellington P9226
Damaged by intruder on training flight. P/O Bala & crew safe.
54 OTU Blenheim L6835
Shot down by intruder and belly-landed. P/O Calvert & crew safe.

Luftwaffe

4./NJG 1 Bf110D2 3376
Hit by return fire and crash-landed at Bergen. Oblt E. Zur Lippe-Weissenfeld
& crew wounded. Aircraft 10% damaged.
III./NJG 1 Bf110E 3684
Damaged by German nightfighter and force-landed at Rheine.
Aircraft 40% damaged .
III./KG 26 He111H5 3606 1H+CD
Failed to return. Oblt A.Kaden & crew lost.
III./KG 26 He111H5 3608
Ditched off Cherbourg after combat with Beaufighter. Crew rescued. Aircraft lost.
Stab./KG 27 He111P2 1620
Crashed in sea off St.Malo. Fw H.Richter & crew injured. Aircraft lost.
II./KG 27 He111H4 5705 1G+DM
Failed to return. Lt H.Robrahn & crew lost.
II./KG 30 Ju88A5 4226
Crash-landed at Gilze-Rijn due to enemy gunfire. Lt A.Kick wounded.
Aircraft 15% damaged.
II./KG 55 He111P4 2994 G1+GN
Failed to return. Stfw K.Brüning & crew lost.
II./KG 55 He111P4 2989 G1+OP
Failed to return. Ofw K.Singler & crew lost.
II./KG 76 Ju88A5 6236 F1+OP
Failed to return. Fw J.Herrmann & crew lost.
III./KG 76 Ju88A5 7188 F1+BT
Failed to return. Fw G.Unger & crew lost.

13th March 1941

In the morning Bf109s from *II./JG 54* flew a sweep over east Kent and crossed out over Folkestone, where several were sighted and pursued by two 91 Squadron Spitfire pilots. Two Messerschmitts were claimed destroyed by Flight Lieutenant Holland and Sergeant Spears.

Circus No 7 was flown in the early afternoon, six Blenheims of 139 Squadron attacking Calais/Marck airfield under heavy fighter protection. Bf109s of *JG 51* were scrambled to intercept them and 64 Squadron was attacked near the target, where Squadron Leader Aenas Macdonell was shot down, baling out to become a prisoner.

The bombers attacked and withdrew towards Boulogne, where the escorts were engaged by fighters from *JG 51* and more from *I./LG 2*. 610 Squadron, part of the Top Cover Wing, fought off the main attack, 'probables' being claimed by Sergeants Horner and Warden. One Bf109 of *II./JG 51* crash-landed on the coast and a Spitfire was badly damaged. Further Messerschmitts bounced 611 Squadron, shooting down Sergeant Darling, who crash-landed at Dungeness. Spitfires were claimed by *Major* Mölders of the *Stab, Oberleutnant* Staiger of *III./JG 51* and by *Hauptmann* Ihlefeld, *Unteroffizier* Brandt and an unidentified pilot of *I./LG 2* during this encounter.

A little later, three Hurricanes of 302 Squadron patrolled over Worthing, finding a Ju88 of *4.(F)/121* at 11,000 feet. Pilot Officers Karwowski, Wroblewski and Sergeant Nowakiewicz attacked, chasing the bomber down to sea level and claiming it damaged before breaking off the action due to fuel shortage. However the radar 'blip' suddenly vanished in mid-Channel and the three pilots were subsequently credited with its destruction. '7A+LM' had indeed crashed into the Channel, carrying

Hermann Staiger of III./ JG 51. 63 victories. Ended the war flying Me262 jet fighters and died 22.6.1964.

Unteroffizier Egon Schmidt and his crew to their deaths. A second aircraft from this *Staffel* was encountered further to the west by Flight Lieutenant Rook and Sergeant Haywood of 504 Squadron on coastal patrol. The Hurricane pilots chased the Junkers back towards France, Rook claiming damage to it, but Haywood's aircraft was hit by return fire. The Junkers returned safely with the pilot, *Unteroffizier* Franz Jenscher, wounded. During the day, a Spitfire was claimed shot down by a bomber crew, southeast of Portsmouth. This would appear to have the action reported by 504 Squadron.

Bf109s flew a fighter sweep during the late afternoon, engaging a flight of 92 Squadron Spitfires near the English coast. Flight Lieutenant Wright wrote in his logbook:

"Rather hazy. Crossed seven 109s at 28,000 feet. They climbed away, but had a crack at one. Short plume of smoke only."

Allan Wright was credited with a 'damaged', while the Spitfire flown by Adjutant De Montbron. was damaged.

Coastal Command Beauforts flew shipping strikes, crews claiming to have torpedoed a destroyer off Jutland, a vessel sunk near the Frisian Islands and to have attacked shipping in Ymuiden harbour. Flying Officer Morton's 59 Squadron Blenheim was chased for thirty minutes by Bf109s, but escaped after the aircraft was hit several times.

Casualties 13th March 1941

Royal Air Force

12 Squadron Wellington W5353
Crashed landing at Binbrook. Sgt Wheeldon & crew safe.
18 Squadron Blenheim T2232
Crashed landing at Great Massingham. Sgt Owen & crew safe.
19 Squadron Spitfire P7890
Belly-landed at Duxford. P/O Pozluzny safe.
22 Squadron Beaufort L9798
Crash-landed. Sgt Pitman & crew safe.
59 Squadron Blenheim TR-H
Damaged by Bf109. P/O Morton & crew safe.
64 Squadron Spitfire P7555
Failed to return from sortie. S/L Macdonell DFC lost.
64 Squadron Spitfire P7291
Belly-landed at Rochford. P/O Roberts safe.
64 Squadron Spitfire P7645
Belly-landed near Faversham. P/O Campbell safe.
65 Squadron Spitfire YT-
Strafed on ground by Ju88.

Flt Lt X de Mont-bron of 92 Squadron. He was reported missing on 3rd July 1941 during a Circus operation.
- Brian Cull

72 Squadron Spitfire X4621
Overshot Acklington. P/O Fordham safe.
85 Squadron Havoc BJ500
Crashed at Wimbish after take-off. F/L Allard DFC & crew killed.
92 Squadron Spitfire QJ-
Damaged by Bf109. Adj De Montbron safe.
111 Squadron Hurricane P2886
Crashed force-landing near Fraserburgh. Sgt Bryson killed.
207 Squadron Manchester L7313
Crashed: no further details.
300 Squadron Wellington R1327
Force-landed at Charmy Down. W/C Makowski safe.
504 Squadron Hurricane V6812
Damaged by return fire from Ju88. Sgt Haywood safe.
603 Squadron Spitfire R7543
Crashed landing at Acklington. Sgt Neill safe.
610 Squadron Spitfire DW-
Shot down by Bf109: no further details.
611 Squadron Spitfire P7368
Damaged by Bf109s and crash-landed at Dungeness. Sgt Darling safe.
5 BGS Blenheim K7068
Missing. Sgt Sutherland & crew interned in Eire.
18 OTU
Two Wellingtons and a Magister bombed at Bramcote.

Luftwaffe

Stab I./JG 1 Bf109E1 6056
Crash-landed at Jever. Aircraft destroyed.
I./JG 1 Bf109E1 6257
Crashed at Loddenheide. Uffz R.Mohler killed. Aircraft destroyed.
II./JG 51 Bf109E 3770
Force-landed at Gravelines. Aircraft 60% damaged.
10./JG 51 Bf109E1 5677
Crash-landed at Charleville. Gfr W.Doegen injured. Aircraft 90% damaged.
E./JG 53 Bf109E4 1168
Crashed on take-off from St. Aubin, pilot unhurt. Aircraft 30% damaged.
III./KG 1 Ju88A5 3209
Bombed at Gevilliers. Aircraft 60% damaged.

I./KG 53 He111H5 3744
Collided with He111 on take-off from Wittmundhafen. Uffz Roth & crew unhurt. Aircraft 20% damaged.

I./KG 53 He111H5 3810
Collided with above on take-off from Wittmundhafen. Fw Radloff & crew unhurt. Aircraft 30% damaged.

II./KG 77 Ju88A5 4121
Crashed on take-off from Schipol. Aircraft 10% damaged.

IV./LG 1 Ju87B2 5704
Crash-landed at Vaernes. Aircraft 40% damaged.

I./LG 2 Bf109E4 5801
Crashed on take-off from Calais/Marck. Aircraft 25% damaged.

II./ZG 76 Bf110E1 3430
Crashed at Aalborg. Ogfr M.Liederwald & crew injured. Aircraft destroyed.

4.(F)/121 Ju88A5 0419 7A+LM
Failed to return. Uffz E.Schmidt & crew lost.

4.(F)/121 Ju88A5 0408
Damaged by fighters, one man wounded. Aircraft 15% damaged.

13/14th March 1941

Bomber Command Operations	
Hamburg 139	Rotterdam 14
Luftwaffe Operations	
Glasgow/Clydeside 236	
Liverpool 65	Hull 78

As the 5 Group force left, a Manchester of 207 Squadron sustained a burst tyre. This was soon changed and thus Flying Officer Matthews' bomber left Waddington late. It was caught near the base by *Feldwebel* Hahn of *I./NJG 2*, the Ju88 pilot shooting it down in flames at 22.00 hours and claiming 'A Hudson near Waddington'. There were no survivors.

Serious damage was again caused to Hamburg, but several aircraft were lost. A 110 Squadron Blenheim captained by Flight Lieutenant Dickinson DFC was intercepted and shot down over Tolbert at 22.48 hours by *Oberfeldwebel* Gildner of *3./NJG 1*. Paul Gildner achieved a 'double' twenty minutes later by destroying Sergeant Elder's 214 Squadron Wellington near Burlanger. Another Wellington, a 57 Squadron machine flown by Sergeant Harvey, was shot down near Cloppenburg at 00.54 hours by Leutnant Schmidt from *I./NJG 3*, this crew surviving to be taken prisoner. *Feldwebel* Rasper of *4./NJG 1* claimed another Wellington over the sea 10km northwest of Pettten at 03.20 hours, probably a 218 Squadron aircraft which was damaged under these circumstances. Additionally, two Whitleys failed to return; Sergeant Arkwright's 77 Squadron

Top: *The Avro Manchester acquired a fearsome reputation for being under-powered with unreliable engines. Had it been used to re-equip The Rolls-Royce engined Whitley squadrons of No.4 Group, perhaps the situation might have been different. Above left: Paul Gildner of II./NJG 1 was one of the most successful pilots during 1941. He was killed in action on 24.2.43 after his 44th victory. Above right: Gildner (right) inspects the wreckage of Dickinson's Blenheim at Tolbert.*

aircraft was lost at sea and the bomber flown by Sergeant Cook of 102 Squadron crashed near Ohlsdorf. The final loss was a 50 Squadron Hampden, ditched by Sergeant Grainger on the return flight. Two more 218 Squadron Wellingtons received *Flak* damage. One belly-landed with a mortally wounded radio operator while the other sustained two casualties. During the attacks, Flak gunners claimed four victories, two of tthem by gunners aboard naval vessels.

Many RAF fighters were scrambled to meet the heavy German attacks upon Britain and, for the first time, the AI-equipped Beaufighters began to show their true worth.

The first success was achieved by Pilot Officer Hodgkinson of 219 Squadron, who intercepted and shot down a *7./KG 55* Heinkel over Winchester at 20.40 hours. 'G1+MR' crashed at Wood Farm, Bramdean, Hampshire, after *Oberleutnant* Walter Hesse and one crewman had parachuted. Twenty minutes later Sergeant Hilken of 264 Squadron claimed an He111 damaged over the south coast. There was then a lull in fighter engagements until 21.45 hours, when Flying Officer Braham of 29 Squadron intercepted a Do17 'U5+DA' of *Stab./KG 2* off East Anglia. After problems with his armament, Braham decided to ram the bomber, but his observer managed to cure the fault in time for a final attack. With a huge flash *Feldwebel* Rucker's aircraft blew up, spattering the sea with wreckage. West of Liverpool, Pilot Officer Lewandowski of 307 Squadron engaged a Heinkel at 22.00 hours, firing two bursts from 50 yards and chasing it down to sea level. He claimed it probably destroyed after losing it low over the water.

To the north, Flight Lieutenant Denby of 600 Squadron engaged another He111 near Dundee at 22.25 hours. '6N+AH' of *1./K.Gr.100* was shot down at Drumshang Farm, Dunure, after *Oberleutnant* Schulz and his crew and baled out. At the same time Flight Lieutenant Sheen of 72 Squadron engaged a Ju88 off Amble, the Spitfire pilot shooting it down in flames in view of naval observers offshore. It was undoubtedly 'M2+JL' of *3./K.Fl.Gr.106*, flown by *Oberleutnant* Hildebrandt Voightlander-Tetzner. This aircraft was reported missing from a sortie to Glasgow.

219 Squadron was again successful at 22.35 hours, Sergeant Clandillon shooting down '1H+JR', a Heinkel from *III./KG 26*. This crashed on Smokehall Farm, Shipley, killing *Unteroffizier* Friedrich Hermann and his crew. 604 Squadron Beaufighters were also patrolling the south coast, Flying Officer Chisholm claiming an He111 shot down into the sea at 22.40 hours, while at this time Squadron Leader Little of 219 Squadron claimed

another off the Needles. He then damaged another in the same area. Thirty minutes later Wing Commander Charles Widdows of 29 Squadron found a Ju88 over Lincolnshire, the German aircraft breaking up under his fire and the wreckage falling on Smith's Farm, Dovendale, near Louth. When inspected, the aircraft proved to be 'R4+GM', a Ju88C fighter of *I./NJG 2*. Flown by *Gefreiter* Körner, who perished with his crew.

As midnight neared, Pilot Officer Wynne-Wilson of 255 Squadron claimed a Dornier damaged over Hull, possibly a *III./KG 3* machine. Then 604 Squadron struck again. Flight Lieutenant Lawton claimed a Ju88 destroyed off Portland, while Flying Officer Chisholm reported another He111 shot down in the same area. Two further combats occurred at unrecorded times. Flight Lieutenant Skinner of 604 Squadron damaging an He111 and Flying Officer Gilbert of 601 Squadron inconclusively engaging another near Farnborough while on a practice flight.

Besides the losses noted above, *Feldwebel* Herbert Liebs's *6./KG 27* Heinkel was reported missing, another of *Stab./KG 55* ditched in the Channel. Several more bombers crashed on return.

Fighter Command reported several aircraft casualties. One was a 600 Squadron Beaufighter flown by Group Captain Rogers, which disappeared into the sea off Prestwick. Kirton-in-Lindsay was attacked by an intruder. After making an unsuccessful pass on Squadron Leader Smith's 255 Squadron Defiant on final approach, the German aircraft strafed a 65 Squadron Spitfire. St. Eval was also strafed and several aircraft were hit.

To sum up, British fighters had claimed ten destroyed (nine by Beaufighters), two 'probables' and four damaged, while the Luftwaffe had actually lost seven aircraft missing plus six further casualties, two due to accidents.

Casualties 13/14th March 1941

Royal Air Force
10 Squadron Whitley T4157
Crashed landing at Bircham Newton. S/L Holford & crew safe.
25 Squadron Beaufighter R2255
Overshot Wittering. F/L Clayton & crew safe.

50 Squadron Hampden X3146
Failed to return. Sgt Grainger & crew lost.
57 Squadron Wellington T2970
Failed to return. Sgt Harvey & crew lost.
77 Squadron Whitley N1493
Failed to return. Sgt Arkwright & crew lost.
102 Squadron Whitley T4273
Failed to return. Sgt Cook & crew lost.
110 Squadron Blenheim R2278
Failed to return. F/L Dickinson DFC & crew lost.
207 Squadron Manchester L7319
Shot down by intruder near Waddington. P/O Matthews & crew killed.
214 Squadron Wellington N2646
Failed to return. Sgt Elder & crew lost.
218 Squadron Wellington R1183
Hit by Flak and belly-landed. One crewman wounded.
218 Squadron Wellington R1328
Damaged on operations. Two crewmen wounded.
218 Squadron Wellington R1448
Damaged by fighter. One crewman wounded.
247 Squadron Hurricane HP-
Crashed landing at St.Eval. P/O Waechter safe.
255 Squadron Defiant N1770
Overshot Dunholme Lodge. P/O Wright & crew safe
263 Squadron
Six Whirlwinds damaged in strafe of St.Eval.
600 Squadron Beaufighter R2158
Crashed into sea off Prestwick. G/C Rogers & crew lost.

Luftwaffe

I./NJG 2 Ju88C4 0604 R4+GM
Failed to return. Gfr H.Körner & crew lost.
Stab./KG 2 Do17Z2 4248 U5+DA
Failed to return. Fw B.Rucker & crew lost.
I./KG 2 Do17Z 4191 U5+JK
Crashed at Merville, Uffz Hanke and one crewman injured.
Aircraft 20% damaged.
III./KG 26 He111H5 3610 1H+JR
Failed to return. Uffz F.Hermann & crew lost.
II./KG 27 He111H3 3346 1G+AP
Failed to return. Fw H.Liebs & crew lost.
5./KG 30 Ju88A5 0204
Crashed at Molenschott, Ofw H.Koch & crew killed. Aircraft destroyed.
Stab./KG 55 He111P2 2854 G1+HA
Force-landed at Le Bourget after combat, one man killed, one wounded.
Aircraft destroyed.
II./KG 55 He111P4 3095 G1+JM
Force-landed at Cherbourg after combat, Lt E.Barth & two crew wounded, one
killed. Aircraft 90% damaged.
III./KG 55 He111P2 2806 G1+MR
Failed to return. Oblt W.Hesse & crew lost.
III./KG 55 He111P2 2815 G1+GS
Hit by enemy gunfire and landed at le Bourget, three men from Fw Schloms's
crew wounded. Aircraft 25% damaged.

K.Gr.100 He111H3 6865
Crashed at Vannes. Lt W.Kortenmeier & two crew killed, one injured.
Aircraft destroyed.
K.Gr.100 He111H3 3352 6N+AH
Failed to return. Oblt W.Schultz & crew lost.
3./K.Fl.Gr.106 Ju88A5 2234 M2+JL
Failed to return. Oblt H.Voigtlander-Tetzner & crew lost.

14th March 1941

There were several fighter engagements along the south coast. These begane at 08.00 hours when Squadron Leader Ellis, Pilot Officer Grey and Sergeant Warden of 610 Squadron found a bomber over over the Channel. They all attacked, claiming a Ju88 damaged. This is likely to have been a Heinkel of *I./KG 28* that subsequently crashed at Nantes. At 11.42 hours Flight Lieutenant Dawbarn and Sergeant Stehlik of 312 Squadron found and shot down a Ju88 near Bardsey Island. This was 'VB+KJ' of *2.(F)/O.b.d.L.*. There were no survivors from *Leutnant* Fritz Thoms' crew.

Finally, at 18.15 hours, Sergeant Marsh of 152 Squadron claimed a Ju88 damaged south of Portland. '4U+EL' of *1.(F)/123* crashed into the sea off Jersey with the loss of *Feldwebel* Karl-Heinz Jahnke and his crew and is likely to have been Marsh's opponent.

One British aircraft was lost when Pilot Officer Newton's 53 Squadron Blenheim crashed near Brest, shot down by *Oberleutnant* Höckner of *II./JG 77*, who claimed a 'Beaufort' destroyed at 15.32 hours.

Casualties 14th March 1941

Royal Air Force

1 Squadron Hurricane V7464
Crashed landing at Lindholme. Sgt Gill & crew safe.
41 Squadron Spitfire X4177
Overshot Catterick. P/O Ford safe.
53 Squadron Blenheim V5399
Failed to return from sortie. P/O Newton & crew lost.
110 Squadron Blenheim R3832
Crashed near Horsham-St-Faith. Sgt Leadbeater & crew believed safe.
118 Squadron Spitfire N3288
Belly-landed at Aston Down. Sgt Parker safe.
118 Squadron Spitfire R6910
Crashed landing at Filton. Sgt Jenkins safe.
218 Squadron Wellington W5644
Missing en route to Middle East.

253 Squadron Hurricane V7624
Crashed landing at Skeabrae. P/O Barton safe.
263 Squadron Whirlwind P6988
Crashed at Portreath. P/O Thornton-Brown injured.
308 Squadron Hurricane ZF-
Force-landed at Bramcote. F/O Wandzilak safe.
605 Squadron Hurricane Z2335
Crashed at Swaffley. Sgt Kestler killed.
609 Squadron Spitfire P7671
Overshot Biggin Hill. P/O Baraldi safe.
1 PRU Spitfire R7117
Overshot Odiham. P/O Flynn safe.
10 OTU Whitley -----
Missing off Wales. P/O Bridson & crew lost.

Luftwaffe

III./JG 2 Bf109F2 8131
Crashed at Dessau, Stfw H.Klee killed. Aircraft destroyed.
E./JG 3 Bf109E4 1357
Force-landed at Fontenet, pilot unhurt. Aircraft 20% damaged.
III./JG 51 Bf109F1 6632
Damaging taxiing at Hangelar, pilot unhurt. Aircraft 30% damaged.
3./JG 52 Bf109E3 1265
Crash-landed at Vlissingen. Aircraft 25% damaged.
II./JG 54 Bf109E4 5006
Crash-landed at Cherbourg. Aircraft 40% damaged.
I./NJG 3 Bf110C4 ----
Crashed on take-off from Vechta. Aircraft 20% damaged.
I./KG 3 Ju88A5 3302
Crash-landed at Wunstorf, crew unhurt. Aircraft 40% damaged.
I./KG 3 Ju88A5 3308
Crash-landed at Wunstorf, crew unhurt. Aircraft 75% damaged.
I./KG 28 He111H5 3802
Force-landed at Nantes on combat sortie. Aircraft 80% damaged.
III./KG 51 Ju88A5 7119 9K+BS
Crash-landed at Maltragny, Oblt F.Scherer and two crew injured, one killed.
Aircraft 60% damaged.
E./KG 51 Ju88 ----
Crash-landed at Lechfeld,, Oblt W.Willisch and one crewman injured.
Aircraft 95% damaged.
3./KG 53 He111H4 6980
Belly-landed on Texel on combat sortie. Aircraft 30% damaged.
I./KG 77 Ju88A5 8146
Collided on take-off from Schipol. Aircraft 50% damaged.
III./KG 77 Ju88A5 2132
Collided on take-off from Schipol. Aircraft 70% damaged.
K.Gr.806 Ju88A5 2259
Crashed on take-off from Caen. Aircraft 10% damaged.
III./St.G.77 Ju87B1 5306
Force-landed at Etampes-Mondesir. Aircraft 40% damaged.
E./ZG 26 Bf110C1 1357
Collided with Bf110 30km south of Ingolstadt. Lt K.Dahinten and gunner killed.
Aircraft destroyed.

E./ZG 26 Bf110C2 3232
Collided with Bf110 30km south of Ingolstadt. Lt U.Ensslen and gunner killed.
Aircraft destroyed.
2.(F)/O.b.d.L. Ju88A5 382 VB+KJ
Failed to return from sortie. Lt F.Thoms & crew lost.
3.(F)/123 Ju88A5 559
Crashed in sea near Jersey after combat. Fw K-H.Jahnke & crew believed safe.
Aircraft destroyed.
5.(H)/12 Hs126B1 4081
Force-landed at Darmstadt-Griesheim, crew unhurt. Aircraft 50% damaged.
SNF.Kdo.1. Do24 10
Crashed at Brest. Aircraft destroyed.

14/15th March 1941

Bomber Command Operations	
Gelsenkirchen 101	Düsseldorf 24
Rotterdam 12	
Luftwaffe Operations	
Glasgow/Clydeside 203	Sheffield 117
Plymouth 11	

Much damage was caused at the Hydriewerk Scholven synthetic oil plant at Gelsenkirchen, while fires were started at Rotterdam. Just one aircraft failed to return when Sergeant Rogers' 149 Squadron Wellington was intercepted and shot down over Panningen at 22.34 hours by *Hauptmann* Streib of *I./NJG 1*. Two more bombers were intercepted, but both escaped; Flying Officer Elliott's 150 Squadron Wellington was engaged by a Bf110 and was damaged, but the rear gunner scored hits upon the fighter. This may have been Hauptmann Streib, whose fighter was damaged in combat and landed with the *Bordfunker* wounded. Squadron Leader Burt's 82 Squadron gunner inconclusively exchanged fire with a Ju88 near Eindhoven.

Meanwhile, Squadron Leader Gracie of 23 Squadron, intruding

Werner Streib, the 'Father of the Luftwaffe night fighters', achieved 68 victories and survived the war. He died on 15.6.1986.

239

over Merville, claimed a Do17 probably destroyed. A Do17 of *2./KG 2* and a Bf110 of *2./E.Gr.210* crash-landed at this airfield, one possibly due to Gracie's attack.

RAF fighter interceptions began at 21.40 hours when Flying Officer Geddes of 604 Squadron caught *Oberleutnant* Eckhard Henschke's *6./KG 55* Heinkel en route for Glasgow; 'G1+IP' spun into the ground at Brinkmarsh Farm, Falfield, Somerset, killing the crew. Ten minutes later Flight Lieutenant Topham of 219 Squadron engaged an incoming bomber south of Beachy Head and shot it down into the sea. This would appear to have been 'M7+EH', a Ju88 of *1./K.Gr.806* flown by *Feldwebel* Siegfried Helbig, which was reported missing.

The final interception was by Flight Lieutenant Gibson of 29 Squadron.[1] This Beaufighter pilot obtained a 'visual' on a Heinkel off the east coast and, after cannon problems, chased the bomber down to sea level. At 22.00 hours he watched it crash into the sea off Skegness pier after one man had parachuted. It was *Leutnant* Georg Stugg's 'V4+HK' of *2./KG 1* and when Gibson visited the wreckage next morning to obtain a mess trophy, he was told that all the crew had perished.

AA sites claimed three bombers shot down and, besides those losses narrated above, two *KG 55* Heinkels failed to return; *Unteroffizier* Claus Bauer's 'G1+BA' of the *Geschwaderstab* and 'G1+ER' flown by *Leutnant* Wilhelm Rauchle from *6 Staffel*. Several further aircraft suffered damage.

Intruders of *I./NJG 2* were over East Anglia, where a Coastal Command Wellington from 221 Squadron was attacked by a Do17. Pilot Officer Rae's rear gunner returned fire and the bomber escaped undamaged.

St. Eval was again raided. A Harrow transport was blown up and a Hurricane damaged.

Casualties 14/15th March 1941

Royal Air Force

10 Squadron Whitley P4956
Hit by Flak and belly-landed at Bircham Newton, Sgt Watson & crew safe.
149 Squadron Wellington L7858
Failed to return from sortie. Sgt Rogers & crew lost.

---

1. Guy Penrose Gibson, on attachment from Bomber Command, was later to lead the famous 'Dams Raid' in 1943, for which he was awarded the Victoria Cross.

150 Squadron Wellington T2967
Damaged by Bf110 and crash-landed. F/O Elliott & crew safe.
247 Squadron Hurricane HP-
Strafed at St.Eval.
271 Squadron Harrow K6951
Destroyed in raid on St.Eval.

Luftwaffe

I./NJG 1 Bf110 ----
Hit by return fire and force-landed at Eindhoven, Hptm W.Streib unhurt, gunner wounded. Aircraft 50% damaged.
I./KG 1 He111H3 5683 V4+HK
Failed to return from sortie. Lt G.Stugg & crew lost.
2./KG 2 Do17Z1 3310
Crash-landed at Merville. Aircraft 35% damaged.
III./KG 2 Do17Z3 4243
Crash-landed at Cambrai, one man wounded. Aircraft 40% damaged.
I./KG 30 Ju88A5 214
Damaged by fighter and landed at Eindhoven with Fw M.Borchard and two crewmen wounded, one killed. Aircraft 90% damaged.
I./KG 30 Ju88A5 ----
Damaged in combat and force-landed at Gilze-Rijn, one wounded. Aircraft 20% damaged.
III./KG 51 Ju88A1 2272
Force-landed near Le Havre. One man injured. Aircraft 40% damaged.
4./KG 53 He111H3 5613
Belly-landed at Vendeville. Aircraft 65% damaged.
Stab./KG 55 He111P2 2838 G1+BA
Failed to return from sortie. Uffz C.Bauer & crew lost.
I./KG 55 He111P4 3096 G1+JP
Failed to return from sortie. Oblt E Henschke & crew lost.
III./KG 55 He111P2 2795 G1+KR
Failed to return from sortie. Lt W.Rauchle & crew lost.
K.Gr.806 Ju88A5 8200 M7+EH
Failed to return from sortie. Fw S.Helbig & crew lost.
2./E.Gr.210 Bf110E1 3455
Crash-landed at Merville. Aircraft 10% damaged.

15th March 1941

Despite several sweeps over East Kent by German fighters, the sole engagement came off the coast during a convoy patrol by three Hurricanes of 615 Squadron. At 16.20 hours five Bf109s from *II./LG 2* came in at wave-top height to attack the ships. Pilot Officer Timewell fired on one without effect, but Adjutant Lafont, attacking another, saw strikes and last saw it heading for France trailing smoke. Lafont was credited with shooting it down and indeed the fighter-bomber subsequently crashed into the Channel, killing *Oberfeldwebel* Seidel.

Henri Lafont of 615 Squadron made his only claim on 15th March 1941.

- B. Cull

During the day P/O Leedham's 53 Squadron Blenheim crew was reported missing.

Casualties 15th March 1941

Royal Air Force

53 Squadron Blenheim T2132
Failed to return from sortie. P/O Leedham & crew lost.

56 Squadron Hurricane Z2593
Force-landed on Uxbridge Common. Sgt Hoyle safe.

79 Squadron Hurricane P3771
Overshot Pembrey. P/O Haigh safe.

111 Squadron Hurricane P3701
Crashed landing at Montrose. W/O Blaize safe.

145 Squadron Spitfire P7603
Force-landed at Shoreham. Sgt Weber safe.

210 Squadron Sunderland P9624
Crashed landing at Oban. Four men from F/O Butcher's crew killed.

220 Squadron Hudson N7261
Swung landing at St.Eval. F/O Simpson safe.

255 Squadron Defiant N1765
Crashed landing at Kirton-in-Lindsay. Sgt Theisler & crew safe.

269 Squadron Hudson P5121
Crashed on take-off from Wick. Sgt Cheatley & crew believed safe.

308 Squadron Hurricane V6858
Crashed landing at Baginton. P/O Wielgus safe.

Luftwaffe

E./JG 3 Bf109E1 4877
Belly-landed at Frévent. Aircraft 85% damaged.

E./JG 3 Bf109E7 4804
Crash-landed at Fontenet. Aircraft 45% damaged.

E./JG 27 Bf109E1 2954
Crashed at Parndorf. Aircraft 40% damaged.

III./JG 51 Bf109E4 3748
Crash-landed at St.Omer. Aircraft 10% damaged.

III./JG 51 Bf109F1 6639
Damaged taxiing at Sandhofen. Aircraft 75% damaged.
III./JG 51 Bf109F1 6635
Crashed on take-off from Sandhofen. Aircraft 80% damaged.
E./JG 51 Bf109E1 4025
Force-landed at Lavies. Aircraft 15% damaged.
E./JG 51 Bf109E1 3908
Force-landed at Mouelle. Aircraft 80% damaged.
E./JG 51 Bf109E7 3656
Crashed on take-off from Abbeville. Aircraft 25% damaged.
E./JG 53 Bf109E1 1596
Belly-landed at St.Aubin. Aircraft 70% damaged.
III./JG 54 Bf109E7 0697
Damaged taxiing at Le Mans. Aircraft 65% damaged.
I./KG 2 Do17Z 3300
Hit by AA fire and crash-landed at Merville, three crew wounded.
Aircraft 25% damaged
IV./KG 2 Do17Z2 1127
Crashed at Rodach, Lt H.Geider & crew killed. Aircraft destroyed.
I./KG 51 Ju88A5 0206
Tyre damage at Villaroche. Aircraft destroyed.
II./KG 53 He111H3 3301
Crash-landed at Celle. Aircraft 35% damaged.
5./LG 2 Bf109E7 3725 Black L
Shot down in combat, Ofw A.Seidel killed. Aircraft lost.
I./NJG 2 Ju88C4 0630
Crash-landed at Gütersloh. Aircraft 30% damaged.
E./St.G.1 Ju87R1 5387
Force-landed at Würzburg, crew unhurt. Aircraft 30% damaged.
I./St.G.77 Ju87B1 5108
Force-landed at Cherbourg. Aircraft 90% damaged.
3.(H)/21 Hs126 3466
Crashed at Jambol. Lt H.Schulte & crew killed. Aircraft destroyed.
E.St.Rechlin Bf109E7 5183
Crash-landed at Berlin-Schönefeld. Aircraft 40% damaged.

15/16th March 1941

Bomber Command Operations
Lorient 37 Düssseldorf 31 Vannes 5
Luftwaffe Operations
London 93 Southampton 9

There were no casualties from the RAF bombing raids. For the first time Hurricanes from 87 Squadron took part in night intruder operations, Flying Officers Beamont and Ward refuelling at Warmwell before heading for the Caen airfield complex at 01.30 hours. Beamont strafed a searchlight post on the Normandy coast before finding an airfield, where he claimed a bomber destroyed on the ground. He fired the last of his ammunition into a train on the return flight. One He111 of

II./KG 55 sustained damage at Avord, possibly during this attack.

London and the Home Counties were the main targets for the Luftwaffe. At 22.00 hours Wing Commander Pike of 219 Squadron engaged an He111 south of Bognor Regis, which he claimed to have shot down into the sea. This would appear to have been '1G+DL' of *I./KG 27* flown by *Leutnant* Ekkehart von Hoslin, which was reported missing. The only other combat took place at 00.05 hours, Flying Officer Verity of 96 Squadron attacking a Ju88 east of Wrexham. The Defiant crew claimed this probably destroyed. One Ju88 of *II./KG 1* crash-landed on return at Rosieres, possibly as a result of this fight.

AA gunners claimed two bombers damaged, one Heinkel of *I./KG 1* belly-landing on return.

Casualties 15/16th March 1941

Royal Air Force

1 Squadron Hurricane V9379
Crashed landing at Kenley. Sgt Rex safe.

Luftwaffe

I./KG 1 He111H3 6877
Belly-landed at Amiens. Aircraft 60% damaged.
II./KG 1 Ju88A5 4189 V4+BN
Landed at Rosieres. Aircraft 25% damaged.
III./KG 26 He111H4 3627
Damaged by fighter and crashed at Le Bourget with one crewman wounded. Aircraft 50% damaged.
I./KG 27 He111H3 3301
Failed to return from sortie. Lt E von Hoslin & crew lost.
II./KG 55 He111H4 3068
Tyre damage at Chartes. Aircraft 30% damaged.
II./KG 55 He111P4 3091
Damaged at Avord, cause not notified. Aircraft 40% damaged.
K.Gr.100 He111 ----
Crashed at Dijon. Ofw Reinhold Wiessner and one crewman killed, two injured. Aircraft destroyed.

Chapter Eight

The Storms of March

16th March 1941

There was no air activity of any note during the daylight hours.

Casualties 16th March 1941

Royal Air Force

46 Squadron Hurricane V7604
Crashed landing at Church Fenton. P/O Curtis safe.
61 Squadron Hampden AD754
Crashed landing at Kinloss. F/O Stewart & crew safe.
152 Squadron Spitfire P8024
Overshot Warmwell. Sgt Fawcett safe.
220 Squadron Hudson N7281
Undershot Portreath. P/O Milton & crew safe.
224 Squadron Hudson N7369
Overshot Aldergrove. P/O Drummond & crew safe.
320 Squadron Hudson T9279
Overshot Pembrey. F/L Dolman & crew safe.

Luftwaffe

III./JG 2 Bf109E4 1318
Crashed on take-off from Le Havre. Pilot safe. Aircraft 35% damaged.
E./JG 27 Bf109E1 3888
Belly-landed at Parndorf. Arcraft 40% damaged.
Stab./JG 54 Bf109E4 5909
Belly-landed near le Mans. Pilot safe. Aircraft 70% damaged.
E./KG 4 He111H4 3282
Crash-landed at Branderup. Aircraft 25% damaged.
I./KG 27 He111H5 3967
Undercarriage damage at Tours. Crew safe. Aircraft 30% damaged.
I./KG 51 Ju88A5 8086
Undercarriage damage at Villaroche. Crew safe. Aircraft 35% damaged.

16/17th March 1941

The RAF was placed on 'stand down', but isolated German bombers were reported over the British Isles. At 21.50 hours an He111 was attacked and claimed damaged over Studland Bay by Flying Officer Geddes of 604 Squadron. A Ju88 of 2./*KG 51* failed to return. This aircraft, '9K+AK' flown by *Leutnant* Egon

245

An He115B1 floatplane, as used by many of the Küstenfliegergruppen. One such aircraft was lost without trace on 17th March.

- via Simon Parry

Ars, attempted a low level attack upon RAF Chilmark, but was hit by AA fire. The pilot sent the message 'Landing in England!' then ordered his crew to bale out. Three were captured at once. The fourth remained at large for two days before being apprehended at Barford St. Martin.

Four further German bombers crashed, one possibly due to AA batteries at Holton Heath, where gunners claimed a 'probable'.

Casualties 16/17th March 1941

Royal Air Force

604 Squadron Beaufighter R2190
Damaged landing at Boscombe Down. F/O Geddes & crew safe.
604 Squadron Beaufighter R2243
Overshot Charmy Down. Sgt Wright & crew safe.

Luftwaffe

I./KG 51 Ju88A5 8124 9K+AK
Failed to return. Lt E Ars & crew lost.
II./KG 76 Ju88A5 0542
Crashed at Chateaudun. Uffz W Bartels & crew injured. Aircraft 90% damaged.
II./KG 76 Ju88A5 5146
Tyre damage at Chateaudun. Crew safe. Aircraft 30% damaged.
II./KG 76 Ju88A5 0241
Crashed 8km west of Courtelain, near Le Havre. Fw K-H Richter & crew killed. Aircraft destroyed.
II./KG 76 Ju88A5 2213
Crashed near Chartres. Two crew injured. Aircraft destroyed.

17th March 1941

One RAF fighter engaged a German bomber when Flight Lieutenant Walker of 111 Squadron intercepted and claimed to have damaged an He111 east of Scotland at 15.15 hours. A second combat took place when Sergeant Blake's 269 Squadron Hudson fought a Bf110 over the North Sea. The British pilot was mortally wounded, but managed to fly the bomber home before succumbing to his wounds. A Bf110 from *II./ZG 76* flown by *Leutnant* Josef Steininger was lost in the sea, possibly as a result of this action. A second aircraft was lost when *Unteroffizier* G.Wittulski's He115 of *2./K.Fl.Gr.506* was reported missing.

Casualties 17th March 1941

Royal Air Force

10 Squadron Whitley Z6478
Overshot Dishforth. Sgt Sturmey & crew safe.
86 Squadron Blenheim V5464
Collided. Fate of P/O Mace's crew not known.
86 Squadron Blenheim Z8808
Collided. Fate of P/O Cresswell's crew not known.
149 Squadron Wellington T2899
Crashed landing at Mildenhall. Sgt Burch & crew safe.
269 Squadron Hudson -----
Damaged by Bf110. Sgt Blake died of wounds.
300 Squadron Wellington T2608
Damaged landing at Winthorpe. P/O Kurowski & crew safe.
611 Squadron Spitfire P7886
Crashed landing at Hornchurch. Sgt Gilmour safe.

Luftwaffe

E./JG 52 Bf109E1 3199
Crash-landed at Döberitz. Aircraft 35% damaged.
III./JG53 Bf109F2 6696
Crashed on take-off from Sandhofen. Lt E.Klager unhurt. Aircraft 90% damaged.
E./JG 53 Bf109E4 1237 Black 15
Force-landed at Fontenet, Uffz A.Seidl unhurt. Aircraft 75% damaged.
II./KG 1 Ju88A5 6255
Crashed 15km west-northwest of Cherbourg, fuel shortage. Fw H.Haben & crew killed. Aircraft destroyed.
I./KG 51 Ju88A5 7134
Crashed at Villaroche. Uffz K.Lindemaier & crew killed.
Aircraft destroyed.
Stab./KG 55 He111P2 1529
Crashed at Villacoublay. Crew safe. Aircraft 40% damaged.
I./KG 55 He111P4 3102
Crash-landed at Le Bourget. Crew safe. Aircraft 30% damaged.
II./KG 55 He111P4 2954
Crashed at Avord. Two of Uffz H Zeigler's crew killed. Aircraft destroyed.

I./KG 76 Ju88A5 6259
Taxiing accident at Chateaudun. Aircraft 30% damaged.
II./ZG 76 Bf110 3439 M8+CN
Crashed in sea at PQ 8713. Lt J Steininger & crew lost.
2./K.Fl.Gr.506 He115 3267 S4+FK
Failed to return. Uffz G.Wittulski & crew lost.
SNF.Kdo.1. Bre 521 0034
Shot down by own Flak at Royan. One man wounded. Aircraft destroyed.

17/18th March 1941

Bomber Command sent 57 aircraft out to attack Bremen and Wilhelmshaven, three more raiding Rotterdam. All the aircraft returned, although two crews reported engagements with fighters. The gunner from Sergeant Hobday's 82 Squadron Blenheim crew claimed a Bf110 destroyed near Emden, while a second Messerschmitt was claimed destroyed by a Hampden crew near the Dutch/German frontier. Flak batteries claimed a Wellington shot down at Winsen.

Over East Anglia intruders from *I./NJG 2* patrolled until dawn. At 06.53 hours *Feldwebel* Peter Laufs of *1 Staffel* attacked a 221 Squadron Wellington off Cromer, claiming it destroyed. Pilot Officer Robinson actually returned to Langham, his aircraft badly shot-up. Twenty minutes later *Leutnant* Pfeiffer found a 149 Squadron Wellington on final approach to Mildenhall and shot it down in flames at Beck Row, Suffolk. Sergeant Warren and his crew were killed.

Casualties 17/18th March 1941

Royal Air Force
21 Squadron Blenheim R3636
Crashed and exploded on take-off. S/L Allen & crew killed.
75 Squadron Wellington T2835
Crashed landing at Feltwell. P/O Andrews & crew safe.
149 Squadron Wellington R1474
Shot down at Beck Row by intruder. Sgt Warren & crew killed.
221 Squadron Wellington X3161
Damaged by intruder. P/O Robinson & crew safe.
311 Squadron Wellington R1378
Belly-landed at East Wretham with battle damage. Sgt Anderle & crew safe.

Luftwaffe

- nil -

Pilot Officer Bernard Klee of 222 Squadron in his Spitfire 'Zanzibar III'
- A.Long

18th March 1941

The first contact with German aircraft occurred in the late morning. Six Hurricanes of 17 Squadron flew from Croydon to practice flying from Ford and Shoreham when five aircraft were sighted near Bexhill. These aircraft were first taken to be Spitfires but were actually Bf109s from *I./JG 51* engaged on a fighter sweep. As the strangers flew inland, the Hurricane pilots turned to investigate, but were at once bounced by the *Gruppenstab. Hauptmann* Joppien and *Oberleutnant* Busch each selected a Hurricane and opened fire and both were shot down. Sergeants Hughes and Bartlett baled out wounded, having not seen attackers. Shortly after this, three 74 Squadron Spitfires engaged Messerschmitts of *6./JG 51* southwest of Folkestone, where a '109 was claimed destroyed by Pilot Officer Churches. *Unteroffizier* Georg Seidel crash-landed at Wizernes with slight damage.

In the afternoon Flight Lieutenant Van Mentz and Pilot Officer Klee patrolled off East Anglia and intercepted 'F6+KK', a reconnaissance Bf110 from *3.(F)/122*, which was attacked and shot down. *Oberleutnant* Albert Frexer ditched his aircraft safely but, although the crew were seen swimming away, they were not found by the rescue services.

Coastal Command aircraft operated off Holland and the Frisian Islands, where two ships were claimed sunk. Pilot Officer Siddall of 59 Squadron found a surfaced *U-boat*, but as he dived to attack it, his Blenheim was bounced by an escorting Bf110 and was badly damaged.

Casualties 18th March 1941

Royal Air Force

17 Squadron Hurricane Z2704
Shot down by Bf109. Sgt Bartlett baled out wounded.
17 Squadron Hurricane Z2670
Shot down by Bf109. Sgt Hughes baled out wounded.
59 Squadron Blenheim TR-T
Damaged beyond repair by Bf110. P/O Siddall & crew safe.
107 Squadron Blenheim L4885
Undershot Crail. Sgt Wolstenholme & crew safe.
213 Squadron Hurricane R4109
Collided near Castletown. Fate of pilot not known.
213 Squadron Hurricane V6697
Collided near Castletown. Fate of pilot not known.
257 Squadron Hurricane V6952
Crashed near Cromer. Sgt Garner safe.
312 Squadron Hurricane V7028
Force-landed at Dolgarrog. F/O Cermank safe.
1 PRU Spitfire R7070
Crashed landing at Benson. F/O Carthew safe.
3 PRU Wellington T2709
Crashed at Medley Manor, Oxfordshire. Sgt Jones & crew safe.

Luftwaffe

III./JG 2 Go145A1 2850
Crashed at Fontaine-le-Dun, Uffz H-J Knorn killed. Aircraft destroyed.
6./JG 51 Bf109E7 6465
Damaged in combat and landed at Wissant. Uffz G.Seidel unhurt.
Aircraft 10% damaged.
6./JG 52 Bf109E 5038
Force-landed at Maldeghem. Pilot safe. Aircraft 25% damaged.
E./JG 52 Bf109E1 6376
Collided with Bf109 2km south of Döberitz. Ofhr E.Rennert killed.
Aircraft destroyed.
E./JG 52 Bf109E1 4897
Collided with Bf109 2km south of Döberitz, pilot baled out unhurt.
Aircraft destroyed.
II./KG 1 Ju88A5 3316
Crashed on take-off from Rosieres. Crew safe. Aircraft 30% damaged.

I./KG 40 FW200C3 0041
Crashed 50km south of Brest. Lt H Winkler and four men killed, one injured.
Aircraft destroyed.
3.(F)/122 Bf110C5 2179 F6+KK
Failed to return. Oblt A Frexer & crew lost.

18/19th March 1941

Bomber Command Operations
Wilhelmshaven 44 Kiel 99
Rotterdam 19
Luftwaffe Operations
Hull 378 London 36 Southampton 26

One Blenheim failed to return from the night's operations. Pilot Officer Brown's 101 Squadron machine fell to Flak at Wilhelmshaven. A Wellington was abandoned over England, and Sergeant Watson ordered his 10 Squadron crew to do likewise before attempting to force-land at Masham, but he was killed when the Whitley crashed.

378 German bombers struck at Hull. There were no defensive fighter claims and all aircraft returned, although several crashed.

Casualties 18/19th March 1941

Royal Air Force
10 Squadron Whitley T4202
Abandoned at Masham, Yorks. Sgt Watson killed force-landing.
18 Squadron Blenheim Z5802
Overshot Great Massingham. Sgt Mounser & crew safe.
21 Squadron Blenheim R3675
Crash-landed near Manston. P/O Rogers & crew safe.
21 Squadron Blenheim R3761
Crash-landed near Manston. P/O Ogilvie & crew safe.

A burnt-out Ju88 in Holland, probably a KG 30 aircraft, on Gilze-Rijn airfield.
- G J Zwanenberg

59 Squadron Blenheim V5533
Crashed landing at Marham. P/O Munro & crew safe.
75 Squadron Wellington T2763
Hit by Flak and Abandoned near Ryhill. One man from F/O Collins' crew killed.
101 Squadron Blenheim R3846
Failed to return. P/O Brown DFC & crew lost.
218 Squadron Wellington R1387
Missing en route to Middle East. Sgt Arnold & crew lost.
300 Squadron Wellington L7789
Belly-landed at Swinderby. P/O Kula & crew safe.

Luftwaffe

I./KG 1 He111H3 5622
Crashed at Amiens. Uffz H Onken & crew killed. Aircraft destroyed.
II./KG 54 Ju88A5 8183
Force-landed at Evreux. Lt H Mohr & one man killed, two injured.
Aircraft destroyed.
II./KG 55 He111P2 1459
Abandoned on fire over Amiens. Crew safe. Aircraft destroyed.
I./KG 77 Ju88A5 4266
Crash-landed at Juvincourt. Crew safe. Aircraft 10% damaged.
I./KG 77 Ju88A5 8209
Undercarriage damaged at Juvincourt. Crew safe. Aircraft 15% damaged.
K.Gr.100 He111H3 3174
Hit by AA and belly-landed at Vannes. Crew safe. Aircraft 40% damaged.

19th March 1941

The clearer weather continued, bringing considerable German air activity in the Channel area. These were mostly sweeps and defensive patrols by fighters. A few reconnaissance aircraft were reported around the coastline, but no bombs fell. It was against one of the latter aircraft that the first combat occurred. Squadron Leader Bob Tuck of 257 Squadron took off for a solo patrol and was vectored towards a Do17, which he intercepted over Cromer Knoll at 08.25 hours. He attacked, claiming to have shot it down into the sea. No Dornier was actually lost, but a machine of *7./KG 2* crash-landed at Cambrai after a combat sortie while *Unteroffizier* Hilden's *E.Gr.210* Bf110 crashed near Hazebrouck, killing the crew.

No German fighters were encountered until the afternoon, when several British fighter units engaged in combats off the south coast.

Red Section of 609 Squadron was away at 13.15 hours on a convoy patrol and were bounced by Bf109s from an unidentified unit over the Channel. After a burst of gunfire that damaged

Pilot Officer Ogilvie's Spitfire, the Messerschmitts dived away and could not be caught.

Later in the afternoon, at around 16.25 hours, 610 Squadron patrolled over the Channel and were attacked at 18,000 feet by four Bf109s from *II./JG 53*. Sergeant Hale was engaged by *Hauptmann* Bretnütz and crash-landed wounded at Hailsham, his Spitfire badly shot-up by cannon fire. One Messerschmitt was claimed destroyed by Sergeant Payne.

Approximately an hour later, three 1 Squadron Hurricane pilots, patrolling south of Dungeness at 4,500 feet, were also attacked. Two Bf109s from *I./LG 2* dived on them from the eye of the sun, taking them completely by surprise. *Hauptmann* Herbert Ihlefeld shot down two Hurri-

Herbert Ihlefeld again demonstrated his shooting ability when, on 19th March, he shot down two 1 Squadron Hurricanes.

canes in quick succession. Sergeant Stefan crash-landed, his aircraft becoming a 'write-off', while Pilot Officer Kershaw baled out of his blazing aircraft too low and was killed when his parachute failed to deploy. At that moment three Spitfires of 609 Squadron appeared and at once dived to support the lone British survivor. Pilot Officer Ogilvie, airborne again after his disagreeable experience a little earlier, claimed hits on a Bf109 that headed for France emitting white smoke from its exhausts. In these actions no Bf109 sustained combat damage. One of *4./JG 51* belly-landed at Mardyck, cause not known.

The final engagement took place in the north, where a Ju88 was seen and attacked by Wing Commander Richardson and Squadron Leader Maclean of 111 Squadron while on a training flight near Collieston. The two pilots fired almost 1,000 rounds, but claimed no hits. Two Ju88s of *I./KG 30* crash-landed at

Gilze-Rijn after combat sorties. Possibly one was involved in this brief clash.

Casualties 19th March 1941

Royal Air Force

1 Squadron Hurricane Z2810
Shot down by Bf109. Sgt Stefan safe.

1 Squadron Hurricane Z2759
Shot down by Bf109. P/O Kershaw killed.

54 Squadron Spitfire P7980
Belly-landed near Hornchurch. Sgt Woodhouse safe.

92 Squadron Spitfire X4257
Crash-landed near Maidstone. S/L Rankin safe.

92 Squadron Spitfire R6897
Crash-landed. Sgt Le Cheminant safe,

92 Squadron Spitfire R6776
Crash-landed. Adj De Montbron safe.

206 Squadron Hudson N7293
Crashed landing at Langham satellite. F/O Tanner & crew safe.

213 Squadron Hurricane V7664
Crashed landing at Castletown, P/O Schou killed.

220 Squadron Hudson N7310
Crashed into Hoy Island. Sgt Harris & crew killed.

226 Squadron Blenheim L1197
Crashed landing at Sydenham. W/C Harrison & crew safe.

252 Squadron Blenheim V5741
Damaged at Halton. Sgt Brunwell & crew safe.

305 Squadron Wellington R1214
Taxy accident Syerston. P/O Nogal & crew safe.

306 Squadron Hurricane V6950
Taxy accident Ternhill. Sgt Kosmowski safe.

604 Squadron Beaufighter R2056
Damaged landing Boscombe Down.. S/L Anderson & crew safe.

609 Squadron Spitfire P7830
Damaged by Bf109. P/O Ogilvie safe.

610 Squadron Spitfire -----
Damaged by Bf109, force-landed. Sgt Hale safe.

Luftwaffe

E./JG 3 Bf109E1 6250
Force-landed at Burie. Aircraft destroyed.

4./JG 51 Bf109E7 4213
Belly-landed at Mardyck, pilot unhurt. Aircraft 10% damaged.

E./JG 51 Bf109E 5606
Crashed at Abbeville. Gfr Pirschmann killed. Aircraft 95% damaged.

III./JG 53 Bf109F2 ----
Crashed on take-off from Berck-sur-Mer, Uffz F.Zerr injured.
Aircraft 30% damaged.

I./KG 1 He111H3 5553
Crashed at Montdidier. Fw K Lörwald & crew killed. Aircraft destroyed.

*A KG 30 Ju88
comes to grief
at Gilze-Rijn.
The crew
appear to
have emerged
unscathed.
- E.Böttner*

7./KG 2 Do17Z2 1191
Crash-landed at Cambrai, crew unhurt. Aircraft 25% damaged.
III./KG 4 He111H4 5711
Crashed on take-off from Leeuwarden. Three men from Oblt H.Nottelmann's
crew injured. Aircraft 85% damaged.
4./KG 30 Ju88A5 4215
Crash-landed at Gilze-Rijn, crew unhurt. Aircraft 70% damaged.
4./KG 30 Ju88A5 3319
Crash-landed at Gilze-Rijn, crew unhurt. Aircraft 15% damaged.
II./KG 51 Ju88A5 7201
Belly-landed at Bretigny, crew unhurt. Aircraft 75% damaged.
II./KG 51 Ju88A5 7201
Belly-landed at Bretigny. Aircraft 75% damaged.
III./KG 76 Ju88A5 4231
Crashed on take-off from Illesheim. Aircraft destroyed.
K.Gr.806 Ju88A5 2281
Undercarriage damaged at Caen, crew unhurt. Aircraft 10% damaged.
K.Gr.806 Ju88A5 2249
Belly-landed at Caen, crew unhurt. Aircraft 20% damaged.
E.Gr.210 Bf110E1 3463
Crashed at Roanne. Aircraft destroyed.
E.Gr.210 Bf110E1 3825
Crashed at Hazebrouck, Uffz Hilden & crew killed. Aircraft destroyed.
E.Gr.210 Bf110E1 3843
Force-landed at Nieder Hardenburg, one crewman injured.
Aircraft 35% damaged.
E./ZG 26 Bf110C4 3062
Crash-landed at Ingolstadt. Aircraft 15% damaged.

19/20th March 1941

Bomber Command attacked Köln with 36 aircraft, two more
going to Rotterdam. All the bombers returned from the above
operations, although one of 311 Squadron crashed on take-off
and a second of 149 Squadron crashed on return. Two Bf110s of
NJG 1 crashed, one due to combat.

Howard Peter Blatchford, from Canada, eventually commanded the Digby and later the Coltishall Wing. He was killed in action on 3rd May 1943, having claimed at least four victories.

London became the principal target for the German bombers in the heaviest attack of the year thus far. Four hundred and seventy-five crews claimed successful attacks on their target. Only one fighter pilot engaged when Flight Lieutenant Peter Blatchford of 257 Squadron claimed to have probably destroyed a Ju88 off Southwold. A Ju88 of *II./KG 51* crashed on return at Villacoublay, killing the crew, while another of *I./KG 54* crashed near Liseux, killing two. Two He111s from *I./KG 1* and *4./KG 53* also crashed on return, possibly victims to AA gunners who claimed a bomber shot down and a second damaged.

Casualties 19/20th March 1941

Royal Air Force

149 Squadron Wellington R1159
Crash-landed near Swanton Morley. Sgt Hall & crew safe.
257 Squadron Hurricane V7076
Damaged by return fire from Ju88. F/L Blatchford unhurt.
311 Squadron Wellington N5434
Damaged on take-off. S/L Wasse & crew safe.

Luftwaffe

I./NJG 1 Bf110 ----
Damaged in combat and landed at Venlo, Lt J.Bender and gunner wounded. Aircraft 50% damaged.

III./NJG 1 Bf110D3 3669
Crashed at Rheine, Oblt W Winkler & crew killed. Aircraft destroyed.
I./KG 1 He111H3 5643
Crash-landed at Amiens, crew unhurt. Aircraft 35% damaged.
II./KG 51 Ju88A5 2277
Crashed near Villacoublay. Hptm J Meyer & crew killed. Aircraft destroyed.
4./KG 53 He111H5 3643
Belly-landed at Vendeville, crew unhurt. Aircraft 30% damaged.
I./KG 54 Ju88A5 2242
Crashed near Lisieux. Lt G Helms & one crewman killed, two injured.
Aircraft destroyed.
I./KG 54 Ju88A5 4168
Undercarriage damaged at Evreux, crew unhurt. Aircraft 25% damaged.
I./KG 54 Ju88A5 6081
Hit obstruction at Evreux, crew unhurt. Aircraft 20% damaged.
III./KG 55 He111P2 1495
Crashed on take-off from Villacoublay, crew unhurt. Aircraft 30% damaged.
I./KG 77 Ju88A5 8126
Crashed on take-off from Juvincourt, crew unhurt. Aircraft 30% damaged.
II./KG 77 Ju88A5 7204
Tyre damaged at Beauvais, crew unhurt. Aircraft 25% damaged.

20th March 1941

The morning opened with a bang when two Bf110s from
E.Gr.210 made a dawn strafe of Ford airfield. Later in the
morning Bf109s flew a sweep over Kent. One was claimed
damaged by AA gunners, but to interceptions were made by
British fighters.

Bomber and Coastal Commands carried out shipping strikes
during the day. Blenheims from 2 Group made a low level
attack against a convoy off Holland, where an 82 Squadron
aircraft flown by Squadron Leader Kelly was lost to *Flak*.
Coastal Command Beauforts operated further north, bombing
small German naval units off the Frisian Islands. Flying Officer
Boycott's 22 Squadron aircraft also fell to *Flak*.

The night brought small scale raids by Bomber Command.
The *U-boat* pens at Lorient were raided by 21 bombers while 42
more laid mines. A Hampden of 83 Squadron flown by Sergeant
James was reported missing, shot down by *Flak* near Morlaix.
Two of the crew were killed, but one evaded and eventually
returned to England. A lone Blenheim attacked Le Bourget,
where a Heinkel of *E./KG 26* was blown up on the ground.

The Germans switched their objective, 125 aircraft attacking
Plymouth and Devonport. One was claimed probably destroyed
and two more damaged by AA gun-sites. Indeed, three Ju88s of

257

K.Gr.806 were damaged; *Feldwebel* Büse crashed off Argentan, *Oberleutnant* von Bechtolsheim's bomber was lost off Calais and the third machine landed at Caen with battle damage.

Casualties 20th March 1941

Royal Air Force

9 Squadron Wellington W5434
Crashed on take-off Honington. S/L Wasse & crew safe.

22 Squadron Beaufort N1091:U
Failed to return from sortie. P/O Boycott & crew lost.

22 Squadron Beaufort -----
Damaged by Bf110s and crash-landed. F/O Campbell & crew safe.

59 Squadron Blenheim T2433
Hit tree low flying. P/O Miles & crew safe.

72 Squadron Spitfire X4920
Belly-landed at Acklington. P/O Newton unhurt.

82 Squadron Blenheim T3604
Failed to return from sortie. S/L Kelly & crew lost.

145 Squadron Spitfire P8025
Belly-landed at Tangmere. P/O De Hemptinne unhurt.

206 Squadron Hudson AE611
Crashed near Aldergrove P/O Warren & crew killed.

232 Squadron Hurricane W9204
Collided near Grantown-on-Spey. Fate of pilot unknown.

232 Squadron Hurricane P3608
Collided near Grantown-on-Spey. Fate of pilot unknown.

238 Squadron Hurricane Z2331
Force-landed at Wimborne. Sgt Domagala unhurt.

238 Squadron Hurricane Z2826
Belly-landed at East Stoke Dorset. P/O Collyns unhurt.

258 Squadron Hurricane -----
Force-landed near Douglas I.o.Man, engine failure. F/L Campbell unhurt.

315 Squadron Hurricane V7675:M
Belly-landed at Speke. P/O Kornicki unhurt.

320 Squadron Anson W1789
Crashed landing at Silloth. Sgt Van Kooy & crew safe.

612 Squadron Whitley Z6471
Lost: No details.

Luftwaffe

E./JG 27 Bf109 1944
Crashed on take-off from Eisenstadt. Aircraft 40% damaged.

III./JG77 Bf109E7 6437
Belly-landed near Lannion, pilot unhurt. Aircraft 40% damaged.

I./KG 51 Ju88A5 5061
Taxiing accident at Villaroche. Aircraft 20% damaged.

III./KG51 Ju88A5 5067
Undercarriage damaged at Bretigny, crew unhurt. Aircraft 60% damaged.

I./St.G.1 Ju87R2 6041
Taxiing accident at Riem. Aircraft 10% damaged.

1.(F)/122 Ju88A5 0418
Crash-landed at Vendeville. Aircraft 70% damaged.

Casualties 20/21st March 1941

50 Squadron Hampden AD742
Undershot Lindholme. P/O Burrough & crew safe.
83 Squadron Hampden X3132
Failed to return from sortie. Sgt James & crew lost.
102 Squadron Whitley Z6494:M
Undershot Topcliffe. W/C Howes & crew safe.
102 Squadron Whitley Z6485:N
Undershot Topcliffe. P/O Warne & crew safe.
103 Squadron Wellington R1467
Force-landed near Hickling Notts. Sgt Munearo & crew safe.
144 Squadron Hampden AD745
Abandoned near Chelveston. P/O Harrison & crew safe.
149 Squadron Wellington N1159
Crashed at Peasenhall Green Norfolk. Sgt Hall & crew believed safe.
207 Squadron Manchester L7278
Crashed near Wymondham, Sgt Harwood & crew killed.
219 Squadron Beaufighter R2070
Crashed Eastergate, Tangmere. Sgt Gee & crew killed.
236 Squadron Blenheim Z5755:L
Abandoned over Bodmin Moor, one man from P/O Barron's crew missing.
301 Squadron Wellington L7874
Crashed in circuit Swinderby. Three men from Sgt Lenozoski's crew killed

Luftwaffe

E./KG 26 He111H5 3585
Bombed at Le Treport. Aircraft 70% damaged.
K.Gr.806 Ju88A5 8425 M7+GL
Failed to return from sortie. Oblt B von Bechtolsheim & crew lost.
K.Gr.806 Ju88A5 7210 M7+FL
Crashed near Argentan, Fw H Buse & crew killed. Aircraft lost.
K.Gr.806 Ju88A5 2243
Crashed at Caen, crew unhurt. Aircraft 10% damaged.

21st March 1941

Air actions were limited to minor harassing attacks by both sides. Single German bombers ranged far and wide over Britain, enjoying the relative immunity afforded by the low cloud base. Bombs fell on the Kent coast and in Norfolk.

Green Section of 611 Squadron made the only interception when Flight Lieutenant Meares and Pilot Officer Reeves sighted and attacked a Ju88 that they found bombing a ship near Dungeness. Hits were seen, but no claim was made.

Bomber Command shipping strikes continued in the afternoon when nine Blenheims from 139 and 82 Squadrons sought targets of opportunity off the Frisian Islands. During one attack off Borkum at 16.30 hours a tanker was claimed hit and one bomber was claimed by the naval *Flak* gunners.

For Coastal Command, Flight Lieutenant Innes of 236 Squadron flew a convoy patrol near Caldey Island where the Blenheim crew engaged and drove off a pair of He111s that attempted to attack the shipping. Three bursts were fired at one, but no hits were claimed, although a Heinkel of *I./KG 27* crash-landed at Brest with AA damage.

At 07.30 hours, *Oberleutnant* Stolte of *I./JG 1* claimed a Blenheim shot down west of Katwijk, while a bomber crew claimed a Hurricane off Orfordness at 19.25, this latter possibly in combat with 611 Squadron.

Casualties 21st March 1941

Royal Air Force

41 Squadron Spitfire R6893
Crashed landing at Catterick. Sgt London unhurt.

91 Squadron Spitfire P7970
Taxiing accident at Hawkinge. F/S McKay unhurt.

256 Squadron Defiant N3454
Taxiing accident. Fate of crew unknown.

256 Squadron Defiant N3382
Hit by N3454. No casualties.

260 Squadron Hurricane V7133
Belly-landed at Skitten. F/L Bowring unhurt.

311 Squadron Wellington T2553
Damaged landing at East Wretham. F/O Sejbl & crew safe.

311 Squadron Wellington P9224
Taxy accident at East Wretham. F/O Pohlodek & crew safe.

311 Squadron Wellington L7841
Damaged landing at East Wretham. Sgt Styblik & crew safe.

Luftwaffe

I./JG 2 Bf109E7 5986
Crashed at Bourgtherwoude, Lt W Sengerob killed. Aircraft 95% damaged.

E./JG 3 Bf109E4 1323
Taxiing accident at Fontenet. Aircraft 15% damaged.

I./JG 51 Bf109E4 0842
Crashed at Watten. Uffz G.Schwarz killed. Aircraft destroyed.

I./JG 51 Bf109E4 5588
Crashed near Calais. Lt G.Schreiner killed. Aircraft destroyed.

III./JG 51 Bf109E4 1637
Taxiing accident at St. Omer. Aircraft 25% damaged.

12./JG 51 Bf109F1 5650
Crash-landed at Le Touquet, pilot unhurt. Aircraft 25% damaged.

Wellingtons of 311 (Czech) Squadron on a training flight over Norfolk in March. Pictured here are R1410:M, R1378:K and T2561:A. R1378 was wrecked on March 18th. R1410 failed to return on 26th June 1942, while T2561 was reported missing on 10th September 1942.

III./JG 53 Bf109F2 12604
Crashed on take-off from Krefeld. Aircraft 25% damaged.
II./JG 54 Bf109E1 6369
Crashed on take-off from Le Mans, pilot unhurt. Aircraft 85% damaged.
III./JG 54 Bü131 4506
Force-landed at Cherbourg. Aircraft destroyed.
III./KG 2 Ju52 5388
Crash-landed at Brussels. Aircraft 50% damaged.
IV./KG 3 DO17Z2 3292
Crashed on take-off from Kitzingen. Ofw J.Hausch & crew killed.
Aircraft destroyed.
I./KG 27 He111H5 3697
Crashed at Brest-Sud after combat, Uffz F Kukoreit and three crew killed.
Aircraft destroyed.
III./KG 51 Ju88A5 6167 9K+BR
Crashed near Le Havre, Uffz G Unruh & crew killed. Aircraft destroyed.
K.Fl.Gr.506 He115B1 2226
Damaged in storm at Sola. Aircraft 45% damaged.
K.Fl.Gr.706 He115B1 2252
Damaged in storm at Sola. Aircraft 35% damaged.
E./NJG 1 Bf110C3 0981
Belly-landed at Echterdingen. Aircraft 40% damaged.
E./NJG 1 Bf110C4
Force-landed at Echterdingen. Aircraft 25% damaged.

E.Gr.210 Bf110E1 3485
Force-landed at Dieppe, crew unhurt. Aircraft 10% damaged.
E.Gr.210 Bf110E1 3438 S9+LK
Force-landed at Moorsele, Uffz B.Aretz & crew unhurt. Aircraft 20% damaged.
3.(F)/22 Do17M1 2346
Crash-landed at Nieder-Mendig. Aircraft 50% damaged.
2.(F)/O.b.d.L. Do215B4 0088
Taxiing accident at Villeneuve. Aircraft 35% damaged.

21/22nd March 1941

Bomber Command despatched 66 aircraft to Lorient, six to Ostend and seven minelaying, while one OTU aircraft dropped leaflets. Although only one aircraft failed to return - Flight Lieutenant Barber's 57 Squadron Wellington being shot down by *Flak* over Ostend - several incidents took place on return. Four crews died in crashes and a 21 Squadron aircraft, hit by *Flak* at Lorient, lost the gunner who baled out into the Channel.

Plymouth and Devonport were again pounded by the *Luftwaffe*, the 150 participating crews causing great destruction. One bomber was claimed damaged by AA gunners.

Casualties 21/22nd March 1941

Royal Air Force

7 Squadron Stirling N3637
Damaged taxiing at Newmarket. F/O Blacklock & crew safe.
12 Squadron Wellington W5358
Overshot Binbrook. F/S Kellaway & crew safe.
18 Squadron Blenheim P6931
Crashed at Great Massingham. Sgt Anderton & crew safe.
21 Squadron Blenheim T2038:M
Crashed on return. P/O Cowings injured, one killed, one missing.
25 Squadron Beaufighter R2206
Overshot Wittering. P/O King & crew safe.
41 Squadron Spitfire R6893
Crashed on take-off from Catterick. Fate of pilot unknown.
44 Squadron Hampden X3137
Crashed landing at Boscombe Down. P/O Hazelden & crew safe
49 Squadron Hampden X305?
Crashed at Hamel Down Tor, Dartmoor. P/O Wilson & crew killed.
50 Squadron Hampden P2093
Crashed landing at Lindholme. F/O Hook & crew safe.
51 Squadron Whitley N1488
Crashed landing at Dishforth. Sgt Purdon & crew safe.
57 Squadron Wellington R3169
Failed to return from sortie. F/L Barber & crew lost.
57 Squadron Wellington R3275
Damaged landing at Middle Wallop. P/O Bridger & crew safe.

Night Raider. An He111 of KG 55. This unit played a leading part in the night Blitz on England and lost many aircraft and crews.

- via Simon Parry

83 Squadron Hampden AD794
Force-landed near Newton. F/L Thompson & crew safe.
103 Squadron Wellington R1452
Taxy accident at Newton. S/L Mellor & crew safe.
105 Squadron Blenheim T1892
Crashed Rednal, Birmingham. P/O Shirlaw & crew killed.
105 Squadron Blenheim Z5899
Crashed at Woolfox Lodge. Sgt Willsher & crew safe.
150 Squadron Wellington R3228
Crashed on return at Blaenau Ffestiniog. F/O Elliott & crew killed.
214 Squadron Wellington R1136
Taxy accident at Wittering. P/O Oliver & crew safe.
214 Squadron Wellington R1465
Overshot Waddington. Sgt Paramore & crew safe.
214 Squadron Wellington R1380
Damaged landing at Swinderby. Sgt Williams & crew safe.
218 Squadron Wellington L7798
Crashed landing at Marham. F/O Smith & crew safe.

Luftwaffe

III./KG 77 Ju88A5 5092
Belly-landed at Juvincourt, crew unhurt. Aircraft 35% damaged.

22nd March 1941

Harassment by German cloud cover raiders continued. Several claims were made by ground defences in the afternoon and early evening and, at 19.45 hours, an He111 of *5./KG 4* crashed at the County Hotel, Immingham, Lincolnshire. This aircraft, '5J+KN' flown by *Feldwebel* Walter Kössling, had been hit by light AA fire during an attack upon Leeming airfield. It then hit a balloon cable and crashed. Three men baled out, but one parachute caught on the tail unit, carrying the unfortunate crewman to his death. A Heinkel from *4 Staffel* was also hit by AA fire and crashed at Soesterburg with one wounded crewman aboard.

Coastal Command aircraft ranged along the enemy-held coastline during the day sustaining several casualties. Pilot Officer Dale of 59 Squadron failed to return from a dawn patrol to Brittany and a second aircraft from this unit flown by Pilot Officer Villa crashed on the Isle of Wight on return. The last casualty was again a Blenheim. Pilot Officer Duff's 254 Squadron Blenheim fighter was shot down near Haugesund, Norway by naval *Flak* gunners

No Bomber Command night raids were scheduled, neither were there German raids upon Britain.

Casualties 22nd March 1941

Royal Air Force

19 Squadron Spitfire P7301
Belly-landed at Fowlmere. P/O Cowley unhurt.
42 Squadron Beaufort L9869
Overshot Leuchars. Sgt Cannell & crew safe.
59 Squadron Blenheim T2433:X
Failed to return from sortie. P/O Dale & crew safe.
59 Squadron Blenheim V5396:J
Crashed on Isle of Wight. P/O Villa & crew safe.
220 Squadron Hudson N7297
Crashed landing at Thornaby. P/O Bennett & crew safe.
242 Squadron Hurricane LE-
Hit by 605 Squadron Hurricane. No casualty.
254 Squadron Blenheim L9406
Failed to return from sortie. P/O Duff & crew lost.
260 Squadron Hurricane V7166
Belly-landed at Skitten. Sgt Black unhurt.
317 Squadron Hurricane V6534
Crashed on take-off from Acklington. Sgt Koscik unhurt.
485 Squadron Spitfire R6765
Damaged landing at Driffield. Sgt Thomas unhurt.
605 Squadron Hurricane -----
Taxy accident with 242 Squadron Hurricane. P/O Dawick unhurt.

Luftwaffe

II./JG 54 Bf109E4 0837
Belly-landed at Le Mans, pilot unhurt. Aircraft 25% damaged.
4./KG 4 He111P4 3099
Hit by AA fire and crash-landed at Soesterburg. One man wounded. Aircraft 60% damaged.

5./KG 4 He111P4 2938 5J+KN
Failed to return from sortie. Fw W Kössling & crew lost.
I./KG 51 Ju88A5 6208
Abandoned near Orleans, crew unhurt. Aircraft destroyed.
III./KG 55 He111P2 1707
Undercarriage damaged at Villacoublay, crew unhurt. Aircraft 15% damaged.
K.Gr.806 Ju88A5 3019
Crash-landed at Caen, crew unhurt. Aircraft 80% damaged.
2.(F)/122 Ju88A5 0417
Crash-landed at Evére. Aircraft 25% damaged.
3.(H)/41 FW189A1 0085
Crash-landed at Maria ter Heide. Aircraft 15% damaged.
Kur.St.1 Fi156C2 4219
Crashed. No further details.

Casualties 22/23rd March 1941

Royal Air Force
213 Squadron Hurricane V7019
Belly-landed at Castletown. P/O Janicki unhurt.
612 Squadron Whitley T4287
Crashed at Stoneywood, Dyce. Three men from Sgt Durbridge's crew killed.

Luftwaffe

- nil -

23rd March 1941

The morning brought an unexpected 'visitor' to the flying-boat base of Sullom Voe in the Shetlands. At 11.30 hours a Bf110 was seen approaching, flying fast and low. It was from *Stab./ZG 76* and was welcomed by heavy and accurate gunfire from the naval Bofors batteries. 'M8+WE', hit by 40mm shells, dived into the sea just offshore, carrying with it *Unteroffizier* K.Rudiger and his *Bordschütze*.

Several lone *Luftwaffe* bombers were plotted in the south and, almost an hour later, two Hurricane pilots from 238 Squadron found a Ju88 of *4./KG 77* over Sussex. Flight Lieutenant Morris and Sergeant Bernard harried it relentlessly for five minutes before *Oberleutnant* Werner Lode admitted defeat. He attempted to belly-land on Parson's Farm, near Poling, but hit an anti-landing obstacle and crashed. One crewman was killed. There was no further action until 14.30 hours, when Pilot Officer Draper and Sergeant Healey of 41 Squadron reported

How the well-dressed fighter pilot went to work. Sgt Joe Pipa of 43 Squadron, in helmet, mask, Mae West and boots, clips his parachute on. Drem, spring 1941.
- Andy Saunders

damaging a FW200 off Whitby.

The last interception occurred at 15.30 hours. Flight Lieutenant Mortimer-Rose of 234 Squadron, leading Pilot Officer Masters and Sergeant Shepherd sighted a Ju88 near the Isle of Wight. They attacked and claimed damage before it disappeared into the inevitable cloudbank. Their shooting was accurate however, for a machine from *1.(F)/123* subsequently crashed near Amsterdam after combat. It was probably *Oberfeldwebel* Hund's crew, who claimed a Spitfire destroyed.

Coastal Command aircraft continued harassing German shipping and coastal installations during the day. Pilot Officer Villa of 59 Squadron found trouble again when he ventured too close to Calais. He attracted the attention of a Bf109 patrol from *II./JG 53* and, although his gunner defended the Blenheim bravely, he could not prevent the aircraft from being seriously damaged before they escaped in cloud. One Messerschmitt crashed on return at Arques with *Gefreiter* Franz Leitner wounded.

235 Squadron fared worse however. Three Blenheims, patrolling off the Hook of Holland, were discovered by Bf109s from *3./JG 1*. The aircraft flown by Pilot Officer Newman and Sergeant Evans were both shot down into the sea by *Oberleut-*

nant Stolte and *Unteroffizier* Schubert. Pilot Officer Green's aircraft escaped with serious damage.

Casualties 23rd March 1941

Royal Air Force

1 Squadron Hurricane Z2498
Damaged taxiing at Kenley. P/O Raymond unhurt.
59 Squadron Blenheim -----:G
Damaged by Bf109. P/O Villa & crew safe.
105 Squadron Blenheim R3682
Crashed landing at Swanton Morley. Crew safe.
118 Squadron Spitfire X4232
Belly-landed near Tetbury. Sgt Jones unhurt.
141 Squadron Defiant N1795
Force-landed near Gravesend. F/O Williams & crew safe.
235 Squadron Blenheim V5452
Damaged by Bf109. P/O Green & crew safe.
235 Squadron Blenheim Z6085:N
Failed to return from sortie. P/O Newman & crew lost.
235 Squadron Blenheim L9494:D
Failed to return from sortie. Sgt Evans & crew lost.
252 Squadron Blenheim L8047
Undershot Chivenor. Crew safe.
263 Squadron Whirlwind P6991
Overshot Portreath. Sgt Lawson unhurt.
300 Squadron Wellington R1273
Crashed on take-off from Langham. Crew believed safe.
610 Squadron Spitfire P7685
Hit hill near West Dean. Pilot believed killed.

Luftwaffe

III/JG 2 Bf109E7 0813
Crash-landed at Le Havre. Aircraft 40% damaged.
10./JG 51 Bf109E7 5945
Crash-landed at Dieppe, pilot unhurt. Aircraft 65% damaged.
II./JG 53 Bf109F2 5681
Crashed on take-off from Arques, Fw F Leitner wounded. Aircraft 90% damaged.
II./KG 2 Do217E 1019
Crash-landed at Achmer. Aircraft 35% damaged.
I./KG 54 Ju88A5 5161
Belly-landed at Evreux, crew unhurt. Aircraft 20% damaged.
4./KG 77 Ju88A5 7103 3Z+DM
Failed to return from sortie. Oblt W Lode & crew lost.
III./K.Gr.z.b.V.1 Ju52 6142
Crashed at Nikolsburg. Fw Brenner & crew injured. Aircraft destroyed.
Stab./ZG 76 Bf110E2 3774 M8+WE
Failed to return. Uffz K Rudiger & crew lost.
1.(F)/123 Ju88 201
Crash-landed at Schipol, crew unhurt. Aircraft 60% damaged.
1.(F)/123 Ju88 398
Crash-landed at Le Havre, crew unhurt. Aircraft 35% damaged.

E./(F)/O.b.d.L. Ju88A5 0516
Crashed at Wenigtreben. Ofw L.Martin & crew killed. Aircraft destroyed.

23/24th March 1941

Bomber Command Operations
Berlin 63 Hannover 26
Channel Ports 7 Minelaying 5
Luftwaffe Operations
cancelled

No losses were sustained against the heavily defended capital city, although several aircraft crashed on return. One Blenheim failed to return from Kiel, however, Sergeant King's 105 Squadron machine falling near Bremen. A Bf110 of *I./NJG 3* crashed near Vechta, cause not notified, while a Ju88 of *I./NJG 2* crashed near Alphen due to fuel shortage.

Casualties 23/24th March 1941

Royal Air Force

7 Squadron Stirling N3643
Crashed on Hazelwood Common, Leiston S/L Robertson & crew fate unknown.

12 Squadron Wellington W5360
Overshot Binbrook. Sgt Wheeldon & crew safe.

21 Squadron Blenheim R3673
Overshot Bodney. Sgt Sprason & crew safe.

21 Squadron Blenheim R3875
Overshot Bodney. P/O Marshall & crew safe.

53 Squadron Blenheim T2396
Overshot St. Eval. P/O Bannister & crew safe.

61 Squadron Hampden X3005
Abandoned near Driffield; Flak. P/O Pritchard & crew safe.

68 Squadron Blenheim L1207
Crashed near Malton. Sgt Kirkland & crew fate unknown.

87 Squadron Hurricane P2825
Overshot Charmy Down. Sgt Walbank unhurt.

87 Squadron Hurricane V7646
Overshot Charmy Down. Sgt Thompson unhurt.

105 Squadron Blenheim Z5903
Failed to return from sortie. Sgt King & crew lost.

105 Squadron Blenheim R3682
Overshot Swanton Morley. Sgt Wood & crew safe.

214 Squadron Wellington R3233
Overshot Stradishall. Sgt Meadows & crew safe.

252 Squadron Blenheim L8407
Undershot Chivenor. F/O Blennerhassett & crew safe.

256 Squadron Defiant N3423
Crashed landing at Colerne. Sgt Leonard & crew safe.

300 Squadron Wellington R1273
Crashed on take-off from Langham. S/L Cwynar & crew safe.

300 Squadron Wellington T2719
Crashed on take-off from Langham. Sgt Hazierczak & crew safe.
300 Squadron Wellington T2886
Crashed landing at Langham. Sgt Nowakowski & crew safe.
301 Squadron Wellington P9214
Damaged landing at Swinderby. Sgt Kleindeschmidt & crew safe.

Luftwaffe

I./NJG 2 Ju88A1 6119
Force-landed at Alphen, crew unhurt. Aircraft 10% damaged.
I./NJG 3 Bf110C4 3061
Crashed at Vechta, Lt E Schmidt & gunner killed. Aircraft destroyed.

24th March 1941

The morning began with a Jabo attack upon Martlesham Heath by Bf110s of *E.Gr.210, Oberleutnant* Wolfgang Schenk leading his pilots in a gliding attack from 12,000 feet. Bombs were dropped on the airfield and a successful strafe was reported by *Leutnant* Kloss. This attack had been timed to coincide with a strafe of Lympne by Bf109 *Jabos* from *II./LG 2* and in neither case were any claims submitted by the defences. *E.Gr.210* had recommenced operations on 11th March and, from 13th March, had also begun night strafing attacks.

Fighter Command pilots were kept busy hunting lone German raiders around the coastline and engaging Messerschmitt patrols along the Channel. At 06.22 hours, Flying Officer Forster of 605 Squadron tracked down an elusive Heinkel

A member of 242 Squadron ground staff points out the unit emblem to a WAAF. This insignia was perhaps not the wisest choice for operations over France!
- Andy Saunders

269

off Felixstowe. This was attacked and claimed damaged. It was not until the late morning however that the next fight took place. Sergeant Kucera of 1 Squadron engaged a Ju88 near Montrose and claimed damage to this also.

The skies fell quiet until 15.00 hours, when Bf109 formations were encountered off the Kent coast by RAF fighters. Flying Officer J E Demozay of 1 Squadron caught a Bf109 off Deal, claiming it shot down, while fifteen minutes later Flight Lieutenant Holland of 91 Squadron reported another probably destroyed near Hastings. A Bf109 of *II./JG 53* force-landed at St. Inglevert, possibly following this engagement. Two Hurricane pilots from 17 Squadron also encountered Bf109s when Squadron Leader Miller and Sergeant Tomlett briefly sparred with a *Staffel* over the Channel, but these withdrew without a shot being fired.

The final engagement came at around 15.30 hours when Pilot Officer R L Spurdle and Sergeant Dales of 74 Squadron engaged a Ju88 of *3.(F)/11* near Dunkirk. They attacked, claiming it probably destroyed, and it crash-landed near Calais with *Oberfeldwebel* Otto Lilienthal and one other crewman wounded. A second reconnaissance Ju88 was lost when a machine from *4.(F)/121* crashed near Biarritz, out of fuel.

Blenheims from 2 Group flew strikes along the French coastline and attacked targets off Holland and Norway. One ship was claimed hit off the Dutch coast, but one aircraft failed to return. Flight Lieutenant Black and his 82 Squadron crew fell victim to Flak at Heligoland.

At 19.45 hours, *Leutnant* Geisshardt of *I./LG 2* claimed to have shot a Spitfire down into the Channel.

The night brought terrible weather and no operations took place

Casualties 24th March 1941

Royal Air Force

19 Squadron Spitfire P7429
Collided, landed safely. P/O Anderson unhurt.
19 Squadron Spitfire -----
Collided, landed safely. Sgt Charnock unhurt.
40 Squadron Wellington R1166
Overshot Alconbury. Crew safe.

Jean Demozay of 91 Squadron was a former civilian pilot. He was rejected by the Armee de l'Air but was accepted for the Royal Air Force. He flew under the Nom de Guerre of 'Moses Morlaix' to protect his family from reprisals. He became the top-scoring French fighter pilot to fly with RAF by achieving at least 21 victories. He was killed in a flying accident on 19th December 1945.

43 Squadron Hurricane N2436
Belly-landed at Dunbar. P/O West unhurt.
82 Squadron Blenheim L9839
Failed to return from sortie. F/L Black & crew lost.
82 Squadron Blenheim R3767
Crashed landing at Bodney. Sgt Harrison & crew safe.
92 Squadron Spitfire X4279
Damaged on take-off, crash-landed. P/O Wade unhurt.
144 Squadron Hampden P1295
Force-landed near Lincoln. P/O Hamilton & crew safe.
209 Squadron Lerwick L7252
Ditched off Pembroke Dock. S/L Banks & crew safe.
222 Squadron Spitfire P7847
Crashed at Salthouse, Sgt Cockram killed.
501 Squadron Hurricane V6959
Overshot Charmy Down. Sgt Blackshaw unhurt.
615 Squadron Hurricane Z2510
Crashed in Surrey. Sgt Davidson safe.

Luftwaffe

III./JG 2 Bf109E4 5042
Belly-landed at St. Martin, pilot unhurt. Aircraft 35% damaged.
II./JG 53 Bf109F2 6646
Force-landed at St.Inglevert. Aircraft 20% damaged.
II./KG 1 Ju88A5 3352
Force-landed 60km north of Bordeaux. Oblt K-H Müncheberg & crew killed. Aircraft destroyed.
III./KG 51 Ju88A5 6154 9K+KT
Crashed at Villacoublay, Uffz H Jenkel & crew killed. Aircraft destroyed.
K.Gr.z.b.V.101 Ju52 5699
Crashed at Rehhorn in bad weather. Fw A.Krause & crew killed. Aircraft destroyed.

K.Gr.z.b.V.101 Ju52 5277
Force-landed at Rehhorn in bad weather. Aircraft 70% damaged.
K.Gr.z.b.V.101 Ju52 6246
Force-landed at Rehhorn in bad weather. Hptm K.Thomas & two men injured.
Aircraft 75% damaged.
K.Gr.z.b.V.101 Ju52 6414
Force-landed at Rehhorn in bad weather. Uffz K.Mauerhofer injured.
Aircraft 50% damaged.
3.(F)/11 Ju88 495
Crash-landed at Calais. Ofw O Lilienthal and one crewman wounded.
Aircraft 60% damaged.
4.(F)/121 Ju88 498
Force-landed at Biarritz due to fuel shortage, crew unhurt. Aircraft destroyed.

Casualties 24/25th March 1941

Royal Air Force

236 Squadron Blenheim T1806
Crashed landing at Carew Cheriton. P/O Chappell & crew safe.
255 Squadron Defiant N3739
Taxiing accident Sgt Woolley & crew safe.
255 Squadron Defiant N3422
Hit by N3739. No casualties.

Luftwaffe

- nil -

25th March 1941

A small number of *Luftwaffe* reconnaissance aircraft were plotted around the British coastline. Coastal towns in the south and southwest became the targets for 'hit and run' raids, mainly by lone bombers. A few German fighter sweeps were also flown and one of these caught a pair of 17 Squadron Hurricanes, which had taken off at 10.25 hours on convoy patrol. *Hauptmann* Herbert Ihlefeld of *I./LG 2* bounced the unsuspecting RAF fighters from astern. Although Flight Lieutenant M.B.Czernin evaded the attack successfully, the aircraft flown by Squadron Leader H.de C.A.Woodhouse took many hits. He would probably have been killed had not Manfred Czernin driven Ihlefeld off.

Four interceptions were made against bombers. At 11.40 hours Pilot Officer R L Spurdle and Sergeant Dales attacked and claimed damage to a Do215 over East Kent. Pilot Officers Seghers and Curtiss of 46 Squadron had an inconclusive fight with a Ju88 off the east coast, as did Flight Lieutenant Tamblyn of 242 Squadron, engaging a Do17 in the same area. Sergeant Wright of 605 Squadron fared better by claiming damage to a Bf110 off Corton at 16.45 hours. One German bomber crew claimed the destruction of a British fighter during one of these engagements.

Bomber Command aircraft were again active off Holland and the Frisian Islands. Returning crews claimed hits on a *Flak*-ship off Ameland, a patrol boat near Borkum and a convoy, attacked off the Dutch coast. All the aircraft returned safely. Coastal Command aircraft on similar duties fared less well. Beauforts patrolled the German Bight, losing Squadron Leader Kelly's 22 Squadron bomber to *Flak* from a patrol boat. One 59 Squadron Blenheim crew, looking for trouble in the Channel, suddenly found more than they could handle. Two Bf109s came in fast, hammering shells into the bomber and badly wounding the gunner before Flight Lieutenant Palmer could escape. The heavily damaged Blenheim was crash-landed in England without further injury to the crew.

Bad weather again prevented all night operations.

Casualties 25th March 1941

Royal Air Force

17 Squadron Hurricane Z2794
Damaged by Bf109. S/L Woodhouse safe.
22 Squadron Beaufort W6486:A
Failed to return from sortie. S/L Kelly & crew lost.
51 Squadron Whitley P5027
Belly-landed at Holme-on-Swale. S/L Bouwens & crew safe.
59 Squadron Blenheim -----:J
Damaged by Bf109. One man from F/L Palmer's crew killed.
114 Squadron Blenheim R3766
Overshot Thornaby. Sgt Locke & crew safe.
142 Squadron Wellington W5393
Damaged taxiing at Benson. W/C Maw & crew safe.
238 Squadron Hurricane V7655
Belly-landed at Silloth. P/O Sellar unhurt.
303 Squadron Spitfire P8038
Damaged taxiing at Northolt. P/O Kolaczkowski safe.
308 Squadron Hurricane W6858
Damaged in accident at Sealand. F/O Wielgus unhurt.
401 Squadron Hurricane P3769
Crashed near Digby, P/O Henderson killed.

Luftwaffe

I./JG51 Bf109F1 5638
Crashed near Marquise. Lt J.Gallasch killed. Aircraft destroyed.

6./JG 51 Bf109E4 1118
Force-landed near Mardyck, pilot unhurt. Aircraft 10% damaged.
K.Gr.100 He111H3 3320
Crashed at Laval. Ofw R Wiessner & one man killed, two crewmen injured.
Aircraft destroyed.
E./St.G.77 Ju87B1 5142
Collided with unidentified Ju87 at Wertheim. Fw E.Naumann killed.
Aircraft 95% damaged.
7.(H)/12 Hs126B1 3196
Crashed at Allenstein. Uffz H.Gerstadt & crew killed. Aircraft destroyed.

Casualties 25/26th March 1941

Royal Air Force and Luftwaffe

- nil -

26th March 1941

The day followed the same general pattern as the 25th, with lone German aircraft reconnoitring the coastline, bombing shipping and attacking towns in the south and southwest. A few more adventurous *Luftwaffe* crews droned in over the coast using cloud cover to make pinpoint attacks upon targets in London and the Midlands. There were several claims by AA sites for bombers damaged and, at 12.30 hours, the airfield defences at Andover shot down a Ju88. It was 'F1+FP' of *II./KG 76*, which took direct hits as *Leutnant* Otto Peper attempted a low level attack. There were no survivors. In addition a Do17 of *5./KG 3* crashed at Antwerp on return after failing to find Leeuwarden and diverting to Eindhoven. All four men were killed.

Two fighter pilots made contact; at 09.06 hours Flying Officer D N Forde and Pilot Officer Thompson of 605 Squadron intercepted a Do17 off Orfordness, claiming it destroyed. It was an aircraft from *2/KG2* flown by *Oberfeldwebel* Fischer, which was slightly damaged but returned with the pilot wounded and the gunner claiming both British fighters shot down.

Squadron Leader Little of 219 Squadron had a disagreeable experience at Northolt. He was at the end of the runway in a Magister, the squadron 'hack', when a Ju88 streaked down from the low cloudbase and peppered the 'Maggie' with bullets, fortunately without injuring the pilot.

Coastal Command aircraft flew more patrols, Pilot Officer McMillan's 59 Squadron Blenheim failing to return from a reconnaissance. Pilot Officer Emms' 612 Squadron Whitley crashed into the sea off Wick with the loss of the crew and another 59 Squadron Blenheim crashed on return from Brest. On the credit side, Beauforts carried out a torpedo strike against a convoy off Holland, Flying Officer K.Campbell's 22 Squadron crew claiming to have hit a supply vessel.

For the third night in succession no operations took place.

Casualties 26th March 1941

Royal Air Force

17 Squadron Hurricane Z2571
Abandoned near Odiham. P/O Sowrey unhurt.
21 Squadron Blenheim -----
Damaged by bird strike. Sgt Fryer & crew safe.
56 Squadron Hurricane Z2573
Force-landed near Guildford. Sgt Hoyle unhurt.
59 Squadron Blenheim V6065
Crashed Winterboune Abbas. P/O Sandes & crew killed.
59 Squadron Blenheim V5648
Failed to return from sortie. P/O McMillan & crew lost.
118 Squadron Spitfire X4820
Crashed landing at Filton. P/O Milne safe.
219 Squadron Magister -----
Strafed on take-off from Northolt. S/L Little unhurt.
238 Squadron Hurricane Z2458
Crashed near Winchester, P/O Davis killed.
306 Squadron Hurricane -----
Force-landed near Eastchurch. P/O Skalski unhurt.
308 Squadron Hurricane -----
Crashed near Cottesmore, Sgt Parafinski killed.
402 Squadron Hurricane W9137
Crashed near Lincoln. P/O Smith safe.
609 Squadron Spitfire P7785
Crashed St.Martins Plain, Cornwall. Fate of pilot unknown.
612 Squadron Whitley T4290
Ditched off Wick. P/O Emms & crew safe.

Luftwaffe

E./JG 52 Bf109E1 3406
Crashed 1km west of Döberitz, Ofhr G.Albrecht killed. Aircraft 90% damaged.
3./NJG 2 Ju88C2 0173
Crash-landed at Gilze-Rijn, crew unhurt. Aircraft 35% damaged.
2./KG 2 Do17Z1 3442 U5+CK
Damaged by fighter over Channel, Ofw K.Fischer wounded. Aircraft 10% damaged.
5./KG 3 Do17Z2 2534
Crashed near Eindhoven, Fw H Schramme & crew killed, Aircraft destroyed.

I./KG 51 Ju88A5 6162
Crash-landed at Villaroche, one crewman injured. Aircraft 40% damaged.
II./KG 76 Ju88A5 4259 F1+FP
Failed to return from sortie. Lt O.Peper & crew lost.

Casualties 26/27th March 1941

Royal Air Force and Luftwaffe

- nil -

27th March 1941

A few daylight raiders were again in evidence over south and southwest England, where a few bombs fell. Several German fighter sweeps were flown over the Channel area and a number of combats took place.

Action began in the late morning when two Spitfires from 74 Squadron, flown by Squadron Leader Wood and Pilot Officer Smith, patrolled the Dungeness area. Here at 11.00 hours they were bounced by Bf109s from an unknown unit, which shot down and killed Smith. Wood fought on, claiming a 'probable' before the Messerschmitt pilots withdrew.

Precisely three hours later, a pair of 616 Squadron Spitfire pilots patrolled over Littlehampton, where a Bf110 of *2.(F)/122* was seen and engaged by Flight Lieutenant C H MacFie, who delivered several attacks and damaged it. The Messerschmitt limped back to France and crash-landed at Théville with the pilot, *Unteroffizier* Alfons Munz, wounded.

Bf109s from *I./LG 2* flew a *Freijagd* over Kent at 16.30 hours. Six Spitfires from 609 Squadron were scrambled to intercept, but it was the German pilots who achieved surprise by bouncing the Spitfires southwest of Dungeness. The '109s came down fast and hard and the Spitfires scattered. The Germans did not stay to fight, but rocketed out to sea leaving the Spitfire flown by Sergeant McSherry going down like a blazing torch, victim to *Leutnant* Geisshardt.

Widespread anti-shipping strikes were flown by both Bomber and Coastal Command aircraft. The latter lost two Blenheims of a formation from 53 Squadron sent to attack shipping near Ushant. They were attacked by Bf109s from *II./JG 77*, which shot down the aircraft flown by Pilot Officer Philpott and

Colin MacFie, Commanding 'B' Flight of 616 Squadron.
- A.Saunders

Sergeant Fothergill, one being claimed by *Unteroffizier* Bochmann. Of ten 2 Group aircraft sent out to Holland, one Blenheim of 139 Squadron returned with severe *Flak* damage.

The Royal Navy achieved success off Milford Haven when a convoy was attacked by He111s at 09.30 hours. Gunners aboard HMS *Leith* shot down '1G+EL' of *3./KG 27*, which crashed near the Smalls lighthouse. *Leutnant* J Crenz and his crew were rescued and made prisoners. A second Heinkel was claimed damaged.

Casualties 27th March 1941

Royal Air Force

53 Squadron Blenheim V5865:O
Failed to return from sortie. P/O Philpott & crew lost.
53 Squadron Blenheim -----:P
Failed to return from sortie. P/O Fothergill & crew lost.
56 Squadron Hurricane Z2635
Force-landed near Guildford. Sgt Myall unhurt.
66 Squadron Spitfire P7744
Damaged taxiing at Exeter. P/O Durrant unhurt.
74 Squadron Spitfire P7328
Failed to return from sortie. P/O Smith lost.
75 Squadron Wellington R3171
Crashed landing at Feltwell. Sgt Sargent & crew safe.
118 Squadron Spitfire N3127
Crashed landing at Upavon. Sgt Jones unhurt.

277

118 Squadron Spitfire X4675
Crashed landing at Filton. P/O Robson unhurt.
139 Squadron Blenheim L9386
Damaged by Flak, one man from P/O Sydney-Smith's crew wounded.
145 Squadron Spitfire P7908
Damaged taxiing at Tangmere. F/O Bachman unhurt.
222 Squadron Spitfire P8028
Collided near Norwich, P/O Logan killed.
222 Squadron Spitfire P7857
Collided near Norwich, Sgt Wilson killed.
242 Squadron Hurricane Z2511
Damaged taxiing at Martlesham Heath. P/O Oak-Rhind unhurt.
272 Squadron Beaufighter R2198
Belly-landed at Chivenor. F/O Holgate & crew safe.
315 Squadron Hurricane V7187
Collided near Fleetwood, Sgt Paterek killed.
315 Squadron Hurricane V7188
Collided near Fleetwood, F/L Szulkowski killed.
315 Squadron Hurricane V7656
Dived into sea near Fleetwood P/O Hojden killed.
315 Squadron Hurricane P3936
Ditched out of fuel, F/O Wolinski rescued unhurt.
601 Squadron Magister N3922
Crashed at Northwood. Sgt Weightman safe.
609 Squadron Spitfire P7785
Shot down near Hawkinge by Bf109, Sgt McSherry killed.
616 Squadron Spitfire P7732
Force-landed at Durrington. Sgt Sellars unhurt.

Luftwaffe

I./NJG 2 Ju88C4 0363 R4+AH
Crash-landed at Rheims, Fw H.Strüning & crew unhurt. Aircraft 90% damaged.
I./KG 27 He111H5 3747 1G+EL
Failed to return from sortie. Lt J Krenz & crew lost.
I./KG 28 He111H 3511 1T+KK
Crashed at Nantes, Lt R Freudenberger & crew killed. Aircraft destroyed.
3.(F)/122 Bf110E3 2317
Crash-landed at Théville, one crewman injured. Aircraft destroyed.

27/28th March 1941

Bomber Command Operations

Köln 39 Düsseldorf 39
Channel Ports 13

Luftwaffe Operations

Minelaying 7

As the bombers tracked in towards the Ruhr, many nightfighters were waiting along their defensive line. Only two Bf110 crews from *3./NJG 1* were successful however. At 23.05 hours *Oberfeldwebel* Herzog claimed a Wellington destroyed 10km north of Meijel. This was actually a 78 Squadron Whitley flown by Sergeant Mills.

The wreckage of a 78 Squadron Whitley somewhere on the continent

Twenty-five minutes later Herzog discovered Flight Lieutenant Siebert's 207 Squadron Manchester over Bakel and shot it down 10km southeast of Helmond. The last claim came from *Oberleutnant* Fenske of I./NJG 1, who intercepted and shot down Flight Lieutenant Shore's 9 Squadron Wellington near Hertogenbosch at 23.50 hours. The British pilot subsequently escaped from captivity and returned to England. Two further British casualties were sustained when Flight Lieutenant Leroy's 110 Squadron Blenheim crashed at St. Eval after raiding Brest, while Squadron Leader Holford's crew abandoned their 10 Squadron Whitley over Cottesmore.

No German raids were reported over Britain.

Casualties 27/28th March 1941

Royal Air Force

9 Squadron Wellington R1335
Failed to return from sortie. F/L Shore & crew lost.

10 Squadron Whitley Z6477
Abandoned near Pickworth, engine failure. S/L Holford & crew safe.

12 Squadron Wellington W5381
Crashed landing at Binbrook. S/L Baird & crew safe.

57 Squadron Wellington R1441
Undershot East Wretham. Sgt Emmerson & crew safe.

75 Squadron Wellington R1518
Damaged landing at Feltwell. Sgt Kilsby & crew safe.
78 Squadron Whitley Z6470
Failed to return from sortie. Sgt Mills & crew lost.
110 Squadron Blenheim L8787
Crashed on return. F/L Leroy & crew injured.
144 Squadron Hampden AD829
Damaged taxiing at Hemswell. P/O Harrison & crew safe.
207 Squadron Manchester L7303
Failed to return from sortie. F/L Siebert DFC & crew lost.
311 Squadron Wellington R1441
Crashed landing at East Wretham. Crew safe.

Luftwaffe

- nil -

28th March 1941

Only a few reconnaissance aircraft were reported around Britain and some bombs fell in Kent. At 09.45 hours Pevensey AA gunners opened fire on a Heinkel, claiming it probably destroyed. Such an aircraft of *I./KG 28* crash-landed at Nantes on return.

It was not until shortly after noon that fighters made contact. Three Hurricane pilots of 302 Squadron patrolling over the Channel came upon a Ju88, '3Z+EN' of *II./KG 77*. Pilot Officers Lapka, Kaminsky and Sergeant Lysek attacked, shooting it down into the sea near the French coast. *Oberfeldwebel* Hohdorf's crew was lost. Thirty minutes later Flight Lieutenant P P Hanks and Flying Officer McIntyre of 257 Squadron intercepted an He111 off Happisburgh. Both pilots attacked, claiming a shared 'probable' before it escaped in cloud.

Coastal Command aircraft maintained pressure on the *Kriegsmarine* by attacking convoys near the Frisian Islands and upon naval installations on the French coast, but eighteen Bomber Command aircraft saw nothing. Night operations were again cancelled.

Casualties 28th March 1941

Royal Air Force

139 Squadron Blenheim V5498
Crashed at Risborough. Sgt Jennings & crew believed safe.
242 Squadron Hurricane Z2588
Crashed at Bradfield St. George. P/O Smith killed.
501 Squadron Hurricane V6841
Crashed on take-off Filton, Sgt Laws killed.

501 Squadron Hurricane V7540
Hit HT cable. Sgt Smithers fate unknown.

Luftwaffe

E./JG 54 FW44 0640
Crashed at Cazaux. Aircraft 80% damaged.
Stab./KG 3 Do17Z3 2827
Crash-landed at Wunstorf. Aircraft 35% damaged.
I./KG 28 He111H5 3758
Crash-landed at Nantes, crew unhurt. Aircraft 70% damaged.
III./KG 76 Ju88A5 4223
Crash-landed at Illesheim. Aircraft 20% damaged.
IV./KG 76 Ju88A1 3184
Taxiing accident at Roth. Aircraft 70% damaged.
II./KG 77 Ju88A5 2257 3Z+EN
Failed to return from sortie. Ofw E.Hohdorf & crew lost.
E./K.Gr.100 Ju52 7068
Crashed at Kölloda, Fw H.Wallbaum & two crew killed. Aircraft destroyed.
1./196 Ar196B 0060
Crashed off Ostend. Ofw J Westphal killed, one crewmen rescued injured.

29th March 1941

A few cloud cover raiders were plotted over Britain, but no fighter interceptions took place. 601 Squadron sent Hurricanes out on Rhubarbs, Squadron Leader O'Neill strafing Mardyck. The diarist of *I./JG 51* wrote 'One Hurricane attacked the airfield. One hangar hit twice, two Bf109s slightly damaged'. A Messerchmitt from *6./JG 51* crash-landed at this base, cause not notified. *Flak* gunners claimed a Hurricane destroyed at 11.08 hours, west of Calais.

Bomber and Coastal Command aircraft continued shipping strikes. A 21 Squadron Blenheim returned with severe *Flak* damage.

Casualties 29th March 1941

Royal Air Force

21 Squadron Blenheim -----
Damaged by Flak. W/C Bartlett & crew safe.
54 Squadron Spitfire P7979
Belly-landed at Rochford. P/O Batchelor unhurt.
500 Squadron Anson W1673
Overshot Detling. W/C Candler & crew safe.
1 PRU Blenheim K9143
Damaged taxiing at Benson. F/L Wise & crew safe.

Luftwaffe

I./JG 51 Bf109E -----
Slightly damaged in strafe of Mardyck.
I./JG 51 Bf109E -----
Slightly damaged in strafe of Mardyck.

6./JG 51 Bf109E4 3766
Crash-landed at Mardyck, Gfr A Hafner injured. Aircraft 80% damaged.
10./JG 51 Bf109E1 5389
Crashed at Camiers, Ofhr G Ulms killed. Aircraft 95% damaged.
E./JG 51 Bf109E4 3750
Force-landed at Fleurus. Aircraft 50% damaged.
III./KG 1 Ju88A5 3187
Force-landed near Le Havre, crew unhurt. Aircraft 10% damaged.
I./KG 26 He111H5 3588
Crashed south of Stavanger, Oblt E.Hippel & crew killed. Aircraft destroyed.
II./KG 51 Ju88A5 8130
Force-landed near Rixingen, Fw R Spanheimer & two crew injured.
Aircraft 70% damaged.
II./KG 51 Ju88A5 6108
Crashed at Schramberg, Uffz R Erdmann & crew killed. Aircraft destroyed.
E./LG 1 Ju88A5 8220
Crashed at Wachtersbach, Fw K.Dietlof & one crewman killed.
Aircraft destroyed.
II./LG 2 Bf109E7 4149
Crashed at Butweilerhof, Uffz A.Kuhn killed. Aircraft destroyed.
II./LG 2 Bf109E7 5595
Damaged taxiing accident at Butweilerhof. Aircraft 90% damaged.

29/30th March 1941

Twenty-five Bomber Command aircraft were sent out on minelaying duties. A Hampden of 83 Squadron, flown by Pilot Officer Reynolds, failed to return from the Brest area, shot down by *Flak* some 60km north of the target.

For the first time in a week the *Luftwaffe* launched a concentrated raid when fifty bombers struck at Bristol and Avonmouth. A Ju88 was claimed damaged by AA gunners at 21.30 hours, likely to have been a *I./KG 27* aircraft that reported damage under these circumstances.

Casualties 29/30th March 1941

Royal Air Force
25 Squadron Beaufighter R2205
Crash-landed near Wittering. F/S Smythe & crew safe.
83 Squadron Hampden AD800
Failed to return from sortie. P/O Reynolds & crew lost.

Luftwaffe
I./KG 27 He111 ----
Damaged by AA fire. Aircraft 30% damaged.
II./KG 76 Ju88A5 8057
Crash-landed at Chateaudun, crew unhurt. Aircraft 45% damaged.

A smoking crater marks the last resting place of '4U+GH' of
1.(F)/123, shot down from 24,000 feet by Anthony Lovell of 41
Squadron, 30th March 1941.

30th March 1941

Several lone raiders were reported over Britain, particularly
over the south coast and over Scotland. The only interception
took place at 15.00 hours. Ten Spitfires of 41 Squadron had
been scrambled in pairs to patrol over Seaham, Flight Lieutenant Lovell spotting a high-flying Ju88. He and his wingman
climbed steeply to 24,000 feet, Lovell engaging the aircraft, a
Ju88 of *1.(F)/123*. After several bursts the '88 nosed down and
dived into the ground at Barnaby Moor, Hillsborough, where it
blew up. One man from *Leutnant* Werner Schlott's '4U+GH'
baled out, but was subsequently discovered dead from gunshot
wounds.

Two 91 Squadron Spitfires patrolled near Dunkirk at 18.10
hours, meeting a few Bf109s from *IV./JG 51*. One was attacked
and claimed destroyed by Flight Sergeant McKay. It crash-
landed at Etaples with battle damage.

A Coastal Command Blenheim was intercepted by Bf109s off
Calais at 17.30 hours. The aircraft was badly shot-up, but Pilot
Officer Griffiths managed to return to base with his gunner
wounded.

Casualties 30th March 1941

Royal Air Force

48 Squadron Anson W1768
Overshot Port Ellen. Sgt Irwin & crew safe.

54 Squadron Spitfire P7818
Overshot Hornchurch. P/O Powling unhurt.

59 Squadron Blenheim V6064:A
Damaged by Bf109 and crash-landed at Hawkinge. One man from P/O Griffiths' crew wounded.

91 Squadron Spitfire P7783
Damaged before take-off from Hawkinge. Sgt Mann unhurt.

229 Squadron Hurricane V6872
Failed to return from sortie. Presumed collided. P/O Dewar lost.

229 Squadron Hurricane W9307
Failed to return from sortie. Presumed collided. P/O Du Vivier lost.

238 Squadron Hurricane Z2382
Undershot Chilbolton. P/O Remy unhurt.

247 Squadron Hurricane P3164
Belly-landed at St.Eval. Sgt Renvoise unhurt.

300 Squadron Wellington T2574
Crash-landed at Swinderby. Sgt Leszkiewicz & crew safe

310 Squadron Hurricane Z2643
Crashed landing at Fowlmere. Sgt Dvorak unhurt.

607 Squadron Hurricane V7061
Crashed near Dunbar, P/O Lane injured.

609 Squadron Spitfire P7668
Belly-landed near Sevenoaks. Sgt Rouse unhurt.

Luftwaffe

10./JG 51 Bf109E1 5695
Crash-landed at Etaples, pilot unhurt. Aircraft 65% damaged.

I./JG 52 Bf109E7 1959
Crashed on take-off from Vlissingen, pilot unhurt. Aircraft 40% damaged.

I./JG 52 Bf109E 1187
Crashed on take-off from Vlissingen, pilot unhurt. Aircraft 50% damaged.

I./JG 77 Bf109E1 3212
Crash-landed at Sola, pilot safe. Aircraft 35% damaged.

II./KG 2 Do217E1 5055
Crash-landed at Achmer. Aircraft 45% damaged.

1.(F)/123 Ju88A 115 4U+GH
Failed to return from sortie. Lt W Schlott & crew lost.

30/31st March 1941

Brest was attacked by 109 bombers, while thirteen raided Calais, ten laid mines and two OTU aircraft dropped leaflets.

Flak gunners at Brest claimed two Blenheims, but all the bombers returned, although two crashed. There were no reported German raids, but the *Fernnachtjäger* were patrolling over East Anglia, where two Wellingtons were attacked.

Pilots of 41 Squadron. (l to r) Plt Off J.N.MacKenzie, Flt Lt A.D.J.Lovell, Sqn Ldr D.O.Finlay, Flt Lt E.N.Ryder and Plt Off R.C.Ford. Lovell brought down the Ju88 on the 30th.

- Andy Saunders

Squadron leader Coleman's 150 Squadron Wellington was slightly damaged. One of the long-range fighters failed to return. *Gefreiter* Ottomar Kruger's *I./NJG 2* Ju88 disappeared without trace.

Casualties 30/31st March 1941

Royal Air Force

35 Squadron Halifax L9486
Belly-landed at Linton-on-Ouse. P/O Franklin & crew safe.
58 Squadron Whitley -----
Crashed landing at Linton-on-Ouse. P/O Joshua & crew safe.
101 Squadron Blenheim T2281
Crashed on return at St. Eval. Sgt Riddle & crew safe.
103 Squadron Wellington R1043
Crashed on return at Yeovil. Two men from W/C Littler's crew killed.
150 Squadron Wellington R1444
Damaged by intruder. S/L Coleman & crew safe.
252 Squadron Blenheim Z6254
Overshot Chivenor. S/Lt Crane & crew safe.
Fighter Interception Unit Defiant N1811
Crashed landing at Northolt. W/C Chamberlain & crew safe.

285

Luftwaffe

I./NJG 2 Ju88C4 0618 R4+HM
Failed to return from sortie. Gfr O Kruger & crew lost.

31st March 1941

There was an uneasy respite over Britain. The sole fighter engagement occurred when Sergeant Jack Mann of 91 Squadron flew a solo patrol and was bounced by Bf109s from *7./JG 51* over Griz Nez at 09.20 hours. He was cruising at 24,000 ft when four Messerschmitts attacked from above. Mann saw them coming and threw his Spitfire into a vertical dive, which ripped away his canopy, goggles and helmet. Glancing in his mirror he saw the '109 still behind. As he eased out of the dive at low level, he saw the grey-dappled German fighter streak past him and crash into the sea, witnessed by nearby naval observers. *Leutnant* von Saalfeld was killed when his 'White 3' plunged into the Channel a few moments after he had radioed that he had shot down a Hurricane.

Jack Mann of 91 Squadron, pictured here in later civilian life as an airline pilot, had a narrow escape on 31st March. Four days later, however, he was to have another, which effectively ended his fighting career.

- *Andy Saunders*

Blenheims from 2 Group continued their anti-shipping campaign, claiming several vessels damaged as well as attacking German facilities on Terschelling Island. Two aircraft from 21 Squadron were lost. Those flown by Pilot Officer Rogers and Sergeant Adams both fell to *Flak*.

A further loss was sustained when a Spitfire of 1 PRU failed to return from Rotterdam. It is believed that Pilot Officer Punshon was intercepted and shot down into the Channel northwest of Calais at 11.35 hours by *Major* von Maltzahn of *Stab./JG 53*.

Two losses were suffered by the Luftwaffe; a Ju88 from *1.(F)/124* flown by *Feldwebel* Josef Goldbrunner was reported missing from a sortie to Peterhead, while a Bf110 of *4.(F)/122* crashed near Antwerp due to enemy fire, probably from a ship.

Casualties 31st March 1941

Royal Air Force

15 Squadron Wellington N2843
Crashed landing at Wyton. Sgt Nutt & crew safe.

21 Squadron Blenheim R3884
Failed to return from sortie. Sgt Adams & crew lost.

21 Squadron Blenheim R3900
Failed to return from sortie. P/O Rogers & crew lost.

40 Squadron Wellington T2974
Damaged taxiing at Silloth. P/O Trench & crew safe.

74 Squadron Spitfire P7428
Damaged beyond repair. No details.

88 Squadron Boston AW399
Belly-landed at Sydenham. P/O Meakin & crew safe.

91 Squadron Spitfire -----
Damaged in combat. Sgt Mann unhurt.

93 Squadron Havoc BJ473
Belly-landed at Middle Wallop. F/L Hayley-Bell & crew safe.

263 Squadron Whirlwind P7000
Damaged taxiing at Portreath. P/O Stein safe.

264 Squadron Defiant N3326
Damaged taxiing at Biggin Hill. P/O Curtice & crew safe.

601 Squadron Hurricane V7539
Crashed at Keswick in blizzard, F/O Seddon killed.

601 Squadron Hurricane -----
Crashed at Keswick in blizzard, P/O Smith killed.

1 PRU Spitfire X4029
Failed to return from sortie. P/O Punshon lost.

Luftwaffe

I./JG 1 Bf109E7 1272.
Crashed at Bergen, pilot safe. Aircraft 40% damaged.

3./JG 51 Bf109E1 6648
Crash-landed at Coquelles, pilot safe. Aircraft 15% damaged.

6./JG 51 Bf109E7 4208
Crash-landed at Mardyck, Lt G Rübell injured. Aircraft 60% damaged.

7./JG 51 Bf109F1 6624 White 3
Failed to return. Lt E.v.Saalfeld lost.

III./JG 51 Bf109E 6644
Crash-landed at Wizernes, pilot safe. Aircraft 70% damaged.

I./JG 54 Bf109E4 0918
Crashed near Wesermünde, pilot safe. Aircraft 50% damaged.

III./KG 1 Ju88A5 4220
Force-landed near Albert, crew safe. Aircraft 50% damaged.

II./KG 77 Ju88A5
Crash-landed at Beauvais-Tille. Aircraft 10% damaged.
K.Gr.z.b.V.104 Ju52 6673
Force-landed at Schmalkalden. Aircraft 10% damaged.
K.Gr.z.b.V.105 Ju52 5336
Crash-landed at Zwölfaxing. Aircraft 15% damaged.
K.Fl.Gr.406 Do18G1 0858
Crashed on Tarva Island, one man killed, one injured. Aircraft destroyed.
4.(F)/122 Bf110C5 2294
Crashed near Antwerp due to enemy gunfire. Lt H Vanderleeden & crew
wounded. Aircraft 65% damaged.
1.(F)/124 Ju88D 0792 G2+OH
Failed to return from sortie. Fw Josef Goldbrunner & crew lost.
Kur.St. OKM Caudron C445 03936
Crash-landed on a flight from Berlin to Le Bourget. Aircraft 80% damaged.

31st Mar/1st April 1941

Thirty-nine British bombers attacked Bremen, Emden and
Rotterdam, two Wellingtons carrying the first 4,000 lb light-case
blast bombs (later to become known as 'cookies') to Emden. A 15
Squadron Wellington failed to return. Sergeant Kelly's aircraft
was intercepted by *Feldwebel* Heinz Scherfling of *7./NJG 1* en
route to Bremen and was shot down in flames over Bahndorf
Haren, southeast of Gröningen, at 2236 hours. Another Wellington crashed on return and was burnt.

Although many German raiders were plotted over Britain,
mostly attacking Tyneside, the southwest and Wales, no claims
were made by the defences.

Casualties 31st March/1st April 1941

Royal Air Force
15 Squadron Wellington T2703
Failed to return from sortie. Sgt Kelly & crew lost.
149 Squadron Wellington R1229
Crashed on return at Mildenhall. One man killed and two injured
from Sgt Morhen's crew.

Luftwaffe

I./KG 53 He111 3553
Crashed on take-off from Vitry-en-Artois. Aircraft 20% damaged.
4./KG 53 He111H2 3339
Crash-landed at Vendeville, crew safe. Aircraft 15% damaged.

1st - 7th April 1941 Overview

Royal Air Force

Fighter Command

Note: Events will be covered up to and including April 7th. Further movements during April 1941 will be proper to Volume Two, which will commence with an Order of Battle from that date.

The rotation of squadrons and improvements in equipment continued. On the 3rd, 306 Squadron moved from Ternhill to join the Polish Wing at Northolt, while 3 Squadron arrived at Martlesham Heath from Castletown, changing places with 17 Squadron, which moved next day. Further movements were:

1st	238 squadron	Chilbolton to Pembrey, sending a detachment to Carew Cheriton.
5th	111 Squadron	Montrose to Dyce.
7th	1 Squadron	Kenley to Croydon.
	118 Squadron	Filton to Colerne.

One new unit was formed on the 8th, when 452 (RAAF) Squadron was established at Kirton-in-Lindsay with Spitfire Is. During April, 1, 257 and 302 Squadrons re-equipped with Hurricane IIs, while 72 and 152 Squadrons received Spitfire IIs. It had been realised that the days of the Hurricane as an air superiority fighter in northwest Europe were numbered. Therefore plans were underway to re-equip all front-line Hurricane units with Spitfires. Thus during April, 111 and 308 Squadrons took Spitfire Is on charge.

Bomber Command

The only unit movement came on the 3rd, when 18 Squadron moved to Oulton. 2 Group instructions were expanded on this date in response to an enquiry from Air-Vice Marshal Stevenson. All enemy vessels including fishing vessels were now to be attacked whenever opoortunities presented themselves. Trains were also now regarded as military targets, but passenger trains were excluded, to avoid causing casualties to civilians in the occupied territories.

Coastal Command

On the 1st, 612 Squadron transferred from Dyce to Wick and two days later, 252 Squadron moved from Chivenor to Aldergrove, changing places with 272 Squadron, which commenced re-equipment with Beaufighters.

The Luftwaffe

Fighter Forces

There were several changes during this first week. On the 1st, *JG 26* returned from Germany after its period of rest and re-equipment. *Stab* and *I Gruppe* arrived at Brest, *III./JG 26* went to St. Brieuc and *II./JG 26* arrived at Morlaix two days later. This permitted *II./JG 2* to leave Brest for its old home at Beaumont-le-Roger on the 7th. On this date *III./JG 53* also moved, from St. Brieuc to Berck-sur-Mer.

Bomber Forces

During the first week of April, several units changed bases. *III./KG 4* transferred from Eindhoven to Leeuwarden, *II./KG 76* from Chareaudun to Criel and *III./KG 76* from Gilze-Rijn to Cormeilles. *E.Gr.210* moved from Wevelghem to Abbeville on the 4th. *I/KG 1* also moved, to Brest/Lanveoc, where it was renumbered as *III./KG 40*, while *Stab./KG 40* was newly established at Bordeaux. One unit left, *II./KG 4* leaving Soesterburg for Italy.

Widening Theatres

Since late October 1940, the Italian forces had been waging a bitter campaign in Greece but with little success. The Greeks, aided by a small British Expeditionary Force, had fought the Italians to a stalemate. Hitler was unhappy with this. He had already laid plans to invade the Soviet Union and required a secure southern flank for this plan to proceed. Meanwhile the Yugoslavian government had recently been overthrown by a military coup, which repudiated the Axis Tri-partite pact, signed on 25th March. It was therefore imperative that this vulnerable southern flank be secured immediately, which required an invasion of Yugoslavia. The German forces would then be in a favourable position to assist Italy and to drive southwards into Greece, thus preventing Allied interference with his Balkan adventure. It would consolidate the whole of southern Europe as an Axis stronghold, provide support for the coming campaign in Libya, where the Italians were also in trouble, and would place his embarrassed ally, Mussolini, very firmly in his debt.

Thus, on 6th April, *Operation Marita* was put into effect. The *Wehrmacht*, with massive air support, moved into Yugoslavia and northern Greece. The campaign was to last a scant three weeks, the evacuation of British forces from Greece commencing on 25th April. meanwhile the arrival of *General* Erwin Rommel's *Afrika Korps* in North Africa had quickly led to a sharp reversal of British fortune there also. The theatres of war were slowly expanding.

Chapter Nine
Warming Up

1st April 1941

The first day of the month brought forth a veritable swarm of interceptions of reconnaissance aircraft and bombers. These were engaged upon harassing raids on coastal towns and convoys, or making cloud cover attacks upon selected airfields.

The first aircraft to be lost fell without a shot being fired. A Ju88 was tracked in across Shropshire, flying fast and low. It was 'V4+BS' of *8./KG 1* flown by *Unteroffizier* Heinz Ewald, which was heading for Birmingham. Visibility was poor and, at 09.45 hours, the Junkers flew straight into the mist-shrouded Brown Clee Hill, where it blew up. There were no survivors.

Weather conditions frustrated the efforts of Fighter Command to catch raiders until mid-afternoon, when at 15.15 hours a Heinkel of *3./KG 4* attacked Leeming airfield. AA gun-sites opened fire, claiming it damaged, while three 41 Squadron Spitfires were scrambled. They discovered the German aircraft one mile north of the airfield and Flight Lieutenant Anthony Lovell engaged. He chased it eastwards and fired a long burst. Pieces were seen to fly off, but then Sergeant Powell 'cut in' on his leader, making three firing passes from dead astern. More chunks of metal flew off and oil spurted from one engine. Powell, who had closed to fifty yards, suddenly found his windscreen covered in oil. He broke away violently to avoid a collision and last saw it vanishing into thick cloud over Seaham harbour. This aircraft, claimed as damaged, later crash-landed at Soesterberg.

Over an hour later, at 17.20 hours, Flying Officer Edmond and Pilot Officer Crowley-Milling of 242 Squadron patrolled over a convoy off Harwich. The Hurricane pilots saw a Ju88 approaching and fought it off, claiming a 'damaged'. This unit was in action again five minutes later, probably against the

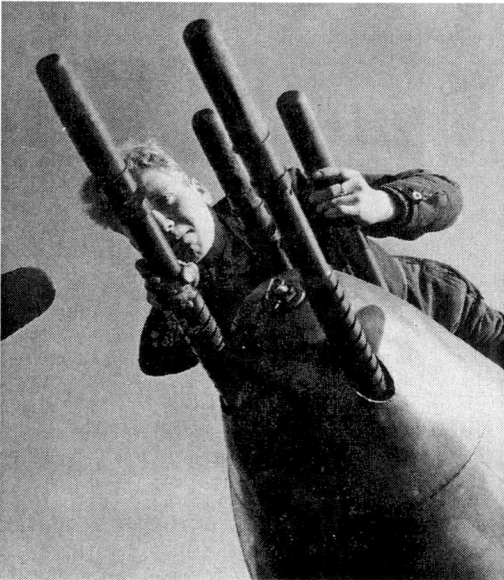

The sting in the nose. An armourer examines the four 20mm cannon in the nose of a 263 Squadron Whirlwind. The concentrated firepower made it a formidable ground attack aircraft, but it was not as effective against bombers as were the more agile single-engined RAF fighters.
- *British Official*

same bomber. Squadron Leader Treacey and Flying Officer Grassick, on a convoy patrol off Suffolk, intercepted a Ju88 from *II./KG 77*. The fighter pilots harried their adversary towards England where, after two men had baled out, *Leutnant* Paul Meyer's '3Z+LN' nosed over and dived into the ground at Worlingham. Pilot Officer North and Sergeant Warminger of 257 Squadron had also been directed to intercept this bomber and appeared on the scene just as the 242 Squadron pilots closed in. They could not get within range and were denied a 'share' of the victory.

During the afternoon. *I./KG 27* sent several He111s out on anti-shipping strikes in the Bristol Channel and along the south Wales coastline. Several fighter patrols were despatched to counter them. First to engage were Hurricane pilots from 79 Squadron, who caught '1G+HL' of *3./KG 27* while it was attacking a convoy west of St. David's Head. Flight Lieutenant Haysom attacked through a concentrated naval AA barrage and shot it down into the sea. *Oberfeldwebel* Reinhold Böer and one crewman were rescued by the ships. This victory was also claimed by AA gunners. The German unit lost another Heinkel to Hurricanes of 316 Squadron. Pilot Officers Anders and

Gabsewicz took off at 17.05 hours and intercepted *Oberfeldwebel* Ernst Lorra's '1G+LH' off Milford Haven. The two pilots attacked, claiming to have shot the Heinkel down into the sea. Apparently they lost sight of it in the sea mist, for Lorra headed his badly damaged bomber westwards towards Eire. He finally crash-landed it at Ballyristeen, County Wexford, where the crew were interned. Twenty-five minutes later, *I./KG 27* lost a third bomber when '1G+FL' of *3 Staffel* suffered engine failure over the Bristol Channel. *Unteroffizier* Günther Nicolei attempted to force-land on Lundy Island, but crashed into the cliff some 75 feet below the crest. Amazingly, three men survived, although badly hurt.

Cloud cover raiders were still over England and, at 18.10 hours, a Ju88 bombed Hornchurch airfield and was claimed damaged by the defences.

An hour later two Whirlwinds from 263 Squadron flown by Squadron Leader Donaldson and Flight Lieutenant Crooks patrolled along the north coast of Cornwall. At 19.00 hours they sighted a Dornier north of Predannack and attacked from astern. The German *Bordschütze* threw back a hail of gunfire, which shot Crooks' Whirlwind down into the seas in flames, killing him instantly. Donaldson managed to put a burst into the German aircraft, but could only claim a 'damaged' before the *Luftwaffe* crew found sanctuary in the clouds.

As dusk fell, the last combat of a somewhat hectic day occurred. Two Hurricane pilots from 247 Squadron sighted a FW200 accompanied by two He111s near St. Eval and Sergeant Renvoise attacked the Focke-Wulf, firing a long burst and claiming damage to it before the three German bombers were lost in the gathering gloom.

The daylight airfield attacks had caused more confusion than damage. When a lone Ju88 bombed St. Eval, a 53 Squadron Blenheim was fired on by a 247 Squadron Hurricane pilot!

The Hampdens of 61 Squadron had been temporarily placed under control of Coastal Command and had flown down to St. Eval. From here they departed on a daylight sortie to attack the German battlecruisers at Brest. Weather conditions were foul and the formation turned back. The aircraft flown by Pilot Officer Hartop lost touch with the rest and was not seen again.

Blenheim IVs of 235 Squadron, Coastal Command.

Hartop was intercepted and shot down 25km northeast of Brest by *Feldwebel* Bock of *II. / JG 2*

Other Coastal Command bombers made attacks along the coastline of the occupied territories and claimed to have torpedoed a ship off Terschelling. A Blenheim of 235 Squadron ditched off Hunstanton. Pilot Officer Annan's crew was rescued.

During the day the *Luftwaffe* fighter forces were strengthened when *Major* Adolf Galland's *JG 26 'Schlageter'* commenced its return to the Channel front. Bf109s from *I* and *III. / JG 26* flew out to St. Brieuc. Galland himself would shortly arrive with the rest of the *Geschwader*.

The first night of the month, unlike the daylight hours, was peaceful, no raids being carried out by either side.

Casualties 1st April 1941

Royal Air Force

41 Squadron Spitfire EB-
Damaged by debris from He111. Sgt Powell safe.
41 Squadron Spitfire R6775
Crashed on take-off from Catterick. Sgt Wilmott safe.
50 Squadron Hampden P4409
Crashed on take-off from Lindholme. Crew safe.
53 Squadron Blenheim T2398
Damaged by Hurricane at St.Eval. P/O Reade & crew safe.
61 Squadron Hampden X3129
Failed to return from sortie. P/O Hartop & crew lost.
79 Squadron Hurricane V6959
Crashed landing at Pembrey. F/L Denison safe.
85 Squadron Havoc BT463
Crashed landing at at Debden. F/O Bailey & crew safe.
234 Squadron Spitfire P7898
Damaged landing at Warmwell. P/O Masters safe.

235 Squadron Blenheim V5764
Crashed on Heacham Beach. P/O Blake & crew killed.
235 Squadron Blenheim Z6022
Crashed into sea. P/O Annan & crew rescued.
263 Squadron Whirlwind HF-
Failed to return from sortie. F/L Crooks lost.
311 Squadron Anson K6296
Damaged in flight. F/O Stransky & crew safe.
602 Squadron Spitfire LO-
Crashed at Ayr due to engine failure. Fate of pilot not known.
602 Squadron Spitfire X4557
Crashed landing at Prestwick. Sgt MacKay safe.

Luftwaffe

I./JG 51 Bf109F1 6610
Crashed on take-off from Calais/Marck. Aircraft 60% damaged.
III./JG 54 Bf109E7 4116
Crash-landed at Waldenburg. Aircraft 60% damaged.
I./KG 1 Ju88A5 6245 V4+BS
Failed to return. Uffz H Ewald & crew lost.
I./KG 4 He111P2 1623 5J+NL
Crash-landed at Soesterberg. One man wounded. Aircraft 35% damaged.
I./KG 27 He111H5 3635 1G+LH
Failed to return. Ofw E.Lorra & crew lost.
I./KG 27 He111H4 6993 1G+HL
Failed to return. Ofw R.Böer & crew lost.
I./KG 27 He111H5 3837 1G+FL
Failed to return. Uffz G.Nicolei & crew lost.
I./KG 27 He111 ----
Hit by AA PQ6234/15 West, one man wounded. Aircraft 10% damaged.
III./KG 51 Ju88A5 6293 9K+ET
Crash-landed at Schwechat. Lt K.Capesius & crew unhurt.
Aircraft 70% damaged.
III./KG 51 Ju88A5 5073 9K+CS
Crashed south of Saverne. Ogfr G.Müller & crew killed.
Aircraft destroyed.
III./KG 51 Ju88A5 8206
Crash-landed at Wiener-Neustadt. Aircraft 30% damaged.
III./KG 51 Ju88A5 5109
Crash-landed at Wiener-Neustadt. Aircraft 60% damaged.
III./KG 51 Ju88A5 4084
Crashed on take-off from Wiener-Neustadt. Aircraft 60% damaged.
III./KG 51 Ju88A5 8199
Crash-landed at Wiener-Neustadt. Aircraft 70% damaged.
I./KG 53 He111H5 3565
Crashed on take-off from Vitry-en-Artois. Aircraft 10% damaged.
II./KG 77 Ju88A5 0614 3Z+LN
Failed to return. Lt P.Meyer & crew lost.
K.Gr.z.b.V.104 Ju52 6095
Crashed at Wildbad. Lt R.Springing & crew killed. Aircraft destroyed.

2nd April 1941

Luftwaffe aircraft attacked targets in East Anglia and the northeast of Scotland, while reconnaissance sorties were intercepted along the south coast during the morning.

Early in the day, at 07.30 hours, Flight Lieutenant Mortimer-Rose of 234 Squadron claimed to have probably destroyed a Ju88 near Lyme Regis. A Ju88, 'M7+DL' of *3./K.Gr.806*, was lost, but this is recorded by German sources to have fallen to AA fire. *Leutnant* Willi Haas and his crew were reported missing. At the same time a Hurricane patrol from 504 Squadron found an He111 of *7./KG 55* off Budleigh Salterton. This aircraft, 'G1+JR', was shot down off the coast by Flight Lieutenant Parsons. Of *Unteroffizier* Hans Wagner's crew, only the body of the commander was recovered from the sea.

The final encounter took place at 12.50 hours, when Squadron Leader Heyworth led a 79 Squadron Hurricane patrol off Linney Head. They intercepted a Ju88, which was claimed probably destroyed by Heyworth. It appears to have been a reconnaissance machine from *3.(F)/121*, which crashed at Dinard following a fighter attack. One Hurricane was badly damaged by return fire.

One fighter pilot had a fruitless encounter, Sergeant John Shepherd of 234 Squadron finding a Ju88 over the Channel, but losing it in cloud before a shot could be fired. More fortunate were AA gunners aboard HM paddle minesweeper *Lorna Doone*, who claimed a Do17 destroyed during a shipping attack.

Apart from defensive patrols, Fighter Command aircraft were despatched on *Rhubarbs*, one of which prompted *Leutnant* Hans Strelow, a young fighter pilot from *5./JG 51*, to write in his diary:

"We saw an aircraft come quite smoothly out of the clouds. A Hurricane. He was already very close and sprayed the airfield with his eight guns. As he turned towards us, we hastily vanished behind the barracks and as we emerged we saw him go straight up into the clouds again. During the attack the airfield loudspeaker played merrily and a voice stressed our air superiority on the Channel Front!"

Bomber and Coastal Command aircraft also went inland, attacking the airfields of Haamstede, Maupertus and Carpiquet. Meanwhile Coastal units flew shipping strikes, claiming to have badly damaged an armed merchant vessel off Holland. A 53 Squadron Blenheim that attacked two small ships was chased away by a Bf109, but an 82 Squadron aircraft piloted by

Sergeant Haynes was reported missing. Coastal Command sustained a loss when Pilot Officer Milton's 220 Squadron Hudson failed to return. It was attacked by Bf109s while patrolling the Western Approaches. Although it evaded them, it was then caught in an electrical storm. One engine cut and the pilot was forced to belly-land north of Poitiers. Every man evaded capture, however, and all returned to England between 1941 and 1943.

Casualties 2nd April 1941

Royal Air Force

21 Squadron Blenheim R3661
Damaged by Flak. One man from P/O Ogilvie's crew killed.
41 Squadron Spitfire P8049
Crashed near Richmond, Yorks. Fate of pilot not known.
82 Squadron Blenheim Z5818
Failed to return from sortie. Sgt Haynes & crew lost.
82 Squadron Blenheim T2165
Damaged by Bf109. W/C Elworthy & crew safe.
82 Squadron Blenheim T2118
Damaged by Bf109. P/O Munro wounded, one crewman killed.
220 Squadron Hudson P5146
Failed to return from sortie. P/O Milton & crew lost.

Luftwaffe

Stab./KG 53 He111H3 6943
Hit by AA fire at Norwich. Aircraft 10% damaged.
III./KG 55 He111P2 2137 G1+JR
Failed to return from sortie. Uffz H.Wagner & crew lost.
K.Gr.806 Ju88A5 2198 M7+DL
Failed to return from sortie. Lt W.Haas & crew lost.
E./St.G.77 Ju87B1 0273
Force-landed at Wertheim. Aircraft 30% damaged.
II./ZG 76 Bf110 3446
Force-landed at Wittmundhafen. Aircraft 40% damaged.
E.Gr.210 Bf110E1 3830
Crash-landed at Wevelghem. Aircraft 10% damaged.
3.(F)/121 Ju88A5 0447
Belly-landed at Dinard after combat. One man wounded. Aircraft 65% damaged.
1.(H)/11 FW189 ----
Damaged in flight near Köln-Wahn. One man killed. Aircraft 5% damaged.
2./406 Do18 0861
Crashed into Skaggerak. Crew believed safe. Aircraft lost.

3rd April 1941

The previous night had been peaceful but, as dawn broke, several fighter patrols were sent out to protect shipping and to oppose reconnoitring German aircraft. Squadron Leader 'Paddy'

Originally designed as a shallow-draught river patrol boat, HMS Locust was pressed into service to escort convoys in the Thames estuary. Here, on 3rd April, her crew claimed a German bomber shot down by the Boulton-Paul four-gun turret mounted amidships.

- W Armstrong

Treacy of 242 Squadron led a section of Hurricanes out to Orfordness at dawn. This pilot intercepted an aircraft identified it as a Do17, and claimed to have damaged it.

At the same time, 07.00, a pair of Spitfires from 610 Squadron flown by Flight Lieutenant Norris and Sergeant Ballard patrolled off Beachy Head. They accounted for 'V4+KU', a Ju88 of 5./KG 1, which was engaged and blasted into the sea three miles off Seaford Head. Two bodies were later recovered from *Feldwebel* Rudi Twartz's crew.

More Hurricanes from 242 Squadron were airborne later in the morning when Flight Lieutenant Tamblyn and Flying Officer Rogers escorted a convoy off Norfolk. At 09.00 hours a Do17 was sighted, but Hugh Tamblyn ventured too near and was shot down into the sea. Rogers could not close sufficiently to open fire before the German aircraft was lost in cloud. A Bf110 of *E.Gr.210* landed damaged at Wevelghem and was possibly that engaged by one of the two 242 Squadron patrols.

There were no further engagements until 17.25 hours, when Hurricanes of 504 Squadron patrolled near Portreath at 15.30 hours. Squadron Leader Tony Rook and Pilot Officer Hunt intercepted a Heinkel, '1G+MH' of 1./KG 27 flown by *Leutnant* Fritz Hühle, which was seeking shipping in the Channel. The two fighter pilots shot it down into the sea near Stepper Point, Padstow. No trace of the crew was found. The Royal Navy also claimed a success when a convoy was attacked in the Thames estuary by three German bombers. HMS *Locust* opened fire, claiming a raider shot down into the sea.

II. / JG 26 made its transfer flight from Düsseldorf to Morlaix. Galland himself did not plan to to join them until the following day.

Casualties 3rd April 1941

Royal Air Force

25 Squadron Beaufighter X7451
Spun in near Wittering. Sgt Maxwell & navigator believed killed.

54 Squadron Spitfire P7610
Hit hangar on take-off. Sgt Thompsom injured.

66 Squadron Spitfire LZ-
Damaged in strafe.

66 Squadron Spitfire LZ-
Damaged in strafe.

66 Squadron Spitfire LZ-
Damaged in strafe.

86 Squadron Blenheim V6140
Damaged by Hurricane and crash-landed at Ipswich. P/O Gubbins & crew safe.

222 Squadron Spitfire P7780
Broke up over Southborough. Sgt Scott killed.

242 Squadron Hurricane Z2692
Failed to return from sortie. F/L Tamblyn lost.

257 Squadron Hurricane V6873
Belly-landed at Coltishall. P/O Blackburn safe.

316 Squadron Hurricane V6735
Overshot Pembrey. P/O Stegman safe.

Luftwaffe

Stab./Jafü 2 Bf108 1599
Crash-landed at Antwerp. Aircraft 15% damaged.

II./JG 2 Bf109E7 2047
Force-landed near Brest. Aircraft 45% damaged.

II./JG 26 Bf109E7 4957
Belly-landed at Brest. Aircraft 50% damaged.

III./JG 26 Bf109F2 5724
Taxiing accident at St. Brieuc. Aircraft 80% damaged.

9./JG53 Bf109F2 6700
Hit by a landing Bf109 at St. Brieuc. Aircraft 90% damaged.

III./JG 53 Bf109F2 6720
Hit another Bf109 when landing at St.Brieuc. Ofw J.Krobschnabel unhurt. Aircraft 90% damaged.

III./JG 53 Bf109 6701
Rammed by landing aircraft at St.Brieuc. Aircraft 80% damaged.

II./KG 1 Ju88A5 7208 V4+KU
Failed to return from sortie. Fw R.Twartz & crew lost.
I./KG 3 Ju88A5 6277
Crash-landed at Wunstorf. Aircraft 50% damaged.
2./KG 26 He111H5 3742
Hit by enemy gunfire and crashed at Sola. Aircraft 30% damaged.
I./KG 27 He111H5 4014 1G+MH
Failed to return from sortie. Lt F.Hühle & crew lost.
Zerst.E.Gr.Vaerlose Bf110D3 3713
Taxiing accident. Aircraft 50% damaged.
1./E.Gr.210 Bf109E2 3467
Damaged by enemy gunfire and landed at Wevelghem. Aircraft 25% damaged.
1.(F)/121 Ju88A5 0613
Force-landed at Homs. Aircraft 60% damaged.

3/4th April 1941

A Whitley of 51 Squadron flown by Pilot Officer Harrington failed to return from the main target, shot down by *Flak* near Lannion. A Blenheim flown by Wing Commander Addenbrooke, CO of 101 Squadron, was also reported missing. Another from this unit crashed and blew up at Frampton, killing Sergeant Burrows and his crew, while a 75 Squadron Wellington crash-landed at Boscombe Down, having collided with another aircraft - reportedly a Blenheim - over Lyme Bay. This may explain Addenbooke's loss. Several more bombers crashed on return, but accidents were not the only danger; A 115 Squadron Wellington piloted by Sergeant Thompson was peacefully droning back to Marham when *Leutnant* Völker's black *I./NJG 2* Dornier slid in behind it. Those on the ground at Marham heard the bomber pass overhead, closely followed by the fighter. Then came the thumping of gunfire, punctuated by the terrible crash as the Wellington went into the ground near Kingley at 01.20 hours. A further 51 Squadron Whitley was lost when Pilot Officer Sharp's aircraft was shot down in error by a Hurricane of 87 Squadron. Four of the crew baled out safely. Flight Lieutenant Carver had been informed that the aircraft was hostile, apparently confirmed by incorrect recognition signals from the bomber crew.

Bomber Command Operations		
Brest 90 Ostend & Rotterdam 7		
Minelaying 15		
Luftwaffe Operations		
Bristol/Avonmouth 94 Hull 9		

Following a dusk attack upon St. Eval, the Germans again headed for Bristol in an attack lasting four hours. Only one claim was made by the defences however. Flight Lieutenant John Cunningham of 604 Squadron intercepted a bomber identified as a Heinkel and claimed it shot down into the Channel at 00.50 hours. No such loss occurred, but a Ju88 'V4+AR' of *7./KG 1* flown by *Leutnant* Ernst Menge is known to have crashed into the Channel south of The Needles at this time. It is this aircraft that Cunningham is believed to have destroyed.

Casualties 3/4th April 1941

Royal Air Force

42 Squadron Beaufort W6499
Crashed landing at at Dumfries. F/O Garbett & crew safe.

49 Squadron Hampden P4403
Overshot St Eval. Sgt Ball & crew safe.

51 Squadron Whitley Z6556
Failed to return from sortie. P/O Harrington & crew lost.

51 Squadron Whitley T4299
Shot down near Sturminster Newton. P/O Sharp and three crewmen baled out, one killed.

75 Squadron Wellington R1161
Force-landed at Boscombe Down after collision over Lyme Bay. F/O Pritchard & crew safe.

77 Squadron Whitley P4947
Crashed at Waddington. Sgt Kyle & crew safe.

77 Squadron Whitley Z6583
Crashed at Tangmere. Three men from Sgt Dowlings' crew killed.

78 Squadron Whitley Z6408
Damaged landing at Boscombe Down. Sgt Dunlop & crew safe.

83 Squadron Hampden AD748
Crashed on Dartmoor. F/L Thompson & crew killed.

101 Squadron Blenheim N3552
Failed to return from sortie. W/C Addenbrooke & crew lost.

101 Squadron Blenheim T2439
Crashed at Frampton. Sgt Burrows & crew killed.

115 Squadron Wellington R1470
Shot down by intruder near Kings Lynn. Sgt Thompson and four crew killed.

141 Squadron Defiant T3913
Crashed near Gravesend. F/O Williams & crew killed.

144 Squadron Hampden AD783
Overshot St.Eval. Sgt Young & crew safe.

144 Squadron Hampden AD791
Overshot St.Eval. Sgt Curtis & crew safe.

604 Squadron Blenheim L6671
Crashed on take-off from Middle Wallop. Sgt Luing & crew safe.

John Cunningham of 604 Squadron (left) claimed his fifth confirmed victory on the night of 3rd April. He is pictured here with Edward Crew, who was also to become a leading RAF nightfighter pilot. Crew claimed his first success on the night of 4th April.

Luftwaffe

III./KG 1 Ju88A5 4224 V4+AR
Failed to return. Lt E.Menge & crew lost.
I./KG 76 Ju88A5 8142
Crashed 30km North of Verdun. Fw W.Kröger and three men injured, one killed. Aircraft destroyed.

4th April 1941

Following a quiet morning, Spitfires were sent out on *Rhubarbs*. Group Captain Harry Broadhurst led a section from 611 Squadron to strafe Calais/Marck in the afternoon, where the defences put a single bullet into the windscreen of his fighter.

Two Spitfires of 222 Squadron left Wittering at 15.40 hours and were vectored towards a reported raider northeast of Cromer. It was identified as a Ju88, which was first attacked by Flight Lieutenant Thomas, who saw hits but experienced heavy return fire, which put his guns out of action. Then Sergeant Ramsay continued the engagement, firing until his ammunition was exhausted and leaving the bomber diving into cloud. It was claimed probably destroyed.

Approximately an hour later, at 16.45 hours, 91 Squadron was scrambled from Hawkinge to search for raiders in the Channel area. A Ju88 of *II./KG 76* was seen near Deal, which was attacked and damaged by Pilot Officer Gage. *Oberleutnant* Kröner brought his aircraft back to force-land at Amiens, with

Sgt Spears wedding. Jack Mann is on the left, front row.
- Andy Saunders

one man killed and two wounded. The squadron then began to patrol the southeast coastline in pairs. At this time two Bf109s from *Stab. / JG 26* were flying on a transfer flight to Brest, flown by *Major* Adolf Galland and *Oberfeldwebel* Robert Menge. Galland decided to come 'the long way round', via the English coast where, he felt, the Tommies might provide him with 'something to shoot down.' This was unauthorised, but in such matters Galland was his own man. Thus the Messerschmitts appeared shortly after Sergeants Spears and Mann had been detached to seek another Ju88. The two *Luftwaffe* pilots attacked them, Galland shooting down Spears, who baled out wounded, while Menge, equally accurate, brought down Jack Mann, who crash-landed his blazing aircraft at Hawkinge. As the Spitfire slid to a halt the pilot scrambled from the cockpit, but then the petrol tanks exploded, badly burning him.[1]

Bomber Command despatched fourteen bombers on anti-shipping sorties. Eight Blenheims of 82 Squadron operated along the coast of Denmark and Sergeant Fearns' aircraft failed to return. It was shot down into the sea by *Flak*, exploding in impact.

---

1. 'Jackie' Mann, after pursuing a career in civil aviation, finally retired to Beirut in the Lebanon. He is now well known as one of the hostages, held for several years before hiis release.

Upper: Jack Mann's 91 Squadron Spitfire after the crash-landing. Although burnt, he was able to pull a camera from his flying suit and take this remarkable photograph. - Andy Saunders
Lower: Adolf Galland clambers from his 'Emil' after another combat sortie. On 4th April he and Robert Menge bounced Mann and Spears, shooting both down. - via Author

The *Luftwaffe* made a third fighter claim. *Feldwebel* Wurmheller of *II./JG 53* reported the destruction of a Spitfire, 20km north of Wissant, at 11.18 hours.

Casualties 4th April 1941

Royal Air Force

21 Squadron Blenheim V6073
Crash-landed at Chivenor. P/O Ogilvie & crew safe.

77 Squadron Whitley T4200
Damaged landing at Topcliffe. P/O Tyrie & crew safe.

82 Squadron Blenheim L9270
Crashed into sea. Sgt Fearns & crew killed.

87 Squadron Hurricane R4228
Damaged landing at Charmy Down. Sgt Castle safe.

91 Squadron Spitfire P7565
Shot down by Bf109. Sgt Spears baled out wounded.

91 Squadron Spitfire P7783
Shot down by Bf109. Sgt Mann crash-landed near Hawkinge wounded.

114 Squadron Blenheim T2224
Crash-landed at Thornaby-on-Tees. Sgt Mansfield & crew safe.

222 Squadron Spitfire P8074
Damaged by return fire from Ju88. F/L Thomas safe.

224 Squadron Hudson N7307
Overshot Limavady. P/O Barwood & crew safe.

245 Squadron Hurricane V7678
Crashed at Carrickfergus. Sgt Gault killed.

308 Squadron Hurricane X4388
Crashed on take-off from Kirton-in-Lindsay. S/L Orzechowski safe.

601 Squadron Hurricane Z2576
Force-landed at Gaddesdon, Herts. Sgt Briggs safe.

611 Squadron Spitfire H-B
Damaged by Flak. G/C Broadhurst safe.

Luftwaffe

II./JG 26 Bf109E7 5970
Crash-landed at Etaples, Lt Reiche wounded. Aircraft 85% damaged.

III./JG 51 Bf109F 5652
Crashed on take-off from Wizernes. Aircraft 50% damaged.

Z./JG 77 Bf110C4 3527
Force-landed at Herdla, reportedly following combat.
Aircraft 35% damaged.

II./KG 3 Do17Z3 2901
Crash-landed at Wunstorf. Aircraft 25% damaged.

I./KG 28 He111H5 3882
Hit obstruction landing at Nantes. Aircraft 65% damaged.

I./KG 30 Ju88A5 5127
Force-landed at Deelen. Aircraft 40% damaged.

IV./KG 30 Ju88A5 6130
Crashed on Heustädter Heide. Uffz H.G.Bouvier & crew killed.
Aircraft destroyed.

II./KG 54 Ju88A5 6146
Force-landed at Rugles. Aircraft 70% damaged.

A *Stirling of 7 Squadron is 'bombed-up'. Designed to pre-war specifications, the Stirling could carry no larger bomb than the 500lb weapons shown here. It also had a limited ceiling, since the wingspan of 99 feet was designed to fit pre-war hangars.*

I./KG 76 Ju88A5 8142
Force-landed at Amiens. Fw Oblt Kröner unhurt, one man killed & two injured. Aircraft 30% damaged.
E./St.G.77 Ju87B1 5209
Force-landed at Wertheim. Aircraft 75% damaged.
E.Gr.210 Bf110E1 3435
Crashed at Abbeville. Oblt W.Krause & gunner killed. Aircraft 50% damaged.
1.(F)/120 He111H2 5513
Crash-landed at Bardufoss. Aircraft 40% damaged.

4/5th April 1941

From the attacks one Hampden was lost when the 106 Squadron machine flown by Wing Commander Polglaise was seen shot down by *Flak* while flying low over Brest. A direct hit was claimed upon *Gneisenau*, which was actually a 'near miss'. The bomb landed in the dry dock and the battlecruiser was moved out into the harbour for safety. Flak gunner claimed three bombers shot down in this area.

The first raiders approached the English southwest coast as dusk was falling. Visibility was sufficient for two Hurricanes of

| **Bomber Command** |
| **Operations** |
| Brest 54 Köln 11 Rotterdam 3 |
| Minelaying 6 OTU 2 |
| **Luftwaffe Operations** |
| Bristol/Avonmouth 105 Great |
| Yarmouth 18 |

79 Squadron to make the initial interception. Flying Officers Haysom and Bryant-Fenn found a bomber identified as a Heinkel (although without doubt a Ju88 of *II./KG 54*) over Linney Head at 20.31 hours and inflicted damage upon it. The squadron sustained a casualty, however, when Pilot Officer Robinson's Hurricane was seen to dive into the sea while on patrol in the same area.

604 Squadron Beaufighters were ordered away as the gloom turned to full darkness and, at 22.15 hours, Pilot Officer Lawton made contact with a bomber near Frome. He attacked and claimed an He111 probably destroyed. This would appear to have been another Junkers from *II./KG 54*, which returned having been damaged by a fighter. Lawton and his navigator were force to bale out due to damage sustained in this encounter. The only confirmed success did fall to a 604 Squadron crew. Flying Officer Edward Crew hunted down *Oberfeldwebel* Herbert Rose's He111 of *III./KG 26* and, over Weston-Super-Mare, caught the bomber with a withering burst of fire. Three men took to their parachutes as '1H+ED' went down in flames at West Huish, carrying two more crewmen to their deaths. AA sites claimed two bombers destroyed and three more damaged.

Casualties 4/5th April 1941

Royal Air Force

59 Squadron Blenheim V5530
Abandoned over Wattisham. P/O Morton & crew safe
79 Squadron Hurricane P3661
Crashed into sea off Linney Head. P/O Robinson killed.
79 Squadron Hurricane V7013
Undershot Pembrey. F/O Clift safe.
106 Squadron Hampden AD738
Failed to return from sortie. W/C Polglaise & crew lost.
604 Squadron Beaufighter R2259
Abandoned over Hungerford in fog. F/L Lawton & crew baled out.

Luftwaffe

III./KG 26 He111H5 3595 1H+ED
Failed to return. Ofw H.Rose & crew lost.

I./KG 54 Ju88A5 4149
Undercarriage damage at Evreux. Aircraft 30% damaged.
II./KG 54 Ju88A5 5226 B3+KP
Damaged by fighter on sortie to Bristol. Lt H.Mally & crew unhurt.
Aircraft 20% damaged.
II./KG 54 Ju88A5 4230
Damaged by fighter on sortie to Bristol. Aircraft 40% damaged

5th April 1941

Bad weather prevented all but minimal air activity. Although German aircraft ventured forth to bomb targets in northwest Scotland, they went unchallenged by the defences.

The Hampdens of 61 Squadron again set out to attack the battlecruisers at Brest. As before, the mission was aborted and again an aircraft was lost. Pilot Officer McCrossan's bomber crashed into the sea during a storm.

One combat took place when a 53 Squadron Blenheim was engaged by a Bf109, but escaped unscathed.

Casualties 5th April 1941

Royal Air Force

41 Squadron Spitfire P7320
Undershot Catterick. Sgt Hopkinson safe.
61 Squadron Hampden AD753
Failed to return from sortie. P/O McCrossan & crew lost.
66 Squadron Spitfire LZ-
Three aircraft damaged in strafe.
71 Squadron Hurricane V6757
Crashed near Louth. F/O Morantz injured.
79 Squadron Hurricane P3092
Crashed landing at Angle. Sgt Round safe.
87 Squadron Hurricane P3380
Belly-landed at Exeter. P/O McLure safe.
88 Squadron Battle RH-
Destroyed in raid on Sydenham.

Luftwaffe

E./JG 53 Bf109E7 6177
Crash-landed at Evreux. Aircraft 30% damaged.
II./KG 77 Ju88A5 3284
Crashed after take-off, 6m from from Couvron. Ofw E.Schwarz & crew killed. Aircraft destroyed.
III./KG 77 Ju88A5 0546
Collided landing at Juvincourt. Fw F Goletz and two crew killed. Aircraft destroyed.
III./KG 77 Ju88A5 8219
Collided landing at Juvincourt. Lt F.Siegl and two crew killed. Aircraft destroyed.

5/6th April 1941

Bomber Command operations were cancelled, but a handful of

German aircraft crossed the British coastline in the southwest and eastern Scotland. No fighters made contact, but AA gunners claimed a bomber destroyed and a second damaged. Coningsby was attacked by an intruder and a number of Hampdens were slightly damaged by bomb splinters. St. Eval was also attacked.

Casualties 5/6th April 1941

Royal Air Force

106 Squadron Hampden -----
Several aircraft slightly damaged in strafe.
118 Squadron Spitfire R6883
Crashed landing at Colerne. Sgt Fairbairn safe
255 Squadron Defiant N3321
Crashed landing at Kirton-in-Lindsay. Sgt Feruga & gunner safe
485 Squadron Spitfire X4662
Belly-landed near Market Weighton. P/O Barrett safe
502 Squadron Whitley T4268
Crashed on take-off from Limavady. P/O Ramsay & crew safe
504 Squadron Hurricane TM-
Four aircraft damaged in raid on St.Eval
504 Squadron Magister TM-
Damaged in raid on St.Eval

Luftwaffe

- nil -

6th April 1941

At dawn Coastal Command mounted yet another raid upon Brest. Six Beauforts of 22 Squadron were detailed, three carrying torpedoes, however, only four were actually despatched. All three torpedo aircraft and one bomber departed between 04.30 and 05.15 hours. The first Beaufort, piloted by Flying Officer Kenneth Campbell, reached the target area at 06.30 hours. As the lone Beaufort roared into sight all hell broke loose. The Beaufort continued steadily on its suicidal course through the hail of tracer fire over the harbour, tracking straight for *Gneisenau*. The torpedo fell clear, passing over the concrete mole and hurtled towards the big warship, striking astern and doing considerable damage. Then the bomber took a heavy barrage from *Flak* gunners. There was no escape and the bomber crashed in flames into the harbour. When the wreckage was recovered, the Germans believed that the pilot's seat was occupied by the navigator. German aircraft normally had the

Top: A Beaufort drops a practice torpedo. The attacks on the German warships at Brest were carried out from this clearly low altitude and through a wall of Flak. - British Official

Left: Kenneth Campbell of 22 Squadron, who was posthumously awarded the Victoria Cross for his attack on the Gneisenau on 6th April 1941.

pilot's seat on the right, as opposed to the left in British aircraft and it seems that some confusion has arisen. An experienced Beaufort airmen and author Roy Conyers Nesbit has expressed the opinion that it would not have possible for Sergeant James Scott, the Canadian navigator, to have pulled Campbell clear and taken the controls in the short space of time between the aircraft being hit and finally crashing into the water. Campbell was posthumously awarded the Victoria Cross. In the words of his citation, which first described the heavy concentration of shore *Flak* batteries and *Flak*-ships:

"....Flying Officer Campbell must have run the gauntlet of all these guns, flying almost at sea level and have flown past the anti-aircraft ships at less than mast height in the very mouths of their guns. He would then have skimmed the mole and fired the torpedo at point-blank range. The damage caused was such that the battlecruiser returned to the dock from which she had but recently emerged.

"By pressing his attack to a successful conclusion in the face of the most formidable anti-aircraft fire, Flying Officer Campbell displayed determination, skill and daring of a quite outstanding character."

The destruction of his aircraft was credited to *Flak* gunners

Thirty minutes after Campbell's heroic sacrifice, Sergeant Alan Camp also of 22 Squadron brought his Beaufort in over Brest:

"When I arrived at Brest it was full daylight. I crossed the spit of land at the southwest corner of the harbour, coming under fire from shore batteries. I then came down to a few feet above the harbour and flew towards the mole protecting the Rade Abri, behind which the battlecruiser lay. I passed three Flak-ships moored just outside the mole and nearly reached the end of the mole itself. By then I was being fired at by shore batteries all around the harbour and by the guns of the three Flak-ships. Continuous streams of fire seemed to be coming from every direction. It was by far the worst Flak I have ever encountered. When I was up to the mole I saw that the battlecruiser herself was completely hidden from me by a bank of haze. I therefore turned away to the east and climbed into cloud."

The third torpedo-armed Beaufort, flown by Flying Officer Hyde, also made an unsuccessful sortie to Brest. His aircraft was badly damaged by *Flak* and crashed on return.

At noon, Beauforts of 22 Squadron were out again, hunting German warships at sea. A minesweeper and a destroyer were attacked with torpedoes north of Brest, but Bf109s appeared and Flying Officer Hicks' aircraft was shot down into the sea.

Shortly afterwards, two Whirlwinds of 263 Squadron took off to patrol along the Cornish coastline. At 13.05 hours they intercepted an He111 off Lizard Point. This was attacked and claimed damaged by Flying Officer Howe and Pilot Officer Tooth and would seem to have been an aircraft of *I./KG 27*, which returned with the *Bordfunker* wounded.

Shortly after 16.30 hours, two Spitfires of 74 Squadron flew a 'Rhubarb' to St. Omer, where *Luftwaffe* fighters were encountered. Pilot Officer Robert Spurdle claimed a Bf110 probably destroyed, while Flight Lieutenant Tony Bartley claimed damage to a Bf109, which he watched force-land in a field. Bartley's aircraft was shot-up and he force-landed at Hawkinge on return. Several other *Rhubarbs* were flown during the day and the War Diary of *JG 53* noted: '...one Spitfire strafed Berck.' During the day Coastal Command lost two further crews, both in Blenheims. The 107 Squadron aircraft flown by Wing Commander Cameron crashed into the sea off the British coast while returning from a shipping strike, while Pilot Officer Lishman's 53 Squadron aircraft was shot down by a Bf109 after reporting a U-boat off St. Brieuc.

The German fighters submitted four claims during the course of the operations against Brest. *II./JG 2* reported three fights. *Feldwebel* Bauer claimed a Blenheim 40km north of Morlaix at 12.45 hours (believed to have been Lishman); *Oberleutnant* Hepe claimed another 6km north of Plouestat at 13.40 and *Hauptmann* Greisert claimed a third at Brest at 16.00, this latter clearly a 22 Squadron Beaufort. *Oberfeldwebel* März of *II./JG 26* claimed an Anson at Brignogan Plage, at 13.30 hours.

Casualties 6th April 1941

Royal Air Force

22 Squadron Beaufort N1016
Failed to return from sortie. F/O Campbell & crew lost.
Pilot awarded posthumous Victoria Cross.

22 Squadron Beaufort N1147
Failed to return from sortie. P/O Hicks & crew lost.

59 Squadron Blenheim V5962
Failed to return from sortie. P/O Lishman & crew lost.

74 Squadron Spitfire JH-
Force-landed at Hawkinge. F/L Bartley safe.

107 Squadron Blenheim V6023
Crashed into sea. W/C Cameron & crew believed lost.

111 Squadron Hurricane R4086
Damaged taxiing at Dyce. Sgt Hanes safe.

118 Squadron Spitfire X4826
Collided over Chippenham, Wilts. Fate of pilot not known.

118 Squadron Spitfire X4822
Collided over Chippenham, Wilts. Fate of pilot not known.

206 Squadron Hudson T9298
Crashed landing at Aldergrove. P/O Harwood & crew safe.

232 Squadron Hurricane W9699
Belly-landed near Stonehaven. Sgt Christian safe.

272 Squadron Blenheim L9252
Crashed landing at Weston-Super-Mare. Sgt Rouse & crew safe.

312 Squadron Hurricane V6536
Belly-landed on beach. Sgt Stehlik safe.

315 Squadron Hurricane P2974
Damaged landing at Speke. P/O Fiedorczuk safe.

313

Luftwaffe

8./JG 53 Bf109F2 6681
Crash-landed at St Brieuc. Aircraft 85% damaged.
I./KG 27 He111H5 3687
Damaged by enemy gunfire, one man wounded. Aircraft 20% damaged.
I./KG 27 He111 3973
Crash-landed at Tours. Aircraft 30% damaged.
III./KG40 He111 ----
Hit by own Flak at Brest. Hptm B.Stärcke wounded, one man killed.
Aircraft 60% damaged.
I./K.Gr.z.b.V.1 Ju52 5337
Crashed. No further details. Aircraft destroyed.

6/7th April 1941

One loss was sustained during the listed attacks. Pilot Officer Jackson's 83 Squadron Hampden failed to return from a minelaying sortie, shot down by *Flak* at Brest.

Bomber Command Operations

Brest 71 Calais 6 Airfields 10
Rotterdam 3 Minelaying 24

Luftwaffe Operations

Minelaying & isolated attacks 57

Over Britain, one combat took place when Flight Lieutenant Hayes of 600 Squadron was fired on by an He111. Undamaged, the Beaufighter out-turned the Heinkel, which went into a steep dive. Hayes fired four drums of 20 mm shells, but vibration rapidly caused the gunsight to become unusable. Hayes then lost sight of the German aircraft and his claim for a 'probable' was disallowed.

The Reinforcement Flight (218 Squadron) at Stradishall despatched seven Wellingtons to the Middle East during the night but one aircraft, piloted by Flying Officer Kimberly, was lost without trace.

Casualties 6/7th April 1941

Royal Air Force

49 Squadron Hampden X7899
Failed to return from sortie. P/O Jackson DFM & crew lost.
114 Squadron Blenheim L9020
Crashed on take-off from Thornaby-on-Tees. Sgt Cash & crew safe.
218 Squadron Wellington N2812
Missing en route to Middle East. F/O Kimberley & crew lost.

Luftwaffe

I./KG 27 He111H5 3973
Landed at Tours with motor damage. Aircraft 30% damaged.
II./KG 55 He111P4 3079
Believed to have hit another He111 landing at Chartres. Aircraft 30% damaged.

II./KG 55 He111P4 2992
Hit by landing He111 at Chartres. Aircraft 45% damaged.

7th April 1941

Fighter Command aircraft were despatched on *Rhubarbs* to Furne and Middelkerke shortly after dawn. At the same time Blenheims of Bomber and Coastal Commands set out on anti-shipping sorties and attacks upon airfields and troop concentrations. Nine bombers from 139 Squadron, operating in two flights of six and three, attacked a convoy off Ijmuiden, but were roughly handled by the Germans. The first flight flew through a wall of *Flak* to carry out their bombing runs and one was badly hit, limping back across the North Sea to crash-land in England. The second flight approached at wave-top height, but were attacked by Bf109s of *I./JG 1*. Sergeant Bennett's aircraft was shot down 25km west of Ijmuiden by *Unteroffizier* Krause, but a fighter was claimed shot down by a gunner.

During the course of the day's anti-shipping operations a Blenheim of 53 Squadron flown by Pilot Officer Nicholson was reported missing. Two 59 Squadron Blenheims were attacked by Bf109s, Pilot Officer Scarfe encountering one Messerschmitt and Pilot Officer Buchan two. Both British aircraft escaped undamaged.

Over England, two Spitfire pilots from 222 Squadron made the only contact with intruding German aircraft at 09.35 hours. Sergeants Marland and Ramsay were on convoy patrol off Yarmouth when Marland suddenly saw a bomb explode in the middle of the convoy. He attracted his companion's attention and a Do17 was then seen. They chased it right through a heavy naval AA barrage. Marland fired three bursts, reporting that the crew had baled out before the aircraft crashed into the sea.

Just over thirty minutes later, two Spitfires from 74 Squadron flew a *Rhubarb* along the French coast and were engaged by Bf109s over Griz Nez at 10.00 hours. In the fight that followed, Pilot Officer Rogowski claimed a Messerschmitt destroyed, while Pilot Officer Howard reported strikes on a second. More *Rhubarbs* were despatched in the afternoon and Wing Commander Peel led six Hurricanes on a sortie to Berck, where two Bf109s of *III./JG 53*, rolling down the airfield on an *Alarmstart*, were attacked. Both were slightly damaged and *Gefreiter*

Frankhauser was wounded. *Flak* gunners claimed a Spitfire destroyed near Ostend at 19.45 hours.

Fighter Command sustained a loss in the early evening during a convoy patrol by six Hurricanes of 249 Squadron; Pilot Officer Wynne crashed near Ongar for no apparent reason and died.

Casualties 7th April 1941

Royal Air Force

53 Squadron Blenheim T2398
Failed to return. P/O Nicholson & crew lost.

59 Squadron Blenheim TR-C
Damaged by Bf110. P/O Scarfe & crew safe.

59 Squadron Blenheim TR-F
Damaged by Bf110. P/O Buchan & crew safe.

64 Squadron Spitfire P7500
Belly-landed near Great Dunmow. Sgt Blackman safe.

74 Squadron Spitfire P8140
Damaged landing at Manston. Sgt May safe.

139 Squadron Blenheim L9386
Failed to return . Sgt Bennett & crew lost.

139 Squadron Blenheim XD-
Damaged by Flak and crash-landed. One crewman killed, one injured.

249 Squadron Hurricane Z2663
Crashed at High Ongar after operational sortie. Sgt Wynne killed.

Luftwaffe

E./JG 51 Bf109E4 0991
Crashed on take-off from Abbeville. Gfr A.Ketzel injured. Aircraft 90% damaged.

7./JG 53 Bf109 5459
Strafed by fighter during a scramble from Berck-sur Mer. Gfr J.Frankhauser wounded. Aircraft 5% damaged.

7./JG 53 Bf109 5651
Strafed by fighter during a scramble from Berck-sur-Mer. Aircraft 10% damaged.

Wekusta 76 He111 5326
Crashed at Aspern. Fw Heinz & crew killed. Aircraft destroyed.

The story continues......

Volume Two will present the heavy *Blitz* of April and May 1941, followed by the withdrawal of the Luftwaffe forces to the East for the assault upon Russia, the hunt for the battleship *Bismarck*, the suicidal low-level anti-shipping offensive known as *Operation Channel Stop* and ends at beginning of the Non-stop Offensive, with the commencement of the massive *Circus* operations over France.

Index

Personnel - Royal Air Force
Note: Names indexed in squadron order

319

329

Personnel, Luftwaffe

Mobius, Ofw H. Tr.St. I Fk.K. 75
Mohler, Uffz R. I./JG 1. 231
Mohr, Lt H. II./KG 54. 252
Mölders, Maj W. Stab./JG 51. 111, 122, 156, 157, 171, 177, 221, 229
Moller, Fw F. IV./JG 51. 206
Moritz, Ofw H. III./KG 27. 155
Much, Fw H. 3./KG 26. 163, 164
Müller, Uffz. 1./JG 3. 93
Müller, Ogfr G. III./KG 51. 296
Müncheberg, Oblt K-H. II./KG 1. 271
Muth, Fw W. 2./KG 30. 87
Naumann, Fw E. E./St.G.77. 274
Nelson, Lt E. I./ZG 76. 208
Neumann, Fw E. III./JG 77. 68
Nicolei, Uffz G. I./KG 27. 294, 296
Nies, Ofw W. SNFKdo 4. 42
Nottelmann, Gfr H. III./KG 4. 255
Oesau, Hptm W. III./JG 3. 107, 108, 109
Olejnik, Ofw R. 2./JG 3. 106, 107
Onken, Uffz H. I./KG 1. 252
Ostholt, Oblt. III./JG 3. 107
Ottmer, Lt M. I./JG 51. 198, 199
Pabst, Oblt H. II./St.G.77. 213
Patscheider, Lt H. 4./KG 2. 174
Peper, Lt O. II./KG 76. 274, 276
Peter, Uffz H. 10./KG 3. 210
Peterburs, Ofw H. III./ZG 76. 118
Petry, Lt M. 6./KG 53. 94
Pfeiffer, Kt R. I./NJG 2. 248
Pichler, Uffz J. 7./JG 77. 157
Piep, Fw E. I./KG 1. 133
Philipp, Fw W. II./JG 26. 106
Pirkner, Oblt G. 4./JG 51. 177, 179
Pirschmann, Gfr. E./JG 51. 254
Plumecke, Oblt W. I./KG 28. 85
Pohland, Fw H. I./LG 2. 156, 158
Ponzet, Fw P. I./JG 54. 211
Pöpel, Uffz G. I./JG 3. 91, 93
Port, Oblt G. E./LG 1. 44
Presia, Fw W. 1.(F)/120. 133, 134
Pütz, Fw A. 8./KG 27. 166, 167
Raab, Uffz. SNF.Kdo 4. 196, 197
Rademacher, Uffz H. E./KG 1. 84
Radloff. Fw. I./KG 53. 232
Rasper, Fw H. 4./NJG 1. 223, 232
Rauchle, Lt W. 6./KG 55. 240, 241
Reiche, Lt. II./JG 26. 306
Rennert, Ofhr E. E./JG 52. 250
Richter, Fw H. Stab./KG 27. 228
Richter, Fw K-H. II./KG 76. 246
v.Richthofen, Fhr Manfred. 177
Riemenschneider, Ofw K. II./KG 27. 161

Rinck, Oblt F-K. III./KG 30. 84
Robrahn, Lt H. 4./KG 27. 226, 228
Rohde, Uffz H. Stab./ZG 26. 207
Roming, Uffz J. E.Gr.210. 96, 97
Rose, Ofw H. III./KG 26. 308
Rosner, Fw E. I./KG 77. 152
Rossbach, Ofw H. I./NJG 1. 73
Roth, Uffz. I./KG 53. 232
Rowold, Uffz W. II./LG 2. 31
Rübell, Lt G. 6./JG 51. 171, 173, 287
Rücker, Fw B. Stab./KG 2. 234, 236
Rücker, Oblt J. I./KG 2. 38, 39, 97
Rudiger, Uffz K. Stab./ZG 76. 265, 267
Rudiger, Fw W. III./KG 26. 200, 201
Rusche, Lt B. 4./KG 27. 162, 164
Ryback, Uffz K. I./LG 2. 121, 124
Rybiak, Uffz E. 6./JG 3. 97
v.Saalfeld, Lt E. 7./JG 51. 286, 287
Schaarschuch, Fw H. 198, 199
Schaller, Lt W. E./JG 53. 210
Schenk, Oblt W. E.Gr.210. 269
Schentke, Fw. III./JG 3. 107
Scherbaum, Fw R. I./NJG 3. 160
Scherer, Oblt F. III./KG 51. 238
Scherfling, Fw H. 7./NJG 1. 288
Schiffner, Lt H. 6./KG 2. 34
Schimmelpfennig, Lt E. 9./St.G.1. 105, 162
Schindler, Uffz M. 4./KG 3. 65, 66
Schlagregen, Fw W. I./KG 1. 216, 218
Schleef, Uffz. 9./JG 3. 107
Schlether, Lt W. II./LG 2. 116, 117
Schloms, Fw. III./KG 55. 236
Schlott, Lt W. 1.(F)/123. 283, 284
Schmal, Ofw J-T. I./KG 30. 46, 47
Schmidt, Uffz E. 4.(F)/121. 230, 232
Schmidt, Lt E. I./NJG 3. 269
Schmidt, Stfw G. I./KG 27. 117
Schmidt, Lt H. 3.(F)/123. 180, 181
Schmidt, Uffz R. 5./JG 77. 38, 96, 144
Schmidt, Uffz W. 1./JG 1. 139
Schmidt, Lt. I./NJG 3. 232
Schneegold, Uffz B. Kur.St.OKM. 170
Schneider, Hptm K-F. II./KG 30. 211
Schneider, Ofw. SNF.Kdo 5. 220
Schramme, Fw S. 5./KG 3. 205
Schreiber, Fw E. 4./NJG 1. 223
Schubert, Uffz H. 3./JG 1. 269
Schüle, Fw E K.Gr.100. 69
Schulte, Lt H. 3.(H)/21. 243
Schulz, Oblt A. 2./NJG 2. 65, 67, 125, 126, 127
Schulz, Oblt W. K.Gr.100. 234, 237
Schüster, Fw J. I./NJG 2. 168

Personnel, Miscellaneous

Units, Royal Air Force

Groups

1 Group, Bomber Command. 17
2 Group, Bomber Command. 18, 28, 30, 42, 46, 88, 101, 108, 110, 187, 257, 270, 286, 289
3 Group, Bomber Command. 18, 112, 165
4 Group, Bomber Command. 18, 24, 112, 131
5 Group, Bomber Command. 18, 41, 118, 198, 232
9 Group, Fighter Command. 14
10 Group, Fighter Command. 14, 66
11 Group, Fighter Command. 15
12 Group, Fighter Command. 16
13 Group, Fighter Command. 16
14 Group, Fighter Command. 17
15 Group, Coastal Command. 19
16 Group, Coastal Command. 19
17 Group, Coastal Command. 19
18 Group, Coastal Command. 20, 186

Wings

Biggin Hill. 185
Kenley. 185
Tangmere. 186, 204-205
North Weald. 186
Northolt. 186
Duxford. 186
Hornchurch. 185, 204

Squadrons

1 Sqn. 15, 33, 90, 91, 92, 101, 105, 106, 111, 116, 121, 134, 185, 202, 237, 244, 253, 254, 267, 270, 289
3 Sqn. 17, 27, 56, 61, 67, 69, 72, 100, 106, 153, 184, 192, 196, 289
7 Sqn. 18, 28, 38, 119, 124, 128, 186, 200, 262, 268, 307
9 Sqn. 18, 55, 56, 94, 110, 119, 123, 124, 128, 147, 168, 193, 194, 223, 227, 258, 279
10 Sqn. 18, 36, 37, 40, 68, 69, 74, 112, 147, 168, 180, 194, 200, 227, 235, 240, 247, 251, 2793
12 Sqn. 17, 116, 172, 230, 262, 268, 279
15 Sqn. 18, 57, 124, 128, 145, 147, 200, 287, 288
17 Sqn. 15, 92, 100, 101, 121, 184, 249, 250, 270, 272, 273, 275, 289
18 Sqn. 18, 67, 230, 251, 262, 289
19 Sqn. 16, 57, 100, 106, 158, 164, 172, 182, 186, 192, 230, 264, 270

21 Sqn. 18, 124, 126, 128, 178, 197, 227, 268, 251, 262, 268, 275, 281, 286, 287, 298, 306
22 Sqn. 19, 64, 66, 77, 78, 81, 82, 119, 131, 132, 209, 230, 257, 258, 273, 275, 310, 311, 312, 313
23 Sqn. 15, 34, 36, 37, 47, 52, 56, 67, 68, 70, 71, 169, 173, 179, 184, 200, 212, 216, 217, 219, 239
25 Sqn. 16, 62, 116, 165, 174, 197, 235, 262, 282, 300
26 Sqn. 206
29 Sqn. 16, 100, 128, 174, 193, 207, 234, 235, 240
32 Sqn. 14, 45, 52, 67, 100, 114, 160, 213
35 Sqn. 18, 61, 216, 217, 285
40 Sqn. 18, 68, 69, 101, 114, 128, 165, 223, 227, 228, 270, 287
41 Sqn. 15, 30, 49, 50, 52, 76, 96, 100, 105, 106, 114, 156, 157, 158, 164, 199, 237, 260, 262, 265, 283, 285, 292, 295, 298, 309
42 Sqn. 20, 113, 116, 118, 119, 123, 188, 199, 264, 302
43 Sqn. 17, 74, 84, 94, 104, 119, 130, 184, 199, 266, 271
44 Sqn. 18, 146, 147, 197, 215, 217, 262
46 Sqn. 16, 61, 101, 122, 123, 164, 184, 206, 245, 272
48 Sqn. 19, 30, 43, 44, 61, 62, 134, 169, 284
49 Sqn. 19, 42, 54, 97, 99, 124, 127, 128, 262, 302, 315
50 Sqn. 19, 32, 83, 139, 140, 194, 223, 228, 233, 236, 259, 262, 295
51 Sqn. 18, 36, 37, 45, 47, 66, 82, 111, 131, 132, 151, 167, 168, 180, 193, 194, 262, 273, 301, 302
53 Sqn. 19, 38, 47, 51, 52, 96, 135, 155, 218, 219, 237, 242, 268, 276, 277, 294, 295, 297, 309, 313, 315, 316
54 Sqn. 17, 91, 96, 100, 101, 123, 138, 172, 175, 178, 184, 185, 198, 199, 202, 204, 214, 221, 222, 254, 281, 284, 300
56 Sqn. 15, 49, 92, 101, 105, 106, 111, 121, 138, 178, 186, 206, 242, 275, 277
57 Sqn. 18, 144, 180, 232, 236, 262, 279
58 Sqn. 18, 68, 69, 132, 197, 285
59 Sqn. 19, 40, 41, 47, 92, 93, 96, 99, 122, 168, 180, 188, 230, 250, 252, 258, 264,

338

Training Units

Units, Luftwaffe

Note: Where only a Geschwader is referred to in the text (i.e. JG 51, KG 55 etc.), this reference will be indexed to the relevant Geschwader Stab entry.

Fighter Units

Stab./KG 53. 21, 74, 95, 298
I./KG 53. 21, 47, 95, 200, 201, 232, 288, 296
  1./KG 53. 56, 92, 93
  2./KG 53. 65, 66, 88, 89, 113, 115
  3./KG 53. 134, 135, 182, 238
II./KG 53. 21, 99, 102, 173, 243, 251
  4./KG 53. 33, 75, 153, 154, 241, 256, 257,
    288
  5./KG 53. 67, 68
  6./KG 53. 76, 78, 94
III./KG 53. 21, 102, 130, 155, 199, 215
E./KG 53. 21
Stab./KG 54. 24
I./KG 54. 24, 39, 256, 257, 267, 309
II./KG 54. 24, 306, 308, 309
E./KG 54. 24, 89, 113, 155, 158, 220, 222
Stab./KG 55. 24, 35, 140, 235, 236, 240, 241,
  247, 263
I./KG 55. 24, 241, 247
II./KG 55. 24, 228, 236, 244, 247, 251, 314,
  314
  5./KG 55. 225
  6./KG 55. 226, 240
III./KG 55. 24, 34, 35, 60, 220, 222, 236, 241,
  257, 265, 296
  7./KG 55. 234, 297
E./KG 55. 24, 86, 94, 154, 155
Stab./KG 76. 189
I./KG 76. 86, 93, 152, 189, 207, 210, 248,
  303, 307
II./KG 76. 46, 72, 102, 145, 149, 152, 167,
  199, 212, 228, 246, 274, 276, 282, 290,
  303
  6./KG 76. 150, 225
III./KG 76. 73, 85, 189, 210, 228, 255, 281,
  290
  9./KG 76. 224
IV./KG 76. 281
E./KG 76. 152
Stab./KG 77. 23, 102, 189
I./KG 77. 23, 102, 152, 154, 159, 189, 238,
  251, 257
II./KG 77. 23, 53, 74, 97, 102, 189, 212, 220,
  232, 257, 276, 280, 281, 293, 296, 309
  4./KG 77. 265, 267, 288
III./KG 77. 23, 102, 147, 192, 193, 203, 220,
  238, 263, 309
E./KG 77. 23, 152, 215
K.Gr.100. 23, 32, 33, 69, 75, 89, 155, 159,
  180, 221, 234, 244, 251, 274
E./K.Gr.100. 23, 97, 154, 158, 237, 281
K.Gr.606. 24, 155, 258
  3./KGr.606. 152, 153, 240

K.Gr.806. 24, 40, 56, 58, 74, 134, 135, 143,
  145, 213, 215, 238, 241, 255, 257, 265,
  297, 298

Dive-bomber Units

Stab./St.G.1. 22, 150
I./St.G.1. 22, 120, 160, 258
II./St.G.1. 102
  5./St.G.1. 132, 133
III./St.G.1. 22, 106
  7./St.G.1. 105, 112
  8./St.G.1. 113
  9./St.G.1. 135, 1136
E./St.G.1. 208, 222, 243
III./St.G.2. 39, 84, 102
Stab./St.G.3. 70
Stab./St.G.77. 25, 102
I./St.G.77. 25, 112, 243
II./St.G.77. 25, 213
III./St.G.77. 25, 238
E./St.G.77. 135, 274, 298, 307

Specialised Combat Units

Stab./LG 1. 24, 102
I./LG 1. 24, 70, 89, 102, 179
II./LG 1. 29
III./LG 1. 24
  7./LG 1. 102
IV./LG 1. 25
E./LG 1. 24, 44, 282
IV./LG 1. 45, 232
I./LG 2. 22, 70, 78, 91, 120, 121, 124, 129,
  137, 143, 155, 158, 172, 175, 176, 190,
  200, 206, 207, 213, 229, 232, 253, 270,
  272, 276
  3.(H)/LG 2. 75
II./LG 2. 22, 31, 112, 117, 190, 241, 269, 282,
  5./LG 2. 116, 243
  9./LG 2. 164
E.Gr.210. 22, 79, 80, 96, 102, 113, 189, 212,
  220, 255, 257, 262, 269, 290, 298, 307
  1./E.Gr.210. 97, 210, 301
  2./E.Gr.210. 200, 208, 240, 241
  3./E.Gr.210. 155, 158

Reconnaissance Units

2.(F)/11. 62
3.(F)/11. 44, 270, 272
4.(F)/14. 41, 181
1.(F)/22. 190
2.(F)/22. 25, 46, 158, 193, 222, 223
3.(F)/22. 25, 98, 99, 262
3.(F)/31. 62
1.(F)/120. 25, 133, 134, 201, 202, 307
1.(F)/121. 124, 301

Coastal Units

Transport Units

Miscellaneous Units

Regia Aeronautica Units

343

Ships, British

Ships, German

Airfields

Places

Blitzed! The Battle of France May-June 1940

The struggle to halt the German invasion of Europe. Includes RAF and Luftwaffe loss listings.

256 pages ISBN 1-871187-07-9 Price £15.95

Battle over the Third Reich

A photographic account of the battle for air supremacy over Germany as seen by the Luftwaffe

184 pages ISBN 1-871187-10-9 Price £17.95

1944 - Over the Beaches

The Allied air offensive over Normandy and against Germany during June 1944, with full Allied victory and loss listings, supplemented by accounts and combat reports giving views of the campaign from all viewpoints and also providing an insight into the activities of the *Luftwaffe*.

338 pages ISBN 1-871187-26-5 Price £14.95

Readers Research Service

The author, an accredited independent researcher at Public Record Office, offers readers a comprehensive research sevice based upon the day-by-day record compiled during his past twenty-five years research into WW2 air operations over northwest Europe. This independent facility, operating under the trade name of **A.C.E.** *(Air Combat Europe) Services*, is available at competitive rates to anyone requiring such information.

For prospective authors, the facilities to transfer information from *Amstrad* PCW word processors to *IBM* format to meet publishers requirements and to have limited-edition books etc. edited, typeset and produced, are also available.

For further details, contact John at **A.C.E. Services** at the address below:

83, Watford Road,
Radlett,
Hertfordshire.
WD7 8LU
Tel: 0923-858379